THE
BROAD GAUGE
ENGINES
OF THE
GREAT WESTERN RAILWAY
1846-1852

Published by LIGHTMOOR PRESS

© Lightmoor Press & Brian Arman 2022

Designed by Neil Parkhouse

British Library Cataloguing-in-Publication Data. A catalogue record for this book is available from the British Library

ISBN: 9781915069 01 6

LIGHTMOOR PRESS
Unit 144B, Lydney Trading Estate, Harbour Road,
Lydney, Gloucestershire GL15 4EJ
www.lightmoor.co.uk

Lightmoor Press is an imprint of
Black Dwarf Lightmoor Publications Ltd

Printed in Poland
www.lfbookservices.co.uk

This fine study of the 'Iron Duke' Class 4-2-2 *Sultan* was taken near the entrance to Westbourne Park goods yard in 1856 (a favoured spot for engine photography at this period), shortly after the end of the Crimean War. Note the iron-bodied Loco Coal waggon behind on the right. In the centre background, the Royal Saxon public house still stands today, although is now named The Metropolitan, but the other buildings in this view are all now gone. A contemporary print of an enlargement of the locomotive only also features on page 114 but of note here is the tender lining with its 'scalloped' corners, typical of the period though it was not universally applied. The photograph clearly demonstrates the application of the tender lining, which was divided into four panels, the first and fourth of which followed the contours of the tender to the front and rear.

THE
BROAD GAUGE
ENGINES
OF THE
GREAT WESTERN
RAILWAY
PART 3: 1846-1852

THE REVEREND CANON
BRIAN ARMAN

CONTENTS

FOREWORD AND ACKNOWLEDGEMENTS . . . . .PAGE 5

PREAMBLE: SIR DANIEL GOOCH'S DIARIES . . . . .PAGE 7

COLOUR SECTION . . . . .PAGE 9

SECTION 1:
SWINDON AND GOOCH

CHAPTER 1:
SWINDON . . . . .PAGE 17

CHAPTER 2:
GOOCH'S LOCOMOTIVE POLICY 1846-1864 . . . . .PAGE 57

SECTION 2:
PASSENGER ENGINES DESIGNED BETWEEN 1846 AND 1852

CHAPTER 3:
GREAT WESTERN . . . . .PAGE 63

CHAPTER 4:
THE 'PRINCE' CLASS . . . . .PAGE 75

CHAPTER 5:
THE 'IRON DUKE' CLASS . . . . .PAGE 91

CHAPTER 6:
THE 'BOGIE' CLASS. . . . . .PAGE 149

SECTION 3:
THE GOODS CLASSES DESIGNED BETWEEN 1846 AND 1852

CHAPTER 7:
THE 'PREMIER' CLASS . . . . .PAGE 163

CHAPTER 8:
THE 'PYRACMON' CLASS . . . . .PAGE 179

CHAPTER 9:
THE 'CAESAR' CLASS . . . . .PAGE 189

CHAPTER 10:
MISCELLANEOUS ENGINES: AVALANCHE AND BACCHUS . . . . .PAGE 197

SELECT BIBLIOGRAPHY. . . . . .PAGE 200

APPENDIX 1: THE EXPERIMENT WITH GREAT WESTERN . . . . .PAGE 201

APPENDIX 2: THE BLEASDALE PHOTOGRAPHIC COLLECTION . . . . .PAGE 205

APPENDIX 3: GWR ENGINE STOCK, OCTOBER 1849 . . . . .PAGE 207

FOREWORD AND ACKNOWLEDGEMENTS

In the first two parts of this series, we have investigated the GWR's earliest engines of highly variable quality ordered by Brunel and delivered between 1837 and 1841 (Part 1), and then analysed the four designs which might be termed 'Gooch's early standard engines', delivered by contractors between 1840 and 1842 (Part 2). Here in Part 3 we move forward to 1846 to study the exceptionally important period of the development of Gooch's earlier work. This resulted in the construction, largely in the Company's own newly established workshops at Swindon, of engines which were of a size and power that, in their time, were beyond parallel both nationally and internationally. Indeed, it would not be to overstate our case by proposing that the years covered in this part, 1846-1852, saw Daniel Gooch rise to the pinnacle of his profession, marking him out as one of the great locomotive engineers of his and subsequent eras. Not only did he design ground-breaking engines, he also instituted a programme of research and testing – in the course of which he designed and built the first dynamometer car – which was perhaps the first initiative of its type ever attempted in the new world of locomotive engine development. This earned for Gooch the appreciation and admiration of many of his peers, and is best summed up by D.K.Clark, who used Gooch's data to produce a formula of train resistance: *'Mr Daniel Gooch is the only experimentalist whose results are worthy of implicit confidence … it is our conviction that they* [the tests] *were conducted with the strictest impartiality … worthy of the high character of Mr Gooch as an experimentalist and observer'*.

If all this was not enough, Gooch was also intimately concerned with the planning, construction and equipping of the new workshop establishment at Swindon. This was in itself a mammoth task, for Gooch, Brunel and their assistants were not just building new workshops, they were literally building a new town in one of the least industrialised and poorest parts of the country. The means by which these challenges were overcome is, in its way, an epic story, which I have attempted to tell in the first chapter of this book and will follow up in later volumes. I feel, however, the need to explain my purpose in doing so here, for there are already two well respected histories of Swindon Works, not to mention several official guides that were published by the GWR and BR(WR).

My very first attempt at public speaking, outside of the school environment, was in 1970 when I was just sixteen. My father gave annually a series of WEA (Workers Education Authority) lectures about the history of Swindon to local students and he asked me to talk about the railway and its locomotives. He, of course, was a great support and helped and encouraged me every step of the way. I vividly remember the occasion, a room full of old Swindonians both male and female and mostly sixty or older, all of whom had GWR connections! Daunting the experience certainly was but I somehow managed to engage the audience to such an extent that between them they gave the lecture for me. In its way it was a triumph of bare-faced cheek over experience but I learnt some very valuable lessons that night which have never left me. One

lovely old gentleman came up to me afterwards, took my hand and said that I really had *'not left much out'*. I remember thanking him and thinking actually he and his colleagues had not left much out because I had been very much the pupil and they the teachers. The most important lesson that I learnt that evening was that behind every official history of facts and dates there is a very real human story, often of great endeavour and hardship. It is that narrative I have tried to present here but told through my own eyes.

Later in his life and after the final closure of Swindon Works in 1986-87, I got to know Alan Peck who wrote *The Great Western at Swindon Works*. Alan was a Swindonian through and through and had spent the whole of his working life in the factory; no-one living really knew it as well as he did. On one occasion our conversation turned to the work of the 'P2 Shop' or the 'Cylinder Shop' as it was sometimes called, which was later redesignated 'W Shop'. Alan had spent some time there and told me about one of the cylinder boring machines that had been made in the Works in the mid 1840s, which was still in use and working to a high degree of accuracy when steam locomotive repairs ceased in 1964. This opened my eyes to another façet of the output of the Works, of which I had previously been only hazily aware, namely that Swindon, like other workshops of a similar kind, manufactured and maintained much of its own plant. Alan told me that an audit carried out in 1938, the last truly full year of independent GWR management, revealed that approximately 60 per cent of all the machinery in the workshops in use at the time had been manufactured locally – an astonishing achievement. He therefore taught me that there was much more to Swindon Works than simply building and maintaining rolling stock and thus, how important it was to look beneath the surface to reveal what was a far more complicated story than might otherwise be apparent. I owe him a tremendous debt of gratitude.

Since my first attempts at public speaking all those years ago, I have given literally hundreds of lectures about Swindon Works up and down the country. Interestingly, the poor individual to whom it was deputed the task of giving a vote of thanks often seemed to say much the same kind of thing, namely *'We thank Canon Arman for explaining the complexities of the history of Swindon Works. Previously I have never quite been able to grasp all the details of the story from the written word'*. When you hear those kinds of comments made a multiple number of times, you soon realise that some things need clarification, which is why I have included a Swindon Works timeline in my narrative, hoping that it will add clarity to what is undoubtedly a complex story.

As before I am indebted to a number of very generous people who have contributed to this work. Paul Garnsworthy has drawn the very fine map of Swindon Works as it was in 1849, which matches the beautiful painting of 'The Works and New Town' executed by Edward Snell in the same year. Paul has helped in numerous other ways, particularly when it comes to photographs included in this book. Through careful research with old Ordinance Survey maps, he has been able to identify locations and probable dates which otherwise I might only have been able to offer a best guess at identifying.

Gerry Nichols, the SLS Librarian, has once again been able to dig out obscure material held in the library collection as well as a number of contemporary newspaper reports which have enhanced and coloured the narrative. To both Paul and Gerry I offer my most sincere thanks.

As mentioned also in Part 2, Alan Garner was a great help when we were able to visit Didcot to study the Gooch Coke Books kept there. He remains my 'go to' technical man, from which many fruitful discussions have emanated. I thank him for his help and support.

Once again Neil Parkhouse and his dear wife Heather have done a wonderful job through this most challenging period of lockdown and furlough. Not only was Part 2 published during the pandemic but this part has been wholly written and produced within it. The two of them, with the support of their little team of young ladies, have done a remarkable job with their usual optimism and good humour. I cannot thank them enough.

Sean Bolan is a railway artist of the very highest calibre. Once again his work adorns these pages capturing, as it does, not only the detail but the spirit of the age as well; it is a skill that few possess and even fewer can equal. I thank him most generously.

The support of friends has, for reasons that I will shortly explain, been of particular significance to me through the course of writing this volume. I would therefore especially like to thank Tudor Watkins, John Hembury, Michael Wyatt, Stephen Park, Malcolm Barton, Dave Murdoch, Jon Hewlett, Dr Andrew Cowie and Tony Reynalds among many others for offering generous friendship and great kindness throughout a most challenging and painful time.

On 13th August 2020, when the manuscript of this book was about half finished, I suffered a very sudden heart attack in the kitchen of our home in Bristol. My wife, a former Sister at the Bristol Royal Infirmary, was on the point of going out when the event occurred. Her quick reactions and nursing skills kept me alive until the paramedics could arrive and take over the CPR which she was doing. There followed three operations and seven weeks in the Bristol Heart Institute and a lengthy period of convalescence and rehabilitation which, as I write, is still ongoing. Quite simply I owe my life to my wife, Terri, whose love, devotion – she visited me every day during my period of hospitalisation – skill as a nurse, carer, mother and lifetime companion, to number just a few of her capabilities and achievements, has been inspirational. To her I owe everything, including thanks for typing this book, and I therefore dedicate this work to her for her ongoing love and devotion through this, the most challenging period in all our lives. Most appropriately, the manuscript was delivered to my publishers one year later to the day – 13th August 2021!

Rev'd Canon Brian Arman
Filton, Bristol

Publisher's Note

The Great Western Railway was built to a gauge of 7ft 0$\frac{1}{4}$in. and in the days when it was solely a broad gauge railway, always referred to other railways built to Stephenson's 4ft 8$\frac{1}{2}$in. gauge as being 'narrow gauge'. Your author, being a Great Western man and broad gauge in particular, also leans to that view. However, as publishers we felt that such a reference nowadays could be confusing, when the terms 'narrow', 'standard' and 'broad' are generally taken to define the three basic forms of railway gauge – albeit both the first and last of those cover a 'multitude of sins' between them so to speak. Therefore we have used just 'broad' and standard' in reference to gauge in the text, the only codicil being that any direct quotes from other sources that refer to 'narrow' have been left as they are. They can all be taken, however, to mean 'standard'.

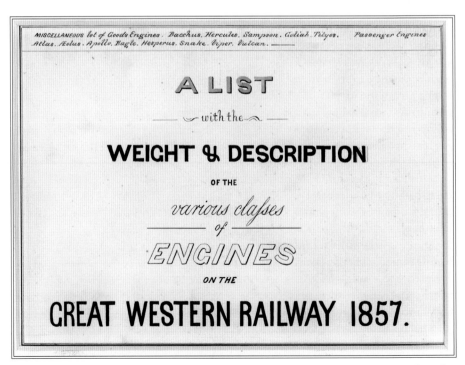

The title page of the Greast Western Railway's 1857 book of engine and tender watercoloured drawings and specifications, all of which are presented through this series of books.

PREAMBLE
SIR DANIEL GOOCH'S DIARIES

I have owned a copy of Gooch's Diaries for upwards of forty-five years and have read and re-read it many times. For a very long time I treated it with great respect and quoted from it in articles and whilst giving lectures in, what I now realise, was an historically uncritical way! I suspect that I am far from being alone in making the not unreasonable assumption that these are the words of the great man himself, someone who is rightly held in the very highest esteem in engineering and railway management circles. I am also a Swindonian – and proud to be so. Even today, though memories are fading fast, Gooch is thought of with respect and even affection among its older citizens and his name is still attached to the town in various ways, not least in there being a street named after him. Therefore it is almost akin to some secular blasphemy to cast aspersions on the memory of a man who more or less was responsible for founding the New Town and who took such a strong, some might say paternalistic, interest in Swindon's growth and the needs of the workforce for over forty years. He even represented the town, then a part of the 'Cricklade Hundreds', in Parliament for twenty years; though, by his own admission, he found the responsibility and the practical demands of Parliamentary life irksome.

In the light of the foregoing it is hard to admit that in a significant number of cases the details contained in the diaries are inaccurate. I am of course not the first person to draw this conclusion but until the discovery of Gooch's original manuscripts in June 1969 we had only the heavily edited and redacted 1892 version of his diaries to work with, which gives, at best, a rather disjointed narrative. What is more it is now evident that in preparing the diaries for publication much of a personal nature was omitted. Gooch's somewhat difficult handwriting was inaccurately transcribed and his grammar and spelling corrected. Nor was any effort made to check the facts presented in the diary which has led many subsequent authors up the garden path, as it were! One such example to demonstrate the point must suffice. The 1892 diary states that Gooch was educated at 'Condhall' School. In fact, this is a misreading of Crow Hall which is the accurate rendering of the name. There are a number of other similar errors spread throughout the 1892 publication, so casual readers who, like myself, come to the diaries with a certain amount of reverence, need to beware of falling into the trap of honouring a great man's memory in preference to engaging one's critical historical faculties.

Fortunately, help is at hand. When the previously unknown manuscripts of Gooch's life were offered for sale by the auctioneer Sotheby & Co. on 23rd June 1969, they came to Roger Burdett Wilson for analysis and transcription. They could not have been placed in any better hands. His very careful work of editing this important material, accompanied by copious notes and drawing on considerable advice from many historians and academics, was published by David & Charles in 1972 under the title *Sir Daniel Gooch: Memoirs and Diary*. No serious historian or researcher should be without a copy of this work, which should always be consulted in preference to the 1892 version of the diary.

Yet no one person, even with the best available contemporary advice, can possibly know everything. Considerably more original material has come to light since 1972 that has illuminated the early history of the GWR and in particular the engineering aspects of the Company's development, which Gooch was intimately associated with. These discoveries sometimes contradict Gooch's

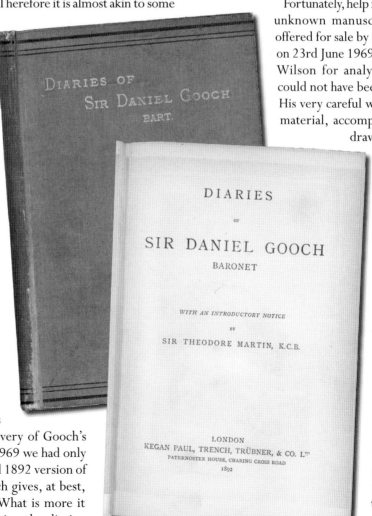

Cover and title page of an 1892 first edition of the *Diaries of Sir Daniel Gooch, Baronet*.

memories or at least cast some doubt upon the way in which he recorded his thoughts and intentions, and how and when they were eventually executed.

To give one particular example Gooch writes: '*During the year 1844 I tried the experiment of using corrugated copper fireboxes in our engines, thinking that by that means I would greatly enlarge the heating surface. Experience shewed me what perhaps a little more reflection might have told me beforehand that it did no good. The temperature of the gasses escaping from the chimney was not higher than it ought to be, and therefore as all the heat given out by the fire was already taken up, I did not obtain any benefit, as I did not increase the bulk of the fire. It made a strong box but a very costly one, and I only put it to two engines.*'

Without any possible means of verifying this statement, one can only accept it at face value and move on. Yet some drawings uncovered in Swindon Works in the 1980s directly contradict the date of the experiment quoted above. Gooch was right that two engines were experimentally fitted with a corrugated firebox, the 'Sun' Class 2-2-2s *Assagais* and *Gazelle*, but the drawing is dated January 1864 and relate to a period when the engines concerned were being rebuilt with new boilers and fireboxes of a more modern design than the Haycock type originally fitted. Perhaps Gooch conceived the idea in 1844 but only brought it to fruition much later on? What is more, with the benefit of much hindsight, one wonders where and how he might have executed such an idea in 1844. Swindon Works had opened in the previous year but was initially only equipped for repair and maintenance work. Such special one-off jobs might just have been within its scope then but I am bound to say that I wonder if such was the case. My guess is that Gooch conflated his memories into an entry which expresses more about his thinking rather than

their practical application?

The fundamental problem with Gooch's diaries is that all the entries dated before 1867 are not really diaries at all but memoirs. Gooch did not begin to write them until October 1867, as Roger Burdett Wilson observes: '*Daniel Gooch was fifty-one when, in October 1867, he began to write an account of the main events of his life down to that time, but there was already more to record than many men gather in a lifetime. After the completion of the memoirs he began to keep a diary, the first entry in which is dated February 1868. This he continued at rather irregular intervals until about 6 months before his death. With the memoirs the diary filled eight volumes. Of these, two covering the period 1870-73 and 1886-89 have not survived so far as is known.*'

Sir Daniel Gooch in 1866, after being made a baronet.

The obvious question which arises from these observations is, without contemporary written notes can you be sure of what you said and did thirty-five years ago with any accuracy? I am sure that I cannot. Certain memories stand out but as to the accuracy of what was said and done or thought at the time, I could not be absolutely content – neither it seems could Sir Daniel Gooch, as he became after being made a baronet in 1866.

Finally, it is worth pointing out that any history written before the publication of Roger Burdett Wilson's book could not have benefitted from his discoveries. This unfortunately includes MacDermot's *History of the GWR* and C.R. Clinker's revision published by Ian Allan in 1966. As I have had to learn the hard way, it is very important to double check one's facts even when they appear to emanate from unimpeachable sources. Even with all the care that it is possible to take, mistakes will still be made – that is the nature of our humanity. Perfection is not granted to us and Sir Daniel Gooch, very great man though he was, is no exception to that rule.

Sean Bolan has also kindly granted us permission to use his evocative painting of Bridport circa 1858. This carefully researched scene gives a graphic impression of the station in its earliest guise – it was rebuilt in 1893 – complete with contemporary motive power of both the four-coupled and four-legged variety. The 'Bogie' Class 4-4-0 tank *Hesiod* is reported to have worked the branch inspection train on 5th November 1857 and then seems to have been replaced by classmate *Theocritus* as the branch engine sometime in 1858 or early 1859. Thereafter, the branch was largely worked by the little 'Leo' Class 2-4-0 tanks though larger engines were not unknown. In fact, the only broad gauge photograph that exists of Bridport illustrates *Brindley* of the 'Victoria' Class, a 2-4-0 tender engine, posed at the shed in the mid 1860s (this photograph will appear in Part 4 of this series). The last broad gauge train ran to Bridport on Thursday 18th June 1874.

Sean Bolan's captivating watercolour brings life to an everyday event of the late 1850s at Oxford station. *Queen* has arrived at the south end with a train from Birmingham and with Oxford being the engine's home shed, it will shortly be relieved for the run to Paddington by *Great Western* – seen here in all its magnificent elegance. *Great Western* would be returning back to base too, having worked down to Oxford from Paddington earlier in the day, and with the footplate crew also going home, a fast run could be anticipated. *Great Western* will take all of this in its stately stride for, when it was built, it was perhaps the fastest running engine in the world and subsequently spent the greater part of its working life doing much the same thing as illustrated here. Sean's great talent is that of opening a window into the everyday events of the past, thus allowing the modern observer to see into a world that was every bit as innovative and exciting as is our own.

This is one of only three or four fully coloured illustrations in Lane's archive. I am not an expert on colour pigments but I am informed by those who are that originally the paint colour was a dark green which, over many years, had the yellow pigment 'bleached out' of it (this has been 'corrected' here using computer imaging software). This, apparently, is because Lane, along with the person or persons responsible for the 1857 specifications, used inks and not paints as colourisers. With that important caveat in mind the details of the paint scheme illustrated here can confidently said to represent contemporary practise in 1849, the print being dated 3rd July. As the illustration on page 5 of Part 2 proves, the general paint scheme had not changed since at least 1840 and with few embellishments was to remain in use until the mid 1960s. Tenders had their side and end panels lined out but otherwise followed the same general scheme.

SECOND LOT OF GOODS

ALLIGATOR. BEHEMOTH. CALIBAN. MAMMOTH. PYRACMON. STEROPES.

DESCRIPTION

CYLINDERS 16 ins in diamr. and 24 ins stroke. Steam ports 1½ ins by 13 ins. Exhaust port 2¾ ins by 13 ins.
BOILER 10 feet 6 ins long and 4 feet 3 ins diamr inside. Fire Box 4 feet 11 ins long by 5 feet 3½ ins wide.
TUBES. 219 Tubes 10 feet 11 ins long and 2 ins in diamr outside. Heating Surface of Box 121.33. Tubes 1134. 40 sq.ft.
WHEELS. Leading Driving and Trailing 5 feet in diamr and all coupled.
FIRE GRATE area 18.44 Superficial feet.
BEHEMOTH with 7 cwt of Coke and 7 ins of water in the Glass weighs Leading T.C.Q. Driving 10.2.0. Trailing T.C.Q. 9.18.0. T.5.0.

The GWR 1857 specification colour-washed drawing of the '2nd Lot Goods' or 'Pyracmon' Class engines as they are more commonly known. The whole class of six engines were of uniform design, as represented here.

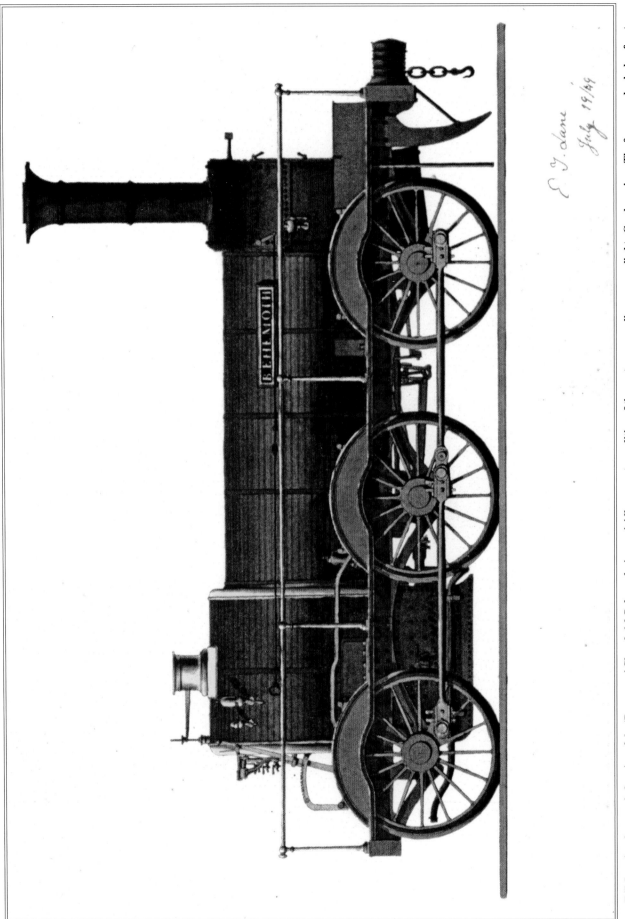

E.T. Lane's colour wash drawing of the 'Pyracmon' Class 0-6-0 *Behemoth* gives a vividly accurate rendition of the contemporary livery as applied to Goods engines. The frames and splasher fronts are Windsor brown, whilst the wheels are green with black tyres. The main superstructure is green and the boiler bands are black. Other fittings are black and the brightwork is highly polished. The drawing is dated July 19th 1849 which is, presumably, when Lane executed the illustration. Apart from the addition of a leading sandbox, which seems to be a little on the large side, the engine is in original condition. *Behemoth* entered service in March 1848 and was withdrawn in December 1873.

FIRST LOT . COUPLED .

AJAX . ARGO . BELLEROPHON . BERGION . BRIAREUS . BRONTES . DREADNOUGHT . FURY . JASON . PREMIER . TELICA . VESUVIUS .

It was decided to take the opportunity in this volume to present some of the 1857 drawings in colour. However, it should first be noted that in the 165 years since they were executed, the yellow pigment has faded and they all now have a strong blue tinge. To an extent this has been possible to correct on the computer although the spokes of the wheels have proved resistant to alteration. Howver, they do give a reasonable idea of how these engines would have appeared whilst the livery arrangement will be useful for modelling purposes. These first two illustrations show members of the 'Premier' Class (Chapter 7), Above, and 'Caesar' Class (Chapter 9), Below.

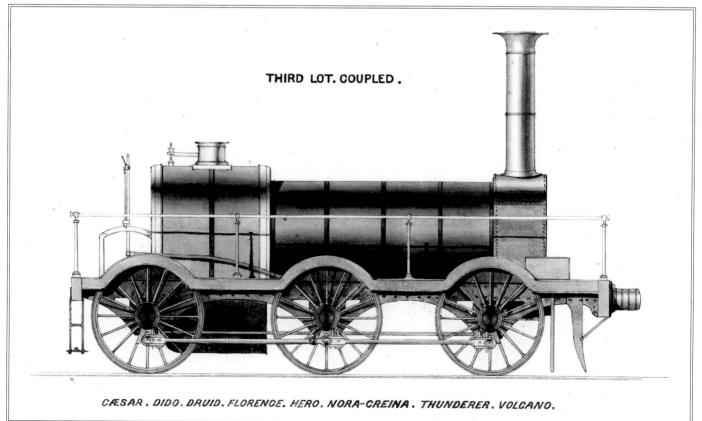

THIRD LOT. COUPLED .

CÆSAR . DIDO . DRUID . FLORENCE . HERO . NORA-CREINA . THUNDERER . VOLCANO .

ABOVE: An 'Iron Duke' Class '8ft Single' (Chapter 5)

BELOW. The drawing for the Express Tenders – these are also covered in detail in Chapter 5.

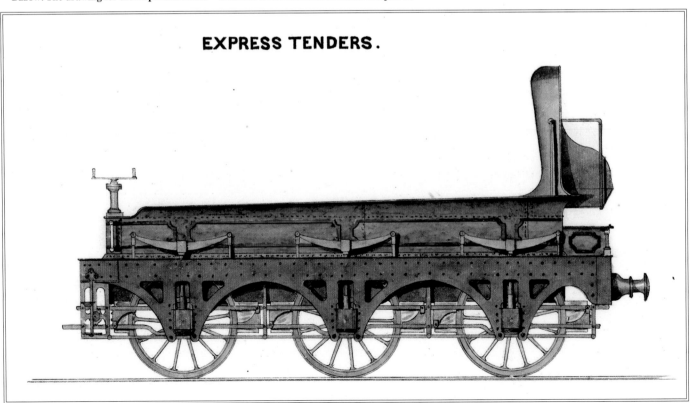

SECTION 1: SWINDON AND GOOCH
CHAPTER 1
SWINDON

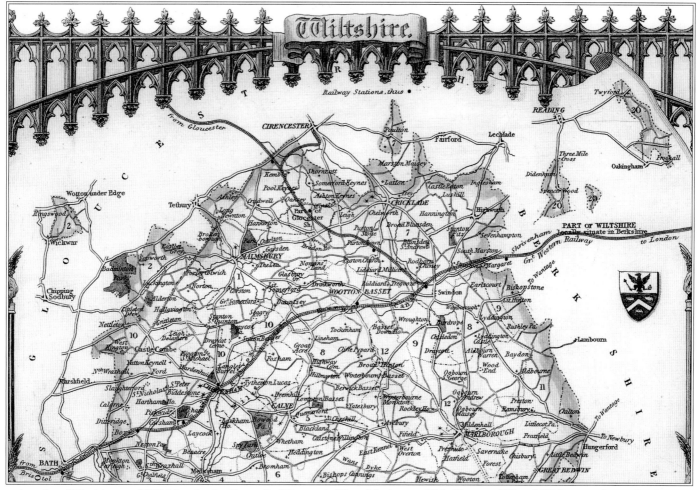

A portion of Moule's map of Wiltshire, showing the north of the county. The original was published between 1830 and 1836 but was then updated circa 1845 to include the new railways. Note that Swindon was still just a village at this date, its status below that of the nearby market towns of Wootton Bassett and Cricklade. The GWR main line through the county had opened in stages, in 1840 and 1841, with Swindon station situated over a mile from the village. The Cheltenham & Great Western Union Railway's line to Cirencester also opened in 1841, with the line north from Kemble to Gloucester finally opening in 1845. The stations are shown as black dots. Due to problems with the local squire, the first Kemble station was situated alongside the Cirencester to Tetbury road; it was closed when a new station at the junction for what had become the Cirencester Branch was opened in 1882.

I was born in Swindon in 1954, some 114 years after Daniel Gooch and Isambard Brunel, with the backing and agreement of the Great Western Railway Board, had decided that the low water meadows adjacent to the main line and in the 'V' of the junction made with the quasi-independent Cheltenham & Great Western Union Railway would be an appropriate place to site a series of workshops. These were to form '*Our principal engine establishment*', as Gooch described it in a letter to Brunel dated 13th September 1840.

Though I was born in the Old Town, the origins of which reach back to Saxon times and perhaps earlier, mine was very much a GWR family though the 'Old Company' – as it was habitually referred to – had sadly ceased to exist six years before. Our people were employed largely on the locomotive side of the works, either as blacksmiths or boilermakers, though my father had driven a steam hammer in the No. 18 Carriage Shops, until he retrained as a draughtsman after the war. After this he worked in the main offices until leaving railway employment in the mid-1950s.* Though various branches of the family came originally from Gloucestershire, Somerset and Hertfordshire, most to find work on the GWR, the Armans were solidly of North Wiltshire stock, having been continuously employed as blacksmiths (among

---

* Father went to work as a draughtsman for Swindon Borough Council after leaving the railway, where, for those who know Swindon's road system, he draughted the original design of the town's (in)famous multi-layered 'Magic' Roundabout!

other things) in the town of Wootton Bassett since late medieval times. Indeed, my rather unusual surname is believed to have derived from the middle English word for armourer – 'armurer'.

Swindon in 1840, with a population of barely 2,000 was then just one of a number of small towns in what was a largely agricultural area bereft of any major manufacturing activity, which included nearby Wootton Bassett and Highworth. It is true that there was some quarrying on Swindon Hill – which would in time provide materials for the construction of the railway works and village – but this was relatively unimportant when compared with the agricultural basis of the town's existence. That said Swindon was hardly a prosperous place in 1840. The boom in agriculture which had been precipitated by the Napoleonic Wars had subsided into a period of lengthy depression through the decades that followed. A government survey of the Counties of England, made in the early 1840s, identified Dorset, Wiltshire, Cumberland and Westmoreland as the four poorest shires in the country.

The arrival of two canals nearby had done little over time to alleviate this malaise. These, the Wilts & Berks Canal, sanctioned under an Act of 1795, linked the Kennet & Avon Canal at Semington with the River Thames at Abingdon. The second canal, the North Wilts, made a junction with the Wilts & Berks a mile or so from the bottom of Swindon Hill and linked up with the Thames & Severn Canal at Latton. This was promoted in 1813. Though in theory they provided links to London, Bath, Bristol and via a long tunnel at Sapperton to Stroud, Gloucester and the Severn Basin, they do not appear to have had a significant long-term impact on the wealth of the town other than the quarrying activities. They did enable coal to be brought in more cheaply, while stone, timber and agricultural products could be moved around more quickly and at advantageous rates. However, there had to be a ready market for these commodities as, excepting the stone, Swindon was simply too far away from the larger areas of population to benefit from these new transport links. In 1840, England was still overwhelmingly an agricultural nation and cities like Bath, Bristol, Oxford and London could be supplied more cheaply from sources nearer at hand.

Having painted a rather gloomy picture of pre-railway age Swindon, it is worth pointing out that the town had enjoyed four fairs annually since at least 1629, and perhaps rather longer, while a weekly market, which had begun as far back as 1257, was still in existence and in fact continued until recent times. *Pigot's Wiltshire Directory* of 1842 describes Swindon as '*a Market Town with two main streets that were lit by gas supplied by a company formed in 1841*'. The regular market dealt with cereals weekly, fat and lean cattle fortnightly, and cheese monthly. The four fairs were held in early April, mid-May, mid-September and mid-December. Those in April and September were 'Hiring Fairs' but all offered numerous opportunities to purchase livestock, consumer goods, cloth, clothes, sweetmeats, fruit, vegetables in their season, spices, other luxury goods and naturally the chance to enjoy a pot or two of locally brewed ale and cider. All things considered matters could have been perhaps a little better but they might have been worse. Then the navvies arrived and many people's worst fears were soon realised.

Swindon already knew a lot about 'navigators', i.e. those who dug the canal navigations – navvies for short. During the previous forty years, two canals had been dug nearby so their roistering, unpredictable and sometimes violent behaviour was well within living memory. In some quarters there was an ambivalence about the arrival of the navvies. They worked long hard hours and were well paid for their labours, so they ate and drank prodigiously and, for some, their arrival in the area offered an opportunity for profit from their presence. The prevailing feeling, however, was one of fear and dread, accompanied by the not unreasonable supposition that as there were no major earthworks required in the immediate Swindon area – though there were some to both east and west of the town – their stay would not be prolonged. What is more, the local militia of the Wiltshire Yeomanry were nearby should matters get out of hand.

A glimpse of the original part of Swindon circa 1895, looking east down Newport Street. It is likely that the cottages on the left were around 200 years old when this picture was taken, so the street still looked pretty much as it would have done when Gooch and Brunel first came here. However, the 'modern age' had finally arrived in this part of Old Town in 1881, when the Swindon, Marlborough & Andover Railway (which later became a constituent of the Midland & South Western Junction Railway) opened its Swindon station on what was to become a line linking Cheltenham and Southampton; the wall on the right covered in advertisements marks the entrance to the M&SWJR station. Almost nothing of this scene remains today.
Neil Parkhouse collection

Sadly, the good people of Swindon were soon to discover that these hopes were ill-founded. For no sooner had one set of contractor's navvies moved on than another group arrived, to begin laying out the new workshops. The work began by digging conduits, drainage ditches and laying in mains water pipes. From there it proceeded in stages over the forthcoming decades in a way which could not possibly have been envisaged in 1840. In the process, a New Town would be laid out at the foot of Swindon Hill which, in time, would become the beating heart of one of the nation's great railway companies. Though the Old Town would continue to retain much of its pre-industrial character, the simple fact remains that from the moment Daniel Gooch wrote his letter to Brunel recommending that a locomotive manufactory should be built at Swindon, the whole of North Wiltshire would be dragged into the new industrial age whether it liked it or not!

Though hard evidence is somewhat difficult to find, the general impression that one gains is that many people locally looked favourably on the railway. A few, such as those involved in the local transport network, rightly feared for their livelihoods but even they could see that the railway offered plenty of new opportunities. For the majority, who were employed in agriculture, the prospects, if a little daunting, were cheering. The railway seemed to offer the chance of regular wages, better working conditions and possibly better housing. Certainly, members of my family with their blacksmithing skills took that view. They, however, had skills which the railway was keen to employ and living then just four miles away, they did not require housing either. Small wonder then that at least one of the family, soon followed by others, grasped the opportunity offered with hope and enthusiasm.

Others who decided to remain on the land soon realised that they too could enhance their livelihood by becoming what today we would describe as 'part of the supply chain.' Hard working people need to be fed as do their families. Industrial workers had then few, if any, means of growing their own food so they were dependent on others. In fact, it took a little while to establish a locally sourced food chain. The company initially established their own shops, known generally and unpopularly as 'tommy shops', which tended to charge fixed prices for basic foodstuffs. This system proved unsustainable in the long run and there is evidence that, by the mid-1840s, local market gardeners and farmers were setting up stalls in the railway village on a more or less regular basis. These developed to such an extent that a formal covered market building was erected in 1853 and interestingly, a successor to the GWR market, though now located a little away from the old railway village, still thrives in Swindon today.

So much for the local community. However, Gooch and his assistants had other problems. Not only did the new workshops have to be constructed, a matter that Brunel with his able assistant T.H. Bertham had in hand, but they also had to be equipped with the appropriate machinery. Actually, Gooch and his team were well placed to achieve this aim. He was already in touch with a number of machine tool manufacturers, quite a few of which, such as Nasmyth, Gaskell & Co., were also locomotive builders. He had also made the formative decision to adopt Joseph Whitworth's standards for measures, gauges and screw threads. His policy was to purchase the best available equipment from the most reputable suppliers. In this context he succeeded admirably, witness the fact that a number of machines purchased in the 1840s and 1850s were still in use a hundred years later and, in a very few instances, survived until the works closed in 1986. One of Gooch's wisest and most far sighted purchases was a Nasmyth steam hammer. The first of these was installed in 1844 and a larger and heavier example in 1846. These required a shop of their own to be erected, which had to have a specially prepared floor with a slewing crane provided to enable large forgings to be handled successfully. Steam to operate the hammers was initially supplied by the locomotive *Apollo*, adapted for stationary use (see Part 2, Chapters 2 and 3, for much further detail on all this).

In addition to purchasing machine tools from outside suppliers, a gradual process began of in-house manufacture of tools and tooling to satisfy very specific needs and to high levels of accuracy. As the decades elapsed this became a significant aspect of the workshop's capabilities, to such an extent that in the years just before the outbreak of the Second World War, it was reckoned that upwards of sixty per cent of the tools and tooling in use in the workshops were manufactured in the works themselves. In this context, Alan Peck, who spent forty-three years working for the GWR and BR(WR) of which more than thirty-five of those years were in Swindon Works, tells an illuminating story. Speaking of the equipping of the original 'Turning Shop' or 'D Shop' as it was known, he comments:

'One machine which is definitely known to have been installed soon after, presumably in the turning shop, was a cylinder boring machine. It was constructed at Swindon, as was the case with many other machines. This particular boring machine, with later additions, lasted the whole life of steam locomotives and was disposed of with other old machines during the 1960s when it was still working to the high degree of accuracy required.'

Much of the stonework required to build the factory was supplied by Pictor & Brewer from their quarries at Corsham and Bath, including probably the two well known bas reliefs of a broad gauge locomotive that graced the original 1842 engine shed. However, it now seems unlikely that any of the stone came from the tunnel workings at Box (as has been rumoured in the past) but small amounts of Pennant stone were supplied from further afield. Swindon stone was also used and brought to the site from the quarry on Kings Hill by means of a temporary tramway. Swindon stone is a dark yellow sandstone and is harder than the Bath stone which is easier to work and was therefore used for the more decorative parts of the buildings, such as the façade of the office block which faces the main line and the original decorative stonework located on either end of the running shed.

Brick was also used in small quantities in the initial construction of the works buildings. These were supplied by an E. Oldham who received a total of £3,900 between October 1841 and April 1842 for his services. Bricks were presumably brought to Swindon by barge but there is some evidence of local production, which probably accounted for some of the materials supplied. Since little use was made of brick in the construction of the works, it is probable that much of what was purchased was used to build some coke ovens to supply fuel for locomotive purposes. Brick

The pumping engines at Kemble which, from 1903, supplied water to Swindon Works. Originally steam driven, by the time of this December 1966 view inside the pump house they were electrically operated. Interestingly, a pumping station is shown here on the 1877 25 inch OS. The pump house still stands – just – but is abandoned and roofless.
JOHN STRANGE/NEIL PARKHOUSE COLLECTION

was also used in the construction of the station and to line the internal walls of the cottages in the railway village.

Brunel adopted what architects refer to as a 'pier and panel principle' for the construction of most of the main works buildings. In essence this entails the erection of stone piers as load bearing members, supporting timber panels into which windows were inserted at regular intervals. Roofs were generally tiled and were supported by inverted timber A frames – though iron supports were sometimes substituted. Readers wishing to know more about the details of the construction of the works buildings are directed toward two publications, Alan Peck's *The Great Western at Swindon Works* and the RCHME's *Swindon: The Legacy of a Railway Town*. (Accounts in these two books do not always agree and dates can vary slightly. Where I have used specific dates and material, I have endeavoured to ensure that they are accurate but they may thus differ from one or other of the sources mentioned – see also the Swindon Works timeline 1840-61 at the end of this chapter.)

When Gooch wrote his letter to Brunel recommending Swindon as the site of the new workshops, the one concern that he expressed was about the supply of water and in fact this was to be a major issue for the works and town for many years to come. The Old Town was supplied by naturally occurring springs that surfaced around the south side of Swindon Hill but the New Town, which was built on the clay measures at its foot, was not so well provided for. Recourse had to be made to the canals and specifically the North Wilts Canal; Alan Peck describes it thus: '*The water supply to the Works and the village was obtained from the North Wilts Canal through a valve and was fed into two reservoirs immediately to the north of the passenger station … from here water gravitated by pipe across the canal under the Cirencester (later Gloucester) line by a syphon to a well near the boiler house at the east end of the works. From this well it was pumped via a filter house to the tanks provided above both the east and west boiler houses and was then fed to the works*

and estate by gravity. In the village there were stand pipes in the streets, but this supply was not intended as drinking water.'

All the available evidence suggests that drinking water was brought to the works and village by horse drawn water carriers, the water being sourced from the Old Town supply as already described. This situation persisted until 1866, when a local water company was formed and piped drinking water was made available.

Reverting to the matter of the original water supply for a moment, it should be mentioned that the regularity and quality of the water supplied by the canal company was never very reliable. Problems continued until the early 20th century, when wells were sunk at Kemble and water was supplied to the works from there by a system of pumps and pipes. These continued in use until the works closed. Meanwhile the reservoirs behind the station were filled in and the carriage and wagon repair shops were built on the site. Memories are hard to eradicate, however, for the sidings beyond the station were always known as the 'water sidings', a term that remained in use until recent times.

During the early 1840s, the infant GWR was far from being a financially sound organisation. The cost of building and equipping the railway had greatly exceeded Brunel's original estimates and income was still a long way from balancing expenditure. Seen from a purely financial perspective, the decision to base the 'locomotive manufactory' at Swindon was a surprising one, for not only would workshops need to be erected and equipped but a whole town with attendant infrastructure and amenities would have to be provided. Clearly, operating considerations outweighed the purely fiscal ones. Viewed from the perspective of history, self-evidently the correct decision was taken. Nonetheless, the GWR was not in a secure enough position to finance such a project on its own and it therefore turned to a contractor to undertake the construction of the railway village. A director's report of February 1841 makes the following statement:

'*The final determination of working these two railways* [the Bristol

& Exeter and the Cheltenham & Great Western Union railways] upon Lease has imposed upon the directors the necessity of providing an increased stock of locomotive engines, carriages, waggons and other plant adequate to the trade which may be reasonably expected.

It has also decided the directors to provide an engine establishment at Swindon, commensurate with the wants of the company, where a change of engines may be adequately made, and the trains stopped for the purpose of the passengers taking refreshment as is the case at Wolverton on the London and Birmingham Railway. The establishment there would also comprehend the large repairing shops for the locomotive department and this circumstance rendered it necessary to arrange for the building of cottages etc for the residence of many persons employed in the service of the company.

The directors have under these circumstances made an arrangement with responsible builders for the erection of refreshment rooms and cottages without the employment of any capital from the company. The profits of the refreshment business are to remunerate them for their outlay in the accommodation required at Swindon by passenger's consequent upon the trains stopping at that place. The company are to provide the land for the cottages and to secure the builders a fixed rent upon lease, which rent will of course be reimbursed by the tenants of the cottages. The only increased demand upon the company for capital at Swindon will be to defray the cost of that additional land and of the engine establishment and repairing shops there, which are indispensably necessary.'

The contractor who acquired the lease was J.D.&C. Rigby of Millbank, Westminster. Rigbys had already been involved with the company and had built the station at Slough – from which Queen Victoria would make her first rail journey in 1842 – and all the stations between Steventon and Corsham. They were now commissioned to build and operate the station refreshment rooms and 300 cottages for the workmen. They were also the main contractors for building the workshops, though this was financed directly by the company. Almost immediately Rigby's sub-let the catering provision at the refreshment rooms to Samuel Young Griffiths, manager of the Queen's Hotel, Cheltenham. The sub lease was for a term of seven years at an annual rental of £1,100 and an additional payment of £6,000. This was entered into on 24th December 1841 and initially was focussed on a temporary station structure, which was superseded when the new permanent building was opened in 1842. Griffiths would prove to be a poor choice for such an important position with near disastrous consequences for the GWR. It is certainly at this time that the name Swindon was corrupted to 'Swindle-us' by many disgruntled passengers who were forced to avail themselves of the facilities and fare available there.

The enormous extent of the building work required at Swindon soon proved to be beyond Rigbys' capacity to fulfil all the demands being made upon them and work in the Railway Village soon began to lag behind. The whole sorry story is well told in the RCHME volume. Suffice it to say that the original intent was that the 300 cottages should have been completed by Christmas 1842 but that aim was not finally achieved until 1855. It is tempting to place all the blame upon Rigbys for the delays but that would be unjust, the GWR Board has also to shoulder much of the responsibility, as the aforementioned history states:

'... the GWR was equally to blame for the delays in building the cottages. It had been over optimistic in expecting a single contractor to build at its own expense 300 cottages in a little over a year. The General Committee minutes also show that the company adopted a penny-pinching approach when dealing with contractors, holding up payments for months and sometimes even for several years. The company also sought to slow down building works deliberately during periods of recession. For all these reasons the 300 cottages were not to be completed until 1855 fourteen years after Brunel made his original sketch plan for the village.'

Those who suffered most from these unfortunate shortcomings, however, were the workforce themselves and the families which accompanied them to this new and no doubt previously unheard of part of North Wiltshire. Thus, it is to their situation that our attention must now turn.

The first question to address is where, indeed, did all the skilled and not so skilled workforce come from? There were no nearby industrial hubs with a ready supply of such labour. As I have indicated a small proportion of the local population possessed appropriate skills but they were not boilermakers, turners and fitters, coppersmiths or metal workers of all but the most basic of kinds. These were not enginemen or firemen, policemen or engineers, coppersmiths or wheelwrights. Once again Gooch, with his many links in Scotland, Northumberland and Durham, Lancashire and South Wales, was well placed to recruit staff and he seems to have used these contacts, coupled with the inducement of better wages and living conditions, to encourage people to make the arduous journey to Wiltshire. The 1851 census can be used to give some basic indication of people's origins by birth, though it cannot tell us from which town or county individuals moved from to come to Swindon.

In 1842, the landscape gardener J.C. Loudon visited Swindon and gave a memorable description of the refreshments rooms: '*At the station, which is considered half way between London and Taunton, there are four large refreshment rooms, two on each side of the road, of noble proportions and finished in the most exquisite style with the walls panelled, Sylvesters fireplaces and beautifully painted ceilings. Such rooms cannot fail greatly to improve the taste of everyone who enters them; and in this respect alone the proprietors of the railroad are entitled to the best thanks of the country*'. Perhaps he looked but did not sample the fare which did not match the surroundings in which it was served. Brunel certainly hated it.

Swindon station from the west in 1845, looking towards London, from an illustration first published in the *Illustrated London News*. The two infamous refreshment blocks linked by an open bridge are visible on either side. However, the track layout as illustrated here is rather problematic. Even in 1845 there were two through roads that were used for stabling stock, with each platform served by a loop, which does not appear to have been included on the Down (right) side. Presumably the engine is meant to be shunting empty stock, otherwise it is running 'wrong line'. Part of the Up side (left) building still exists, otherwise the rest of the buildings shown here have been swept away. Note the point capstan on the right-hand side, which does not appear to be serving any useful purpose, though it is presumably meant to operate the point in the centre foreground.

Looking west from the station footbridge in 1845, towards the village and workshops. This sketch is vivid rather than realistic though perhaps gives an idea of an industrial landscape transplanted into an otherwise rural setting. The four track layout through the station is, however, more accurately shown, whilst on the right is train is seen arriving off the Gloucester line. Note the waggon turntable on the left.

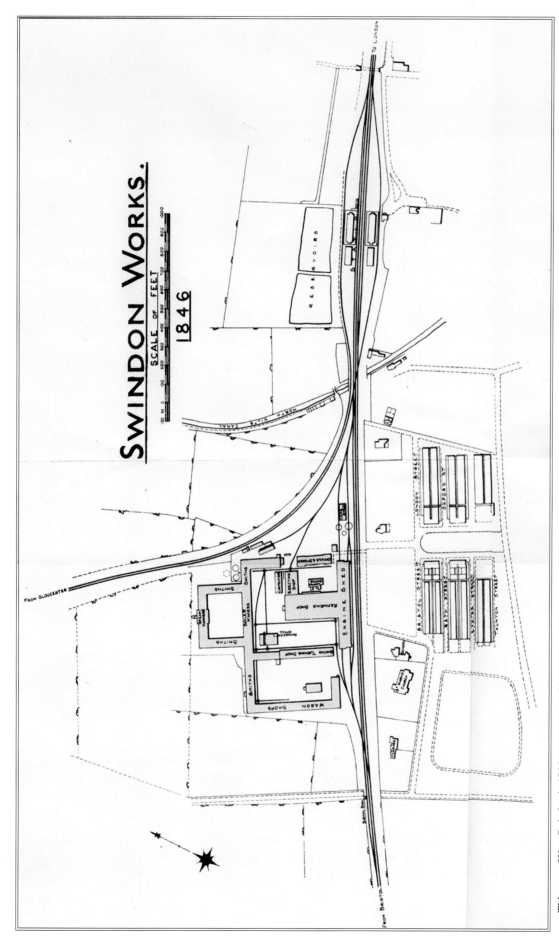

This map of New Swindon in 1846 conveys a sound impression of the extent of the works and village at this time. It is notable that the housing was far from complete, which was a major inconvenience at the time leading to vast overcrowding in the cottages which were habitable. The only supply of water available was from the canal reservoir behind the station, one or two local streams and the Croft Spring up in Old Town, about an hour's walk away. St. Mark's Church and school are shown as are the two large detached houses for senior staff, to the north of London Street and alongside the running lines. The workshops themselves had been erected in two phases of construction, 1841-43 and 1844-46. Although there would be some further minor additions there would be little major changes until the Rolling Mills were built in 1860-61. Some minor 'ribbon development' along the canal is illustrated in the area known as Queens Town, which would slowly expand over the coming years. The other area where some accommodation was available, apart from the Old Town, was at Westcott Farm which was off to the left of the map and not illustrated. The field adjacent to the west end of the village was provided for exercise and sports, including cricket matches and other such activities. Known as 'The Park', it still exists today alongside the much renovated railway village.

This copy of the famous Edward Snell painting of New Swindon in 1849, executed just before he left the GWR for a new life in Australia, was photographed by the author from an early print. Interestingly, the version reproduced in the *Great Western Railway Magazine* in January 1911 differs slightly in minor details, possibly as a result of restoration at some stage. The painting vividly illustrates the extent of the whole site at the time. Most of the cottages in the village had been erected though there were minor additions made in the early 1850s. The vicarage, Church of St. Marks, Bristol Street School (note the children dancing around a Maypole) and the two villas occupied by senior staff are all carefully laid out on the south side of the main line. In the middle distance, the route of the North Wilts Canal is defined as a line of trees crossing from left to right to pass beneath the railway just this side of the

station, whilst further to the right, the confluence of the two canals is visible (there is a barely visible overbridge just beyond the junction). Just before the station on the right is the Queen's Tap public house and the few dwellings which constituted 'Queens Town', as the area was known locally. The Works site is vividly portrayed and the various workshops can be identified from the accompanying diagram. The artist has imagined hovering with his back to Bristol, so the painting is orientated from west to east looking toward London. The strikingly rural nature of North Wiltshire in 1849 is very evident in the illustration and contrasts strongly with the industrial activity of the works site. The painting conveys a very strong sense of order and cleanliness in the new town and workshops – ordered they may have been, however, clean they certainly were not.

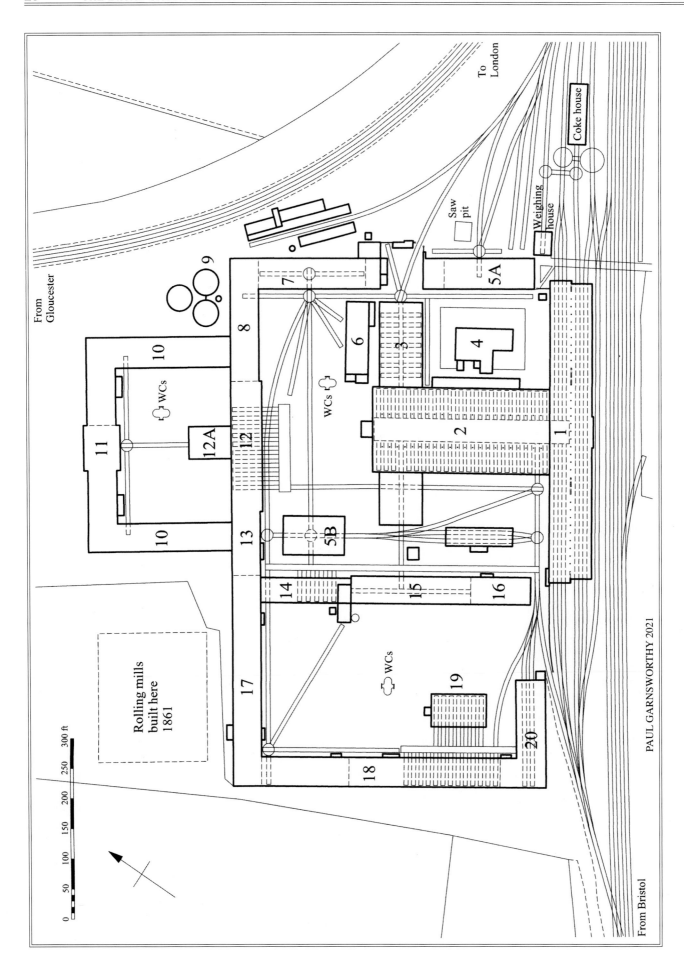

PAUL GARNSWORTHY 2021

SWINDON WORKS IN 1849 – LEGEND

1. 'A' Shop. Running shed, engine maintenance, running repairs, inspection, storage of engines, etc. Building erected in stages between 1841 and 1846.

2. 'B' Shed. Always referred to as such but properly known as 'B' Shop. Main engine repair shed accessed by a traverser via the running shed. Built 1841-43

3. 'C' Shop. Engine Erecting Shop; *Great Western* constructed here 1846. Built 1842-43

4. Copper Smiths & Brass Foundry. Copper and brass fittings, pipework and castings made and finished. Built 1842-43. Demolished circa 1873 when the 'B' Shed extension was erected, opened in 1874

5. Stores. Storage for tools and materials. Built 5A: 1842-43, 5B: 1845-46

6. Carpenters Shop. Production and maintenance of all woodwork involved in locomotive, carriage and waggon construction. Built 1842-43

7. 'D1' Shop. A two-storeyed building which also incorporated some office space and a boiler house. The ground floor was initially the Fitting Shop and was equipped with heavy machinery for cylinder boring, etc. By 1849 it seems in most part to have been turned over to the construction, repair and maintenance of wheels. The upper floor was a light machine shop. It may be here that the first meetings of what would become the Medical Fund took place in 1843-46. Built 1841-43

8. Brass & Locksmiths. Brass finishing & machining, polishing & grinding, Lockmaking. Built 1841-43

9. Gas Works. Built to supply gas to the various shops for lighting, heating annealing and brazing etc. Built by 1849

10. Smiths Shops. Most early engine construction was effected by smithing and forging, mainly the former. Across the whole works complex by 1849, there were about 180 smiths hearths, of which about 50 were in these two Smiths Shops. Built 1842-44

11. Steam Hammers. Originally a smithy, this building was enlarged in 1844 to house the first Nasmyth steam hammer to which at least one larger hammer had been added by 1849. Built 1842-44

12. Boiler Shop. Used initially for boiler repairs, waggon construction and other heavy forging work. *Great Western's* boiler was built here in 1846. Built 1842-43

12A. Boiler Shop extension. Built 1844

13. Wheel Shop. The original works wheel shop, by 1849 had been incorporated into the Boiler Shop. *Premier* and *Great Western's* wheels were made here in 1846. Wheel work was taken over by 'D1' and 'D2' Shops. Built 1842-44

14. Boiler House & Furnace. Power mainly for the range of buildings on the west side of the Works that date from 1845-47. Built 1845-46

15. 'D2' Shop. Like 'D1' Shop this was a two-storey building. Its not clear what the upper floor was first used for though it was laid out as a machine shop. It may have been a store of some sort for it was used for meetings of what became the Mechanics Institute and even for dancing and other entertainments. In later years it became the 'O' Shop or Works Tool Room. The lower floor was a Machine Shop used for locomotive valve gear manufacture and fitting, wheel boring and tyre grinding. This is now the entrance area of the Steam Museum where *Lord of the Isles'* wheels are displayed, in perhaps the same place that they were finished in 1851. Built 1845-46

16. Smiths Shop. An adjunct to 'D2' Shop. Now also part of the Steam Museum complex. Built 1845-46

17. Smiths Shop. This, by 1849, incorporated a spring making facility. Tyre welding was its main activity initially. Built 1845-47

18. Waggon Shops. Manufacture and erection of waggons, many of which were made of iron or had iron components. Built 1845-47

19. Tender Shop. Tender tank and frame construction and erection. Was initially a waggon paint shop. Built 1845-46

20. Waggon Paint Shop. Painting and finishing of waggons. Built 1846-48

NOTES

1. 1849. Because of the turndown in work and the significant layoff of men, activity, especially in the waggon works, was at a low ebb or had been suspended. Part of the waggon paint shop was in use as a store for machinery, some of which was new and still housed in its original packing cases. The situation continued into the early 1850s.

2. 1843-49. Even in the six years from the opening of the Works in 1843 to the date of Edward Snell's drawing in 1849, some of the activities in the various shops changed from their original usage but the available information is contradictory in parts and can be hard to interpret. The information contained above is based on original sources and the notes about the Works given in the *GWR Magazine* between 1911 and 1914, written by A.J.L. White.

3. Shop Lettering. In later years all the Locomotive Workshops were given letters beginning with 'A' and concluding with 'X'. A scheme begun in the early years but not carried forward beyond 'D' initially. This situation seems to have persisted until the late 1860s when Armstrong's expansion and reorganisation of the workshops began. From 1868, the new carriage and waggon shops were numbered from '1', after which all carriage and waggon shops were known by their numbers alone. This situation continued until the consolidation and reorganisation of the Works by British Railways in the 1960s.

Nonetheless, the information gives a vivid impression of the cosmopolitan complexion of the early workforce. By percentage it breaks down in the following way:

- 31% – the North of England or Scotland
- 18% – Gloucestershire and Bristol
- 8% – Greater London
- 10% – Cornwall, Devon and Somerset
- 8% – Wiltshire

The remaining 25% of those recorded as employed at Swindon in 1851 came from just about all the other areas of the British Isles including Ireland. However, notable for their almost total absence are people from the industrialised West Midlands. Gooch had no personal connections there, whilst in all probability there was already plenty of work available to the skilled workers in that region, so uprooting to Swindon would not have been much of an attraction. It is possible that initially there were more people from the north but the financial difficulties of the late 1840s, which we will reflect on later, may have induced many, especially the unmarried, to move away to find work elsewhere. As far as skills were concerned over half the workforce, which also included engine drivers, firemen, policemen and administrative staff, was covered by five categories:

- 13.5% – Fitters and Turners
- 12.5% – Labourers
- 11.5% – Smiths and Smith Strikers
- 9.4% – Boilersmiths and Boilermakers
- 7.0% – Engine Erectors

Most of those who are categorised as labourers had been recruited locally. Wages ranged from £3 12s 7d per month for labourers to £7 4s 6d for foremen. The latter were men of exceptional skill and talent who carried great weight among the workforce and who almost universally originally hailed from the North East.

The average age of the workforce in 1851 was 32. A few were very young, ranging from 12 years of age upwards, whilst an apprentice scheme was already up and running comprising mainly 15-18 year olds. A few women are shown as employed as home workers, i.e. as cleaners and laundresses. Those who did have jobs connected to the railway were almost without exception widows of GWR employees. This may be an early example of a company practise which, in later years, became a source of much

This photograph is believed to have been taken in 1860 before the erection of the Rolling Mills had begun. It shows part of the 1844-46 range of buildings, with the two-storey 'D2' Shop on the right. The ground floor was used by the wheelwrights and the upper storey for machining and storage, and also may have been one of the places first used by the workmen who formed the Mechanics Institute for meetings. The high roofed building behind and to the right is the original Boiler Shop and the one with the water tower and tall hexagonal chimney housed two larger furnaces. The low roofed building at the left rear was used for tyre welding. The Rolling Mills later occupied the site behind this shop. The broad gauge waggon with the wheels outside the frames in the left foreground is interesting and unusual, and note the line to Kemble and Gloucester heading away north in the left background.

comfort in Swindon. The GWR management always looked very favourably upon families who had through accident or illness lost their chief, i.e. male, wage earner. The families of men who were injured or killed in the company's service were given financial compensation and where possible a wife or a daughter was found employment in the company's service. After 1868, when the carriage works opened, the opportunities for women workers became more varied. Many were employed as French Polishers or worked in the upholstery and uniform makers' shops. Some made the netting which, in ages past, was strung between ornate cast iron supports and upon which we placed our bags or cases in the company's coaches. As the years progressed others became clerks and secretaries and operated the Works' own telephone exchange. However, we are now getting very much ahead of ourselves but these examples are proof positive of the GWR's benevolent attitude to its employees to whom they owed so much and who, sometimes, made the supreme sacrifice in their service.

The last point brings me to the grim story of life in the new town in its earliest years. We have already noted that the housing situation was tenuous for a number of years because of delays

in erecting the 300 cottages which had been initially envisaged. When the works formally opened on 2nd January 1843, there were approximately 180 men on the payroll. In addition to these, there were enginemen, firemen and thirty-two others made up of policemen, porters and station staff. One of our chief sources of information about these early years comes from Edward Snell, who became Assistant Works Manager under Archibald Sturrock, who occupied the chief role of Works Manager under Gooch's leadership, from 1842 until he left to become the locomotive engineer of the Great Northern Railway in 1850.

Snell had come to Swindon in February 1843, following an apprenticeship with Henry Stothert of Bath. He started work at Swindon on 1st March as a fitter, earning £2 per week. Over the following years he successively became an erector, inspector of engines and draughtsman, becoming head draughtsman in August 1845 at two guineas a week. In 1846 he was sent by Gooch to visit various machine tool and locomotive manufactories in the North West. Among others he visited Whitworths in Manchester, the Haigh Foundry in Wigan and Jacksons Rolling Mills in Saltford. Snell travelled via Gloucester and Birmingham

This view of the storage area at the back of what had originally been the Erecting ('C') Shop (demolished in 1911) is looking towards the two-storey 'D1' Shop of 1843. Though reroofed and altered in various ways, it is still recognisable with its panel and pier style construction. The mixed gauge waggon turntable in the foreground, still aligned to some broad gauge track, was the last remaining example of its type in the Works complex and is now preserved. This photograph dates from the 1950s, by which time the old 'D1' Shop had been converted into office accommodation. The whole area in the foreground, including the turntable, storage space and the trackwork where the rail-mounted hand crane is standing, was cleared in the 1960s. A traverser was built in its place to enable DMU vehicles and other stock to access the newly refurbished 'B' Shed and 'B' Shed extension. These shops were completely reorganised for DMU maintenance and the neighbouring 'R' Shop (now the Steam Museum) for bogie repairs, becoming respectively '19' and '20' shops. The workman in the photograph is operating a hydraulic capstan.

and on his journey back visited Liverpool, Birkenhead, Chester and Crewe. On his return he commenced design work on some new shops for the works and on 8th November 1846 was made 'general superintendent of the factory', in other words Assistant to the Works Manager. He was now earning at least £2 15s 0d a week but though his position was secure, he was asked to take a significant cut in wages in 1849 during the financial crisis of that year – to £2 a week. Disillusioned by this turn of events he resigned and emigrated to Australia in the latter part of 1849. This was a shame because not only was Edward Snell a highly competent man, he also kept a journal which gives us a fascinating view of day to day life in the railway village and workshops. For example, having newly arrived in Swindon to discover there was already a 'housing crisis' he wrote:

'*Rather queer lodgings mine, at present the house only one storey high,*

walls of rough brick inside and most of the rooms occupied by a barefoot Scots woman and her family.'

Over the next few years, he moved about between one lodge and another at least nine times between 1843 and 1846. He also noted that since he had arrived in Swindon in 1843, he had never felt '*really well*'. The land on which the new town was being built was low lying on a clay sub soil, the drainage was poor and the water quality – except that which was brought from the Old Town spring – undrinkable until it was boiled. The chief problem, however, was the total lack of sanitation. Each cottage was supplied with a small backyard with a privy in the corner. Each pair of cottages had their privy placed side by side and they were arranged in such a way that they both drained into a covered sewer that ran down the middle of the rear alleyway between the blocks of houses, which was accessed by a series of

The earliest known photograph inside the works, this important and historic view shows the interior of 'B' Shed in about 1870. Also referred to as the Repair Shop, it is the building illustrated in J.C. Bourne's famous lithograph (see Part 2, page 90). However, by the time this picture was taken, the building's structure had undergone some modernisation, carried out in 1863-64. As originally constructed the locomotive bays, which were fed by the central traverser, had a low roof which not only made them dark and oppressive to work in but precluded the installation of overhead cranes. To improve working conditions and install overhead equipment it was necessary to raise the roof over the repair bays. To this end the old wooden supports were replaced by cast iron columns, evident here, and the outside wall on either side extended upward. The original 'double rise' roof over the traverser area was left untouched at this time, as the photograph proves, though it was replaced in 1874 when the 'B' Shed extension was added. The traverser had originally been propelled by human power but at some unrecorded date the rather pretty little donkey engine shown here was fitted, which perhaps added to the ease of working in the shed but certainly also made the atmosphere in the building fuggy and dismal. Behind the photographer, the traverser extended all the way into 'A' Shop, illustrated on pages 38-39. It is also noteworthy that mixed gauge trackwork had been laid on the traverser. It is impossible to identify any specific class of engine stabled over the pits on the left-hand side, though two pairs of 8ft 0in. diameter driving wheels suggests the presence of at least two members of the 'Iron Duke' and/or 'Courier' classes.

manholes. In addition, household rubbish was disposed of through a hole in the rear wall of the yards behind each house or pair of houses. The rubbish seems simply to have been pushed out into the alleyway where it was left to be collected by the night soil men, an unenviable job if ever there was one. Other than the rain there was no means of flushing out the sewers so that they soon overflowed, hardly surprising when one recalls that each two roomed cottage could be home to ten people!

The household rubbish would also have built up to a considerable extent, so it is hardly surprising that the atmosphere in the new town soon became putrid and stinking. This was quickly followed by illness and infection, an outcome that any modern epidemiologist would immediately be able to predict. Regrettably, the doctors of the 1840s were not equipped to deal with such a crisis for that indeed was what was to occur. Typhus, smallpox and cholera outbreaks occurred periodically between 1847 and 1852. Such were the ravages of these infections that I estimated in 1980 – though working from less than complete records as I now recognise – that child mortality figures during those dark years approached 50% of live births and that may have been an underestimate during the peaks of the epidemics. Some efforts were made to alleviate the problem; for example, Gooch ordered Sturrock to have all the drains cleansed while the inside of the houses should be thoroughly cleaned and whitewashed. Yet the epidemic only grew worse.

Indeed the sufferings of those who had come to this new 'El Dorado' to find secure work and homes was to be multiplied, for these public health problems went hand in hand with a disastrous downturn in the nation's economy, political instability and in 1848, the year of revolutions, international turmoil on an almost unprecedented scale. This had dire consequences for the Works and the workers. Gooch was forced to make swingeing cuts to the locomotive department's budget, a fair proportion of which

The reverse of the *carte-de-visite* view of the interior of Swindon Works, left, showing the photographer's details. Intriguingly, W.H. Fox was not local, hailing from Weymouth, where he had a prestigious Royal Baths address. This suggests he would have travelled up to Swindon on the Wilts, Somerset & Weymouth line, which ran from Weymouth to Chippenham via Westbury. Having run out of money after only building part of its route, the WS&WR had passed to the GWR in 1851. It was converted to standard gauge in 1874, so was still broad gauge when Fox travelled up to Swindon to take his photographs. The plural is deliberate; it is inconceivable that he took only this picture, leaving us with the tantalising thought that there could be more photographs out there still to find, if they have survived!

involved short time working and redundancies at Swindon. At the beginning of 1847, the numbers employed in the workshops had risen to 1,800 but by the end of 1849, as the nation's financial difficulties were just beginning to turn around, that figure had reduced to just 618. Many moved away from the new town at this time, while others tightened their belts and tried to hang on. Initially it was unmarried men who were laid off, as they were considered to be the most mobile and could attempt to find work elsewhere but there was not sufficient of these to prevent families from suffering terrible depredations as well. Members of my family were fortunate, as they could return to their old lifestyle and family home. Few were so lucky and with only the provision of the Poor Law and Parish relief to fall back on, circumstances, in the light of the challenges already outlined, must have been almost unbearable.

There was in fact a light in the darkness, though few would have recognised this at the time. The GWR had provided for the spiritual life of the community by founding and erecting a new Parish and parish church, which was consecrated on 25th April 1845 and dedicated to St. Mark the Evangelist. A school had also been founded in 1844 for the education of the company's employees' children; a most enlightened move when one remembers that the nation did not introduce compulsory education for children aged 5 to 11 years until 1870. Beyond these established means of support the men were motivated to work together to help themselves. Though *Pigot's Directory of Wiltshire* in 1842 gives the names of four doctors that were resident in the Swindon area, it seems that the early workforce found it hard to access medical care. However, they seem to have been motivated to do something about this problem for Edward Snell mentions in his diaries the existence of a 'sick club', which was evidently already in existence before he arrived in Swindon early in 1843.

Reading Daniel Gooch's diaries, one gains the impression that he was instrumental in setting up several organisations to satisfy the social and medical needs of New Swindon's workforce. In fact, the opposite was the case in that what would become the GWR Medical Fund and the Mechanics Institute was initiated by the workforce and then, which does stand to Gooch's credit, rapidly endorsed and supported by the company. Thus, with the management's backing, the Sick Club became the GWR Locomotive & Carriage Department Sick Fund Society in 1844, which in turn became the GWR Medical Fund Society in 1847. This organisation was to play a major role in overcoming the health problems of the late 1840s and early 1850s, and would go on to be one of the jewels in the crown of Swindon's growth and prosperity. It was a condition of employment that everyone paid into the medical fund and subscriptions towards its support were deducted at source from the men's wages. A Medical Officer of Health, Stuart Rea, was appointed and he in turn instigated a regular programme of monthly inspections of the company's houses to ensure that they were clean and inhabitable – an important innovation for the time.

This most interesting of photographs, which I only came across recently and have not seen reproduced anywhere before, shows the north side of the Rolling Mills and is looking east circa 1885. Careful study of the picture shows that mixed gauge trackwork was in place. The numerous internal user waggons are of considerable interest and that doyen of GWR rolling stock, John Lewis, was able to identify some of them. The wooden open waggon with the white cross on the side and the number 211, for example, is an ex-West Midland Railway coal or coke waggon. Note also the universal application of 5-link shackled couplings. Rebuilding work was to mean that this scene would be virtually unrecognisable within a couple of decades.

The Mechanics Institute, which had also begun at the instigation of the workforce, initially as a library which collected volumes that could be lent out among its members, was formally inaugurated on 8th January 1844. It was formed '*for the purpose of disseminating useful knowledge and encouraging rational amusement among all classes of people employed by the Great Western Railway Company at Swindon.*' Meetings were initially held in a part of the workshops which remarkably is still used for educational purposes today, for the Railway Museum's upper lecture theatre occupies the same site that was first used for meetings in the mid-1840s. Later, the School Room was also used for theatricals and other social events and ultimately a purpose-built building was provided in the centre of the Railway Village, in Emlyn Square, in 1855.

By the time this was opened, conditions in the New Town had radically changed. Gone were the temporary huts that had been erected in lieu of permanent housing, for not only had the company houses finally been completed but a building known as 'The Barracks' was also finished in 1854. This was intended to house single men in a two to a room dormitory and had been started in 1847 but fell victim to the recession and social hardships of the time. Construction, alongside the final elements of the Village, began again in 1851 and its first occupants moved in either in late 1853 or early 1854. By this time numbers employed in the works had exceeded those at the peak of employment in 1847 and further accommodation was required. As an aside it must be remarked that young men, ever inventive, will soon find ways to get around prohibitions aimed at preventing members of the opposite sex from entering their accommodation. In my Theological College in the early 1970s, there was a well attested story that men were ordered for many years to dismantle their beds and place them outside of their rooms if they intended to entertain a female member of the university in their lodgings. This rule persisted for many years until someone pointed out to the Principal (an unmarried man) that beds were not a prerequisite for – well, you can supply the rest of this sentence for yourselves!

What was the case in the 1970s was very certainly applicable in the 1850s and the building soon gained a shameful reputation, to such an extent that it was finally closed down and re-equipped as temporary family accommodation for those who came to Swindon from South Wales in the early 1860s to work in the new rolling mills. Following that, the whole building was transformed into a Wesleyan Church in 1867. In 1962, the building, by now redundant as a church, was transformed into the first railway museum and is now a local social centre.

Alongside the railway's own housing, several local entrepreneurs grasped the opportunity to develop speculative accommodation on their own land. The first such example of this appears to have taken place on Westcott Farm, a little to the west of the company's own houses. In 1843, William Plummer, who owned the farm, had purchased some land adjacent to the farm estate. Here he began erecting houses, generally built in local stone, along the west side of what became Westcott Place and Westcott Street. By 1851, Westcott was described as a modern village and, by 1853, over seventy cottages had been erected. By 1848, the emerging village already had twelve shops, most of which are recorded as either shoemakers or beer houses. Let us not forget that beer was routinely drunk at this time in lieu of the contaminated water. Nonetheless, it was often drunk to excess, which despite the work of the churches and the ongoing social engineering that was developing at the time, became a significant problem in the early life of the New Town.

At this juncture it is important to return to the purpose for

This interior view of 'B' Shed circa 1906 shows the original five-arc roof along with a new and much shallower steam driven traverser that remained in use until the early 1920s.

The original Erecting Shop or 'C' Shop as it was designated, seen here in 1907; it was demolished in 1911. Used initially for waggon construction, it had to be cleared quickly to allow locomotive erection to begin at the end of 1845. All the early Swindon-built broad gauge engines were made here, including *Premier*, *Great Western* and *Iron Duke*. The limited capacity of the shop helps to explain why production of some of the larger classes of engines took place over prolonged periods of time. Note the overhead crane, one of the first such installations in the workshops. Of the engines seen here, on the far left is 'Standard Goods' 0-6-0 No. 423, built in August 1867 and withdrawn in February 1912 and next to it are the frames and cab of 'Dean Goods' 0-6-0 No. 2479, new in April 1896. This engine was withdrawn by the GWR in October 1940 but then went into War Department service, as WD No. 169, although was not one of those sent abroad, instead with others of the class being employed at one of the various ordnance depots around the UK. Its final fate is unknown.

which the New Town and the Works were founded. The initial building at Swindon was intended to supply repair facilities for the company's locomotives and some rolling stock. Gooch, however, was intent on extending the facilities to allow new locomotive construction to commence as soon as was practical. To achieve this he needed additional workshops, new facilities and tooling, not to mention the skilled labour to make boilers, cast and bore cylinders and make driving wheels. To this end we have already noted that he ordered a Nasmyth steam hammer in 1844 at a cost of £300. This was accompanied by an order to a '*Mr Napier*' for a '*traversing frame*' (i.e. table) and lifting apparatus. Further machine tools arrived and Napier installed his traverser in the new erecting shop in May 1845 and his hydraulic lifting apparatus – an overhead crane – in August. At about the same time as these new tools were being ordered, the board, in November 1844, approved an invitation of tenders from '*good makers for six boilers for the six new goods engines which are proposed to be built at Swindon*'. Unfortunately, no record exists of the firm which was contracted to supply these boilers. I once asked Alan Peck, who I got to know very well in the years before he died,

if he knew who the contractor was. He replied that though he could not prove it conclusively he believed that it was Robert Stephenson. So far, I have not been able to verify this assertion but research continues.

In fact, the very first pieces of rolling stock produced at Swindon in 1843 were iron waggons. An order for eighteen such vehicles was placed in October of that year, which states that they are in addition to those '*already ordered*'. This evidence is contained in the company's General Committee minutes for 26th October 1843. Erection of the first engines began in the new 'C' Erecting Shop, which was an adjunct to the Repair Shop, in 1845. *Premier* was the first completed, in February 1846, and was followed by eleven other similar engines (ordered in two batches) delivered between May 1846 and May 1847.

Meanwhile, the board had authorised Gooch to proceed with the construction at Swindon of a '*little engine*' – as Gooch enigmatically refers to it in a contemporary letter – to be built with 8ft 0in. driving wheels and a 6ft 0in. firebox. Gooch confided that '*the great object in building her is to have her ready to start when the Gauge Question commences in Parliament next session or* on the first of April'. This engine, a much enlarged 'Fire Fly', was initially to be named *Lightning* but was rapidly rechristened *Great Western*. Edward Snell was responsible for the detail drawings and the engine mounted the very first boiler to be built at Swindon. It is therefore properly accurately described as the first engine wholly built at Swindon but not the first outshopped and was indeed ready at the beginning of April. *Great Western* was manufactured and erected in just thirteen weeks, a remarkable achievement when one recalls that the workforce was still new and facilities untried.

Fortunately, we know something of the individuals involved in the manufacture of components and erection of the first waggons and engines. These details are contained in what is known as 'the Fawcett List' – a copy of which can be found in Appendix II of Alan Peck's book. It is named after one John Fawcett, who comments, '*I myself contracted for and made the first 8ft wheels for the engines* Great Western *and* Lord of the Isles. *Mr J.Waterson and Mr William Hogarth made the remainder of all the other driving wheels'*. There is a list of all the senior officers, beginning with Brunel and the foremen from each department, covering the years 1843-1865. There then follows a list of contractors - including Mr Fawcett – which suggests that a number of the early and highly skilled artisans attracted to Swindon were semi-independent contractors who employed their own staff or were brought in to train the staff but retained their independence. It is not quite clear to me how the system worked initially but it would seem that those who stayed – and they were too valuable to lose – were eventually absorbed into the company's employ. Alongside the contractors' names is the briefest description of what they were employed to do. These remarks are fascinating, for example:

• *Mr William Laverick – First Contractor for Steam Hammer Work; forgings etc*

• *Mr Richard Pattison – New Engine Erector, built* 1st engine Premier
• *Mr Robert Wardle & Mr Thomas Chilton – 1st Boilermakers & Contractors*
Mr John Brack & Mr Richard Tilley – came from Wigan and were the 1st contractors for building Iron trucks.

There are of course many other names mentioned but the entries copied above are perhaps the most interesting. I was particularly drawn to the comment about Messrs Brack & Tilley, who had been brought in from Wigan. To me this indicates that the majority of the others mentioned had perhaps a 'common' background probably on Tyneside and may have been well known to each other. One further entry is worthy of note:

• *Mr Henry Appleby – First Superintendent of the Running Department and the 'A' Shed was removed from Hay Lane to Swindon before the new works were completed.*

The 'A' Shed was the name of the broad gauge engine shed on which the two 'Fire Fly' Class carvings were placed initially. Both Alan Peck and, with more caution, the RCHME volume tell us that this building was erected in 1841, presumably because that is what is implied in the entry above. However, evidence has more recently emerged to challenge that assumption. My good friend Jack Hayward of Swindon has researched this in some depth and has come to the conclusion that the facilities for engine maintenance that were originally erected at Hay Lane – the railway's temporary terminus before the opening to Chippenham on 31st May 1841 – were removed to Swindon as a temporary measure until the new shed could be built. A reading of the entry above could certainly justify such a conclusion but there is more. When inspecting the temporary facilities at Hay Lane the Board of Trade Inspector Sir Frederick Smith stated:

'*Although Hay Lane station is merely intended as a temporary terminus, the company are forming it, in regard to sidings, switches and other*

In 1873, work commenced on building a new and much larger Boiler Shop. When completed the old one, shown here, was taken over by the millwrights, whose large lathes and boring machines, some of which were first installed in the 1840s, are apparent here. The timber framed overhead crane may well be the one installed when the shop was first brought into use in 1845-46. This photograph was part of a series of internal views of the workshops taken in 1885.

ABOVE: 'O' Shop, seen here circa 1910, was located in the upper floor of 'D2' Shop and housed the Works' Tool Room, a most important and significant part of any workshop complex. The Tool Room was later moved elsewhere and this space became a bolt store. Today it is part of the Steam Museum complex.
BELOW: Some of the works' steam hammers at the same period with, just visible on the far left, what is thought to be one of Naysmith's early hammers. On the right, note the former locomotive boiler providing steam and the tall elegant gas lamp.

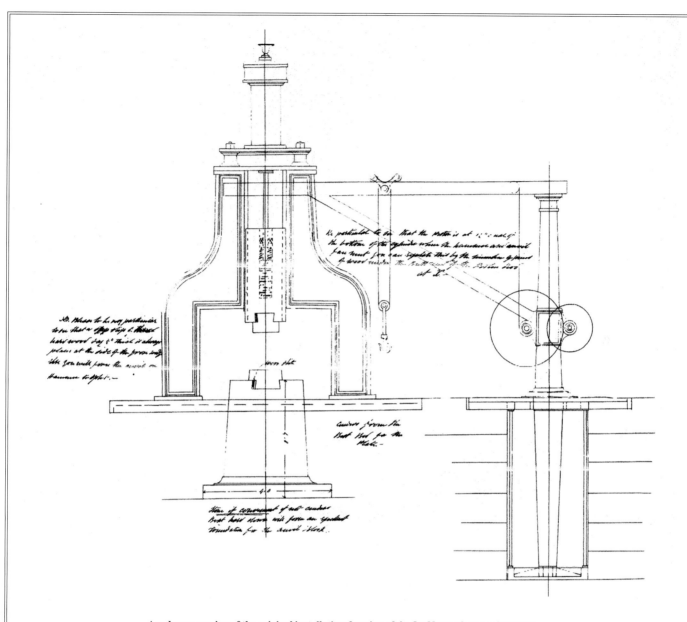

A redrawn version of the original installation drawing of the fist Naysmth steam hammer.

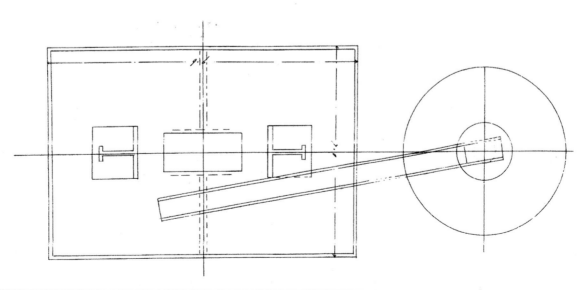

The original 'A' Shop. This building was the original broad gauge locomotive running shed, built and erected in stages between 1841 and 1846, and seen here in 1928-29 shortly before demolition commenced. The oldest part of the complex is to the left, with the substantial stone buttresses; note the set of curved top double doors on the far side entrance. There is evidence to suggest that part at least of this original construction was brought from the temporary terminus at Hay Lane (about 2 miles west of Swindon) and re-erected. However, this small shed soon proved to be inadequate and was extended in stages over the next five years. The two finely carved cartouches of 'Fire Fly' Class engines were mounted at the tops of the stone buttresses, with their Normanesque curved details, which faced the main line at each end of the newer building. These were removed in 1906 and placed in the wall of the new office block where they remain today. When in full use, the double track building nearest the main line appears to have been the running shed, whilst the older building, nearest the workshops, was used for storage and maintenance. Access to 'B' Shed, the main repair shed, was through these buildings via a traverser, access to which was gained via the double sliding doors visible halfway down. Rail access was, of course, also available within the shed itself, which must have been inconvenient at times. Old Swindonians will tell you that if you stand by the $77^{3}/_{4}$ mile post outside the works, visible here, you are roughly speaking, standing at the same height above sea level as the top of the cupola of St. Paul's cathedral in London. This example was always given to explain the genius of Brunel, who designed his magnificent railway with such easy gradients. By the late 1860s, these buildings were proving to be ever more challenging to use effectively and in 1871 a new running shed was opened alongside the Gloucester line. Thereafter, these building were increasingly given over to repair and maintenance work, and were incorporated into the main works complex, although stabling of broad gauge engines continued at the east end of the shed and in the adjacent yard until 1892. After demolition in 1929, the buildings behind the sheds, partly in view on the left, were extended outwards to increase capacity and ease of access.

The opposite end of the original 'A' Shop or broad gauge engine shed, taken after removal of the 'Fire Fly' cartouches from the ornamental buttresses in 1906. Engines visible here are, from right to left, a Beyer, Peacock 0-6-0, a 'Barnum' 2-4-0 and a 'Dean Goods' 0-6-0.

mechanical arrangements in the same extensive and substantial manner as is the ordinary practise at permanent terminals.'

Furthermore, *Herepath's Railway Journal* noted in its November 1841 edition that:

'… *the whole of the locomotive department of the GWR has been removed from Wootton Bassett to Swindon.*'

A final piece of this jigsaw relates to Charles Collett who, as Chief Mechanical Engineer in 1929, was given permission to demolish the old '*1846 engine shed*'. If Collett was accurate with his date – and why should he not have been – then we can assume that, from 1841, the temporary engine shed or house, as it was known, which had been removed from Hay Lane was used until a new building could be completed and brought into use. This seems to me to be the most satisfactory conclusion which can be drawn from all the available evidence. In passing it should be mentioned that Henry Appleby was also a most significant individual. He was among the elite group of early enginemen who Gooch mostly recruited from the Liverpool & Manchester and the Manchester & Leeds railways, though Appleby is said to have come from the North East – he certainly spoke with a strong Geordie accent. That he was in the confidence of Gooch is borne out by his presence with his boss on the footplate of *Orion* when the engine made its epic journey from Paddington to Exeter and back on 1st May 1844. He was certainly a most competent man, who occupied the post of what would later be known as the District Locomotive Superintendent, which he held for the rest of his life.

Of course, the story of Swindon Works as recounted here is far from complete. This essay is only intended to give a flavour of its early history from a slightly personal perspective. What I have attempted to do is to paint a more human picture than a purely chronological account of the building of the factory and the new railway town that grew up around it could supply. I am a proud Swindonian but I am not blind to the challenges, toils and travails of those who first came to North Wiltshire in the 1840s and '50s. Yet they laid the foundation for what would become one of the world's great locomotive, carriage and wagon workshops. Though these volumes are about the company's locomotives, it is also from here on very much the Works' story too, a very small part of which was played by a member of my own family. If some of the locomotives that they built would become the mechanical celebrities of their day, then those who built them were, undoubtedly, the heroes of this new age of engineering – an age which would change the world for all time and one whose achievements created the modern world, the fruits of which we enjoy today.

A VISIT TO THE GREAT WESTERN RAILWAY COMPANY'S WORKS AT SWINDON

From *Mechanics Magazine*, February 1853

By the favour of the Superintendent of the Great Western Company's works at Swindon, Minard C. Rea, Esq., we were afforded an opportunity, a few days ago, of witnessing some of the principal of the numerous engineering operations which are performed in this vast establishment, and of observing the wonderful division of labour, and the admirable dispositions of arrangement and discipline by which so much and such critically intricate work is performed. These works have been little more than ten years in existence, and in that comparatively short space of time they have grown to an extent, and have acquired an importance worthy of the gigantic scale of working which we see in everything incidental to the broad-gauge system of locomotion. They now extend over an area of fourteen acres, which is extremely well laid out for the convenient performance of the numerous subsidiary operations which go to make up the rolling stock of a railway company. In this space, with but few and unimportant exceptions, the manufacture of new locomotives, tenders and carriages, and the repair of old ones, are carried on. This work gives constant occupation to 1,500 hands, including fitters, moulders, smiths, erecters, and various other classes of workmen. At the present moment, more hands would be engaged if they were to be had; but the gradually increasing demand for skilled labour has affected, in a sensible degree, the working staff of this splendid establishment. The opening of the Oxford and Birmingham line, in particular, has added very largely to the demands upon the constructive department, and, together with a gradually extending traffic on the main line and its branches, must still further tend to augment its activity.

Swindon Works are situated upon the northern side of the main line, about 300 yards to the west of the station, where the Cheltenham, Gloucester and South Wales line branches off upon a sharp curve. Occupying a large space in the angle included between the main line and the branch, and having a number of sidings entering from the main line, the works have a very considerable footage on either side, and are laid out in rectangular blocks of stone buildings, separated by a number of communicating squares. Between these squares and the lower floors of the principal buildings there is a ready access with the line by means of trains of the same gauge, which communicate with it. They are accordingly filled with innumerable pairs of wheels united by their axles, which have been so accurately finished, in the lathe or by the grindstone, that a very feeble effort will suffice to set them in motion upon the level rails. In one part of the works we find the engines which impel the innumerable machines in the general shops. These are two in number, but are not in the same apartment. The one is an engine on the Cornish principle – that is, using steam at a high pressure, and condensing it on the other side of the piston. It was made at the well-known Hayle Foundry, Cornwall, and has two cylinders, nominally of 30-horse power each. The other engine is of the same power, but is on the ordinary condensing principle. It was made originally at Bath, but has since been almost completely reconstructed here. From the crank-shafts of these engines the power is carried to all parts of the works by long shafts running underground or overground, or by straps. Adjoining the latter, is an old blower of the double-acting description, for the smiths' forges; but this has for some time been abandoned for the fan. In another place we find a number of men engaged in making the huge axles for the bearing wheels of the locomotives, welding and beating up their component parts of iron, with the help of that most effective instrument – Naysmyth's steam hammer. Passing further on, into another building in the vicinity, we witness the highly interesting and elegant operation of proving, or shaping the tyres. We see too, imperfect or doubtful welds in the tyre cut through and renewed, and the metal rendered of uniform thickness and density, with the most wonderful ease of manipulation. Further on we see the manufacture of the spokes, and the formation of the inner peripheries of the running wheels of the carriages, and the metal framing of their floors. The manufacture of the tube-boilers, fire-boxes, and casing, is a department of the works on a very large scale, and of the greatest interest. In one long upper room we find forty-nine lathes, on the most modern construction, and twenty other machines for boring, slotting, cutting, and shaping the innumerable pieces of metalwork which go to make up the several parts of a locomotive engine. The grinding of the tyres for the locomotives, and especially of the great eight-feet driving wheels now in common use on the Great Western railway, is another of the more important subdivisions of labour in this great storehouse of skill and industry. Of the more striking of these we propose to give a general description, as it will serve to convey some idea of the present state of these arts of construction in metals, at the same time that it will probably be considered a matter of sufficient interest to deserve notice. Our own limits, the vast extent and variety of the works we saw, and the very short time we gave ourselves in the place, prevent us from undertaking anything more than endeavouring to present in a popular manner the ordinary routine of operations in their more important particulars.

Before passing on to notice these, we must say a word or two with references to the men themselves. On the south-side of the line, immediately opposite to the works, is a considerable village, of modern and neat appearance which the wants of this community have called into existence. It has received the name of New Swindon, to distinguish it from Swindon proper, the old Wiltshire market town, which stands upon an inconsiderable eminence about a mile from the railway. New Swindon is conveniently laid out in streets of commodious buildings, which are the residences of the men and their families. These have been drafted from nearly all the large manufacturing towns of the centre and north of England, and display in their physiognomy and general appearance a superiority over the rural population of the neighbouring country, with whom they have little, if, indeed, anything, in common. The affairs of New Swindon appear to go on with great smoothness; and, thanks to the liberal and kind treatment its principal inhabitants receive at 'the Works', and the intellectual character of the work they are engaged upon, they are tolerably well reconciled to the comparatively limited enjoyments at their disposal in this isolated situation. There is one great point of attraction, however, provided for them within the precincts of the works themselves, of the most admirable character, which is undoubtedly a great source of benefit to the Company itself, as well as to the men. In the year 1843 was founded the New Swindon Mechanics' Institution, which has now attained a considerable importance, and is deservedly cherished by the men as a source at once of instruction and entertainment. Its President is Mr Daniel Gooch; its Vice-president and Treasurer, Mr Minard C. Rea; and its Secretary, Mr Alfred Wickenden, under whose administration it enjoys a highly prosperous and efficient condition.

The annual soirée of the Institute had just taken place previously to our visit, and presented a scene of the most gratifying description. The 'great room' of the works was set apart for the occasion, and was profusely decorated with flowers and evergreens, while a fountain made in the works – very creditable in point of design – played in the middle. On one side of the room were displayed a quantity of steam and electro-magnetic machinery, the work of the men during their leisure hours. A great number of varieties of the steam engine were represented in this highly interesting collection, all of which derived motion from a model boiler with which their cylinders were connected. Among the electrical apparatus were two small but energetic electro-magnetic engines; one of the horse-shoe form, with a reciprocating arrangement (by a workman named Squires), employed to drive a section to scale of the engine of the *Lord of the Isles*; and the other a double-acting one, by another workman.

The *soirée* was attended by a very large number of the men and their families, whose dress and general appearance indicated their being very comfortably settled. A concert of vocal and instrumental music, comprising some of the most celebrated works of Boieldieu, Mozart, and Bellini, besides some modern English, formed the first part of the evening's entertainment, which was followed by a very creditable dramatic performance by members of an amateur club formed in the institution, the remainder of the night being devoted to dancing.

Having now endeavoured to convey some idea of New Swindon and its population, we proceed at once to notice some of the more striking of their avocations, within the walls of the works.

One of the most interesting operations carried on here, is that of constructing the axles for the carriages, and for the bearing wheels of the locomotives. As the ordinary weight of the latter, when loaded, is about forty tons, and this enormous mass of matter is frequently impelled at the rate of sixty miles per hour, it is necessary that these axles should be of great strength and perfect workmanship. The utmost care is accordingly observed in their manufacture, and the certainty of the result is in great measure ensured by the admirable adaptation of the appliances to the objects in view; at the same time, there is a complete economy of the material employed. Old iron of all descriptions, scraps of all sizes and shapes, broken bolts, nuts, screws, eyes, bars, plates, filings and turnings, are brought together, and made into heaps of nearly equal weight, and in bulk equal to a cubic foot. These are put into the furnace, brought to the welding heat, and then beaten out into bars of the required length – about eight feet. Several of these are heated over again and welded together into one compact mass, approximating in form to that usually given to

railway locomotive axles. This is a spindle, narrow in the middle, and increasing in length towards the places for the bearings, at which the figure becomes a cylinder of smaller dimensions. The final operation, and that which gives to the fabric all the strength it requires, is exceedingly beautiful to witness. Naysmyth's steam hammer is the machine used. The axle has a portion of its length heated in the furnace, and that portion laid upon the anvil under the hammer. To receive the axle, the anvil is furnished with a 'swage', or hollow mandril, of the form which that part of the axle is intended to receive, and the hammer has a similar one to beat up the hot metal with. The weight of the hammer is 30 cwt; and this huge mass of metal is lifted at rapidly recurring intervals through a space of about two feet, from which height it falls upon the heated axle. A chain passes round the longer end of the axle whilst undergoing this process, and over a wheel; and thus suspended, it is easily turned in the anvil-swage by means of a bar which is clamped upon it, and worked with great skill by a man who watches intently the gradual development of the form. During this operation, cold water is occasionally dashed upon the heated metal, in order, by its sudden contraction, to detach the scales from its surface, which would otherwise be driven into it, and produce a bad description of iron, technically described as 'laminating'. When water is thrown upon it, a sudden disengagement of steam takes place, and globules of hot water are scattered around in all directions by the fall of the hammer. A curious circumstance was mentioned to us in reference to this part of the subject. When a flat surface of heated iron is being operated upon in this manner, and water is dashed upon it, the fall of the hammer produces an explosion which is heard in the trains for a very considerable distance along the line. The explanation of this seems to be, that the great momentum of the hammer overcomes the repelling force which exists between the heated surface and the spheroids of water, causing it to flash instantly into a steam under an enormous pressure, which is suddenly liberated upon the rise of the hammer, or which may even possibly be decomposed. The appearance of the glowing mass under the vigorous action of the hammer, the brilliant scintillations which emanate from it, and its gradual approximation to the desired form, invest the whole operation with a degree of interest which very much strikes the spectator who witnesses it for the first time. If the metal should cool before the part is formed, the crane by which it is suspended is swung round to the fire, and the iron is re-heated. The hammering process is now continued until the particular portion is formed, and then a new swage is put into the anvil and the hammer, which forms two other portions of the iron at equal distances from the centre. By a continuation of this process, the axle of a pair of bearing wheels of a locomotive engine is made in something less than a working day, and turned out of hand as perfectly as the present advanced state of the metallurgical art admits.

A further economy is exhibited in this portion of the works, by employing the same furnace to vaporize the water in the boiler, for impelling the piston of the steam hammer, as heats the iron in the above process. This is effected simply by a judicious arrangement of the flues, which assist the combustion in the furnace itself, at the same time that they convey the vaporizing heat around the boiler. Another ingenious expedient is resorted to for the purpose of keeping the furnaces clear of slag, or scoriæ. This consists in the removal of a small portion of the wall at the back of the furnace near the ground, and surrounding the opening loosely with brickwork, having large interstices. Within this little open chamber the fire of the furnace circulates with great intensity, and so enables the slag to pass out of the main body of the furnace in a fluid state.

In the same part of the works are appliances for proving and shaping the tires of the engine wheels. Some portions of this department of the operations which we witnessed, were interesting in the extreme. A furnace, on the usual underground flue principle, contained a tire about to undergo the process of 'forming', or 'proving'. The apparatus provided for the purpose consists of a large iron bed-plate let in flush with the ground, and firmly fixed in a horizontal position. Upon this plate rest five framed circular sectors, of a radius somewhat smaller than that of the tire, and these are disposed around a central space which is occupied by a conical wedge having its broader end upwards. This wedge is actuated by a slow-threaded screw working in a fixed nut below, which in descending thrusts the segments radially from it. The tire having been heated to a point at which the metal becomes manageable for this purpose, it is brought to the mouth of the furnace and sustained there by the ordinary appliances, until its flange is grasped by three hooks in which the chain from a crane close by terminates. By swinging the arm of the crane from the furnace, the tire is brought concentrically over the proving-plate, upon which it is then let down, and the hooks are removed. The men in attendance then seize a long lever which is run through the head of the screw, and walking round the plate with it force the sectors out against the inner surface of the tire, which all this time is at a glowing white heat. Their motion now becomes more slow, in consequence of the resistance of the tire, but the creaking of the metal indicates that it feels the strain, and yields to it. At length it is impossible to continue this process any longer, and for a minute or two the tire is allowed to contract against the circular peripheries of the sectors. The next step is to shape the exterior of the tire wherever necessary. This is accomplished by means of 'flats', and 'swages'. The former are small masses of metal having a flat surface, one of which, fixed in a twisted osier, is held by one workman upon the upper surface of the tire, whilst another beats upon it with a heavy hammer, which flattens the vertical face of the flange, and at the same time removes the scales from the surface of the metal, which would otherwise produce the effect usually described by the word 'laminating'. Curved swages are then used for producing a uniformly curved edge to the flange; and this portion of the process, which is applicable in the case of a bearing wheel tire, is complete. For the large driving wheel tires, larger sectors and proportionately increased means are employed.

It sometimes happens that tires will give way in their proof, thus indicating the presence of an imperfect weld. This is a circumstance of extremely rare occurrence, but the proof is always resorted to; and a defective tire on the Great Western Railway is a thing hardly ever heard of. When a weld has to be re-made, the appliances are at hand by which it is to be done. The tire is suspended by clamps fixed upon opposite points of its figure to short chains attached to

the fall from the balance arm of a crane. By means of this crane, the tire is easily swung into or out of a smith's fire, where the blast soon brings it up to the welding heat. Thus it is readily heated, re-heated, and welded up. Sometimes the edge of the flange is too thin at one or more points, and in this case it is surprising to see the ease with which the remedy is applied. The tire, suspended as before, is swung round to a suitable support, and turned upon its points of suspension into a convenient position. A thin piece of cold steel, of the size requisite to make good the defect in the tire, is then inserted in a chink, or slit, in the metal at the defective point. This operation is performed in general by the uncovered fingers of men, the skin of which has become all but insensible to heat, by repeated exposure to red-hot surfaces of metal. We witnessed the insertion of a piece of steel into the flange of a tire, just swung out of the smith's fire at a red heat. A man took it up in his fingers, and, after a few trials, inserted it with his own fingers. It was then lightly hammered up, the tire brought back into the fire – where the whole was heated up again, and then removed and beaten up. Operations of this kind on circular masses of red hot steel nearly five feet in diameter, as in the case in the bearing wheel tires, excite a strong interest in the casual spectator.

The formation of the spokes and inner peripheries of the running wheels of the carriages is another great feature in the routine of operations at Swindon Works. In one description of wheel, two spokes are cast together in one length, with their central portions, which resemble wedges with their apices cut off, united in the middle. The small thickness of metal in the centre is then cut through, and the wedge-shaped ends of the single spokes so produced pack concentrically round a centre, which forms the space for the nave. Another description of wheel is also made, which admits of considerable strength in the construction, and of as much facility. Bars are cast, the length of which is equal to the sum of the two spokes, and the arc of the inner periphery of the wheel included between each pair of spokes. The centre of each bar has a small hole cast in it, which determines readily the position of the bar in the machine to which it is next removed, in a red hot state, for the purpose of being shaped. This consists of a simple arrangement of levers and metal faces so disposed, that all that is necessary is to place the bar in it, with its hole passed over a fixed stud, and then to swing the levers round forcibly, which is easily done by means of two large iron balls cast upon them. When taken out of this machine, each bar is formed into a sector of the wheel, consisting of its two radii and their included arc, these sectors pack round a centre, two radii in juxtaposition uniting to form a single spoke. Around the frame thus made the iron tire is placed, the nave is added in the centre, and the whole is complete.

The construction of the iron framework of the carriages is carried on here in several departments of the works, though the orders for new carriages come at very irregular intervals, and are equally irregular in extent; depending, of course, upon the circumstances of traffic and of convenience which exist at any particular time. This part of the work does not present much that is worthy of notice, as it chiefly involves the ordinary operations in iron cutting, boring, shaping, punching, riveting, etc., there are one or two matters to which only it is necessary to direct attention. First, with regard

STEAM FORGING.

BOILER HOUSE.

EXPANDING FIRE.

HEATING WHEEL.

THE GREAT WESTERN RAILWAY COMPANY'S WORKS AT SWINDON.

The illustrations on this and the following page are taken from *The Illustrated Exhibitor & Magazine of Art*, published in 1852. They were later reproduced as independent engravings. Though interesting they give a somewhat false impression of the contemporary working conditions, which were far more challenging than they appear in the illustrations.

Top: *Steam Hammer*.
By 1852, the GWR had acquired two steam hammers from Naysmith. This appears to be the earlier, smaller example acquired in 1844.

Centre: *Boiler House*.
Though giving a false impression of the spaciousness of the original Boiler Shop, the sketch nonetheless illustrates boiler makers at work riveting a seam, a round topped firebox (introduced in 1847) and the combined smokebox cylinder arrangement so beloved of Gooch. I suspect that the boiler illustrated was intended for an 0-6-0 goods engine of the 'Caesar' Class.

Bottom: *Expanding Fire and Heating a Wheel*.
These drawings are intended to demonstrate the process of wheel construction. The left-hand illustration depicts the system used to expand the roughly forged tyre segments out to their proper diameter. On the right, a wheel is being heated in the smiths' fire prior to being swung out for the attention of the hammer welders, seen waiting in the foreground. These processes are more fully described in the text on the previous page.

TOP: *SLOTTING MACHINE*. This giant machine was produced by Whitworth circa 1845 and was invaluable for machining crank axles, as illustrated here.

MIDDLE TOP LEFT: *TURNING AND GRINDING*. This machine, which was still in use 100 years later, was produced by Naysmith and was initially used for grinding tyres in situ on wheels up to 8ft 0ins in diameter.

MIDDLE TOP RIGHT: *CYLINDER BORING*. Alan Peck states that this machine was built in the works and was still in use in 1964.

MIDDLE BOTTOM: *ERECTING SHOP*. This, once again, gives a false impression of spaciousness but shows the 8ft 0ins 'Single' *Swallow*, built in June 1849, under repair and the 0-6-0 goods engine *Hero* of the 'Caesar' Class under construction in what must therefore have been October/ November 1851.

BOTTOM: *TURNING CRANK AXLE*. This illustrates the turning and polishing of the crank axle journals.

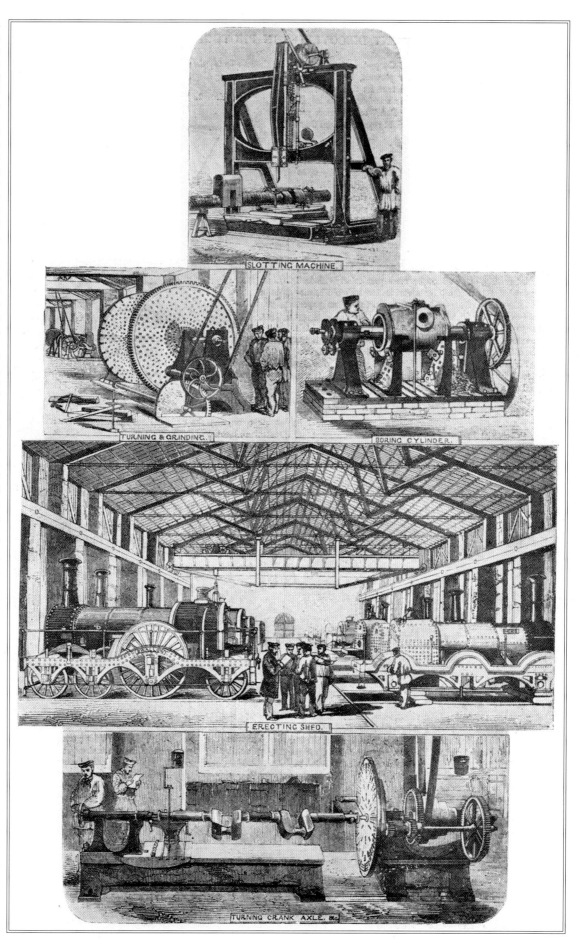

SLOTTING MACHINE.

TURNING & GRINDING.

BORING CYLINDER.

ERECTING SHED.

TURNING CRANK AXLE. &c.

to the long and broad angle-irons which form a portion of the framework of the floors. These have to be flattened out, and must have a perfectly straight line for the intersection of the two planes of which they consist. It is found that if these large angle-irons are drawn from the long furnaces in which they are heated up for flattening, with their ridge or intersection a true straight line, they cool into a curve, and are consequently unfit for the purpose for which they are destined. To remedy this, they are subjected to certain pressures, until, upon being withdrawn from the furnace, they are found to have a curved ridge of a form which is judged of with the greatest precision by the eye of the men. When left to cool in this state, the iron comes out ultimately a combination of two flat rectangles at right angles with one another. The making of the 'horn-plates', or vertical framework in which the axleboxes are suspended by the springs, is also carried on in this part of the work. The lines are chalked out, and large punching engines, worked by cams, are employed to cut out the portions to be removed.

Passing on to another part of the works, we come to the place where the tires are reduced on their exterior, or conical faces, to the true circular form. The steel of which they are made being too hard for the chisel, the only method by which it can be touched is that of grinding. For this purpose grindstones of the ordinary kind are made to revolve with a very high angular velocity, and the tires are mounted in lathes, and made to revolve in contact with them. By this circumferential action, the formation of the tire is slowly but truly effective. The time of grinding is in general different in different tires; but a pair of tires commonly occupy a day in their completion. So great is the velocity of the revolution, a small irregularity in the friction, arising from any momentary cause, will make the grindstone fly in pieces. When this happens the fragments of the stone are projected with considerable force; and to prevent any accident arising from this circumstance, large sheets of iron are suspended above and in front of them, which prevent the fragments from being thrown in the direction in which workmen might approach.

To the principal lathe room we have already adverted. The collection of machines of this class is of enormous value; many of them of recent manufacture, and all of them kept in the finest order. In passing through the room, several portions of the work of different engines, then in hand, attracted our attention by their extreme accuracy and beauty of finish. Some of Whitworth's cutting machinery was in operation, and presented a remarkable contrast with the slow chisel process formerly pursued. In these machines, the cutting edge is formed at the extremity of an arm which turns upon a centre, and which is furnished with the graduated arc of a circle to determine its position. The work is laid upon a metal slab, the level of which can be varied by a choice of grooves, as also can be that of the centre of the cutter. The impulse of the machine does the rest; so that a cylindrical curve of any form can be cut out with great ease and accuracy. Self-acting screw cutters abound in this room, furnished with full sets of 'changes', for varying the pitch of the screw. As broad gauge engines are manufactured here, all their minute parts partake of the greater magnitude which belong to the engines themselves. The ordinary class of locomotives on this line

have cylinders 18 inches in diameter, and 24 inches stroke. Their driving wheels are 8 feet in diameter, and their bearing wheels, of which they have two pairs, 4 feet 6 inches. Their total length is 24 feet, of which the interval between the centres of the bearing wheels, occupies 16 feet. Without its supply of fuel, and the water for its boiler, the engine alone weighs $28^{1}/_{2}$ tons, the tender alone 10 tons, and the weight of both, when loaded, about 56 tons. And this enormous load is frequently urged along the road at rates exceeding sixty miles per hour.

The boiler and firebox department is one of the most interesting portions of the entire establishment, as might be supposed, when it is remembered that a boiler of a Great Western engine presents 1,750 square feet of heating surface. Here the plates of copper and iron are cut, punched, and riveted; and the long screws of inch copper rod for screwing through the casing into the firebox, to prevent expansion outwards, are cut in one machine, and inserted by another, the box and its casing resting on a moveable bed, themselves also moveable upon it, to bring each part of the work successively under operation.

The foundry is necessarily of limited dimensions; as castings are few which occur in the locomotive engine. There, however, we see the cylinders cast, with their slideboxes; and one which was shown to us scarcely cold, struck us as being one of the finest specimens of the interesting art of the founder we had ever seen.

The only remaining part of the works which we propose to notice at this time, is the engine shed. This is entered by a double line siding from the main line, which brings the engines up to a vast lateral extension of the building on the right. When abreast of this wing, the engines have moved from the permanent way on to the top of a huge moveable platform, the upper surface of which is furnished with several pairs of rails, coinciding in gauge and level with those of the permanent way. When resting upon this platform, the latter is moved slowly into the wing by turning a winch, which stands upon it. The platform moves in a deep trench built up with masonry, upon four wide rails, the two extreme ones of which are cogged to impart the motion to it readily, and over these roll sets of large wheels of corresponding figure, arranged in parallel rows. On either side of the trench are pairs of rails, still parallel to the siding, upon any of which an engine may be pushed, or from which it may as readily be removed by an inverse process. This place affords accommodation, with another communicating chamber of large dimensions, for about a hundred engines, and about seventy were actually laid up. There we found that magnificent machine, the *Lord of the Isles*, which attracted so much admiration at the Exhibition, though the repairs she needed were merely nominal. The injury she sustained in the collision at Aynho, on the opening of the Oxford and Birmingham line, appears to have been greatly exaggerated. She was repaired and running to and from London every day, within a very few days of that unfortunate occurrence.

We now take leave of this subject, of which we have pretended merely to give a sketchy outline, fully satisfied that the extensive application of the art of working in iron, which is here seen in its present perfection, cannot be regarded otherwise than with extreme interest by the general body of our readers.

A Chronology of Swindon Works 1840-61
Introduction

I have over the last thirty years, given literally hundreds of lectures about the history of Swindon Works to numerous different groups across the country. The problem that I have often encountered was put most succinctly on one occasion by a gentleman who was asked to give a vote of thanks and said: "*I wish to thank Canon Arman for clarifying for us the complex story of the works' early history. Though I have read and re-read the published accounts of the building and growth of Swindon Workshops, I find the story hard to grasp and confusing to unravel*".

This comment was in fact made in Newcastle, although I have heard, either in conversations or through questions asked at lectures, similar remarks made on many other occasions. Though both the previously mentioned main published books on Swindon Works are easily accessible, they both approach the story of the development of what was ultimately an extraordinary piece of civil, mechanical and social engineering in a thematic way, rather than a chronological one. Therefore, in an attempt to bring some clarity to the matter, I have put together this time line hoping that it aids readers in following what is undoubtedly a most complicated story of both engineering and social endeavour.

As my very great friend and fellow lover of the old GWR Michael Wyatt once said, "*Swindon Works was the crowning glory of the GWR, it needs someone like you, who knows it thoroughly, to make its story illuminating rather than confusing*". This I have tried to do.

1840

April	GWR leased the C&GWUR
13th Sept.	Gooch writes to Brunel recommending Swindon as the site of the new workshops
6th Oct.	GWR Board ratifies decision to build at Swindon
17th Dec.	Line through Swindon opened as far as Hay Lane

1841

Jan./Feb.	Sufficient land to build Railway Village purchased from John Harding Shepherd @ £400 per acre
2nd Feb.	GW Directors appoint J.&C. Rigby to construct works, cottages and station at Swindon
April	Gooch engages Archibald Sturrock (aged 24) to assist him with the setting out and equipment of the Works. Sturrock had been in the employment of the GWR (under Gooch) since Sept. 1840
26th April	Additional land in the south-west corner (Bristol end) of the Works site purchased from Col. Vilett
20th May	Agreement ratified with Joseph Whitworth & Co. of Manchester to supply machine tools, installation to commence in January 1842
31st May	Opening of line from Hay Lane to Chippenham followed by removal of locomotive servicing facilities to Swindon. Opening of C&GWUR between Swindon, Kemble and Cirencester
11th June	It is not known exactly when in 1841 that the first 'sod' was cut to begin the construction of the new workshops. The first priority seems to have been the removal and re-erection of some of the temporary buildings at Hay Lane to the new site. Especially important was the provision of locomotive servicing facilities which needed to be operational by 30th June. The first payment made to Rigby by the GWR for construction work at Swindon was on 11th June
30th June	Opening of line between London and Bristol throughout. Initially all trains changed engines at Swindon
14th Oct.	Revised contract signed with Rigbys stipulating that the contractor should spend no more than £35,000 on the construction of 300 cottages, to be completed by Christmas Day 1842
11th Nov.	Formal handover of land owned by the C&GWUR to the GWR in the 'V' of the junction at Swindon; transferred to the GWR in exchange for locomotive and stock supply and maintenance. This land had been purchased by the C&GWUR in 1837-38
Nov./Dec.	Work begins on digging foundations of and laying in water conduits to the Works site

1842

1st Feb.	GWR Directors resolve that the present facilities available in temporary accommodation at Swindon station, which was itself still unfinished, was '*most objectionable in every respect*'
Feb.	Work begins to construct the first cottages in the Railway Village
April	GWR seeks tenders to build coke ovens at Swindon and to supply the necessary ironwork. The tender was let to Mr William Tiddy on condition that the work was completed in two months. A by-product of the coke oven was gas which would have been of great use in the Works
14th July	Swindon Railway station formally opened
21st Aug.	Death of George Henry Gibbs, sometime Chairman of the GWR. He left £500 in his will toward the erection of a church and school at New Swindon
6th Oct.	GWR Directors set the rental charges on each of the '*new cottages*' at Swindon at 3s 6d per week or £9 2s annually. The first houses were occupied from this time. This coincides with the erection of some temporary wooden houses which may well have been re-erected from the site at Hay Lane
Oct./Nov.	Sick Club. At some time toward the end of 1842, a small group of the new employees who were already concerned by the lack of medical facilities available to them and who could not perhaps afford to pay the local medical practitioners form a 'Sick Fund' to pay for their own medical care
28th Nov.	The machinery in the new shops starts up for the first time

By the end of 1842 it is clear that the first suite of buildings was finished and sufficiently equipped to enable trial working to begin. From the outset, a system of lettering the various workshops was adopted, the first to be completed or at least to begin being used by the end of 1842:

A. Engine House – incomplete at this time

B. Repair Shed

C. Erecting Shop or Lifting Shop

D. Fitting Shop, including main boilers and stationary engines that provided power for the Works. This shop had an upper storey which formed the original machine shop.

In addition to these were Smith's shops, a Coppersmiths and a Boiler shop, which was a higher building than its neighbours to incorporate an overhead crane. Offices were also included in the original build which provided accommodation for Gooch (although he was never resident at Swindon), Sturrock and other officials such as draughtsmen, accountants and clerks.

The Works was initially planned as a locomotive, stabling, repair and maintenance facility. It fulfilled this function adequately but Gooch was eager to build his own engines and thus planned for further developments on the workshop site from the end of 1842, though further building activity on a large scale did not begin again until 1844.

1843

2nd Jan.	The Works officially opens, initial workforce about 180 including enginemen, officials, etc. Archibald Sturrock appointed Works Manager. Note: Peck says 3rd but 2nd Jan. 1843 was a Monday
28th Feb.	Edward Snell arrives at Swindon. He would eventually become chief draughtsman and assistant to Sturrock
March	The Queens Tap public house opens
April	The first school founded in the 'barrack room' (not to be confused with a later building of the same name), probably a temporary building moved from Hay Lane and used there to house enginemen, etc
April	Letter from Station Superintendent Christopher Hill to Chief Traffic Superintendent Seymour Clarke, complaining about the 'insufficient supply of water, defective drainage and the poor state of the roads and fences' at Swindon. No shops had yet been built for provisioning the workforce
Aug.	GWR Board compiles a population table of village residents. 131 cottages had then been built, occupied by 663 persons of whom 216 were men of working age
Sept.	Peck: 'A small number of men in the Works grouped together to set up a Library'. This became the foundation of the Mechanics Institute. The nation's first rate supported library was not set up until 1852, in Salford, Manchester
9th Oct.	A batch of Iron Waggons ordered to be built in the Works. Number not specified
26th Oct.	Order placed on the Works for the manufacture of 18 Iron Waggons, in addition to those already ordered and almost certainly the first items of

rolling stock made there. They were erected in the new boiler shop. There was evidently some urgency about the building of these, which were presumably 'open merchandise waggons', thus indicating the growing demand for the traffic of goods upon the railway

Nov.	Construction of St. Mark's church begins, architects Scott & Moffatt. The church was built of Swindon stone dressed with Bath stone, the interior to be lined with Bath stone

At an unknown time in 1843, work begins at Westcott Farm to build 'speculative housing' at the instigation of William Plummer, the farmer, who had shrewdly purchased adjacent land earlier in 1843.

In addition, Edward Snell mentions that a Methodist Chapel existed in the vicinity of the Railway Village by 1843.

1844

8th Jan.	Mechanics Institute formed. Gooch was the first President. Baths were provided for members, located in the 1842-43 office block. The main aim was to formalise the library and to promote adult learning, etc. It very quickly became a major force for good in Swindon and a source of immense strength and cohesion for the newly arrived workers and their families
8th June	Land donated to the Company by Col. Vilett which became the GWR's park and cricket ground. The conveyance was concluded on this date
Sept.	The GWR Directors General Committee accepts three tenders for the erection of a new gas works and coke ovens. These additional facilities and the requisite piping allowed gas to be supplied in greater quantities to the Works as well as the station and village. In operation by 1846, further expansion took place before 1849
7th Nov.	The GWR Directors General Committee resolved that 'it is expedient to build eight shops [for food and provisioning] at Swindon New Town nearly adjoining to the present cottages'

In 1844, date unknown but towards the end of the year, Gooch's chief draughtsman, Thomas Russell Crampton, left the GWR to work for G.&J. Rennie & Co. Crampton had been responsible for the detail design of the 'Fire Fly', 'Sun', 'Leo' and 'Hercules' classes built by contractors between 1840 and 1842.

Also, 1844 was the year when Gooch seems to have decided to press forward with a scheme to expand the workshops, in order to begin construction of locomotives to new, improved and enlarged designs which he could see would become necessary in the next few years.

1845

This year saw the beginning of a building programme that would see the size of the workshop space available double over the next eighteen months to two years. Planned new construction included further Smiths and Steam Hammer shops, a Spring Shop, a second Machine & Fitting Shop – which included a Wheel Shop – and new and improved office and stores accommodation. A traverser was installed next to the Boiler Shop and hydraulic lifting apparatus was installed in the Erecting Shop. On the Bristol side of the workshop complex, new buildings were erected to facilitate the manufacture of waggons. These appear to have been seen as a priority by Sturrock, no doubt to enable space to be freed up in the Boiler Shop for other works, which included in 1845 some carriage construction.

All of these works, which were progressed with some energy, were undertaken as the GWR's and the nation's finances began to slip into a recession, which really took hold in 1847 and reached a crisis point over the following two years, resulting in many layoffs and great hardship in Swindon.

1st Jan.	Purchase of a steam hammer (ordered in 1844) from Messrs Nasmyth & Co., authorised at the cost of £300. Order to Mr Napier for an engine '*traversing frame*' and a '*hydraulic lifting apparatus*' for the erecting shop. Cost £800
25th April	St. Mark's church consecrated by the Bishop of Gloucester & Bristol – the two dioceses were combined at this time. The parish priest was Rev'd Joseph Mansfield, who became the vicar when the parish proper was constituted in 1846

The new school building seems to have opened at about the same time as the church was consecrated, the children and teachers transferring from the temporary buildings previously used. The first schoolmaster was Alexander James Braid, assisted by his wife and daughter.

28th Aug.	Building of further cottages in the village authorised. The appointed contractor was George Major of Prospect Place, Swindon (Old Town); Rigbys were excluded from the tendering process
Sept./Oct.	Following completion of installation of the hydraulic lifting gear in the erecting shop, work begins to progress on the building of the first engines to be constructed at Swindon
29th Oct.	Edward Snell directed by Gooch to begin making drawings for a large 2-2-2 express engine
Nov.	Gooch writes to Brunel's assistant J. W. Hammond, who was overseeing new housing works at Swindon, urging him to put in hand the completion and construction of new houses. Gooch states that '*10 or 12 people are living in two rooms and when the night men get up the day men go to bed. People are leaving Swindon for want of accommodation*'
Dec. from	The Gauge Trials commenced with three runs Paddington to Didcot by *Ixion*, a 'Fire Fly' Class 2-2-2

1846

Jan.	Work begins on new 2-2-2 express engine
6th Jan.	Second annual report of the Mechanics Institute mentions that the new 'D' Shop (newly opened

and not to be confused with the old 'D' Shop of 1842-43) was in use as a theatre and lecture hall by night, whilst another room in the Works (possibly the upper storey of the old 'D' Shop?) was in use as a library

April	Gooch's 'Little Engine', as he jokingly referred to *Great Western*, is outshopped at the '*end of the month*'. Built in 13 weeks by craftsmen working '*night and day*' and the first engine wholly constructed in the Works, it was a 2-2-2 with 8ft driving wheels and large 18ins x 24ins cylinders. Between Sept. and Nov. 1846, *Great Western* was rebuilt as a 4-2-2, following the failure of the leading axle
Aug.	The Works outshops the first of a new design of 2-2-2 express engine of which six examples were to be built, the last in March 1847. They were smaller and lighter than *Great Western*
3rd Aug.	The GWR Board General Committee authorises building of a further 32 cottages at Swindon. Completed by July 1847, they conclude the scheme of works cottages as first envisaged by Brunel, which should have been finished by Dec. 1842. They were larger than the earlier cottages, each comprising five rooms. Approval also given to construct two 'villas' to house Station Superintendent Christopher Hill and Works Manager Archibald Sturrock. They were built by Thomas Lewis of Bath and cost about £1,200 each

At some unspecified time in 1846, the engine shed was completed with the placing of stone carvings of two 'Fire Fly' Class engines on decorative plinths at either end of the building. Drawings for the building date back to 1841 but the question is did they incorporate a building that was removed from Hay Lane in May 1841, which we know was also of timber construction. There is some evidence to suggest that it might have been so though it is not conclusive but the completed building was, in later years, always referred to in official documents as the '*1846 Engine Shed*'. This suggests that the building was completed in stages over the period 1841-46, the final work, which may have also included the fitting of doors, not being concluded until the latter year.

1847

This year saw the implementation of additional cost cutting measures in the workshops, the commencement of short time working and increasingly the need to lay off men from the Works. The prevalence of disease in the New Town – and the Old – increased with 'low fever', typhus and smallpox outbreaks being recorded. Despite this, new construction of enlarged engine designs continued, albeit at a reduced level. Nonetheless these designs were ground breaking at the time and placed the GWR in a position of national pre-eminence for the next twenty years.

29th April	First trial is conducted of a new design of 4-2-2 express passenger engine with 8ft 0in. driving wheels and 18ins x 24ins cylinders (the same as *Great Western*). The boiler was larger than its

predecessor, making it the most powerful express engine in the country at the time. 29th April being the Duke of Wellington's birthday, the engine is named *Iron Duke* in his honour. The design also incorporated a new type of round-topped firebox replacing the 'Haycock' style used hitherto

26th Oct.   Charles Saunders, GWR Secretary, writes to Gooch advising him of the directors' decision to cut all expenditure until '*better times appear*'. Gooch proceeded to cut the workforce from 1,800 to 618 over the next two years, discharging men in batches of several hundred at a time. Single men were the most affected such that, by September 1849, only three were still employed in the workshops

Nov.   A much improved type of goods engine named *Pyracmon* is produced during this month, larger than *Premier*, with a bigger boiler and a new design of round-topped firebox very similar to that used on *Iron Duke*. It would be followed by five identical engines built in 1848 and many more slightly larger examples over the next fifteen years

1st Dec.   The GWR Medical Fund formally established with Dr Stuart Keith Rae as the first Medical Officer of Health. This was perhaps the first such institution in the country to require all the workforce and their families to be members; subscriptions were stopped from members wages. Without doubt this was the single most important social and medical innovation in the history of Swindon and became a model for the NHS in the 20th Century

1848

In this year the recession began to bite harder, though it is not until the latter half of 1848 that job losses at Swindon became severe. New construction, rebuilding and repairs continued on a restricted basis. The downturn in traffic saw many engines temporarily laid aside.

Work continued in a more desultory manner than before with new building work in the factory. This included an extension to the gas works, further work on the coke ovens, a rear extension to the Boiler Shop, various stores and possibly a Pattern Makers Shop. Work also continued on the Waggon Shops until it was brought to a sudden end in October 1848.

June   An improved 'Iron Duke' named *Courier* is outshopped from the Works. This will be followed by a further 15 very similar engines built in small batches: 7 (*Courier* included) in 1848, 3 in 1849, 4 in 1850 and 2 in 1851. The last of these engines, outshopped in March 1851, is named *Lord of the Isles*. These latter engines had a slightly longer wheelbase than the 'Iron Dukes', with larger boilers, fireboxes and cylinders

14th June   First excursion made under the auspices of the Mechanics Institute, to Oxford. Now recognised as the first tentative steps of what became known

Oct.   as 'Trip' in Swindon – the Works annual holiday Edward Snell records in his diary the financial retrenchment really beginning to bite: '*Everything going on the same as usual. About 200 hands under me building new shops – all busy and bustle – this lasted until October 1848 when our reverses began. Had to sack all the hands and had three or four sweeping sacks through all the shops – since then things have been getting generally worse*'. Snell also appears to have been involved in finishing off the waggon shops at this time

Non-Conformist chapels: Three were built in New Swindon in 1848-49:

Methodist chapel in Bridge Street
Primitive Methodist chapel in Regents Street
Baptist chapel in Fleet Street

Roman Catholicism. There were six Roman Catholic families in Swindon in 1848. The first Masses to be said in New Swindon appear to have been heard in Westcott Place, at the Greyhound Inn, a priest coming down from Horcott near Fairford, some 13 miles away, for the purpose.

Cholera: At some time toward the end of 1848 or early in the following year, an outbreak of cholera occurred but there seems to be no accurate record when the first cases were diagnosed. The company responded by ordering the cleaning of drains, whitewashing internal walls of the cottages and regular inspections. Though bad the outbreak was contained lasting about ten months.

1849

This was perhaps the worst year in the history of New Swindon in the 19th Century. Unemployment and disease ravaged the community and infant mortality rates soared, remaining high for several years to come. This is also the year that George Hudson, 'The Railway King,' was unseated from his throne and the railway industry nationally reached its nadir. Even those in senior roles in the railway works were badly affected and our best evidence of the hardships endured are found in Snell's diary entries:

5th May   '*This present week Mr Sturrock announced his intention of docking my pay from £2.15.0 a week to £2. So today I gave him two weeks' notice and mean to start early in June for New York*'

15th May   '*Left the service of the Company ... I found that although my wages were docked to £2, Budge's [senior draughtsman] were only reduced to £2.10.00 and he had only been there two years ... On the whole I have not done badly at Swindon, I started there as a fitter on 24 shillings a week and before I had left had charge of all the factory under Mr Sturrock*'

He continues with some good words for Gooch, who obviously tried to change his mind and offered to reinstate his higher wages. Snell declined but in the end went to Australia rather than the USA. He stayed in touch with friends at Swindon and later records:

15th Oct.   '*Mrs Sturrock is in the family way again* [her third pregnancy, the family lost their first son Archibald

John on 14th Aug. 1846 when only 6 weeks old. The second child, a girl, Caroline Christina had been born on 21st March 1848]. *The directors examining into the loco accounts pretty severely have overhauled the accounts four times. This day spent as a general Thanksgiving Day on account of the cession of Cholera'*. The last note is without doubt the most significant and joyful event that occurred in an otherwise grim period which was to stretch into 1850 with some easing thereafter

1st May   The Bristol & Exeter Railway takes responsibility from the GWR for providing its own rolling stock and running its own trains. This was a blow for Swindon, having a short term effect on the workload in the workshops and contributing to the increasing problems in the town

Aug.   The first of a new design of 4-4-0 saddle tank named *Corsair* was constructed in the Works. It was followed by a slightly modified sister, *Brigand*, in Sept. These engines were intended for work on the South Devon Railway.

22nd Sept.   Gooch advises the Directors that there are now 23 empty houses at Swindon and 17 were only partly occupied. The Board agree to his recommendation

that rents should be cut by, on average, 1s per week

26th Oct.   Sturrock prepared a report on the available engine stock for Gooch. It shows:

35 engines at work or in stock in good order

12 engines under repair or conversion to tank engine

8 engines in the paint shop

30 engines, including a number awaiting conversion to tank engines awaiting repair or laid aside

Thus 51 out of the 85 listed were out of use – a fairly desperate situation. The report only relates to engines at Swindon

19th Nov.   Gooch makes a complete report to the Directors relating the current state of the engine stock (*Part of this and other relevant material can be found in the RCTS history on pages B17 and B18. Ed.*). Of 170 engines in stock, only 103 were at work

1850

This year continued to be rather grim for the new railway town. It is for this and the following year that I once calculated that the child mortality rate reached about 50% of live births. I now know that the data available then, mainly church registers, was incomplete and the figure may have been even higher, as outbreaks of smallpox and the ever-present typhus were recorded. In many ways the town was at its lowest point. Roads were unpaved, and

The interior of the 1846 engine shed on 28th October 1929, just prior to its demolition. The photograph shows the internal layout of the building after it was adapted for locomotive repair work in 1871, following the opening of the new motive power depot. The original timber construction of the roof is clearly identifiable, as is the traverser, which was the main access to 'B' Shed at the time.

cesspits and drains still overflowing while, despite the best efforts of the various degrees of social engineering that were ongoing, there was much drunkenness and the town lock-ups were often overburdened with miscreants. I have often heard it said in Swindon that for every place of worship that existed in the town, and it was a remarkably observant place, there was always at least one public house and quite as many other less official establishments!

The best news for the town was the opening of the first part of the South Wales Railway between West Chepstow and Swansea, plus various other new stretches of railway, all of which were either owned or, as in the case of the South Wales Railway, worked by the GWR. These include:

18th June	Chepstow West to Swansea High Street
2nd Sept.	Oxford (Millstream Junc) to Banbury
7th Oct.	Westbury to Frome. The line from Chippenham (Thingly Junction) to Westbury via Melksham had opened on 5th Sept. 1848

These, along with a steady upturn in work, led to a slow recovery of employment, a point well illustrated by new orders which are placed in:

Aug.	An order for new motive power and rolling stock is made for working the South Wales Railway. This includes 8 Engines, 75 Coal Waggons and 75 Box Vans at a total cost of £40,000
Nov.	Brunel asks the GWR Board if a large 8-wheeled engine could be exhibited at the forthcoming Great Exhibition. The Board give their consent on the basis that '*no alteration or addition should be made to increase to the Company the cost of the Locomotive Engine in its construction*'

Personnel: On 27th March 1850, Archibald Sturrock was appointed Loco. Supt of the Great Northern Railway on Brunel's recommendation. There were four shortlisted candidates for the post, the other three being George Harrison (Loco. Supt Scottish Central Railway), Francis Trevithick (Loco. Supt L&NWR Northern Division) and John Dewrance (former Loco. Engineer of the Liverpool & Manchester Railway).

Sturrock would later recruit other GWR employees to the GNR, including John Budge and Charles Sacré, who would later become Loco. Supt of the Manchester, Sheffield & Lincolnshire Railway and would be considered as a replacement for Gooch in 1864. At about the same time but separately, the GWR's Traffic Superintendent, Seymour Clarke, was appointed General Manager of the GNR. All these very skilled men left because their salaries were either cut or reductions were threatened.

Works Staff: The ordinary workmen had little bargaining ability and many others left Swindon at this time, either because they were made redundant or for better wages elsewhere. The Railway Village was emptying out as Gooch's report of September 1849 demonstrates. This process reached its nadir in 1850, after which matters began to improve.

In April, Mr Minard Rea — previously in charge of locomotive matters on the B&ER — was appointed to succeed Sturrock as Works Manager. Rea was a friend of Gooch and a fellow Freemason. His appointment was to prove to be a very popular move in Swindon, as he did much to improve the conditions in the Railway Village and oversaw a marked resurgence in the workload and employment in the workshops.

Edward T. Lane is one final member of staff who deserves mention. He came to Swindon in 1847 aged 17 and became an apprentice in the Drawing Office. He was responsible for the numerous drawings which we have of the early broad gauge engines which are now all held in the Science Museum Library. Latterly, he lived at No. 11 London Street in the Railway Village but, most regrettably, he died of typhus in January 1850, shortly before his 20th birthday.

From the end of 1849 or early in 1850, construction of the workshops planned between 1841 and 1847 came to an end. No further extensions were then carried out until 1860, when construction began on the Rolling Mills, which were completed and opened in 1861. This brought an influx of Welsh iron makers to operate the new plant, many of whom came from Tredegar — a town which Gooch had old associations with.

In fact, many of the newly constructed workshops — that is those built between 1845 and 1848 — were working at much less than full capacity. Machinery which had been ordered from Whitworths and others was left fully greased up but unused until the workload began to pick up again from the end of 1850 and onwards.

1851

In the 1851 Census, New Swindon appears for the first time. The population of the Railway Village was given as 1,454 and the average occupancy rate was given as 6 persons per cottage. This is a higher figure than that given in Gooch's report of 1849 and indicates a slow but steady increase in employment from the low point of 1849. In the separate development at Westcott, 104 workers are shown as resident of which only 39% were indicated as working in the workshops. Only 22 people employed in the Works are shown as living in the Old Town.

An idea of the wide range of individuals, their skills and origins can be gained from the residents of No. 7 London Street, which was one of the larger 8-roomed cottages. The main occupier was Peter Appleton, aged 42, an '*engine-driller*' from Haslingden, Lancashire who lived with his wife and two nieces. Lodging with them were three engineers, one of whom, F.A. Bucknell, would become temporary Works Manager in 1864, and J. Fraser, the then assistant to the Works Manager.

The whole ecclesiastical district of St. Marks, which included outlying hamlets, numbered 2,468 souls. This puts the New Town roughly on a par with the old settlement on the hill in terms of population density.

1st May	The Great Exhibition opens in Hyde Park with *Lord of the Isles*, resplendent in its exhibition finish, the largest railway exhibit on display

1852

1st March	The GWR Board contracts Edward Streeter of Bath to carry out repairs to and take general care of the Railway Village houses.

For the following seven years, Streeter is made responsible for roads, drainage, gutters, fences, footpaths, lampposts and water pipes, and their maintenance. Rubbish and ashes were to be cleared from the alleyways and backyards, and privies and drains were to be routinely flushed out.

The 243 cottages, bakehouse and a slaughterhouse located nearby were to have their external woodwork painted twice during the seven year term of the contract. The cottage interiors had to be whitewashed or lime washed. All fixtures and fittings had to be kept in good repair. Footpaths in Reading and Farringdon Streets were to be laid with asphalt $2^1/_2$ins thick, to match a similar footpath in Bristol Street, and the yards and wash houses were to be paved. The GWR also offered its tenants prizes for keeping their dwellings clean and for the maintenance of their front gardens.

Disease: Despite the measures outlined above, various endemic diseases persisted, including typhoid and typhus. Over 400 cases were reported and 14 deaths were recorded in 1852 from these causes. This was almost certainly an underestimation.

1st Oct.	The GWR continues to expand its route mileage with a major new line between Oxford and Birmingham, with 66 miles of mixed gauge double track being opened, albeit with a less than successful special train hauled by *Lord of the Isles*

1853

31st March	Gooch suggests to the GWR Board that building work which had been set aside in 1847 should be restarted. This includes a block of single persons accommodation – known as 'The Barracks' – and some additional housing. The Board agrees to implement this proposal to attempt to alleviate the housing crisis in New Swindon
1st Sept.	Daniel Gooch delivers a prospectus to the GWR Directors outlining a scheme for the formation of the 'New Swindon Improvement Company', to fund the construction of a new building for the Mechanics Institution, along with a covered market to augment the inadequate facilities in the village. The driving force behind this is the new Works Manager, Minard Rea. Shares in the new company were sold to raise the estimated £3,000 required
Sept.	Dr Charles Hind, the GWR's Surgeon (Dr Rae had died earlier in the year), informs the Directors of a serious outbreak of typhoid in the railway village. He requests the company to make urgent improvements to the drains *'thus averting the dreaded approach of Cholera'*
6th Oct.	GWR Board undertakes to pave the backyards and alleyways of all the cottages on the 'railway estate', estimated cost £2,000. Pennant stone to be used for the paving. Reported that by this time water is being supplied to every house in the village. However, it is drawn from the canal and is not reckoned to be safe to drink unless boiled

1854

This was a relatively quiet year for New Swindon. The Works were busy with new construction and major repairs, with twenty-one 0-6-0 engines of the Gooch 'Standard Goods' Class being built. This probably amounts to full production for new building work, since the company also took delivery of nine 4-4-0 saddle tanks of the 'Bogie' Class and the first two 4-2-2s of the 'Courier' ('Iron Duke') Class from outside contractors.

New housing construction continued in the railway village, as did the maintenance of the older cottages and their attendant infrastructures. Yet problems persisted with the many ailments which beset not only New Swindon but many manufacturing areas with poor housing and inadequate drainage. Sewage disposal remained a major problem, which would not be satisfactorily overcome for many years. Having said this, it is also important to point out that the improvements which had recently been put in place, i.e. limewashing the inside of the houses, clearing drains, etc, was beginning to have some positive effect. This can best be appreciated in the church burial registers, which indicate that there was a slowing down in the infant mortality rate in this and the following years.

Work on 'The Barracks' building, which had been halted in 1848-49 during the financial crisis, recommenced in 1854. It was intended for occupation by single men and included facilities for a *'coffee shop and eating house'*.

24th May	The most significant event in 1854 is the laying of the foundation stone of the new building to house the Mechanics Institute situated in Emlyn Square. The stone is laid by Lord Methuen, in the presence of Daniel Gooch, Minard Rea and the architect of the building, Edward Roberts of London. The newly founded local newspaper, the *Swindon Advertiser*, reports that *'a new building designed for the mental, moral and social advancement of the New Town was commenced under the most favourable auspices'*
Dec.	The covered market, situated in front of the new Mechanics Institute in Emlyn Square, opens for business

In the wider context of the GWR, 1854 was a highly significant year:

Jan./May	Opening of the new Paddington station, the departure side on 16th Jan. and the arrivals side on 29th May
1st Sept.	The GWR amalgamates with the Shrewsbury & Chester and the Shrewsbury & Birmingham railways. This brings 77 route miles of a standard gauge railway into the GWR's portfolio and in effect is thus the first major nail in the coffin of the GWR's broad gauge empire

1855

1st May	The Mechanics Institute building opens with much rejoicing. The building includes a library, a reading room, dining room, coffee room, a council meeting room and most significantly for

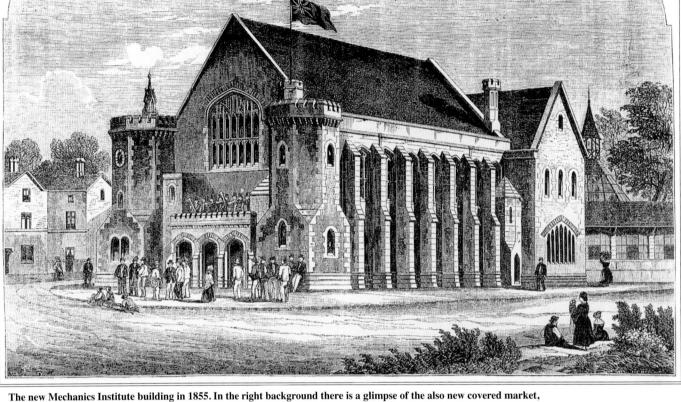

The new Mechanics Institute building in 1855. In the right background there is a glimpse of the also new covered market,

many, a bathroom containing 8 baths — houses in the village had no bathing facilities. It is built of Swindon stone faced with Bath stone

May — This month also sees the outshopping at Swindon of the first of a batch of twelve 0-6-0 standard gauge goods engines, No's 57-68, the last of which appears in January 1856. They are typical Gooch in design, with outside sandwich frames and domeless boilers. They had long lives, though were much rebuilt in the 1870s, the last two withdrawn being No's 58 & 60 in April 1913. Because the standard gauge had not yet arrived at Swindon these engines were transported to Wolverhampton on specially built waggons for final erection

30th July — A local landowner, John Harding Shepherd, who owns a block of land immediately to the east of the Railway Village, puts a number of small plots of land up for sale to any individual who wishes to purchase, with the help of a building society — the Wilts Equitable Property Society & Savings Fund founded in Trowbridge in 1849, which had an office in Swindon in 1855. However, the plots are overpriced and sell slowly, some still being available in the 1870s

1856

Little of major note seems to have happened in Swindon during this year. The Works were busy with a further batch of broad gauge 0-6-0 'Standard Goods' engines of which six were constructed in 1856 and then, from August, a new design of 2-4-0 passenger engine known as the 'Victoria' Class begin to be outshopped. Eighteen engines were built between August and November, which were attached to a new design of 4-wheeled tender, also built in the Works.

The refreshment rooms at the station underwent extensive restoration during 1856. The First Class rooms had their ceilings painted very elaborately, the *Swindon Advertiser* reporting '*no other railway in England presents such magnificent rooms*' in its edition published on 26th May.

1857

20th Jan. — The final part of the Wilts, Somerset & Weymouth Railway, worked by the GWR, opens from Yeovil to Dorchester and Weymouth. The last 6$^1/_2$ miles from Dorchester to Weymouth is mixed gauge to accommodate the L&SWR

2nd Feb. — The link between Bradford Jct and Bathampton opens, completing the final element of the WS&WR

18th June — The highly respected Works Manager, Minard Rea, died from consumption, i.e. tuberculosis. His funeral at St. Marks, which was massively attended,

A photograph of 'Fire Fly' Class 2-2-2 *Leopard* outside Swindon Works awaiting repair following its boiler explosion at Bristol in 1857 appeared in Part 2 (page 85) but this view is different, showing the other side of the severely damaged engine. Despite this, it was rebuilt in August 1859, with lengthened frames and a new boiler, and later still was eventually provided with a cab, before ceasing work in December 1873. It was then sold in January 1879 to the Great Western Pottery (Candy & Co.), manufacturers of glazed tiles at Newton Abbot, for use as a stationary boiler.

caused great sadness in the town. He was replaced by Daniel Gooch's younger brother William
Sept. Following the absorption of the 'Shrewsbury Companies' in 1854, the GWR had begun to feel an increasing financial burden and thus the train service is heavily cut and layoffs and short time working is introduced at Swindon

1858

The layoffs and short time working resulting in a cut in pay grew worse in this year and brought another round of hardship to the town's residents, which was to continue for the next eighteen months or so. In 1858, the GWR paid its lowest ever dividend, just 1.25%, to its shareholders, whilst the slow down affected every aspect of the workshops' workload. Repairs were badly affected, with many engines stood idle and only three new broad gauge 0-6-0 goods engines were turned out, two in August and one in September. A new Class of standard gauge 0-6-0 goods engines, very similar to the '57' Class, were constructed, nine in 1857, with two more in February 1858 and a final one in March. These were known as the '79' Class and had slightly larger boilers and smaller wheels – at 4ft 6ins – than their predecessors.

All things considered, 1858 proved to be one of the lowest points in the history of the GWR. Although matters began to improve in 1859, the next ten years would be ones of great challenge to the company and by implication the New Town of Swindon.

1859

Life in Swindon continued to be challenging, with the Works still very short of work. Only six new broad gauge 0-6-0s were built during this year.

15th Sept. Isambard Kingdom Brunel dies on this day. He had retained the title of Engineer of the Great Western Railway until the end of his life, though much of his work had latterly fallen on the shoulders of his chief assistant, T.H. Bertram, who succeeded him as Chief Engineer.

It is worth pointing out that Brunel's great friend Robert Stephenson died just four weeks later on 12th October. At 56 years of age, he was three years older than Brunel. Thus, the country lost two of its greatest engineers, men who would have graced any age in the nation's history, both worn out by overwork.

Sept. Dr G. Swinhoe is appointed Senior Medical Officer in succession to Dr Hind, who had resigned the previous month. Dr Swinhoe and his twin sons, who also became doctors, were to serve the town for very many years to come

1860

New construction reached its lowest point since locomotive building began in 1846. Only three new engines were built in the company's workshops during this year: one standard gauge 2-2-2 passenger engine, No. 30, at Wolverhampton and two standard gauge 0-6-0 side tank engines, No's 93 and 94, at Swindon. These latter engines embodied the usual Gooch features, domeless boilers with raised firebox and Gooch valve gear but with inside frames only. They were built for shunting in the GWR's Northern Division, which had begun to rid itself of its broad gauge lines by this time.

20th Feb.   The *Swindon Advertiser* reports on a decision taken by GWR Directors to finance and build a new Rolling Mill, '*for the working up of worn and damaged iron*' (scrap by any other name) with the aid of fresh materials. A sum of £20,000 is voted for the mill and machinery.

This Rolling Mill was to produce new rails and was located to the west of the steam hammer and Smiths shops towards the back of the Works complex. As built the mill was able to produce about 250 tons of rails per week, which was later increased by extensions to it in 1862-63, to 400 tons per week. The mills were then driven by two horizontal high-pressure steam engines generating 200hp, which were made at Swindon and powered by eight boilers that also supplied steam to other parts of the Works.

Construction continued throughout the year under the direction of a Mr Thomas Ellis, who probably came from Tredegar along with many of the workforce who manned the new mill. The first rails were rolled in April 1861 and it is said that Thomas Ellis was grabbed by '*his Welsh workmen*', placed in a chair and carried around the whole Works in celebration.

The newly arrived Welsh families had to be housed somewhere so the recently built Barrack House, which had had a difficult few years, was turned over to this influx and remodelled internally to suit family life. Here they stayed until new housing became available in Cambria Bridge Place two or three years later, after which the building lay empty for a while, before becoming a Wesleyan Methodist church in 1867.

In early 1860, about 150 employees formed themselves into the XI Wiltshire Volunteer Rifle Corps, in response to a feared invasion of Britain by the French Emperor Napoleon III. The volunteers drilled on some open ground to the south of the covered market under their leader, Captain William

Gooch, the Works Manager. In 1862, a drill room, armoury and storehouse would be built on this site and these buildings would later be adapted to become the GWR Hospital in 1872.

1861

The 1861 Census showed that, despite the downturn between 1857 and 1859, the population of New Swindon had grown from 2,468 in 1851 to 4,167 ten years later. The combined population of Swindon Parish, i.e. the Old and New towns, now stood at 6,856. In the New Town, the principle areas of expansion had been along Bridge Street, where 48 new cottages were erected in 1861, Fleet Street, and around the hamlets of Eastcott and Westcott.

At this point I will conclude the story of Swindon Works for the moment, as with the opening of the Rolling Mills, the first phase of the development of the workshops comes to an end. We will return to it in later volumes but I hope that I have been able to paint a coherent picture of the development of the Works, Railway Village and the people who came to live and work in the 'Railway Town', as Alfred Williams referred to New Swindon. Those who wish to know more should study the Bibliography on page 200. All the works mentioned therein have been consulted, though sometimes they do give conflicting information and must be read with care. The story is quite hard to unpick, which is why I have included this year by year chronology, ever hopeful that it makes the narrative easier to grasp and follow.

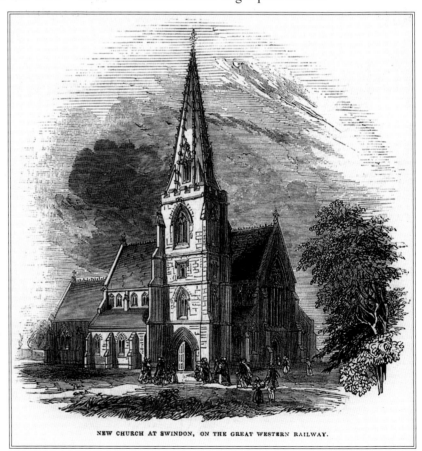

NEW CHURCH AT SWINDON, ON THE GREAT WESTERN RAILWAY.

CHAPTER 2
GOOCH'S LOCOMOTIVE POLICY 1846-1864

Following the opening of Swindon Works and its subsequent developments, which enabled the construction of new designs to be undertaken, Gooch found himself in the happy position of taking a few moments to reflect upon past achievements and the experience gained over the last eight years of both success and failure.

By 1845, he had learnt much about what worked well under Great Western conditions, with its miles of strong but unyielding trackwork, designed by Brunel, on which the rails were laid on top of continuous timber bulks. This gave a steady but hard ride which could, in part, be ameliorated by the retention of the Stephenson pattern sandwich frames. He had also learnt an important lesson from the four classes of engines introduced from 1840. Two of these, the 6ft 0in. singles of the 'Sun' Class, with their 14ins x 18ins cylinders, and the 5ft 0in. coupled 'Leo' Class, equipped with 15ins x 18ins cylinders, had proved to be inadequate for the expanding needs of the railway and were already earmarked for conversion to tank engines as soon as larger replacements could be provided. On the other hand, the larger 'Fire Fly' engines and the derived 'Hercules' Class 0-6-0s had exceeded expectations, and could certainly form the basis from which future designs might be developed.

Though by the latter half of 1845 Gooch, along with Brunel and Saunders for the GWR, was becoming embroiled in the gauge controversy, he must surely have been aware that the broad gauge afforded him the opportunity of building engines of considerably greater capacity than hitherto, without all the perceived challenges of maintaining a low centre of gravity. The wider gauge was inherently stable, which enabled the designer to adopt a greatly enhanced 'loading gauge'. Recognising this, Gooch rightly realised that the key to future success was the steam raising capacity of the boiler and the provision of cylinders of adequate size to use the steam produced efficiently. He also seems to have recognised that the fluidity of steam was best served by the provision of adequate steam passages. However, he initially misjudged the internal layout of the boilers designed for the 4-2-2 'Iron Duke' Class of 1847, by pitching the 303 2ins tubes too closely together, which rather restricted the steam raising capacity of these boilers. Because the boilers were so large this does not seem to have adversely affected the locomotives' performance to any great degree, though the problem was later recognised and when new boilers were required, they were internally redesigned.

In 1843, Gooch perfected his stationary link form of valve gear but how this was actually achieved remains something of a mystery. He certainly did not claim to have invented the form of valve gear which now bears his name – in fact during a court case about patent rights between John Grey and the London & North Western Railway at which Gooch gave evidence, he specifically denied that he was the gear's inventor. It seems that he developed ideas already current in the late 1830s and early '40s. D.K.Clark, writing in 1855, remarks that the original form of Stephenson gear employed a stationary link. He also comments that '*the suspended link motion with the shifting radius link was, we believe, first matured and employed by Mr Gooch*'. To him, he said, '*belonged the merit of having originally apprehended the virtue of this method of adjustment*'. Clark's choice of words here are significant. He is surely implying by the use of the word '*apprehended*' that Gooch developed and perfected rather than invented. Ahrons, writing in Macdermott's *History of the GWR*, comments:

'*In 1843 Gooch produced his well-known stationary link motion, which took the place of the older 'gab' motion and allowed the steam to be cut off in the cylinders at varying points of the stroke according to requirements. Gooch's gear differed from that of Stephenson and Howe which had been invented in 1842* [here Ahrons' might more accurately have employed the word 'perfected'] *in that the curved quadrant link, to which the eccentric rod was attached, was suspended from above and the die block to which the valve rod was connected could be moved up and down within the link. In the Stephenson link motion, the die block is stationary and the quadrant link with eccentric rod attached are moved together. The Gooch link motion was fitted to most broad-gauge engines, as well as to the earlier narrow-gauge engines of 1855-59.*'

It seems reasonably certain that Gooch's form of stationary link motion was retrofitted to members of the 'Fire Fly' and 'Hercules' classes in the mid 1840s, and that *Ixion* and *Hercules* – which took part in the gauge trials – were certainly so fitted. It is also worth recalling that there was more than one 'Mr Gooch' involved in locomotive design in the 1840s. Daniel's older brother, John Viret Gooch, was at this time under the headship of Joseph Locke, in charge of locomotive matters on the London & South Western Railway. The two brothers had previously worked together on the Manchester & Leeds Railway and there is no doubt that J.V. Gooch was a very competent locomotive engineer. It is not beyond the bounds of possibility that the two brothers at least kept each other informed about their ideas and experiences but what is beyond question is that J.V. Gooch first fitted the fixed link motion to the engine *Snake* of the 2-2-2 'Mazeppa' Class, built at Nine Elms in December 1847. Incidentally, this class, which numbered ten engines, were quite similar in capacity to the GWR's 'Fire Fly' Class and proved to be both cost effective and robust. *Snake* was the last in traffic and was withdrawn from Exeter in March 1870. It is also worth recording that though built at Nine Elms, the boilers

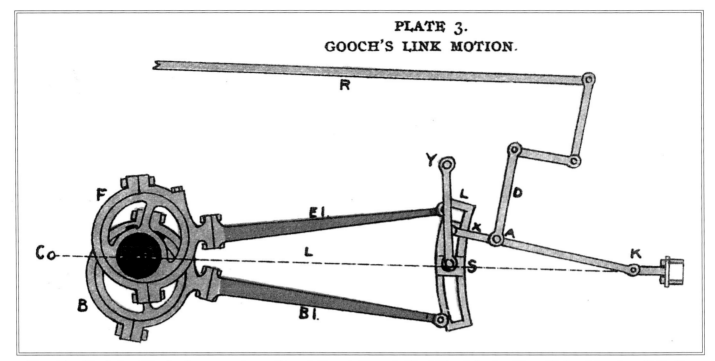

PLATE 3.
GOOCH'S LINK MOTION.

The origins of the design of Gooch valve gear are obscure. It is probably easiest to say that Daniel Gooch developed it possibly in collaboration with his elder brother, John Viret Gooch, though even this is uncertain. According to Ahrons, Gooch first applied this form of fixed link, constant lead, valve gear in 1843 and his brother followed suit in 1847. From 1846 all the new construction included this design of valve gear and it was retro-fitted to the earlier engines as heavy repairs fell due or rebuilding was undertaken. The diagram reproduced here is taken from *The Locomotive Enginemen's and Firemen's Examination Guide* by Maurice George Vaughan, Plymouth Mutual Improvement Class 1920, which was passed onto me by Dick Potts to whom I am very grateful.
Legend: **A.** Coupling of the Lifting Link to the Radius Bar; **B.** Backward Eccentric; **B1.** Backward Eccentric Rod; **C.** Centre Line; **D.** Lifting Link; **E1.** Forward Eccentric Rod; **F.** Forward Eccentric; **K.** Coupling of the Radius Bar to the Valve Spindle; **L.** Suspension Link; **R.** Reversing Gear; **S.** Suspension Link; **X.** Die Block; **Y.** Suspension Link Pivot.
In Gooch gear the concave link faces the cylinder and is fixed in position, with the die block moving within it, making it lighter to operate than Stephenson Gear where the opposite is the case. However, Gooch gear had two disadvantages when compared with the Stephenson arrangement. Gooch gear, no matter what position the gear is set in, gives 'constant lead' in the cylinders. Lead is defined as the amount the valve is open when the piston reaches the end of its stroke, so providing a cushioning effect, essential in a fast-running engine. Stephenson gear, on the other hand, allows for 'variable lead' which, in practise, gives a livelier performance on the road. The other disadvantage is in the line of action between the eccentric and the valve. The motion of the two is indirect, because the eccentric rod and the valve rod are inclined at a considerable angle to each other. The gear is also liable to considerable slip of the block in the link, especially when high mileages have been accumulated by the engine and parts are slack or worn. Some years ago, I was present at a discussion at Swindon with older and retired enginemen. The subject of valve gear and the relative merits of different types came up. I contributed nothing to the debate but was fascinated to listen to those who had practical knowledge of the different types of gear in use over the years. One, very senior, ex-driver summed up the brief comments made about Gooch gear by saying '*He* (Gooch) *nearly got it right*'. At the time I thought it a very apposite remark and I still do.

were supplied by outside contractors – five by the Haigh Foundry and five by W. Fairburn & Son, costing £545 each. Daniel was of course forced to purchase boilers for the 'Premier Goods' Class in 1845-46, though we do not know from whom.

Reverting to matters on the GWR, a detailed report of 1849 states that expansive valve gear had retrospectively been fitted to twenty-six engines which, one assumes, were mainly of the 'Fire Fly' Class. All new construction from 1846 incorporated expansive valve gear and one imagines that it continued to be retro-fitted to the older engines as they fell due for heavy repair. Only at the very end of his period in charge of the locomotive department did Daniel move away from the fixed link gear, when Joseph Armstrong persuaded him to fit Stephenson gear to the '131' Class of 0-6-0 goods engines built at Swindon in 1862 and a batch of twelve engines of the same type built by Slaughter, Grüning & Co. in the same year. Harold Holcroft summed up the relative merits of the Gooch and Stephenson gear in an *Outline of Great Western Locomotive Practise 1837-1937*, writing: '*The latter* [i.e. Gooch gear] *has a constant lead whereas the lead of the Stephenson*

gear is variable and so results in a livelier performance'.

Without going into all the technicalities of 'lap and lead' steam, it is worth noting that Gooch gear, despite its shortcomings, had one distinct advantage. It was much lighter to adjust when using lever reversers than the Stephenson gear, which probably explains why it was retained on the 8ft singles when new engines of much the same design as that of *Courier* of 1848 were built in the 1870s and '80s.

Also, whilst we are considering the matter of technological innovation, it is important to record that in 1847, Gooch built a dynamometer coach of a larger capacity for absorbing power than any other previously applied to locomotive testing. The *Oxford English Dictionary* defines a dynamometer as, '*An instrument for measuring the amount of energy exerted by an animal or expended by a motor in its work, or by the action of any mechanical force*'. The word and presumably the invention seem to have French origins – its first application in English is recorded to have been in 1810.

Gooch is sometimes credited with having been the first to apply a dynamometer to locomotive testing. This is not so, though the first such tests, carried out by the mathematician Charles Babbage, were conducted on the GWR. Gooch, however, used a much more powerful instrument and built a special 4-wheeled carriage – of rather mean proportions – to house it. A dynamometer is in effect a large spring balance which acts as a coupling between the train and the engine. The pull which the spring measured indicates the tractive force exerted by the engine, which was equal to the resistance when the train was moving at a measured speed over a level stretch of railway. Gooch paid careful attention to the design of the spring balance, the leaves of the spring being connected by pivots and rollers to cut down as much as possible friction, which would otherwise impair the results obtained.

Gooch also fitted the vehicle with an 'engine indicator', which

he developed to measure the steam pressure in the cylinders. This was a difficult calculation to make, since the pressure constantly changed. Measurement was achieved by a spring-loaded piston whose movement, as in the dynamometer, was recorded by a pencil on a chart driven from the engine wheels. D.K.Clark, writing in 1855, noted: '*The application of the indicator to the cylinder of the locomotive has aided essentially in giving precision to our knowledge of the behaviour of steam in the cylinder ... Mr Gooch was the first, so far as I am aware, who applied the indicator to the locomotive and he is the only engineer who systematically applies that instrument as a sort of stethoscope for testing their physiological condition*'.

The instrument in question was mounted on the front of the locomotive and was connected to the cylinder by a tube. Gooch, or an unlucky assistant, sometimes Archibald Sturrock,

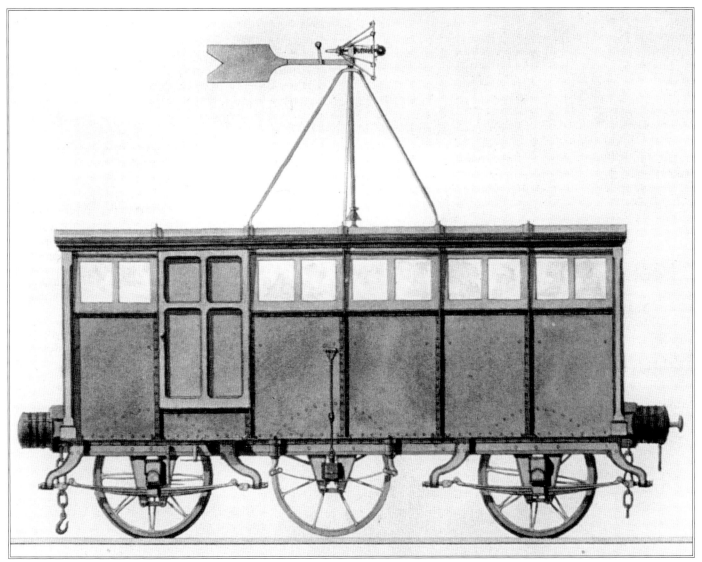

E.T. Lane's colourwash drawing of Gooch's Dynamometer Car of 1847, dated 14th May 1849, is of immense interest since it is the only known detailed illustration of the vehicle. The most significant element in a dynamometer car is the spring balance (seen on the right-hand draw bar) which was coupled to the engine, the pull this measured equalling the tractive force of it. Within the coach (an old Third Class vehicle) the spring balance was attached to an arm mounting a pencil that measured the deflection (*i.e.* pull) by plotting a graph on a paper chart, which was moved along at a speed proportionate to that of the engine by belts and bevel gears driven by a measuring wheel (the carriage's middle wheel) running on the rails. A clock was arranged in such a way that a mechanical device linked to it could mark the paper, say every 30 seconds, so that the speed could be calculated accurately. A wind vane was mounted on the roof to enable the wind velocity and thus the wind resistance to be calculated. Gooch's achievement in designing and equipping this vehicle was immense and marked him out as one of the great experimental engineers of his time. The coach remained in use until September 1876 but in 1879, it was regauged and converted to an Accident Van (also referred to as a Pilot Van) based at Swindon until finally condemned in April 1893.

perched on the buffer beam to take the necessary readings. Gooch comments in his diary that '*it was rather a difficult task to sit on the buffer beam of the engine and take indicator cards at a speed of 60 miles per hour*'.

Clark went further by recognising the danger involved remarking: '*Only those who have undergone the fatigue and risk … with occasionally a brisk side wind to make them conscious of how short a distance there is between time and eternity*'.

Gooch conducted a series of tests in 1847, first with *Great Western* – his large 2-2-2 built in 1846 and then reconstructed as a 4-2-2 when the leading axle broke later that same year – and then with *Dreadnought*, a 'Premier' Class 0-6-0 goods engine on Brimscombe Bank near Stroud. Later in the year, he conducted an exhaustive series of tests with *Great Britain*, the second of the 'Iron Duke' Class of 8ft 0ins 4-2-2 express engines, on a flat stretch of line on the Bristol & Exeter at Banwell, just to the west of Bristol. He made forty-one runs over a measured mile at speeds up to 62.4mph, with trains weighing between 50 and 100 tons. These tests provided Gooch with much conclusive evidence to undermine the narrow (standard) gauge party's contention that the broad gauge, by its bulk, naturally needed to expend greater effort to overcome resistance offered by atmospheric pressure, as well as that which was inevitably produced by the friction created by iron wheels running on iron rails and iron axles running in bronze bearings. It also offered him a considerable amount of data, which allowed him to develop his ideas in both design and train running practises. This resulted in the production, in 1848, of an improved 'Iron Duke' of the '3rd' and '4th Passenger' Lots, commencing with *Courier* in June 1848. As a matter of record, the broad gauge dynamometer vehicle continued in use until 1876. In addition to its internal apparatus, the coach had a large weather vane mounted upon the roof and the whole assemblage must have presented quite a spectacle when in use.

Naturally the history and technical capabilities of this vehicle have attracted much interest and readers wishing to know more about these matters are directed towards the Bibilography on page 200.

From 1847, all new designs, beginning with the 'Iron Duke' 6ft 0in. 'Singles' and the 'Pyracom' Class 5ft 0in. 0-6-0 goods engines, incorporated a new design of firebox. Gooch abandoned the previously ubiquitous Haycock or Gothic type of firebox, with its narrow proportions and deep grate, for the more familiar 'round top' pattern of rather larger proportions, which greatly enhanced the steam raising capacity of the boiler/firebox combination by increasing the heating surface. Mid-feathers continued to be used in the firebed, though how effective these really were remains a matter of contention. Gooch evidently thought that they constituted a useful addition to the steam raising potential of the design but at some extra burden for the maintenance, not to mention the additional cost in labour for fire cleaners, etc. Labour, however, was very cheap, so perhaps these considerations were of little consequence, though Gooch was a consummate keeper of records recording labour, coke, water and lubrication expenditure on a weekly basis, as well as the financial burden placed upon his department by repair

and maintenance costs. The Gooch firebox was the 'raised top' pattern, on which was mounted a brass safety valve cover of a rather pleasing design. Boilers remained domeless. Steam was collected from a perforated pipe, which terminated at a regulator valve mounted in the smokebox.

Gooch having therefore established some fundamental design principles, these may be summarised as:

1. Sandwich Frames, only superceded by plate frames toward the end of his superintendancy
2. Cylinders positioned between the frames, of generous proportions with slide valves mounted between the cylinders
3. Raised top fireboxes
4. Domeless boilers of good steam raising characteristics
5. Fixed link valve gear
6. Steam collection by perforated pipe running the length of the boiler
7. Regulator mounted in the smokebox

Gooch largely stuck to these features for the rest of his period in charge of the GWR's locomotive department and to those of other railways, notably the South Devon Railway, over which he exercised a degree of leadership. His classic goods engines were an enlarged version of the 'Pyracmon' Class and numbered well over a hundred examples, as well as a few tank engines of fundamentally the same design. His celebrated passenger 8ft 0in. 'Singles' of the 'Iron Duke' and 'Courier' classes were perhaps one of the most successful designs of their time, which had some interesting influences on later engineers of significant merit, especially relating to the proportions and steam raising capacity of their fireboxes. Gooch later designed and built a small batch of 4-4-0s of the 'Waverley' Class, which were constructed by Robert Stephenson & Co. in 1855 and had 7ft 0in. diameter wheels and 17ins x 24ins cylinders. Then, the following year, a larger batch of 2-4-0 mixed traffic engines of the 'Victoria' Class were built at Swindon, with 6ft 6ins coupled wheels and cylinders 16ins x 24ins.

In 1849, following the failure of the Atmospheric System, Gooch designed two 4-4-0 saddle tanks featuring a bogie that pivoted around a 'ball and socket' joint, which was attached directly to the underside of the boiler rather in the manner of a traction engine. The leading driving wheels were flangeless and the first of the class, *Corsair*, was fitted with a sledge brake between the coupled wheels, alongside the ashpan. However, his latter feature, whilst effective, had the distinct disadvantage of lifting the rear driving wheels off the rails and was soon done away with. Despite their somewhat ungainly appearance, these two engines proved very successful and were subsequently perpetuated in the form of new builds for the GWR and the South Devon Railway, though with some modification to the framing of later engines built for the latter.

The problem of finding a satisfactory way of burning coal, rather than the expensive coke, was a matter which exercised many locomotive designers in the 1850s. Eventually, the simple expedient of fitting a brick arch in the firebox, a development pioneered on the Midland Railway, was universally adopted in the 1860s. Prior to that, certain other designers, such as Cudworth

Broad Gauge Goods Engine Boilers 8th Lot.
Beattie's patent Smoke consuming.
Scale 3/4 = 1 foot.

This drawing, found in Gooch's notebook, illustrates the proposed fitting of Beattie's patent smoke consuming apparatus to an 0-6-0 goods engine in 1859. As can be readily appreciated, had the device been fitted it would have added to the complexities of construction and required considerable modification to a tried and tested design. However, one can see that Beattie was also on to something here, having in effect invented a combustion chamber, a device whose day was yet to come. The discovery by Brunel that South Wales steam coal was largely smokeless, together with the subsequent adoption of the brick arch to aid combustion, rendered devices such as these superfluous for, as far it is known, this experiment did not proceed beyond the drawing board.

on the South Eastern Railway and Joseph Beattie on the L&SWR, came up with various devices to aid combustion and consume the smoke. In Gooch's notebook, a portfolio of drawings, costings and detailed planning, there are some sketches of a boiler intended to be fitted to a 'Standard Goods' engine of the 8th Lot, introduced in April 1859 and fitted with Beattie's patent smoke consuming apparatus. This appears as a combustion chamber mounted within the rear half of the boiler, through which the hot gasses passed before flowing through the tubes. It was heated by the front half of the grate behind the mid-feather, which was the hottest part of the fire. The obvious disadvantage was that it reduced the heating surface of the boiler. Meanwhile, Brunel, who sadly died in 1859, had discovered that South Wales steam coal when burnt in a locomotive firebox was largely smokeless. It is believed that Gooch did not proceed with a practical application of this apparatus but it at least demonstrates his flexibility of mind and willingness to consider adopting ideas other than those of his own, if only for trial purposes.

Gooch only really departed from some of his cherished design principles toward the end of his superintendentship by adopting, in 1862, Stephenson valve gear for the standard gauge '131' Class of 0-6-0s at Joseph Armstrong's suggestion. Also, plate rather than sandwich frames were fitted to the last five batches of his 'Standard Goods' engines commencing in 1857. He introduced further innovations with the design of twenty-two engines built

for working the Metropolitan Railway, again in 1862. These were 2-4-0 saddle and well tank engines, and were the first in the country to be fitted with condensing apparatus. They had outside cylinders (the only GWR broad gauge design to ever have these) and solid plate frames mounted inside the wheels. The cylinders were steeply inclined to clear the leading wheels and they had 6ft 0in. coupled wheels and 16ins x 24ins cylinders. It is a matter of record that they were not an outstanding success, the condensing gear in particular giving considerable trouble in service.

In conclusion it is interesting to make a comparison which I have often been struck by, between Gooch and Churchward. Neither were great inventors but both were wonderful innovators. Both could see the merits and demerits in others design work, and were prepared to improve and develop the best practice of their day. Both also enjoyed the full confidence of their superiors and magnificent support from their assistants. The end result was the production of some of the most advanced designs of their times, which had profound influences on steam locomotive practise even up to and including the present era. Gooch was certainly at the cutting edge of steam locomotive technology in the 1840s and '50s, which gave the GWR a potential head start over its rivals of about twenty years. Only the mass conversion of the broad gauge, which began in the early 1870s, would see that advantage negated. Gooch, however, would not live to see its final demise in 1892 – that event may have proved a grief to great for him to bear.

E.T. Lane's exceptional drawing of *Great Western* but bearing the name *Lightning*. This finished drawing was worked up from contemporary sketches but was not completed until 22nd March 1849, which begs the question why Lane retained the name *Lightning*? I think the only reason can be that the engine bore this name, if only briefly, before it entered traffic. The only other plausible explanation might be that Lane had become used to referring to it in this vein during construction and so retained it for sentimental reasons. Yet he was a stickler for accuracy so I, very much, tend toward the former explanation. This drawing also gives a good impression of the size and bulk of the engine which, when compared with the earlier types, must have seemed massive indeed. Note the layout of the regulator actuation levers at the front end, with their support bracket riveted onto the smokebox, and the regulator handle curving upwards by the side of the firebox. With this and the contemporary classes, the regulator was placed in the valve chest and worked by the regulator handle, the design of which was subsequently changed from that illustrated here. The positioning of one or two other fittings are also of interest, particularly the siting of the brake whistle away from the engine whistle and the manhole cover on the rear of the firebox where you might expect a conventional regulator to be. This latter feature is also represented on Lane's drawing of *Great Western* as a 4-2-2 (as are also the positioning of the whistles.)

Section 2. Passenger Engines Designed between 1846 and 1852
Chapter 3
Great Western

Introduction

In 1845, the GWR was deeply embroiled in the pressing matter of the gauge question. A Royal Commission had been set up in June 1845 to inquire into this matter asking that: '*A humble address be presented to Her Majesty, praying Her Majesty to be graciously pleased to issue a Commission to inquire whether in future private Acts for the Construction of Railways, provision ought to be made for securing a uniform gauge …?*'

The Commission was constituted of three experts, namely the Astronomer Royal, George Biddel Airy; the retired chief inspector of railways, Lieutenant Colonel Sir John Smith RE; and the Professor of Mathematics at the Military Academy of Woolwich, Peter Barlow. The first meeting was held in August 1845, which was followed by sessions in September, October and then through to Christmas. However, these evidently wearied Brunel, for he suggested that a series of practical trials should take place, which with some hesitation the standard gauge party agreed to. The result of those trials, which was a fairly convincing victory for the broad gauge, are recounted in full in MacDermots *History of the GWR* and are also extensively referred to in Part 2 of this work.

Despite the success in the trials, there was a distinct feeling among the broad gauge party of Brunel, Gooch and Saunders that the margin of their success was not sufficient to entirely overwhelm the opposition. The generous proportions of the broad gauge lent themselves to a significant increase in cylinder and boiler power of the locomotives, while the stability which its dimensions and Brunel's design of continuously supported rails – known as baulk road – would more than adequately support engines of greater weight travelling at higher speeds.

Gooch was only too ready to take on this challenge. Facilities for manufacturing and erecting locomotives at Swindon were already being put in place and the erection of some much-needed goods engines was underway. The boilers for these had been ordered from a contractor but Gooch was convinced that sufficient skills and facilities were available at Swindon to allow in-house boiler making to commence. Despite this and to achieve his aim, various expedients had to be adopted, which included hurrying along the installation of an overhead crane in the new boiler shop and the delay to the building of some waggons which were already in the course of construction. In a letter (now in the National Archives) to Brunel's assistant J.W. Hammond, with whom Gooch was obviously on intimate terms, Gooch darkly comments that he has, '*arranged with Mr Brunel to build a 'little engine' with an 8ft 0in. driving wheel (this I know will please you) and a 6ft 0in. fire box – the great object of building her is to have her ready to start when the Gauge Question commences in Parliament next session or on the First of April*'.

Gooch was, of course, pulling his friends leg. Clearly he meant him to understand that the phrase 'little engine' indicated something entirely the opposite. For her day, *Great Western* – as the 'little engine' would soon become known – would be termed a gigantic engine, far larger and more powerful than anything else then on rails. Built in just thirteen weeks, a truly remarkable achievement, she exceeded all expectations, as we will see, though her weight proved to be a challenge to the Permanent Way Department and she rapidly gained the nickname 'The Mangle' from the platelayers. In fact, there was too much weight on the leading axle, which fractured whilst running through Shrivenham on a Down train after only a few months operation. Rebuilding her with lengthened frames as a 4-2-2 partly overcame the problem. Among the enginemen she was known as 'The Russian', because she consumed so much tallow and oil. Gooch was delighted with her however and with very good reason as will become clear as our story unfolds.

Interestingly, when built the engine was possibly fitted with the nameplate *Lightning* for a very short time. E.T. Lane made a sketch of the engine dated April 1846 bearing this name, below, and those who were involved in building it at Swindon are known to have referred to it as 'The Lightning.' This was probably a nickname, which became attached to it because of the rapidity

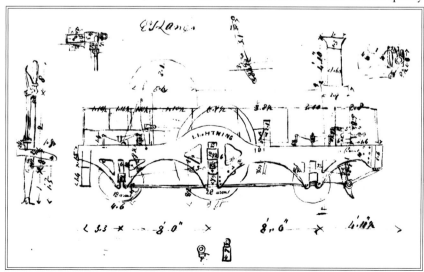

of the build. Perhaps *Lightning* was the name originally given to the engine and Gooch changed it when he or Brunel realised what impact the name *Great Western* would have on the gauge trials and the ensuing debate. We most probably will never quite know the answer, what is beyond question is that *Great Western* never ran in traffic bearing any other name. In fact, it proved to be the first of four engines, two broad gauge and two standard gauge, to bear this most honourable name in the company's service, which stretched from 1846 until February 1963, when the 'Castle' Class 4-6-0 No. 7007 was withdrawn.

Constructional Details

In essence, *Great Western* was a much enlarged 'Fire Fly' and embodied all the best practise which had become apparent from six years of experience gleaned from the work and maintenance of those engines. The drawings for the engine's construction were executed by Edward Snell and were of the most rudimentary kind because they were needed in a hurry. As Alan Platt comments, '*There was no time to produce proper working drawings and so she was built from a few centre-line and outline drawings, pen and ink sketches being used for most of the parts*'.

Frames

These were of typical sandwich frame construction, which provided great strength alongside a degree of elasticity that aided smooth running and haulage capacity. As in the 'Fire Flys' and other earlier classes, the plates were made of $^1/_2$in. wrought iron, bolted through 3ins ash timbers.

Dimensions

TABLE 4.1: DIMENSIONS OF *GREAT WESTERN*		
Wheelbase	8ft 0ins + 8ft 0ins	
Wheels	Driving 8ft 0ins	
	Carrying 4ft 6ins	
Cylinders	18ins x 24ins	These were cast iron and laboriously bored out by hand in the Fitting & Turning Shop. A considerable advance on previous designs.
Boiler Barrel	10ft 6ins	approx. length. 278 2ins tubes
Boiler pressure	100 psi	
Firebox	4ft 10ins x 5ft 4ins	Haycock type
Casing	5ft 6ins	
Tube heating surface	1582.16 sq. ft	
Firebox heating surface	151.05 sq. ft	Again, a very considerable advance on earlier designs.
Total	1733.21 sq. ft	The heating surface figures are calculated for the 'waterside', the fireside equalled 1597.49 sq. ft.
Grate area	22.64 sq. ft	

The boiler was, of course, the very first produced in Swindon Works, erected in the new Boiler Shop and constructed by, among others, Mr George Ditchburn, the first boiler shop foreman, and two skilled artisans, Robert Wardle and Thomas Chilton. Best quality wrought iron plates were used, which were bent into shape by large 'plate rolls' and hammered by the smiths.

The driving wheels were made from over 100 separate parts all forged and then hammer welded into an integral structure of enormous strength. All wheels were fitted with Gooch's patent steel tyres. These were so hard that they could not be turned in the normal way but had to be ground to profile using a specially produced grinding wheel. They were made under the supervision of John Fawcett, a highly skilled craftsman.

The firebox was of the Haycock type, beautifully surmounted by a brass crown topped off by the safety valve and casing.

Valve Gear

The valve gear was of the Gooch, fixed link pattern. Slide valves were placed above the cylinders and were driven by rocking shafts attached to the valve gear.

Regulator

This was of a new design also fitted to the 'Premier' and 'Prince' classes, which were contemporary with *Great Western*. The regulator was placed in the valve chest and was moved by a horizontal curved lever situated above the footplate and positioned to the right of the firebox. The connecting rod between the lever and the valve passed through the front of the smokebox and via the linkage actuated the regulator.

However, this arrangement was later done away with and the standard design of regulator, with slide in the smokebox and a pull out handle on the backhead, was substituted.

Tenders

It is not entirely clear what type of tender was first attached to *Great Western*. Contemporary records give no clue and even Gooch's notebook is silent on the matter. Although E.T. Lane made several drawings of the engine he made none of the engine and tender. Two drawings of the locomotive coupled with a tender do exist, however. One drawing by E. W. Twining in 1934, though beautifully executed, purports to illustrate the engine as built as a 2-2-2 in 1846. Sadly, the drawing is inaccurate in several ways, not least because it shows the engine attached to a sandwich-framed tender which simply did not exist at the time. Because the drawing is so well known I have included it here (page 66) but it must be treated with caution.

A more perplexing 'sketch' is reproduced in G.A. Sekon's *Evolution of the Steam Locomotive*. It shows *Great Western* as a 2-2-2 attached to an iron-framed tender of the sort that Bird and the RCTS history maintain were designed for the 'Iron Duke' Class 4-2-2s in 1847. Since *Great Western* did not run as a 2-2-2 in 1847 this cannot be accurate either, unless of course Bird and the RCTS are wrong about the date of the introduction of these tenders. The sketch in question, reproduced below, is of entirely unknown provenance and, after considerable reflection, I feel it should be treated with great suspicion.

Leaving aside the question of the date of the introduction of these iron-framed tenders, my other major objection to the historicity of this drawing is the published cost allotted to the building of the tender. This was only £365 which, when compared with the overall cost of the engine at £4,342 14s 4d, is of negligible proportions. A comparison with the cost of 'Fire Fly' tenders, delivered between 1840 and 1842 and which, when the extra cost of Gooch's patent steeled tyres is added, equalled £550 is revealing. To my mind the £365 suggests an accountant's figure set against the depreciation of an extant vehicle. It is also worth pointing out that all the available information indicates that the contemporary 'Premier' and 'Prince' Class engines, initially at least, ran with tenders that had been rendered surplus by the rebuilding of 'Sun' and 'Leo' Class engines.

It is with much hesitation therefore that I tentatively suggest that, during its working life, *Great Western* ran with three different designs of tender in the following order:
1. 1846-47: A tender of the design used on the 'Fire Fly', 'Sun' and 'Leo' classes, with 5ft 0ins x 5ft 0ins wheelbase. These were being made spare in 1846 as the 'Sun' and 'Leo' engines began to be rebuilt as saddle tanks. The tenders were also rebuilt, with larger tanks on an iron rather than the original timber frame.
2. 1847-50: An iron-framed tender of the type introduced in 1847 with the 'Iron Duke' Class. These were larger, with a 6ft 0ins x 6ft 0ins wheelbase and a water capacity of about 1,760 gallons (see Chapter 5).
3. 1850-70: Sandwich-framed tender, as described below and with details in **Table 4.2** taken from the 1857 specifications.

TABLE 4.2: SANDWICH-FRAMED TENDER SPECIFICATIONS, 1857	
Wheelbase	6ft 0ins + 6ft 0ins
Wheels	6 – 4ft 0ins dia.
Tank: Length	16ft 6ins
Width	8ft 3ins
Depth	3ft 3ins
Coke Space	102.8 cu. ft
Water Space	301.67 cu. ft, capacity 1,880 gals
Weight: Empty	10 tons 6 cwt
Loaded	21 tons

Probably there were many minor variations in these figures – I have seen the water capacity sometimes described as 1,700 gallons for example. Springing was effected by leaf springs mounted above the footplate and brakes were mounted on the fireman's side alone, actuated by a rather elegant cast brake standard with twin handles. The travelling porter's lookout protection (commonly called 'the coffin') was installed from the late 1840s. Our only photograph of *Great Western* shows the engine as running in the early 1860s, coupled with a sandwich-framed tender that is mounted with this fitting.

The tender which, newly built, was allocated to *Great Western* bore the number 1 in the broad gauge tender lists. Though these records are far from complete, nonetheless they state that it was cut up in 1872. It is not known which engine this tender was attached to at that time – *Great Western* was withdrawn in December 1870 but was not broken up until 1872. It might have remained with the engine throughout its life, having received a larger tank during its latter years? If this could be proved to be the case, then it would

very much be the exception to the general rule, as tenders were routinely swapped between engines on a regular basis.

Costs

This proved to not be a cheap engine to build, the total cost amounting to £4,342 14s 4d, which breaks down as £3,477 14s 4d for the engine and £365 for the tender, plus it also included £500 set against interest on plant, etc. As such, *Great Western* was almost certainly the most expensive locomotive built for the broad gauge and also reflects the excessive cost of labour employed night and day to get the engine finished in record time.

Testing and Working Life as a 2-2-2

The engine was an almost immediate success. One assumes that some initial running-in would have taken place and any necessary adjustments made. It almost goes without saying that there would have been some need for attention, leaking valves, the odd weeping tube or a little steam blow around pressurised joints. Such things almost always occur when an engine is steamed for the first time. Gooch had previously decreed that engines built by contractors should run in a trouble-free way for 1,000 miles before they could be accepted and paid for, so he was well aware of the trials and tribulations of proving new and previously untried designs. It was in the course of this running-in and testing that *Great Western* hauled a gross load of 94 tons at 67mph.

By the end of May, Gooch was sufficiently confident in *Great Western*'s abilities to arrange a test of epic proportions. Two years previously, following the opening of the line through to Exeter, Gooch accompanied by, among others, Henry Appleby, had driven the 'Fire Fly' Class engine *Orion* from London to Exeter and return in one day, with a light load of no more than 30 tons. Gooch in his reportt which was very detailed (see Part 2 pages 64-68) stated that: '*the whole time occupied in running the 388 miles to Exeter and back was 8 hours 29 minutes or 45.7mph, the down trip being 4 hours 21 minutes or 44.5mph and the up trip 4 hours 8 minutes or 46.9mph. the engine arrived at Paddington quite cool and in good order*'. It should be pointed out, however, that these timings were exclusive of stops, of which there were four in each direction.

Imagine, therefore, Gooch's elation when *Great Western* made the same return journey on 1st June 1846 in 6 hours 49 minutes exclusive of stops, 388 miles at an average of 56.9mph; the outward journey occupying 208 minutes and the return 211 minutes of running time. This was a quite outstanding performance which completely eclipsed anything that contemporary standard gauge engines could achieve both in speed and haulage capacity, a fact that Gooch was quick to appreciate.

All these achievements added greatly to the case in favour of the broad gauge. Gooch was at this time involved in writing his *Supplementary Observations of the Published Evidence of the Gauge Commission*, in which he was able to draw upon some of *Great Western*'s early exploits. Then, at the beginning of June 1846, the Board of Trade, having spent four months studying the Gauge Commission's report, published their own views which in many ways favoured the broad gauge. The Board of Trade submission to Parliament recommended what, in effect, was a two-tier system,

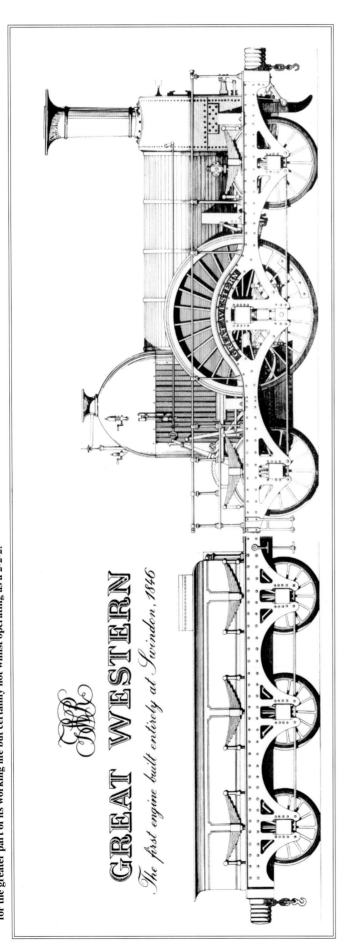

GREAT WESTERN

The first engine built entirely at Swindon, 1846

E. W. Twining's beautiful drawing of *Great Western* dates from 1934 and differs in minor details from Lane's original. For example, the regulator actuation rod is shown at the side of the smokebox in the latter but Twining appears to have it passing through the smokebox. He does not show the positioning of the rear manhole cover either and there are one or two other minor differences. As I mention in the text the details relating to the type of tender originally fitted are very sketchy. One can only say that *Great Western* ran with the type of sandwich-framed tender illustrated here for the greater part of its working life but certainly not whilst operating as a 2-2-2.

allowing already established broad gauge railways to expand in their areas and that broad gauge lines already authorised by Parliament but as yet unbuilt or unfinished should be allowed to proceed. The submission concluded with these words: '*They would therefore recommend that the lines for which Acts have been obtained, but which have not yet been completed to the south of the line from London to Bristol should be permitted to be constructed on the Broad Gauge, as originally intended*'.

This was 'manna' from heaven as far as Brunel and Gooch were concerned and went some considerable way toward vindicating Brunel's decision to adopt the broad gauge in the first place. To further press the case in favour of it, the two of them decided to put on what today we would call a publicity stunt. The five Board of Trade Resolutions were due to be debated in the House of Commons on Wednesday 17th June 1846. Therefore, on Saturday 13th June, a special train was laid on, the exploits of which would be reported in the newspapers in advance of the debate. Consequently, a heavy train consisting of ten coaches — of which three First Class carriages were occupied by the GWR hierarchy and their guests and the rest suitably ballasted weighing in all 100 tons — was assembled at Paddington station. At its head sat *Great Western* with, it is said, both Brunel and Gooch on the footplate. When given the right of way, *Great Western* pulled powerfully out of the station and into immortality. The journey was not trouble free, for a boiler feed pump failed at Slough, holding the engine back somewhat. Despite this minor setback, however, the train forged on, reaching a maximum speed of 69mph (some reports suggest 70mph) and covering one 10 mile stretch at an average of 66mph, the 77 miles to Swindon being covered in 78 minutes at an average of 59.2mph. Had it not been for the set back at Slough, an average in excess of 60mph would have been achieved.

To put this into context, in 1907 A.V. Goodyear timed 'Saint' Class 4-6-0 No. 2904 *Lady Godiva*, then unsuperheated and with a train of 320 tons mainly comprised of what was described as '*old clerestory stock*', between Paddington and Swindon, 77 miles in 78 minutes 40 seconds. Though this train encountered adverse signals at the beginning of the journey, a top speed of 73.5mph was recorded passing Reading and an average speed of 68mph was kept up between Didcot and Swindon, which was passed at 68.5mph; *Great Western*, of course, was required to stop!

Back in June 1846, *Great Western* eventually reached Bristol in 2 hours 12 minutes, exclusive of stops. Great were the rejoicings, Charles Russell calling the trip a '*great feat*', whilst Gooch wrote proudly: '*Had we had this engine ready in time for the gauge experiments how different the results would have been, altho' I don't suppose it would have altered the report*'. He was no doubt right, although when the Regulation of Gauges Bill received the Royal

Assent on 18th August 1846, it protected the extant broad gauge lines and allowed further extensions to be bid for. The GWR may not have won an outright victory but all the effort to build *Great Western* had certainly contributed to an outcome which, in effect, preserved the status quo.

Many newspapers, including *The Times*, *The Morning Chronicle* and *Morning Herald*, gave extended reports of the events that took place on 13th June, the latter two particularly so. As they are largely complementary, I have only reproduced the most complete of the accounts, which was printed in the *Morning Herald* on Monday 15th June 1846 – see Appendix 1. Where details offered in *The Times* and *The Morning Chronicle* differ, I have indicated them below along with a brief resume of the day's events. *The Times* states that the train was driven by Brunel, which seems highly improbable since he had specifically stated that though he often rode on the engines he never drove because as soon as the train was safely underway his attention wavered and he began to think of other things. At least that is what he personally told the gauge commissioners! *The Morning Chronicle* mentions that at Slough '*one of the tubes of the engine burst*' but *The Times* more accurately reported that at Slough one of the pumps on the engine '*gave way*'. On the Down journey, the train stopped at Didcot, no doubt for water and perhaps also coke, for 5 minutes 15 seconds and at Swindon for 4 minutes 27 seconds. The return journey began at 4.00pm and the train arrived at Paddington at 6.30pm, a running time of 2 hours 35 minutes, which included 15 minutes taken for two stops, at Swindon and Didcot. The average speed on the return journey is reported by *The Morning Chronicle* to have been '*about 50 mph*'.

The *Morning Herald* concluded its account with the following paragraph: '*The motion of the carriages at the maximum velocity – viz 70 miles per hour, was perfectly easy. There was not anything approaching the unpleasant oscillation too frequently experienced while travelling in the express trains on the narrow gauge, particularly when the outside cylinder engine is employed*'. Neither Brunel nor Gooch or the GWR's Directors could have hoped for a more ringing endorsement than that. So, the broad gauge was saved.

Following these exploits, *Great Western* became part of the operating fleet of the railway. We do not know where she was based or what exactly her duties were, though it is reasonable to suppose that she took a regular hand in working the Exeter expresses probably between London and Bristol. Frustratingly, no-one seems to have recorded exactly when the leading axle broke. G.F. Bird, writing in *The Locomotive Magazine* in 1901, says that she was hauling a Down express and that the accident occurred at Shrivenham (just east of Swindon), commenting in the September edition: '*Sometime in 1846 or the beginning of the following year the overtaxed leading axle broke whilst the* Great Western *was running with a down train near Shrivenham, fortunately without causing either engine or train to leave the rails. The axle was afterwards tested at Swindon and it proved to be very brittle and crystalline, owing possibly to having been swaged too much at a reduced temperature for the sake of obtaining a neat finish; during the test it flew into several pieces one of which made a slight dent in the wall of the drawing office*'.

Bird was obviously uncertain about the date of the fracture of the axle but there are some contemporary newspaper reports which allow us to draw some confident conclusions about the timing of the incident and *Great Western*'s reappearance into traffic following its rebuilding. First is an entry in the *Western Courier, West of England Conservative, Plymouth & Devonport Advertiser*, dated 9th September 1846:

'THE MONSTER GREAT WESTERN ENGINE

The Great Western Company's Great Western *engine has more than one nickname attached to it. The drivers and stokers call it 'The Russian' from the enormous quantity of tallow and oil which it consumes – being as we are told, as much as 75 per cent more than any other engine on the line. The plate-layers have named it 'the Mangle' from its effects on the rails – and well they may the engine and tender weighing, we are assured not less than 54^1/$_2$ Tons. The Russian has been taken into dock for general repairs and when she will come out no-one ventures to say – we should think, not in the course of the present year. These repairs are estimated to cost from £300-£600; and yet the engine has not run in the whole 9000 miles!*

Another monster engine – it is understood that the Great Western Railway are about to build an engine with eight wheels and still larger than the Great Western *locomotive; but with the weight distributed over a greater number of wheels, it is supposed that it will not press on any one point of the rails with so great an incessant weight as the* Great Western *and will combine all the improvements which the working of the latter has pointed out as capable of being introduced in the monster engines. What next?'*

The paper quotes its source for this information as *Herapath's Railway & Commercial Journal*.

From these observations we can reasonably draw the conclusion that the fracturing of *Great Western*'s leading axle occurred either at the end of August or in the first week of September 1846. This accords with something that Alan Peck told me many years ago when I asked him about this incident, with words to the effect that, "*I have been told that it was in September 1846 but have never been able to prove it*". The conversation took place about forty years ago and I cannot quite recall exactly how Alan phrased his reply but the essence of it is as related here.

We also have no definite date from any official records which I can find that gives a date for *Great Western*'s return to traffic. Yet there is a suggestive newspaper report which helps to narrow the focus down and in addition gives us some interesting information about the locomotive's performance.

This article was first published in the *London Evening Standard* on 7th December 1846 and reprinted in the *Northern Warder*, a Dundee publication, on 17th December 1846. Under the heading '*Progress of the Railway System*', it details a journey from Paddington to Swindon on a train hauled by *Great Western*, which was followed by a visit to the railway works and the new town. Though the actual date of the visit is not given, from information contained within the account it could only have occurred a matter of days before initial publication on 7th December. It mentions that an engine with 7ft 6ins diameter driving wheels was under construction in the '*erecting shop*'. Since the GWR only possessed one broad gauge engine with 7ft 6ins driving wheels this does rather pinpoint the time of the visit. The engine concerned was *Witch* of the 'Prince' Class, which was built in December 1846. Construction probably began a little before this, so the visit may have taken place at the end of November and not later than the first week of December. From our present point of view the following details of the journey are of great interest. The unnamed author writes:

'*The engine, the new* Great Western, *left the Paddington Station at 9hr 46 mins 50 seconds* [1 minute 50 seconds late – the correspondent was travelling on the 9.45 Exeter express] *and not withstanding the driver, a very cautious man, had to reduce his speed on two occasions while passing stations and to run through the Reading station where some obstruction presented itself, at about 30 miles per hour. The entire distance to Didcot, fifty-three miles was performed in fifty-six minutes and twenty seconds – that is from a state of rest at the one station to a state of rest at the other station. A very high velocity was attained from the thirteenth to the nineteenth mile as will be seen from the following notes of the working of the train:*

Reached the	Hr Min Sec	Time per mile in seconds	Miles per hour
12th mile at.	... 10.1.30		
13th mile at.	... 10.2.28	... ...58	....62.06
14th mile at.	... 10.3.25	... ...57	....63.15
15th mile at.	... 10.4.20	... ...55	....65.45
16th mile at.	... 10.5.14	... ...54	....66.62
17th mile at.	... 10.6.9.	... ...55	....65.46
18th mile at.	... 10.7.3.	... ...54	....66.62
19th mile at.	... 10.7.58	... ...55	....65.45'

From the above we can see that *Great Western* was back in traffic by the first week of December 1846 and had no doubt been active for some little time before that. It seems therefore that the engine was out of service for between ten and twelve weeks which, given the work involved in lengthening the frames, adjusting the springing and other requisite tasks, is quite reasonable.

Rebuilding as a 4-2-2

Gooch would obviously have been disappointed by the accident to *Great Western* but he must have been relieved that it was not accompanied by any loss of life and thus loss of prestige. He therefore resolved to make a virtue out of a crisis by rebuilding the engine with lengthened frames, thus redistributing the weight. G.F. Bird takes up the story again: '*The frames were cut in front of the driving wheels and lengthened so that two pairs of 4ft 0in. wheels could be substituted for the single pair of 4ft 6ins leading wheels. These two pairs of wheels were 4ft 4ins apart between centres and the second pair was 6ft 7¹/₂ins in advance of the driving wheel centres thus giving a total wheelbase of 18ft 0in.*'. The new wheelbase was therefore: 4ft 4ins +6ft 7¹/₂ins + 8ft 0in.

It is interesting to note that the old frames were adapted rather than completely new frames cut and erected. This seems to have become a normal procedure when sandwich-frames required extensive renewal or were rebuilt with a lengthened

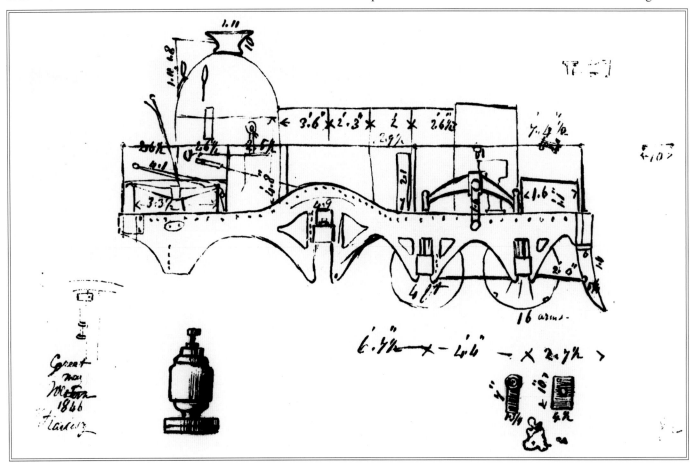

This sketch of Lane's shows the changes made to the framing of *Great Western* following rebuilding as a 4-2-2. The revised system of springing the leading wheels is illustrated and he was careful to note the reduced size of these wheels. He also made accurate measurements of the increased wheelbase and front end extension of the frames. At the footplate end, the trailing wheel appears to have been supplied with a larger spring and the regulator handle design has been modified to make it easier to reach and handle. The water feed clack valve is also shown in some detail, as are several other fittings which are difficult to identify.

Lane sketched the rebuilt engine (ABOVE) and in 1849 worked it up to a fully scaled drawing (BELOW). Unusually, his initial sketch is slightly out of proportion but it is useful because it illustrates the fireman's side of the engine. Most of Lane's sketches and drawings are dated between 1848 and 1849, so this illustration shows the engine after perhaps two years of service and therefore in more or less original rebuilt condition. The finished drawing is a very fine example of the draughtman's art. Note the revised design of the regulator handle and the rodding which runs alongside the base of the smokebox and not through it.

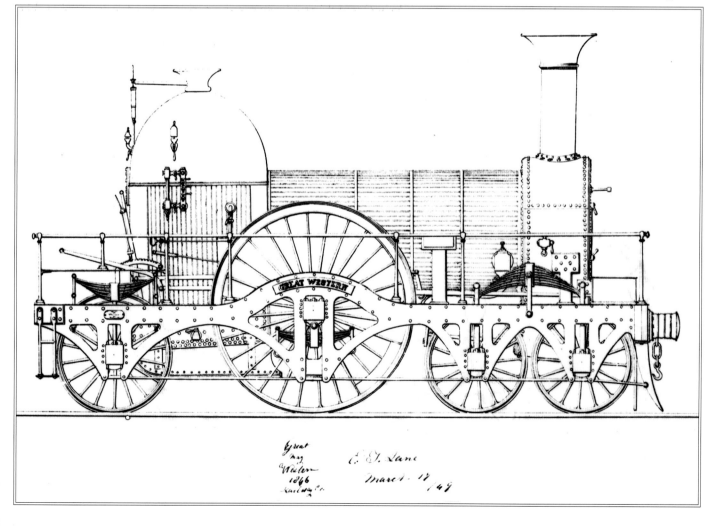

This familiar view remains the only known photograph of *Great Western*, having been taken during the latter years of the engine's working life in, I would suggest, the early 1860s. Though the engine remained largely as rebuilt in 1846-47, a number of modifications and additions are evident here. Beginning at the front end, it had acquired a sandbox on the front of the frames, feeding the leading wheels. Though the engine seems to have retained its original iron capped chimney, a blower has been fitted. The interior of the smokebox has been fitted with a 'draught regulator' (not to be confused with the steam regulator). This may have been fitted from new, though its actuating lever and rodding are not shown on Lane's drawings; however, it is included on Twinings drawing of *Great Western* as a 2-2-2. The draught regulator was a set of louvres placed one above the other on the tubeplate, that could be opened or closed by the driver to control the draught through the tubes. Judging from the spacing of the boiler bands the engine has received, at some time, a new boiler of the modified pattern introduced with the 'Iron Dukes', and the regulator is now in the upper part of the smokebox and actuated by a pull out handle positioned on the backhead (the driver is shown holding the regulator handle). At first glance the footplate appears to have been fitted with a windshield to protect the crew's legs, etc. but a closer inspection suggests that this is not so and the black blob visible at the rear of the firebox backhead may well be part of the background which the photographic retouching has failed to eliminate. The tender is of the usual sandwich-framed type, though fitted with what appears to be a larger tank. In the GWR tender records, this was given the number 1 though it was not, of course, the first tender owned by the company, nor was it the first built. The lining on the tender is faintly visible, executed in four panels of which the front and rear are carried around the curved ends of the tender sides. Each panel has scalloped corners, a design which was in use in the 1850s and early '60s, particularly on express engines. Note also the travelling porter's 'coffin', from which the retouching process seems to have eliminated the associated handrails.

wheelbase – as in the case of some members of the 'Fire Fly' Class. We also noted in Part 2 how *Acheron*, following its boiler explosion at Gloucester in February 1855, had its old frames 'patch repaired' rather than being supplied with a set of new frames. Adding strengthening pieces often around 'horn blocks' was another common practise which was frequently employed as mileage accumulated and frames became worn.

Testing with *Great Western*

In April 1847, Gooch used *Great Western* and the 'Premier' Class 0-6-0 *Dreadnought* to test his new dynamometer car on 'Stroud Bank', also known as Brimscombe or Sapperton Bank. A full description of the tests was printed in the *London Evening Standard* for Monday 26th April 1847. The whole text of the article, which is rather verbose, is contained in the appendix, so I have only reprinted the actual test results here. The tests themselves, by the unnamed author's admission, took place on 'Saturday last', which I take to mean 24th April 1847. He writes:

'*The first experiment made on Saturday last was with 50 tons exclusive of the engine and tender. It was taken by the* Great Western *engine, which has 8 feet driving wheels, 18 inch cylinder, and 2 feet stroke. The train left the 98¹/₂ mile-post at 12h.47m.15¹/₂ s. and reached the 95³/₄ post at 12h.53m.14s., performing the 2³/₄ miles in 3m.58¹/₂ s., or at an average speed of about 27 miles per hour. The top of the incline of 1 in 60 is rather more than a furlong within the tunnel, but the sudden change from light to darkness shut it completely from our sight, so that we are unable to give, from our own observation, to which we confine ourselves, the working over the last quarter of a mile.*

The second experiment was with 60 tons with the same engine. The train started at 1h.26m.12¹/₄ s., and passed the 95³/₄ mile-post at 1h.32m.54¹/₂ s., doing the distance therefore in 6m.42¹/₄ s. or at the average rate of about 24¹/₂ miles per hour.

The third experiment was with 111 tons, drawn by two locomotives – the Dreadnought, *goods engine, with five feet wheels, 16 inch cylinder and two feet stroke and by the* Great Western. *The train started at 3h.55m.47¹/₂ s., and passed the 95³/₄ post at 4h.2m.16¹/₂ s. the distance was therefore performed in 6m.29s., or at the average rate of 25 miles per hour.*

The fourth experiment was with the same load of 111 tons, with the Dreadnought *alone. The train left the starting-place at 4h.34m.57¹/₂ s., and passed the 95³/₄ post at 4h.42m42³/₄ s, doing the distance in 7m.45s., or at the average rate of about 23 miles per hour.*

The fifth and last experiment was with 70 tons with the Great Western. *The train started at 4h.26m7³/₄ s., and passed the 95³/₄ post at 4h.33m.51³/₄ s., being therefore 7m.44¹/₂ s. on the journey, and performing the distance at an average speed of about 23 miles per hour, doing, therefore, not more than the coupled goods engine had just performed with 111 tons. But it is necessary to state that the moment before the* Great Western *started with the 70 tons a slight sprinkling shower came down and wetted the rails; and it will be seen from the details given below that had the run been 5¹/₂ miles instead of 2³/₄ miles, the working of the eight feet driving wheel passenger engine with the 70 tons would have shown a very much higher average velocity than that of the coupled goods engine with the 111 tons.*

It has indeed been stated by railway engineers that a locomotive with eight feet driving wheels cannot start well, even on a level. Some six or eight months since we gave, in disproof of this statement, the working of the Great Western, *with a stopping train of 100 tons, between Paddington and Reading, and in corroboration of the accuracy of the results then furnished by us, and of the groundlessness of such statement, we shall now proceed to show how soon such an engine gets into speed when starting on an incline of 1 in 105, and running over still heavier gradients. To illustrate this point we shall give the average speed attained by the locomotive over the last quarter of the first mile travelled by it after starting from the incline of 105. It is requisite to re-state the gradients of this first mile of running. For a little more than a furlong the gradient is a rising one of 1 in 105. There is then a rising gradient of 1 in 75 for about half a mile; then a rising gradient of 1 in 70 for nearly a quarter of a mile, and the remainder of the mile on a rising gradient of 1 in 75.*

Average speed maintained over the last quarter of the first mile:

Great Western engine	Time of running. Seconds	Speed per mile
With 50 tons	0¹/₂	29¹/₂
With 60 tons	33³/₄	24¹/₂
With 70 tons	42¹/₂	21

We shall now give the average rates of speed at which the several loads

Average speed over gradients as they occur from the starting point					
	Great Western 50 tons miles per hour	Great Western 60 tons miles per hour	The two engines 111 tons miles per hour	Dreadnought 111 tons miles per hour	Great Western 70 tons miles per hour
1 in 105 for about a Furlong	11	10	11¹/₂	11	9
1 in 75 for about ¹/₂ mile	24¹/₂	22	22	19¹/₂	19
1 in 70 for nearly ¹/₄ mile	29¹/₂	26¹/₂	25¹/₂	20³/₄	21
1 in 75 for about ³/₄ mile	33¹/₄	31	29¹/₄	23	26
Level for about ¹/₄ mile	38¹/₄	34¹/₂	33	27¹/₄	31
1 in 70 nearly ¹/₄ mile	39¹/₂	35¹/₂	36¹/₄	29¹/₄	32¹/₂
1 in 60, ¹/₂ mile	38	33	35	26	31

were taken, placing the gradients in the order that they occur from the starting point viz., the 98¹/₂ mile-post:

The advantage of what is called 'running' at a heavy gradient, that is approaching it from a descent or a level, will be easily understood by the reader if he attends to the great increase of speed attained over the level of only a quarter of a mile, and the further increased rate over the heavy gradient immediately beyond it.

We believe that these workings are very far beyond anything that has yet been performed by the locomotive engine. We shall shortly return to this subject, and show how utterly the details given above annihilate the popular, we might say the fashionable, theory of resistances to railway trains at high velocities.'

These tests and the results gained are, in the context of 1847, remarkable. Not only do they throw the performances of the two engines into sharp focus, they also demonstrate Gooch's prowess as an experimental engineer. Nowhere else in the world were tests of this kind being undertaken nor data of such accuracy accumulated. Gooch was in every sense far ahead of his contemporaries in the development of locomotive design, as subsequent events would prove.

This latter point is brought into focus by a further newspaper report found in the *Devizes & Wiltshire Gazette*, published three days later on Thursday 29th April 1847. It reads: '*On Sunday last* [that is the day after the trials on Stroud Bank] *some experiments were made on the Great Western Railway to test the power of the engines. The* Great Western *has undergone alteration and its performance was highly satisfactory between Reading and Swindon; a speed at the rate of 70 miles per hour was easily maintained. The* Iron Duke, *a new eight wheeled engine drew a special train weighing sixty tons up the very steep Gloucester Incline at the rate of 36 miles per hour'*.

From this additional information it appears that Gooch continued his testing work with the newly outshopped *Iron Duke* while *Great Western* was used for what would later be termed '*a loaded road test*'. The purpose behind this testing regime was, of course, to acquire data to aid further improvements in design.

This would indeed bear fruit over the next few years, beginning with an improved *Iron Duke* design introduced in June 1848 and known as the '3rd Lot Passenger' or as the 'Courier' Class.

Gooch's '*little engine*' had indeed proved its worth and would work successfully for a further twenty-three years. In passing, one wonders what is meant in the quotation given above by the phrase '*has undergone alteration*'? It may well be a straight reference to the engine's rebuilding as a 4-2-2 or it might imply some more subtle alterations to the diameter of the blast pipe or perhaps to the travel of the valves but we can only speculate in the absence of more concrete information.

Great Western evidently remained a useful traffic machine and for a time continued to work alongside the 'Prince' Class on the main line, until there were sufficient of the new 'Iron Duke' and 'Courier' Class engines available to fulfil all those duties. From thence it took a lesser part, as will be related in the next section of our story.

Allocation, Works Report, Mileage Analysis as a 4-2-2 and Reflections on *Great Western*'s Work

Though it is not possible to trace the complete allocation history of *Great Western* from its rebuilding in 1846 until its withdrawal in December 1870, all the available records are unwavering in showing the engine to be '*available and in steam at Paddington*'. This was most certainly the case between 1854 and 1862, the period covered by extant '*coke returns*' and though, as time passed, perhaps not employed on the hardest diagrams, the engine gives every appearance of being a reliable member of the passenger stud. It is rare not to find it in steam during the

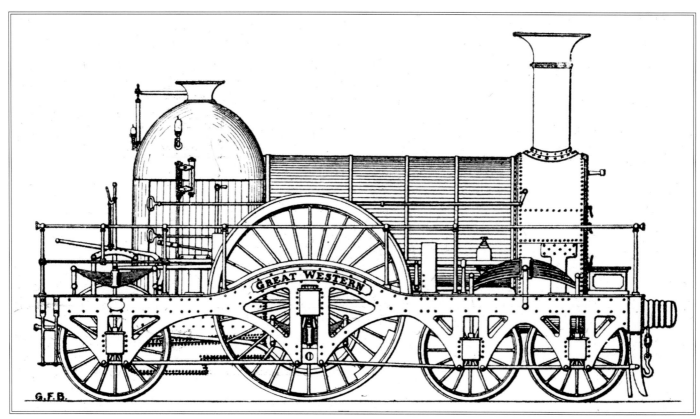

G.F. Bird's drawing of *Great Western*, from the September 1901 issue of *The Locomotive Magazine*, shows various detail differences from Lane's drawing.

four-weekly periods that Gooch employed for record keeping purposes.

Naturally it was stopped from time to time for running repairs, mileage inspections and major works attention. The very scanty evidence for this suggests that it received major attention at Swindon at roughly 18-24 month intervals. It was certainly present for repair in January 1867 and again in July 1868, when it is shown as '*renewed*' – meaning in this instance that it received new cylinders and perhaps a new boiler with increased boiler pressure. Two and a half years later, the engine was withdrawn almost certainly because it was due for another heavy overhaul and was deemed surplus to further requirements. The engine had, throughout all this time, retained its original Haycock firebox so it was also obsolete by this period. Much later, in 1888, a second and completely new broad gauge 4-2-2 named *Great Western* would emerge but other than perhaps the original nameplate, nothing of the old engine was retained or reused as has occasionally been claimed in earlier works. The engine's final mileage was 370,687. Interestingly, it was not broken up until April 1872, which leaves me wondering if thought was given to preserving the engine, for which a cogent case could certainly have been made.

In conclusion it is important to point out that the final mileage figure given above probably only relates to the period that the engine ran as a 4-2-2. As was noted in Part 2, the GWR, in its earlier years at least, treated engines which had undergone major reconstruction as new for mileage purposes. The engine's mileage as a 2-2-2 is said to have been about 9,000 giving a grand total approaching 380,000.

We have little contemporary evidence which gives any definite information about the day to day working life of Great Western in later years. I remember reading somewhere that it frequently worked to Oxford from Paddington but now I need to find the reference I cannot lay my hands upon it. Yet I recall thinking at the time, '*Ah, that explains in part at least why* Great Western's *mileage was so relatively low when compared to other contemporary classes*'. To give but one example, 'Fire Fly' Class *Medusa*, built by Fenton, Murray & Jackson in June 1842 and which ceased work in November 1864, ran a total of 515,205 miles during its twenty-two years of working life – that is 135,518 miles more than *Great Western* over a slightly shorter period. From this one is drawn to the obvious conclusion that, for much of its working life, the engine was involved in short out and back workings such as Paddington to Oxford, Reading or perhaps Windsor. It may also have been maintained as a 'spare' engine at Paddington. Even the near contemporary members of the 'Prince' Class, many of which spent much of their working lives based in Birmingham, managed a considerably greater mileage than

Great Western. Elk, for example, ran 570,940 miles before ceasing work in September 1870, when it was then cut up.

Interestingly, there is, in part at least, a modern comparison. The lowest mileage 'Castle' Class engine, No. 7008 *Swansea Castle*, spent seven of its short sixteen year life based at Oxford and even after its move to Old Oak Common in September 1956, it continued to work regularly on the Oxford, Worcester and Hereford main line. On this admittedly circumstantial basis, I feel confident that the unsubstantiated claim that *Great Western* perhaps worked fairly short out and back diagrams from Paddington or stood spare in Westbourne Park shed yard a reasonable conclusion to draw in light of the available evidence or perhaps the lack of it.

Conclusion

Although built in a hurry to boost the GWR's claims about the superiority of the broad gauge, *Great Western* might be called a 'watershed engine'. However, whilst in this narrow context it succeeded admirably, it achieved more than this. Following its rebuilding as a 4-2-2, Gooch used the engine as a test bed to develop his ideas and to gain experience with locomotives of greater size, weight and power output. This far-sighted engineer could envisage a time when the already-growing demands of commerce and the travelling public would require heavier trains and faster schedules. Experience gained with *Great Western* pointed the way forward. This was indeed a 'watershed moment' in British locomotive development and the cost of building such an important locomotive was thus justified beyond all expectations; she really was a groundbreaking machine.

Finally, as the picture below from the May 1903 edition of the *Locomotive Magazine* indicates, there is just a chance that a small part of *Great Western* still survives. The accompanying text is as follows: '*The very handsome coal scuttle shown was made from the polished brass cover which surmounted the 'haystack' firebox of the veteran 'Great Western' from the date of its building in 1846 to the period of its dismantling in 1870 … The relic is a valued possession of Mr Archibald Sturrock who, as our readers are no doubt aware, was locomotive superintendent of the Great Northern Railway from 1850 to 1866. Previous to that, he was for ten years with Mr Daniel Gooch at Swindon Works, and he was mainly responsible for the building of the famous* Great Western. *On that account when the engine was finally condemned to the scrap heap in 1870 the copper-smith at Swindon reserved some portion of the firebox lagging to work up into the form illustrated and presented the result of his decidedly artistic labours to Mr Sturrock as an interesting memento of the days when that distinguished engineer virtually had charge of the Swindon Shops*'. Where is this interesting relic (left) now I wonder – does anyone know?

This photograph of *Prince* is the best image that we have of a member of this class, taken in the yard at the west end of Swindon Works, possibly following an overhaul. As seen here the engine had undergone some modifications since it was originally built in August 1846. Most notable is the repositioning of the regulator on the backhead, which means that the regulator assembly has been moved from the steam chest to the top of the smokebox. There is also the possibility that new cylinders, with the valves between the cylinders rather than on top, had been fitted; the enlarged balanced weights may be an indication of this. Other minor changes have also occurred, with a blower having been fitted and the whistles regrouped together on the rear of the Haycock. However, the chimney appears to be of the original design adopted in 1846. The tender merits little comment, being typical of its type, though note that the iron axle box covers are painted black and not polished, as may have happened in later years. Note that the outline of the top of the Haycock had been inked in to make it stand out from the sky.

CHAPTER 4
THE 'PRINCE' CLASS

The 'Prince' Class, as the RCTS History refers to it after the first engine, totalled just six engine, built at Swindon in three distinct batches of two between August 1846 and March 1847. The engines of each sub group differed from each other and from other members of the class, in a variety of ways, which will become apparent as our story unfolds. As mentioned in Part 1 of this series, I have maintained the RCTS classifications for clarity but it should also be pointed out here that the GWR referred to the 'Prince' engines as the 'Queen' Class in all their records and official documentation.

The RCTS history comments that, '*This more modest class was produced pending the trials of Great Western*', a thoughtful comment which implies more than it says. Clearly Gooch faced a problem in 1846. Though the gauge trials had proved the superiority of the broad gauge, he evidently felt that he could not rest on his laurels and if it was to stay ahead of its competitors, more power was unquestionably required to work the Exeter expresses which were the GWR's flagship trains of the period. As we have seen, *Great Western* was not without its problems – even before its leading axle broke it was proving to be too heavy for the track – yet its immense power clearly showed the way ahead. In my opinion this explains Gooch's decision to build these engines. Clearly his mind was still in 'experimental mode', hence the many differences which the class exhibited but they did fulfil a useful purpose whilst further developments were taking place and were, in their turn, ideal vehicles to test some of his own new ideas and innovations.

We must now turn to a consideration of the members of the class in detail and **Table 5.1**, below, lists the engines which made up the 'Prince' Class.

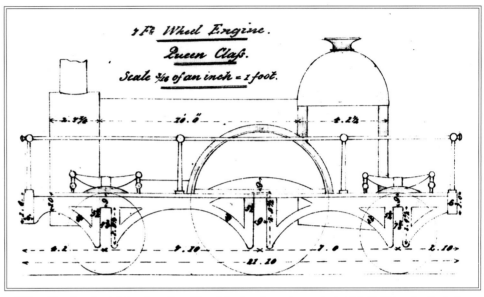

This outline drawing is taken from Gooch's notebook and may demonstrate his initial ideas for the design of these engines which he refers to as the 'Queen' Class, and incidentally is also how the GWR referred to them. The title 'Prince' Class appears to have been given by the RCTS because *Prince* was the first member of the class to enter traffic in August 1846. In fact, only *Elk*, *Peri* and *Sylph* were built with 7ft 0in. diameter driving wheels and straight foot plating as illustrated here.

Note: As in all these early classes, dates when engines ceased work, were written off, broken up or replaced can be contradictory or, at least, confusing. The figures given above are derived from the RCTS History. There are some discrepancies, particularly relating to the disposal of *Witch*, that will be discussed at the end of the chapter. Nonetheless, the dates given above are believed to be as nearly accurate as it is possible to determine.

Construction – General Details

As already mentioned, these engines differed in detail from one another quite markedly. In particular, some had straight footplates with a large polished brass splasher band over the driving wheels, while others had curved frames carried above the leading, driving and carrying wheels. *Witch* had 7ft 6ins driving wheels, whilst all the rest were fitted with 7ft 0ins drivers. Though the length of the wheelbase seems to be constant throughout the class, some had longer frames than others – by perhaps two or three inches – which lengthened the overhang at the front end. These differences can be easily perceived in the various illustrations and photographs accompanying this chapter. Indeed, we are fortunate to possess either a drawing or a photograph of each member of the class, which allows us to pinpoint the individual characteristics of each engine. Unlike *Great Western*, these engines had inside sandwich-frames and

TABLE 5.1: THE 'PRINCE' CLASS		
NAME	BUILT	CEASED WORK
Prince	August 1846	June 1870
Elk	August 1846	September 1870
Peri	November 1846	July 1870
Witch	December 1846	May 1870
Queen	February 1847	January 1870
Sylph	March 1847	April 1870

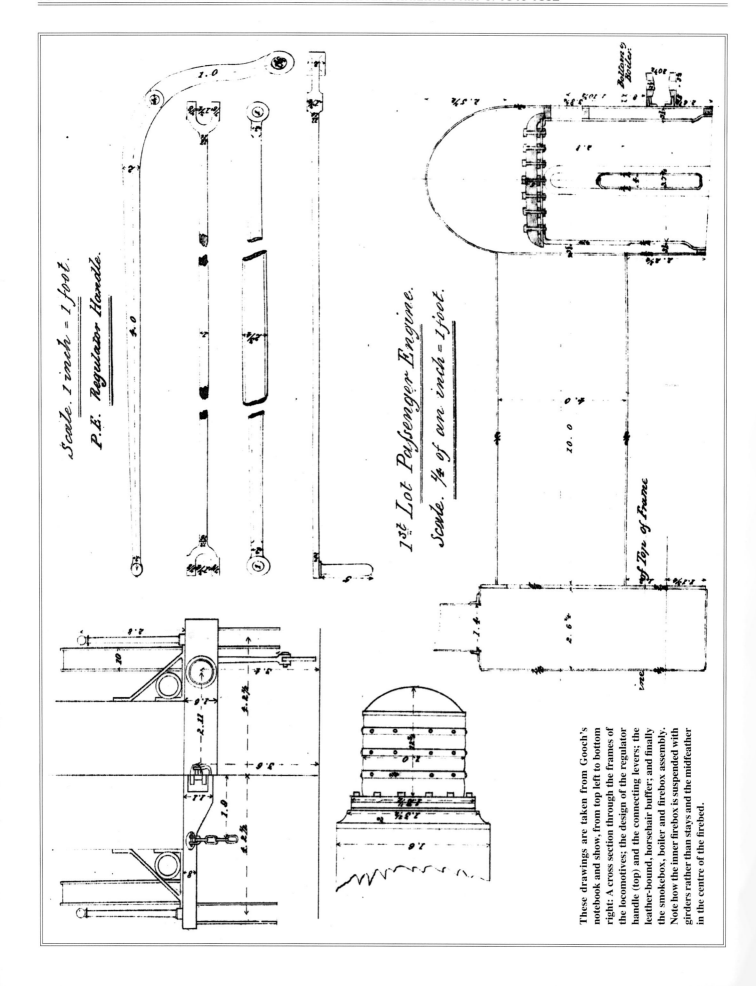

Scale. 1 inch = 1 foot.
P.E. Regulator Handle.

1st Lot Passenger Engine.
Scale. ¾ of an inch = 1 foot.

These drawings are taken from Gooch's notebook and show, from top left to bottom right: A cross section through the frames of the locomotives; the design of the regulator handle (top) and the connecting levers; the leather-bound, horsehair buffer; and finally the smokebox, boiler and firebox assembly. Note how the inner firebox is suspended with girders rather than stays and the midfeather in the centre of the firebed.

all the members of the class were built with and retained the Haycock pattern of firebox throughout their lives. These were the last express passenger engines to be built with this feature.

Cylinders, Valves and Regulators

These engines were built with the Gooch fixed link form of valve gear, which was arranged to drive the valves – placed above the cylinders – by means of a rocking shaft. The regulator was placed in the valve chest and was moved by a horizontal curved lever on the right-hand side of the footplate. The connecting rod between the lever and the valve passed through to the front of the smokebox and there actuated the regulator. This cumbersome arrangement was later modified and the regulator handle was placed in the more normal position on the rear of the backhead. This change would have required extensive modification in the smokebox, boiler and firebox, and was probably only undertaken when significant renewals were necessary.

Cylinders would also have been replaced as time wore on. From 1847, Gooch standardised on a design which saw the valves placed between the cylinders rather than on top of them. This allowed for a more compact arrangement of the valve gear and removed the requirement for rocking shafts. It would seem logical to assume that this arrangement was applied to the 'Prince' Class engines as cylinders fell due for replacement. Unfortunately, I cannot as yet confirm this supposition. Gooch seems to have learnt that slide valves placed above the cylinders could have a detrimental effect on the coasting qualities of an engine's running. When steam is 'on', the valves are held off the faces of the valve chest by steam pressure. However, when steam is shut off, the valves sit back down on top of the valve chest and so impede the engine's coasting capabilities. This proved to be a lesson well learnt and greatly contributed to the free running nature of later designs.

Much of that mentioned above also applies to the contemporary 'Premier' Class of 0-6-0 goods engines, which also exhibited a variety of different designs of splashers and footplate contours, as well as the style of valve and regulator arrangement that have just been described. This class will be dealt with in Chapter 8. The main dimensions of the 'Prince' Class are shown in **Table 5.2**.

TABLE 5.2: THE 'PRINCE' CLASS – MAIN DIMENSIONS	
Wheelbase	7ft 10ins + 7ft 0in.
Driving Wheels	7ft 0in. – except *Witch* 7ft 6ins
Carrying Wheels	4ft 0in.
Cylinders	16ins x 24ins
Boiler: Barrel	10ft x 4ft 0in. (inside diameter)
Tubes	178 x 2ins dia., 10ft 5½ins long
Firebox Casing	4ft 5ins x 4ft 10ins
Tube Heating Surface	876.27 sq. ft
Firebox	105.91 sq. ft
Total	928.18 sq. ft
Grate Area	13.67 sq. ft
The heating surface area is calculated on the fire side, which was standard practise at the time. The total for the water side is 1082 sq. ft	
Elk, with 10cwt of coke and 7¾ins of water in the glass, weights on the wheels were recorded as:	
Leading	8 tons 6 cwt
Driving	11 tons 10.2 cwt
Trailing	6 tons 6cwt

All the figures quoted in the table above are taken from a schedule produced by the GWR in 1857; however, it does not record that *Witch* was fitted with 7ft 6ins diameter wheels.

Individual Characteristics of Each Class Member
Prince

Fortunately, we possess a photograph of *Prince*, which is also undoubtedly the best image of a member of the class that we have. It was taken at Swindon, supposedly by R.H. Bleasdale, although there is mounting evidence to suppose that this was not necessarily the case but it can fairly be described as 'from the Bleasdale collection'. Though the picture is undated I suspect that it was taken in the early 1860s following an overhaul for, despite the posed crew, there is no coke or coal visible on the tender. The driver is holding the regulator which has been placed on the firebox backhead. This is the only illustration that we know of showing this modification. Other later features are the grouping of the whistles together on the rear of the brass Haycock and the provision of a blower, the valve and pipework for which are visible at the rear of the smokebox, behind the chimney.

Prince, of course, was the first member of the class to be built and as the photograph on page 74 demonstrates, was fitted with the longer overhang at the front of the framing. The footplate valance is curved over the wheels and is of polished brass. This exposes the wheels, showing clearly the construction style of each wheel. The very light nature of the frames is also clearly evident, as is the large balance weight on the driving wheel. All these engines were fitted with sanding apparatus from new; the straight delivery pipe – another later modification (compare other illustrations) – was mounted on the fireman's side and, one presumes, activated by him. The larger balance weights (again please compare with other illustrations) may suggest a redesign of the valve gear and the provision of new cylinders, though this remains conjectural.

In passing, we should mention the tender which is of the standard Gooch sandwich-framed design and was common to all members of the class as far as it is known. This design is well known and was used on numerous other broad gauge classes. A standard gauge version was also much in evidence from the mid-1850s.

Elk

Elk was built alongside *Prince* but principally differed from its classmate in the design of its footplate and splashers. The footplate was straight and the splashers had polished rims which, of course, were especially notable over the driving wheels. The handrail was mounted on pillars and it ran in front of the driving wheels rather than behind, as was the case with *Prince*. Otherwise, *Elk* would have been similar to her immediate predecessor with the longer front end, etc.

Peri

The third member of the class was turned out in November 1846 and in many respects resembled *Elk*, though with shorter, 3ft 9ins rather than 4ft 0in. framing at the front end. The design

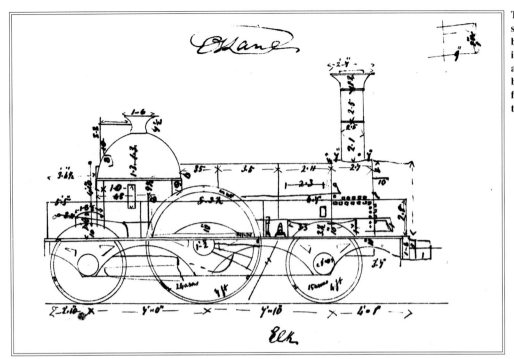

The only illustration of *Elk* we possess is this sketch-cum-drawing by E.T. Lane. Though built at the same time as *Prince*, it differs in the design of the footplate and splashers, as well as the positioning of the handrail but was otherwise similar. The extended frames at the front end are very evident in the drawing.

of the splashers differed in as much that the leading and trailing wheels were surmounted with brass bands similar in profile to the driving wheels. E.T. Lane's sketch, executed in December 1847, also demonstrates the original design of the sand pipe and illustrates the linkage of the valve gear's 'rocking shafts' in front of the smokebox. He also shows the position of the works plate above the driving wheel on the splasher front. As far as I can see, no works plate is visible on any other illustration be it photograph, drawing or sketch.

Witch

In general outline, *Witch*, the fourth member of the class outshopped in December 1846, resembled *Peri*. There were, however, considerable differences not least in the provision of 7ft 6ins diameter driving wheels – which were only fitted to this engine. This in turn required some modifications to the height of the footplate it seems. Consequently, the leading and trailing splashers were of much shallower pattern, with solid polished brass fronts. E.T. Lane's drawing, which dates from 16th November 1848, gives a vivid impression of *Witch*'s appearance – which must have been quite striking to a contemporary observer, an impression that with its high running plate and almost totally exposed wheels, it still presents today.

Queen

Queen was built in February 1847 and, as far as it is possible to tell was more or less a copy of *Prince*, other than the length of the front end which, at 3ft 9ins, was 3ins shorter than that of the latter. We have several illustrations of *Queen* from the pen of E.T. Lane, the first a sketch he made of the engine in Swindon Works yard in February 1848, which he then worked up into a beautiful watercolour dated 3rd July 1849. Especially evident in Lane's

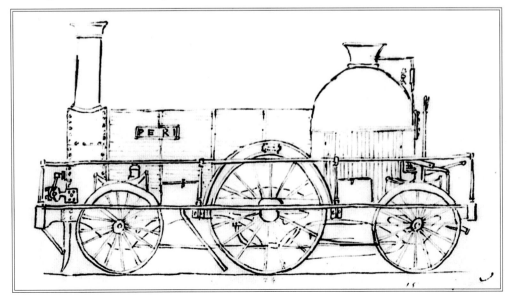

In some respects, *Peri* was similar to *Elk* though built five months later. It retained the straight footplate and the longer framing at the front end. *Elk*, however, had closed or partly closed splashers whilst on *Peri* they were left open, surmounted in each case with a polished brass band. Lane's drawing shows the fireman's side with its sandbox and pipe, and works plate mounted on the driving wheel splasher band. *Peri* was the engine that, it is said, was rebuilt at Wolverhampton with new cylinders and Stephenson valve gear.

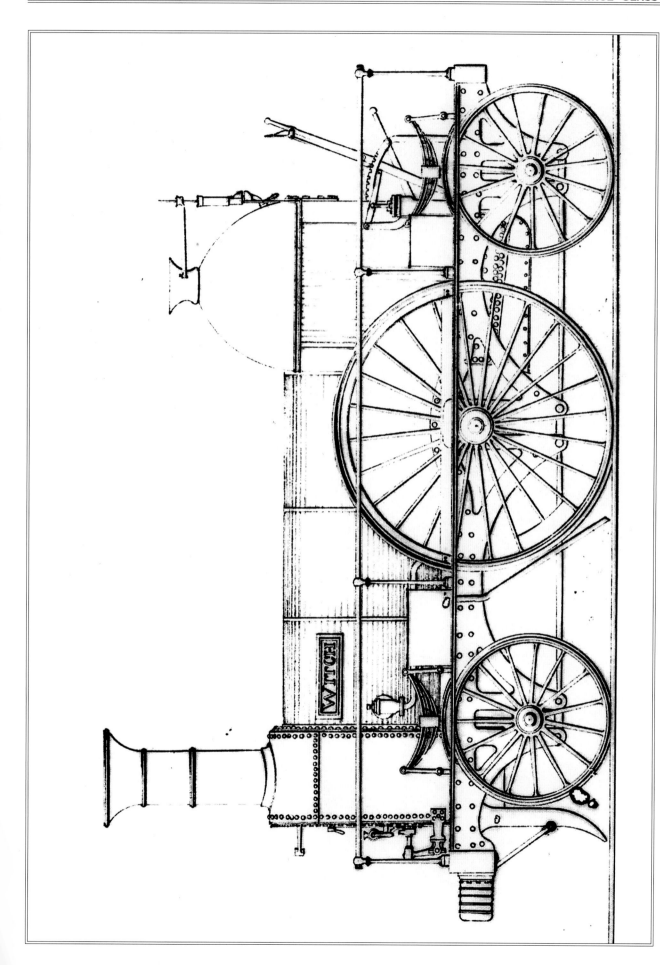

Witch was very similar to *Peri*, though with shorter front-end framing and was also the only one of the class fitted with 7ft 6ins driving wheels. The reason for making this change is not recorded though one assumes that it was for experimental purposes? This particular drawing gives a good impression of the frames, the design of which was common to all members of the class. The larger diameter driving wheel also necessitated a higher pitch for the footplate and a consequent reduction in the size of the leading and trailing wheel splashers, which appear to have had solid faces. Note also the hand pump, positioned alongside the rear of the firebox, which allowed the fireman to top up the boiler in an emergency.

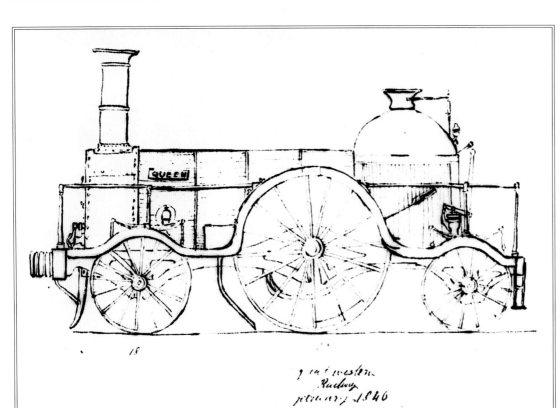

great western
Railway
february 1846

Left: E.T. Lane left several illustrations of *Queen* including the preliminary sketch seen here, a fully scaled drawing and a water coloured version of the same. The engine differed from its immediate predecessors but was much the same as *Prince*, in that the footplate and valancing was carried up over the wheels. *Queen*, however, had a shorter front end to the footplate than *Prince*.

Below: Lane's scaled drawing of *Queen* demonstrates that the engine as built was similar to *Prince* with the footplate and valancing carried above the wheels in a style that would become normal for later designs of the smaller wheeled broad gauge engines. However, *Queen* differed from *Prince* in having a shorter front end to the footplate than her predecessor. Lane's colour washed version of this illustration appears on page 12.

1 0 1 2 3 4 5 6 7 8 9 10 11 12 13 14 15 16 17 18 19 20 FEET.

E. T. Lane
July 2. 18

We are very fortunate to possess this quite early photograph of *Sylph* taken in Swindon Works yard, perhaps about 1857 when several other photographs were taken by A.A. Wickenden in the area. As far as I can tell the locomotive has not received any of the modifications visible and commented upon in the photograph of *Prince*. You will, nonetheless, note that the boiler bands have been polished which was one of the later embellishments mentioned in the caption to the colourised picture of *Queen*. There are eight male figures visible in the picture, whose dress in white fustian attire is typical of the period as is their headgear, which would not be out of place on a soldier recently returned from the Crimea War. In other respects, *Sylph* was very like *Peri* and *Witch* with its straight footplate and open driving wheel splasher. The shallow splashers over the leading and carrying wheels are enclosed and appear to have polished faces.

painting is the arrangement of the driving wheel springs mounted beneath the driving axle. This drawing also well illustrates the locomotive's controls, with the arm of the regulator, the reversing lever and the feed water hand pump all clearly visible on the footplate, while the 'rocking levers' are equally well shown in front of the cylinders.

Sylph

The final member of the class was outshopped in March 1847. In many ways, *Sylph* greatly resembled *Witch* but with 7ft 0in. diameter driving wheels. The engine also had a similar design of footplate, with small polished brass splashers over the leading and trailing wheels.

Our one photograph of *Sylph*, whilst not of the best quality, is interesting in that it apparently shows the boiler lagging covered with iron sheeting, which was increasingly retrofitted after 1848, and with polished boiler bands – usually these were painted black. In my opinion, the photograph, which was taken in Swindon Works yard, is earlier than that of *Prince* and may date from the late 1850s. Perhaps the engine was being readied for some special working? The photograph is additionally useful in illustrating the original positioning of the regulator. On inspection of the image you will note the driver's right hand on the regulator, while his left rests on the reversing lever handle. The whistles are shown in their original positions, with the brake whistle being the one nearest the camera on the side of the haycock, while the shriller 'train whistle' is positioned where it can be easily reached by both members of the engine crew. The gauge glass is also visible on the driver's side of the firebox.

The tender shows clearly the positioning of the travelling porter's protective housing, known colloquially as a 'coffin' or 'iron coffins' by the staff. Introduced in 1847 they were, according to McDermott, finally abolished in 1864 when the Harrison Chord was introduced.

There is a little more to be said about the constructional details of these engines.

Boiler Lagging

The boiler lagging was originally of the contemporary slatted wood (probably ash) construction held in place by iron bands, though brass may have been used instead. E.T. Lane's drawings demonstrate this style of cladding. From the introduction of the 'Courier' Class in 1848, the timber slats were covered with iron sheeting and this was eventually retrofitted to most, but not all, of the earlier engines. The two photographs of *Sylph* and *Prince* indicate that they had both received this modification and I think that it is safe to assume that the other members of the class would have been treated in a similar way. It is also important to remind readers that even when exposed these wooden slats were always painted green and were never simply polished – as has been the case with both modern replicas of broad gauge engines.

Boiler Fittings

During the Gooch era, boilers built after 1846 were universally domeless so this category relates mainly to chimneys, safety valves and clacks.

Chimneys: According to Lane's measurements, these were 4ft 6ins tall and were surmounted by an iron cap that added a further 1ft 2ins to the height, making a total of 5ft 8ins. The outside circumference was 2ft 5ins and the diameter 1ft 4ins, whilst the rather elegant cap tapered out to a maximum width of 2ft 7ins.

Safety Valves: The two safety valves were mounted on top of the haycock firebox – one lock-up valve, and one actuated and graduated by a Salter spring balance. The brass safety valve bonnet rather matched the design of the chimney cap, tapering outwards from a base mounted on the apex of the haycock. Lane gives the height of these covers as 7 $1/2$ins high tapering out to a width of 1ft 6ins.

Clack Valves: Two clack valves were positioned, one on each side of the front ring of the boiler, close to the front tube plate. These are easily identified in the various illustrations.

Springing

The leading and trailing wheels were sprung by leaf springs mounted above the footplate. The driving wheels, however, had heavy underhung leaf springs mounted beneath the axle boxes, supported by the frames. These are difficult to see in the available photographs and some of the drawings/sketches omit them. Fortunately, Lane's drawing of *Queen* gives a clear indication of their positioning and of the way that the frames were designed to accommodate them. Additionally, the frames were kept in tension by tiebars which ran their full length from the leading to the trailing horn blocks.

Injectors

Injectors, replacing the crosshead and hand operated water pumps, were introduced in the 1860s. However, as far as it is possible to tell, none of the class received this modification during their working lives.

Tenders

As we discovered in the previous chapter relating to *Great Western*, it is impossible to be certain what design of tenders were first attached to these engines. I guess (which is all anyone can do) that the pattern of changes followed that set out in Chapter 3. In summary, the probable progression of changes is as follows:
1. 1846-47: Rebuilt iron-framed tenders from 'Sun' and 'Leo' Class engines with 5ft 0in. x 5ft 0in. wheelbase.
2. 1847-50: Iron-framed tenders with 6ft 0in. x 6ft 0in. underframe designed in 1847 for the 'Iron Duke' Class.
3. 1850 onward: Sandwich-framed tenders with a wheelbase of 6ft 0in. x 6ft 0in., initially having a water capacity of about 1,800 gallons, which was subsequently increased by fitting larger tanks to the frames.

It is of course impossible to know if each engine followed this pattern of tender changes. All that can be said with certainty is that what little photographic evidence we possess illustrates the engines concerned attached to sandwich-framed tenders, which implies that these attractive vehicles were the norm, from the mid-1850s, for the whole class.

Brakes

At no point in the lives of these engines was a brake of any sort ever fitted to the actual locomotive. The only available braking was a by means of a handbrake, actuated by a double-handed handle that applied wooden brakeblocks to the fireman's side of the tender.

Addendum

A fascinating letter appeared in the November 1901 edition of the *Locomotive Magazine* from a correspondent who signed himself only with the initials F.S.H. His letter begins with the interesting statement '*when I first went to Swindon Works in 1862 ...*'. He then continues with a number of observations which are not all relevant to the GWR. His comments relating to the 'Prince' Class, which he refers to as the 'Elk' Class, are of especial interest: '*The Elk Class ... had their regulators altered to the dome, worked by a handle with a sector at the back of the firebox in the usual manner. The Peri of this class was placed in the Wolverhampton district, where the late Mr Joseph Armstrong put in new cylinders with the steam chest between them, and a direct acting Stephenson link motion instead of the rocking shafts which were retained in the other five engines. He also added side plates to protect the men from the wind, and I think a weather plate with glasses, but of this I am not certain.*

These engines were remarkable at that period for their high speed and they did good service for many years between Didcot and Birmingham running trains in opposition to those of the L&NWR.'

This is a truly fascinating insight and though I have not been able to corroborate the assertion about the fitting of Stephenson

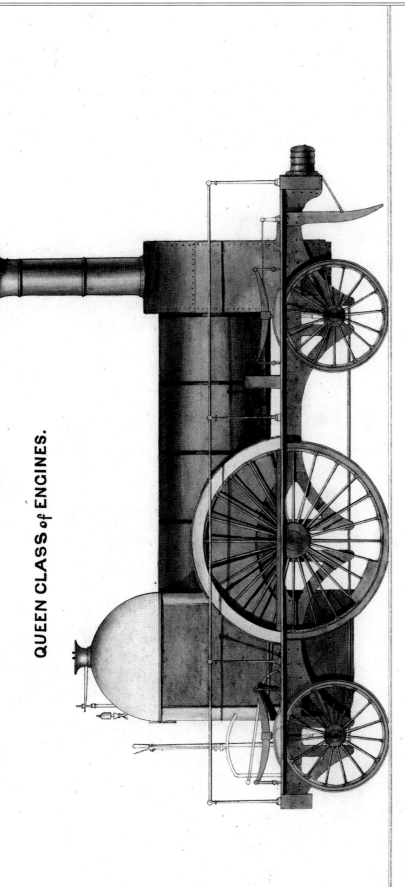

QUEEN CLASS of ENGINES.

ELK . PERI . PRINCE . QUEEN . SYLPH . WITCH .

DESCRIPTION.

*CYLINDERS 16 ins in diam? and 24 ins Stroke. Steam Ports 1½ in? by 13 in? Exhaust 2¾ in? by 13 in?. BOILER 10 feet long and 4 feet in diam? inside. FireBox 4 feet 5 in? long by 4 feet 10 in? wide. TUBES 178 Tubes 10 feet 5½ in? long and 2 in? diam? outside. HEATING SURFACE of FB 105·91. Tubes 876·27. WHEELS Driving 7 feet in diam? Leading and Trailing 4 feet in diam?
FIRE-GRATE area 13·67 Superficial.*
ELK with 10 cwt of Coke and 7¾ in? of Water in the Class weighs. Leading 8.6. Driving 11.10.2 Trailing 6 .. 6 .. 0

T C Q

T C Q

We need to remind ourselves that this drawing (again referring to it as the 'Queen' Class), in common with many others of the 1857 specifications, is only diagrammatic and does not represent the many variations actually present within the class. In fact, hardly two engines in this small class were alike, so the drawing most accurately probably represents *Elk*, though *Peri* and *Sylph* were similar, whilst *Witch*, although fitted with 7ft 6ins driving wheels and 4ft 0in. diameter carrying wheels (a fact not mentioned in the details listed below) was also built with straight footplating.

gear to *Peri*, to me it certainly has the ring of truth. It also bears out the assertion made later that engines of this class periodically visited Wolverhampton Works for routine attention.

He is, however, in error in suggesting that the regulator was placed in the dome, which these engines did not possess. He must mean the smokebox. He also suggests that, aside from *Peri*, all the other members of the class retained the original arrangement of rocking shafts to drive the valves. I do not believe that this last statement is correct, as the photograph of *Prince* on page 74 proves. His observations are nonetheless very interesting and are at least contemporary.

In Conclusion

I feel it is important to remind readers that constructional methods used at the time these and other contemporary classes of engines were erected meant that each was in effect 'hand crafted' so that no two, even if they were outwardly very similar, could be exactly the same. Apart from the specialist wheelwrights and boilermakers, most of the rest of the fitting and fabrication was in the hands of the blacksmiths, who made each component to fit an individual job. To a degree these fitting methods continued throughout the history of steam locomotive construction and remain the case in modern preservation today. Yet it was never so true than in the early days of locomotive construction, where skilled artisans took the often rather meagre drawings and specifications that they were provided with and produced a working locomotive out of them.

Edward Snell records in his diaries how frustrated he became when, having left Swindon and moved to Australia, he received several letters from former colleagues remarking that they had had to amend his drawings – he had in effect been chief draughtsman and Assistant Works Manager – some of which were quite inaccurate. One has to feel some sympathy for Snell, he was given little time to prepare what drawings he could and only had an outline of what Gooch intended. Naturally he made mistakes – it would be impossible not to do so in an environment where the art of the possible far outweighed the blue sky thinking of the designer. In many respects it is remarkable that so much was achieved which proved robust and reliable in service. The 'Prince' Class were without doubt a sound investment and filled a small but significant niche in the GWR's locomotive fleet for the next twenty or more years. That this was achieved with the rudimentary tools available and with a workforce that was still learning the skills involved in locomotive construction and erection, reflects very well not only on Gooch and his senior team but also upon the many skilled and many more semi or unskilled workmen, gathered from around the British Isles, who constituted the workforce at Swindon in the mid 1840s.

Working Lives
1. Accidents

Whilst there were, no doubt, many minor mishaps which involved these engines over the years, there seem to be only two which merited significant attention. The first of these involved the engine *Elk* and occurred at Faringdon Road

station (renamed Challow in 1864) in September 1846, when the engine was a little more than a month old. The *Windsor & Eton Express* of 26th September 1846 reported: '*Luggage van on the 16.45 from Paddington spring bracket broke entering Faringdon Road Station. Engine* Elk, *driven by Robert Patterson GWR driver for 5 years 9 months but 10 years of driving experience, broke away and front of leading passenger carriage was stove in against iron luggage van killing two passengers*'.

This is one of those unfortunate accidents which is not the fault of anyone in particular but through a mechanical failure, in this case a broken spring hanger, which caused a derailment, collision and the tragic death of two innocent persons.

The second, and much better known accident occurred on 25th January 1847 on Wharncliffe Viaduct, between Slough and Hanwell. The story is well known since it is described in L.T.C. Rolt's *Red for Danger*, first published in 1955 and extended and reprinted many times since. Rolt tells a good story so I have taken the liberty of reproducing the paragraph that he devotes to the accident in full:

'*The champions of Brunel's 7ft 0in. gauge always argued that a wider gauge meant greater stability and safety and this contention was certainly borne out by an accident which occurred on the Great Western Main Line at Southall in 1847, soon after the Broad Gauge expresses to Exeter had begun to fly. It was a most extraordinary affair. The locomotive* Queen, *of the 'Prince' Class, then newly delivered from Swindon was approaching Southall at speed with the Up Exeter express when the tyre of one of the 7ft 0in. single driving wheels broke into fragments which flew through the air to bombard a Down goods which was passing at that moment. One broken section killed two drovers who were accompanying cattle while another derailed the goods. The stage seemed to be set for a major disaster, for the express was running on the Wharncliffe Viaduct over the Brent. Yet not only was the goods derailed away from the express but* Queen *held the rails. She ran over the viaduct and was pulled up in Hanwell Station. Here the driver took stock of the damage and then drove his train on into Paddington minus the tyre.*'

Though a good read and accurate as far as it goes, Rolt's narrative lacks detail, which interestingly is filled in by the edition of the *Globe* newspaper published on 26th January 1847. Albeit with some inaccuracies, it reported:

'*Two passengers killed 25th January at Southall by detached tyre from driving wheel of* Queen *on 12pm train from Exeter which continued to Paddington. Engine, built in February 1846 at Swindon and driven by James Almond had been a driver for 25 years, 9 of which on GWR. Train left Swindon at 14.06 with 6 carriages passed Southall at 16.23. driving wheel fitted with Gooch patent tyre supplied by Haigh Foundry of Wigan. 80% tyre is wrought iron and 20% steel – failure occurred at a weld in the iron. Reference to very cold temperature overnight.*'

There is of course some significant misreporting in this piece. The engine was not built in February 1846 but was brand new, possibly on its maiden run in traffic. In fact, it is shown officially as new in February 1847 but bear in mind that the rather vague date concludes a four-week period which usually finished on or about the 19th day of each month. Thus, the engine was as nearly new as it could possibly be always assuming that the *Globe* got all the other details right. It is interesting that Rolt does not actually mention the date of the accident and that McDermot makes no mention of the incident at all.

The tyre was of the Gooch patent design, which he had developed with the collaboration of Edward Evans of the Haigh Foundry in 1840. This produced a tyre which was so hard that it could not be turned in the usual way on a wheel lathe but had to be ground on a special machine developed for the purpose. The method of construction involved a length of wrought iron and a thin steel bar placed together and then passed through a rolling mill to fuse them together. The smiths then hammered the composite bar roughly round a mandrel and made it into a rough tyre which must have involved a 'hammered weld'. This was then finished by grinding the tyre to profile. Presumably it was this weld which failed causing the accident. The process concluded with the tyre being shrunk onto the wheel and then whilst still hot, the tyred wheel was placed in a bath of water to harden the rim.

Unfortunately, the reporting of some of the train times are also inaccurate. The train certainly left Exeter at 12 noon and was indeed the fastest Up train of the day. Following stops at Taunton, Bristol (for a change of engine?) and Bath, the 12.00pm was scheduled to arrive at Swindon at 2.43pm and depart after its 10 minute 'comfort break' at 2.53pm. It was due to arrive at Paddington, following a further stop at Didcot, at 4.30pm. The actual time of the accident as reported by the *Globe*, namely 4.23pm, may then be substantially correct, suggesting that the train was perhaps running a little late but was running fast to make up some time.

Finally, we should mention the driver who demonstrated such presence of mind. James Almond was No. 3 in the GWR's list of drivers, having been employed since March 1838. He was one of three brothers, the others being Thomas and Michael, to drive on the GWR. All were from Tyneside and spoke with a strong 'Geordie' accent, and he and his brothers were all literate. James was 32 years old when he joined the GWR, the oldest of the three. Company records indicate that by 1861 he had been promoted to the post of Locomotive Foreman at Oxford and his younger brothers were also similarly favoured, Michael becoming Locomotive Foreman at Westbourne Park shed.

Two further 'mechanical mishaps' involving members of this class are recounted by T. Houghton Wright in an article in the *Railway Magazine* of October 1898, entitled 'In the Days of Gooch'. He records that on December 28th 1857:

'The engine Prince *(J. Bordiss) broke the right-hand inside connecting rod (when running the express from Oxford down Fenny Compton Bank) and knocked a big hole through the out and inside casing of the firebox, the fire door flew open and the fireman, Frederick Sutton was scalded to death, but Bordiss escaped, though severely injured and both were taken to the Warneford Hospital at Leamington.'*

Houghton Wright later continued:

'I must not forget another curious incident that happened to engineman W. Thompson when he was running the Queen *engine. I have not the date, but it was the up morning express from Birmingham to London and occurred near Heyford. The right-hand driving axle broke short of just inside the boss of the wheel and off it flew across the Down main line through the hedge and into a pool of water.'*

Fortunately no one was hurt in this latter incident, although there was a somewhat amusing addendum as regards the driver:

'Thompson (who had not so much nerve as one would think from his appearance) jumped to the back of the tender and his fireman, Charles Morkott, held on the brake and stopped the train. Then Thompson got down and made a fuss before the passengers, who passed "round the hat" for his bravery in stopping the train!'

Sadly, the author also notes that fireman Morkott was later accidentally poisoned at Slough after mistaking carbolic acid for beer. On a happier note, he also reports that driver J. Bordiss (*Prince*) recovered from his scalding and returned to work for many years thereafter.

Incidents of this sort were fairly commonplace in the early days of railway operation and though now much less frequent, due to the introduction over the decades of better materials and manufacturing methods, remain a potential hazard to this day.

Houghton Wright, who had started with the Company as a pupil at Swindon Works in August 1851 and at the time of writing in 1898 was District Locomotive Superintendent GWR in South Wales, based at Neath, noted one further incident involving a member of the class:

'Tuesday June 27th [1854], *the engine* Witch *(engineman Cuthbert Davison) ran away from Didcot, up the down line, without its tender. This may appear strange but is true. The turn-table at Didcot was too small to take both engine and tender, so they had to uncouple, and while the tender was being turned the regulator flew open, and the sudden start jerked Davison to the ground and away she went. Engineman M. Almond (engine* Great Britain) *was standing in the yard, and seeing what had happened started in chase up the proper line, and overtook her before passing Goring, where he got the switchman to pull over the cross-over and so let the* Witch *follow on the up line, for which feat Almond was awarded £10 by the directors. I was on my way with a train from London to Swindon, and on arrival at Reading was told was told an engine had runaway from Didcot up the down line, and to keep a good look-out.'*

Engineman M. Almond, whose quick actions earned him a handsome reward, is one of the aforementioned 'Geordie' Almond brothers.

Train Services in 1847

Before moving on to consider the later history of the working lives of the 'Prince' Class, it is worth pausing briefly to reflect on the train services on which these engines were employed, before they

MR. T. HOUGHTON WRIGHT
District Loco. Supt., Great Western Railway

were displaced from the best trains by the 'Iron Duke' 4-2-2s, six of which had entered service by the end of 1847.

The so-called 'Battle of the Gauges' induced the GWR management to demonstrate that the claims made on behalf of the broad gauge relating to speed and reliability were not just empty rhetoric. Thus, from 10th May 1845, the 9.30am Exeter express was timed to cover 193¾ miles from Paddington to Exeter in exactly five hours inclusive of stops at Didcot, Swindon, Bath, Bristol and Taunton. Exeter was scheduled to be reached at 2.30pm. This timing, already the fastest start to stop example in the world over such a long distance, lasted just two days before it was cut from 12th May by 30 minutes. The Down train now left Paddington at 9.45am and reached Exeter after observing the same stopping pattern at 2.15pm. The corresponding Up train left Exeter at 12 noon and arrived at Paddington at 4.30pm. However, these timings, which involved a one minute stop at Swindon, were found to contravene the agreement with the franchise of the restaurant rooms there so, from 26th January 1846, the ten minute stop at Swindon was enforced and the nine minutes running time that were lost were absorbed into the overall journey time. Since from the late summer of 1846 the 'Prince' Class became involved in working these trains, initially alongside members of the 'Fire Fly' Class and *Great Western*, it is worth laying out the schedule in full:

Paddington:. .... .dept.	9.45am
Didcot:. .... .arrive	10.50am
.... .dept.	10.52am
Swindon:.... .... .arrive	11.23am
.... .dept.	11.33am
Bath:.... .... .arrive	12.09pm
.... .dept.	12.11pm
Bristol T.M .. .. .arrive	12.28pm
(Express Platform) ... . .dept.	12.33pm
Taunton: .... .arrive	1.27pm
.... .dept.	1.29pm
Exeter:. .... .arrive	2.15pm

The corresponding Up train left:

Exeter:. .... .dept.	12.00 noon
Taunton: .... .arrive	12.41pm
.... .dept.	12.43pm
Bristol: .... .arrive	1.36pm
(Express Platform) ... . .dept.	1.41pm
Bath:.... .... .arrive	1.56pm
.... .dept.	1.58pm
Swindon;.... .... .arrive	2.43pm
.... .dept.	2.53pm
Didcot:. .... .arrive	3.22pm
.... .dept.	3.24pm
Paddington:. .... .arrive	4.30pm

It must be admitted that, by modern standards, trains were very light, probably never exceeding 100 tons and more usually in the 50-70 tons category. Yet it must also be remembered that as recently as 1840, a 'post haste' journey from Exeter to London would have occupied a whole day and more if road conditions were poor, as they often were. Such was the impact of the railways on early Victorian Britain. It should also be pointed out that these trains conveyed only First and Second Class passengers. Third Class passengers could make the same journey but over a much-extended time period and in no great comfort.

In April 1846, another pair of 4½ hour Exeter expresses were put on, leaving Exeter at 6.30am and Paddington at 5.30pm; these stopped at Reading rather than Didcot and also at Chippenham and Bridgewater. To accommodate these extra stops, the five minute wait at Bristol was reduced to two minutes and other running speeds were adjusted accordingly. These fast timings also affected journeys to other intermediate destinations. With a change at Didcot, Oxford could be reached in 1¼ hours from London and by changing at Swindon, Cheltenham was accessible in just 2 hours 47 minutes, which included stops at Tetbury Road and the old Gloucester 'T' station.

As we have noted, the participation of the 'Prince' Class in

The interior of the engine house at Paddington in 1846, with a tender being manhandled onto the centre turntable. As we saw in the earlier parts of this series, locomotive sheds were generally quite small and the yards cramped in the early years, so tenders and engines were routinely separated. On the right is 'Fire Fly' 2-2-2 *Ganymede*, new in July 1842. By the end of 1846, 'Prince' Class engines would be to the fore here, whilst the shed was replaced by that at Westbourne Park in 1855. Eagle-eyed readers who are conversant with this illustration will note that we have erased the name *Etna* from the engine on the far right, as it clearly depicts another 'Fire Fly' and not a member of the Leo Class as *Etna* was. Note too the shed in use for the repair of a wagon in the left background. This is without doubt the best representation that we have of the interior of an engine shed in early broad gauge days.

these workings was short lived. As soon as sufficient 8ft 0ins 'Singles' were available, they were downgraded to lesser jobs and indeed were removed from Paddington, where they had all been allocated initially, altogether. Fortunately, the ever giving *An Historical Survey of Great Western Engine Sheds* notes some early allocations for the period ending 27th July 1850. These show that the six members of the class were divided between Bristol and Swindon, being noted as 'engines in steam' for the two weeks ending 27th July 1850. *Elk, Prince* and *Queen* were at Bristol, with *Peri* and *Sylph* at Swindon. Only *Witch* is unaccounted for but she may have been stopped on shed or been in or awaiting works attention. At this time both these sheds participated in workings on the main line, while the Swindon allocation would also have worked to Gloucester and Cheltenham. Interestingly, both sheds also possessed a small allocation of 'Fire Flys' at the time, with which workings were no doubt shared.

I think it is safe to assume that the situation outlined above persisted until the broad gauge reached Birmingham in October 1852. Thereafter, the 'Prince' Class were largely associated with Bordesley Junction shed and workings between Birmingham and London but particularly north of Oxford. Initially, the shed at Bordesley was a temporary affair that opened on 1st October 1852. Sadly, very little is known about this building

though it is believed to have occupied part of the site which the permanent shed, opened in 1855, was built upon. As far as the extant records show, the whole class, with one minor exception, remained at Bordesley Junction shed until broad gauge workings in the West Midlands ceased in 1869. By this time, these were already also receding across the GWR, so the engines were surplus to requirements and it is highly likely that several members of the class had been laid aside for some time before they were formally withdrawn in 1870. The sole exception is *Queen* which, from 1854 until 1856, spent an extended period allocated to Oxford shed.

From various sources I have been able to put together allocations of engines 'in steam' that covers the ten-year period from October 1852 until July 1862. Unless otherwise mentioned

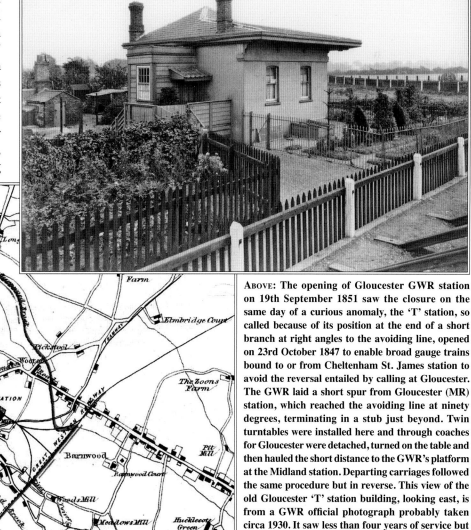

ABOVE: The opening of Gloucester GWR station on 19th September 1851 saw the closure on the same day of a curious anomaly, the 'T' station, so called because of its position at the end of a short branch at right angles to the avoiding line, opened on 23rd October 1847 to enable broad gauge trains bound to or from Cheltenham St. James station to avoid the reversal entailed by calling at Gloucester. The GWR laid a short spur from Gloucester (MR) station, which reached the avoiding line at ninety degrees, terminating in a stub just beyond. Twin turntables were installed here and through coaches for Gloucester were detached, turned on the table and then hauled the short distance to the GWR's platform at the Midland station. Departing carriages followed the same procedure but in reverse. This view of the old Gloucester 'T' station building, looking east, is from a GWR official photograph probably taken circa 1930. It saw less than four years of service but was only finally demolished in 1971, when the sidings just glimpsed on the left were extended.

LEFT: A circa 1850 map of Gloucester showing the position of the T station (between 'Great' and 'Western') and the line running to/from it.

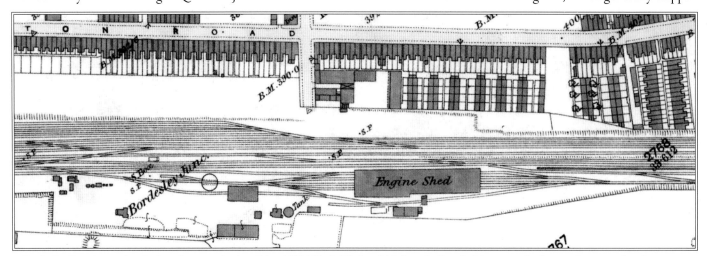

This drawing of Sylph is uncredited but was probably by G.F. Bird and was part of the broad gauge engines history published in *The Locomotive Magazine* in 1901.

all entries refer to Bordesley Junction:

Oct. 1852: *Elk, Peri, Queen, Sylph, Witch*

July 1854: *Elk, Peri, Prince, Sylph, Witch*
: *Queen* (Oxford)

Nov. 1854: *Sylph*

July 1855: *Elk, Prince, Witch*

Dec. 1855: *Elk, Peri, Prince, Witch*

July 1856: *Elk, Sylph*
: *Queen* (Oxford)

Dec. 1856: *Peri, Prince, Sylph, Witch*

July 1857: *Elk, Peri, Prince, Sylph, Witch*

July 1858: *Elk, Peri, Prince, Queen, Sylph*

July 1859: *Elk, Peri, Prince, Queen, Sylph, Witch*

Dec. 1859: *Elk, Peri, Prince, Queen, Witch*

July 1860: *Elk, Peri, Witch*

Aug. 1860: *Elk, Peri, Prince, Queen, Witch*

July 1861: *Elk, Peri, Prince, Queen, Sylph, Witch*

July 1862: *Peri, Prince, Queen, Sylph, Witch*

I found myself wondering if *Queen*'s sojourn at Oxford had anything to do with her potential use on Royal Train duties. By this time, *Lord of the Isles* was the regular royal engine and may have worked the train from Windsor through to Oxford, to be relieved by *Queen* for the journey northwards. The Royal Party was handed onto the L&NWR at Leamington, then used as a royal changeover place which involved, of course, a change of gauge. Whatever the reason for her time at Oxford, *Queen* certainly bore an appropriate name for such workings. One other observation on this engine; the section of *The Locomotive Magazine* series on 'The Broad Gauge Locomotives of the Great Western Railway' that deals with the class refers to the engine as '*The Queen*' and G.F. Bird's accompanying drawing also shows it so named. However, although occasionally referred to in contemporary reports as '*the* Queen *engine*', there is no other evidence to support this alterative version of its name.

The members of the class based at Bordesley took a major share in working the Birmingham to London expresses, hauling them between Birmingham Snow Hill station and either Oxford or Didcot. Though the broad gauge extended to Wolverhampton, trains between there and Birmingham, which generally stopped

Bordesley Junction engine shed as shown on the 1st edition 1888 25 inch OS, by which date the lines had been standard gauge for over a decade.

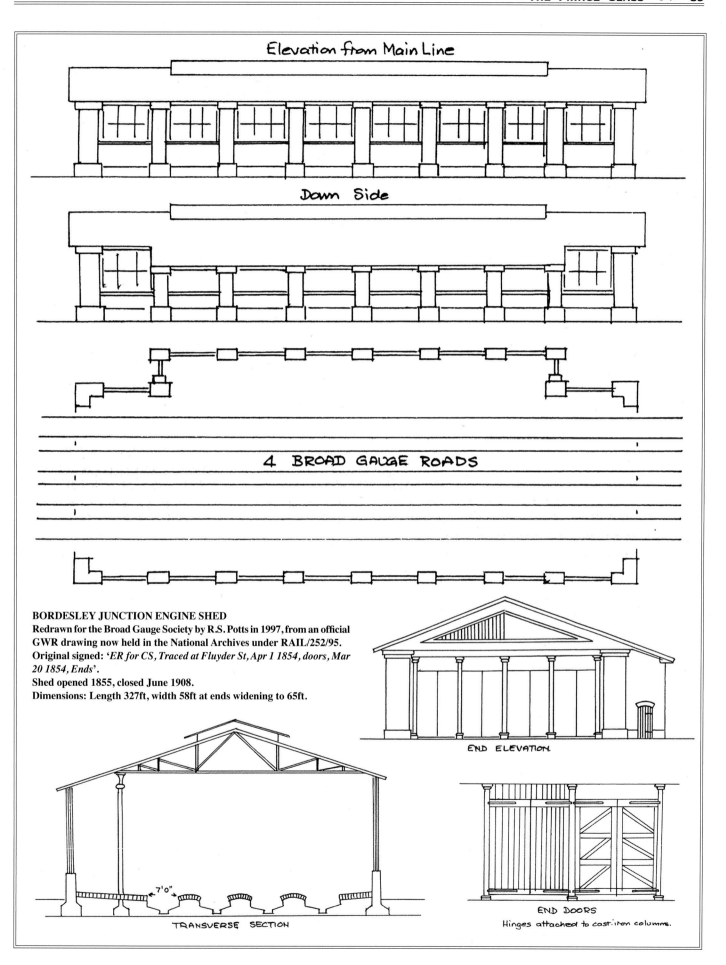

Elevation from Main Line

Down Side

4 BROAD GAUGE ROADS

BORDESLEY JUNCTION ENGINE SHED
Redrawn for the Broad Gauge Society by R.S. Potts in 1997, from an official
GWR drawing now held in the National Archives under RAIL/252/95.
Original signed: *'ER for CS, Traced at Fluyder St, Apr 1 1854, doors, Mar
20 1854, Ends'*.
Shed opened 1855, closed June 1908.
Dimensions: Length 327ft, width 58ft at ends widening to 65ft.

END ELEVATION.

7'0"

TRANSVERSE SECTION

END DOORS
Hinges attached to cast iron columns.

at intermediate stations, were worked by tank engines, usually of the 'Leo' Class. The trains only became fast south of Birmingham, the best of which only called at Leamington on their way to Oxford and vice versa. Having said this, there was normally at least one of the 8ft 0in. 'Singles' also based at Bordesley Junction in the mid 1850s and early '60s, whilst Oxford had quite a stud of the 4-2-2s, so the 'Prince' Class did not quite monopolise such workings. Nonetheless, as the entries show, they were reliable workhorses and fulfilled a useful role on what remained, even by the standard of the time, relatively fast but light trains. One must also be aware that the years 1852-62 mark the high-water mark of broad gauge workings to the West Midlands. In October 1861, the first regular standard gauge passenger train left Paddington for Birmingham and the North. Thereafter, the writing was on the wall for the broad gauge in the so called 'Black Country'. (See also Appendix 3)

Works Report

During the lifetime of the class, most major repairs were carried out at Swindon but in later years, some of the burden was shared with Wolverhampton Stafford Road Works. We know that a number of broad gauge engines received attention there from 1854, the last recorded taking place as late as 1869. Sadly, few details have survived, most of Stafford Road's old records went up in flames when the Works closed in February 1964.

Unfortunately, we only have records of Swindon Works repairs between 1866 and 1869. These include just three entries for members of the 'Prince' Class, the last of which is in 1867. They are: October 1866 – *Witch*; December 1866 – *Queen*; November 1867 – *Witch*. From this information we can safely assume that heavy repairs to members of the class ceased at the end of 1867 and that from then engines were laid aside as major attention became necessary.

Final Disposal and Mileages

As I mentioned at the beginning of this chapter, there are some inconsistencies between the entries shown in **Table 5.3**, above right, and previously published data, *Queen* being a good example. The official records show that she was put to stationary boiler work at Saltney Carriage & Waggon Works in January 1870. Those same records also indicate that *Queen* was formally condemned in July 1870 but no date for the engine's

TABLE 5.3: THE 'PRINCE' CLASS – FINAL MILEAGES & DISPOSAL		
NAME	**MILEAGE**	**DISPOSAL**
Prince	580,562	c/u June 1870
Elk	570,940	c/u September 1870
Peri	612,198	c/u March 1871
Witch	602,729	c/u May 1871
Queen	583,329	stat. boiler Saltney Works, Chester 5th Jan. 1870
Sylph	584,318	condemned July 1870
These figures and dates are taken from records kept at Kew under the Rail 254/148 heading.		

cutting up is given, presumably because she ceased to be reckoned as 'running stock' from July 1870. This was when a general audit of all broad gauge engines was taken and many previously laid aside or indeed already broken up were written off.

Witch is another strange example. Though it is recorded as having ceased work in May 1870, it was not cut up until May 1871 but is shown in the same records as condemned in June that year (the RCTS History says July which is in error). One can only speculate that the engine was laid aside at Swindon in 1870 and because of the pressure of work – at this time literally dozens of broad gauge engines were being broken up – was not dealt with until May 1871. Therefore, it was not formally condemned, i.e. written off, until the then current four-week period, used for accounting purposes, came to an end around 19th June. If that was the case, one wonders why it was not formally condemned in July 1870 with so many others? A possible answer is that the engine was in reasonable condition and was perhaps capable of further work or conversion to a stationary boiler. This is only guesswork of course – as with so much about the broad gauge we will never know conclusively.

Final Reflections

Though the 'Prince' Class lacked the glamour and impact of the 8ft 0in. 4-2-2s that succeeded them, they nonetheless proved to be reliable traffic units achieving high mileages for the time, especially when one considers that most of their working lives were spent running between Birmingham, Oxford and Didcot. This small class which, during the early 1860s was incorporated, with the 'Fire Flys', into the 'Priam' Class, has been largely overlooked. Yet they were a significant step forward in Gooch's thinking at the time and they filled an important niche in the story of the GWR's broad gauge locomotive development that was in the mid 1840s, lest we forget, at the very cutting edge of modern technology.

CHAPTER 5
THE 'IRON DUKE' CLASS

The introduction of the 'Iron Duke' Class in April 1847 marked a major leap forward in 19th century locomotive engineering practice. Trials with the rebuilt *Great Western* had demonstrated the potential that the generous broad gauge dimensions afforded the designer, to increase the boiler power available to feed the cylinders – Gooch having been one of the first mechanical engineers to grasp the relationship between the steam raising capacity of the boiler and firebox, and the size of the cylinders. So many early designs, as Gooch had good reason to know full well, were profoundly 'underboilered'. Additionally, the width afforded by the broad gauge negated concerns, current elsewhere, about the centre of gravity. Gooch was determined to exploit the opportunities presented to him and this he achieved, for though the initial design was a little less than perfect, it was certainly magnificent.

The newly outshopped locomotive made its initial trial run on Sunday 25th April 1847 and its inaugural journey in traffic on 1st May, which also happened to be the Duke of Wellington's 78th birthday. Thus the engine, not inappropriately, was christened *Iron Duke*, a name that became synonymous with the whole class. This eventually numbered twenty-nine engines, built in four separate lots, the last of which, amounting to seven engines, were built by Rothwell & Co. and were delivered between November 1854 and July 1855. The rest were built at Swindon and the last of these, *Lord of the Isles*, was a prime exhibit at the Great Exhibition held at the Crystal Palace in 1851, where it attracted much attention and admiration.

The fact that the whole class of these 4-2-2s has been known as the 'Iron Dukes' by enthusiasts and historians alike for many years presents the serious historian with something of a problem. The first six engines, built between April and November 1847, differed from their later sisters, internally at least, which in turn were slightly different from the later Rothwell-built engines. As originally constructed therefore, the class represented three separate groups, though externally they all came to look much the same. In later years, the Great Western added to the confusion by lumping all the 8ft 0in. 4-2-2' together under the general heading 'Alma' Class. This included *Great Western*, all the 'Iron Dukes' and the later renewals and subsequent new builds, from 1871, which are generally referred to as the 'Rover' Class.

Since I am only dealing here with engines designed before the end of 1852 – although including locomotives built to those designs in subsequent years – I have decided to follow early GWR practise, which broke the 'Iron Duke' Class down into three groups as follows:
1. That which the GWR referred to as the '2nd Passenger Lot',

namely the six engines beginning with *Iron Duke* built between April and November 1847.
2. The '3rd and 4th Passenger Lots', which were built in two batches and differed in some significant respects from the earlier engines. The first member of this group was *Courier*, delivered in June 1848, which headed a sub-class of twelve engines delivered between June 1848 and June 1850. These were supplemented by a further four more or less identical engines of the '4th Passenger Lot', beginning with *Estaffete* in September 1850 and concluding with *Lord of the Isles* in March 1851.
3. The seven Rothwell & Co. engines. Though very similar to the two previous batches, there were one or two small but significant differences which warrant separate attention. This group began with the delivery of *Alma* in November 1854 and concluded with that of *Sebastopol* in July 1855. All were named after places and battles relating to the then ongoing Crimea War.

The 'Iron Dukes'

NAME	BUILT	CEASED WORK
Iron Duke	April 1847	Oct. 1871
Great Britain	July 1847	Sept. 1880
Lightning	Aug. 1847	April 1878
Emperor	Sept. 1847	June 1873
Pasha	Nov. 1847	Feb. 1876
Sultan	Nov. 1847	June 1874

TABLE 6.1: THE 'IRON DUKES' – SIX ENGINES BUILT AT SWINDON IN 1847, '2ND PASSENGER LOT'

Initially, *Iron Duke* was tested on Sapperton Bank during a series of haulage tests in the company of the 'Premier' Class 0-6-0 *Dreadnought*. This, in fact, accounts for the three month gap between the entries of *Iron Duke* and *Great Britain* into traffic, Gooch obviously being keen to prove the many new features included in the design before duplicating them in new production. These 'new' features will be dealt with in detail under the heading 'Constructional Details' but may be summarised thus:
• Domeless boilers, firebox with mid-feather and raised casing. Gooch design of safety-valve cover and the cylinders enclosed in the smokebox casing. Outside sandwich-frames, the driving wheels – which were flangeless – strengthened by inside frames and a centre stay. These supported the crank axle with no less than five bearings. Particularly noticeable was the changeover from the previously ubiquitous Haycock or Gothic firebox to a round topped design which, though greatly enlarged, looked back to Stephenson's *North Star* and *Morning Star* of 1837. These very generously designed fireboxes, with their enormous steam raising capacity, were, without doubt, the best feature of the new engines.

— NEW PASSENGER ENGINE —
— SCALE 1½ IN.·TO 1 FOOT —

IRON DUKE

This large scale drawing – the original was executed at 1½ins to 1ft – shows *Iron Duke* in its original form and is labelled 'New Passenger Engine'. Though my copy of the drawing is undated it must presumably emanate from 1847. Original features which are of note include the initial design of the smokebox with its piano style front, the trailing springing and the lack of any sanding gear. These components would either be modified or, in the case of sanding, added in the coming years. The drawing also conveys a real sense of size. For their days and in the years to come the 'Iron Duke' Class were among the largest express passenger engines in the country. Though the internal layout of the boiler tubes would be amended in succeeding years, these engines, by any measure, were remarkable 'steam raisers', a legacy which would have profound consequences for future locomotive design and performance.

TABLE 6.2: THE 'IRON DUKE' CLASS – MAIN DIMENSIONS	
Wheelbase	4ft 11ins + 6ft 3ins + 7ft 4ins
Wheels – Driving	8ft 0in. flangeless
Leading	4ft 6ins flanged
Carrying	4ft 6ins flanged
Weight	35 tons 10cwt – distributed as 7 tons 2cwt, 7 tons 2cwt, 12 tons 6cwt, 9 tons
Boiler Dimensions	
Barrel	11ft 0in. x 4ft 9¾ins: 303 x 2ins Tubes
Firebox Casing	5ft 0in. x 6ft 0in.
Tube Heating Surface	1,797.12 sq. ft
Firebox	147.87 sq. ft
Total	1,944.99 sq. ft
Grate Area	21.66 sq. ft
Boiler Pressure	100 psi, later increased to 115
The diameter of the boiler barrel shown is the largest of the three rings. The heating surface figures are calculated on the water side. The more usually quoted figures are those of the fire side, which in this instance would give the following dimensions:	
Tube Heating Surface	1,647.39 sq. ft
Firebox	142.80 sq. ft
Total:	1,790.19 sq. ft

Tenders are a source of some uncertainty. A drawing of *Iron Duke* which purports to show the engine in 'as built' condition shows the engine attached to a new design of 6-wheeled iron-framed tender, with a fabricated tank holding approximately 1,760 gallons of water. Springs were mounted beneath the footplate on top of the axle boxes and were suspended from short 'J' hangers and buckles. Wheels were 4ft 0in. diameter, while the wheelbase is variously quoted as 6ft 0in. x 6ft 0in. or 6ft 1ins x 6ft 1ins. Brakes were provided on the fireman's side only. However, with the sole exception of *Lord of the Isles*, all the available photographic evidence shows the 8ft 0in. 'Singles' attached to the sandwich-framed tenders which we have already encountered running with *Great Western* and members of the 'Prince' Class. Furthermore, the 1857 specification refers to a tender of the iron-framed type as *Lord of the Isles* tender, implying that it was the exception rather than the rule. The only certain indication that we have that these fabricated iron-framed tenders ran with the 8ft 0in. 'Singles' is, as mentioned, a drawing dated 1849, which shows *Iron Duke* attached to one. Assuming that the drawing is accurate, it is not a step too far to imply that the initial batch of six 'Iron Dukes' were attached to tenders of this type but by the mid 1850s, when photographic evidence becomes available, they had been exchanged for the sandwich-framed type.

The 'Couriers'

Though generally these sixteen engines were very similar to the six that had preceded them there were some significant differences, especially to the internal layout of the boiler tubes, the length of the boilers and the fireboxes. These were made following experience gained with the first batch of 'Iron Dukes' and were intended to enhance the steaming rate of the boiler/firebox combination. To accommodate the larger firebox and shorter boiler, the wheelbase was slightly altered. All of the authorities agree that these were the first engines outshopped with the wooden boiler lagging encased in sheet iron.

TABLE 6.3: THE 'COURIERS' – 16 ENGINES BUILT IN TWO BATCHES BETWEEN JUNE 1848 AND MARCH 1851: '3RD PASSENGER LOT'		
NAME	BUILT	CEASED WORK
Courier	June 1848	Nov. 1877
Tartar	July 1848	Aug.t 1876
Dragon	Aug. 1848	Dec. 1872
Warlock	Aug. 1848	June 1874
Wizard	Sept. 1848	Nov. 1875
Rougemont	Oct. 1848	Aug. 1879
Hirondelle	Dec. 1848	May 1873
Tornado	March 1849	March 1881
Swallow	June 1849	Sept. 1871
Timour	Aug. 1849	Nov. 1871
Prometheus	March 1850	Oct. 1887
Perseus	June 1850	Dec. 1880
'4th Passenger Lot'		
Estaffete	Sept. 1850	Dec. 1884
Rover	Sept. 1850	Aug. 1871
Amazon	March 1851	July 1877
Lord of the Isles	March 1851	June 1884

TABLE 6.4: THE 'COURIERS' – Main Dimensions	
Wheelbase	4ft 9¼ins x 6ft 4¼ins x 7ft 7ins
Wheels – Driving	8ft 0in. flangeless
Leading	4ft 6ins flanged
Carrying	4ft 6ins flanged
Weight	38 tons 4cwt, distributed as 15 tons, 14 tons, 9 tons 4cwt. There were of course minor differences between individual members of the class
Boiler Dimensions	
Barrel	10ft 9ins x 4ft 9⅜ins, 303 x 2ins tubes
Firebox	4ft 10ins x 5ft 4ins
Firebox Casing	5ft 6ins x 6ft 0in.
Tube Heating Surface	1,757.48 sq. ft
Firebox	161.99 sq. ft
Total	1,919.47 sq. ft
Grate Area	25.47 sq. ft
Boiler Pressure	120 psi
Boiler Pitch	7ft 2¼ins
The heating surface calculations are for the water side; the figures for the fire side are:	
Tube Heating Surface	1,611.45 sq. ft
Firebox	156.56 sq. ft
Total:	1,768.01 sq. ft
Cylinders	18ins diameter x 24ins stroke
Blast Pipe	Orifice 5½ins diameter

It should be mentioned that boiler construction practice at this time resulted in a telescopic arrangement in which each ring was slightly reduced in diameter and was riveted into its larger counterpart. The figures given here are for the largest of the three rings. Ahrons quotes the inside diameter of the smallest ring as 4ft 7⅞ins.

Interestingly, when the boiler of *Perseus* exploded in Westbourne Park shed on 8th November 1862, when the engine was twelve years old, the total heating surface was quoted as 1,768 sq. ft and the boiler pressure was said to be 115lbs per sq inch, thus, corresponding with the normative 'fire side' figures given above. One wonders, however, about the accuracy of the boiler pressure figures? We will return to this sad story in due course.

Ahrons says that the blast pipe measurement was the outside diameter, the actual internal measurement was 5ins, whilst the RCTS history gives a mean diameter of $5^1/_4$ins. The top of the blast pipe was positioned just 2ins below the crown of the smokebox.

The larger firebox and the slightly reduced length of the boiler, coupled to the increased boiler pressure, certainly produced a potentially more powerful engine. As in any steam locomotive, the greatest amount of steam is produced nearest to the fire, so the increased dimensions of the firebox, which even in the earlier design was already substantial, was a major factor in their evident prowess.

As with the 'Iron Dukes', Gooch retained a central midfeather in the lower part of the firebox. Ahrons considers that these were of doubtful value and greatly contributed to the difficulty of firing these engines on account of their height, coming up as they did, to almost the height of the lowest level of the firebox door.

The Rothwell Engines

TABLE 6.5: THE 'ALMAS' – SEVEN ENGINES BUILT BY ROTHWELL & CO. OF THE UNION FOUNDRY, BOLTON		
NAME	BUILT	CEASED WORK
Alma	**Nov. 1854**	**June 1872**
Balaklava	**Dec. 1854**	**Oct. 1871**
Inkermann	**March 1855**	**Oct. 1877**
Kertch	**April 1855**	**Dec. 1872**
Crimea	**May 1855**	**Nov. 1876**
Eupatoria	**May 1855**	**Oct. 1876**
Sebastopol	**July 1855**	**Oct. 1880**

Though this final batch of engines was in the main the same as the previous 'Courier' sub-class, there were two small but significant differences. The first is easily explained – the driving and trailing wheel springs were linked by 'compensation levers'. Gooch was experimenting with compensation beams and levers during the early 1850s, applying rather cumbersome beams to his standard goods engines. They were found to be of little or no value and were later removed.

The other difference is harder to quantify. Though externally the boiler and firebox dimensions were the same as those of the 'Couriers', the recorded heating surface differs as per **Table 6.6**, below.

TABLE 6.6: THE 'ALMAS' – HEATING SURFACE MEASUREMENTS	
Tube Heating Surface	**1,711.9 sq. ft**
Firebox	**171.2 sq. ft**
Total:	**1,883.1 sq. ft**

These figures are given for the water side one assumes. The tube heating surface is a little less and the firebox a little more than the figures given for the 'Couriers'. The difference for the two is 36.37 sq. ft, which in real terms is a minimal amount and is probably accounted for by differences in manufacturing techniques. I suspect that no two boiler/firebox combinations were quite the same.

Constructional Detail –Frames

One of the major challenges facing early locomotive designers was the fragility of the then forged crank axles. Some designs, as in Robert Stephenson's 'long boiler type', sought to do away with the crank axles altogether, by placing the cylinders outside the frames. These, however, proved to be potentially unsteady at speed, as Gooch, from his experiences during the gauge trials, had good reason to know. He therefore sought to alleviate the problem by supporting the crank axle with no less than three sets of frames. He retained the flexible outside sandwich-frames but the driving wheels were also supported by inside plate-frames and a centre stay, thus giving the crank axles the support of five axleboxes in all. The plate-frames ran from the back of the cylinders to the front of the firebox casing. The centre stay was of the same length and was attached to the underside of the boiler shell, as well as to the back of the cylinders and the front of the firebox. By contrast, the leading and carrying wheels were only supported by bearings placed in the outside frames. According to G.F. Bird, writing in *The Locomotive Magazine* of October 1901, '*The outside frames measured 23ft 11ins long, exclusive of the 6ins wooden buffer beam, the overhang being 2ft 8ins and 2ft 9ins at front and back respectively and the top of the plates, so far as the horizontal portion was concerned was 3ft 11³/₄ins above the rail level*'.

The sandwich frames followed the usual pattern of construction using $^1/_2$in. wrought iron plates and 3ins ash timbers. No-one seems to have recorded the thickness of the inside plate-frames, though a close study of the available drawings suggest that they were of substantial proportions, perhaps as much as 1in. thick.

Cylinders

The 18ins x 24ins cylinders were placed horizontally, with their centre lines 4ft $2^1/_2$ins apart. They were completely enclosed within the lower half of the smokebox, which formed a 'warm jacket' around them. The lower part of the smokebox was increased in length to accommodate the cylinders, whilst the front was given a shapely curve below the level of the smokebox door, which made a rather elegant feature out of mechanical necessity. *The Engineer* of 16th June 1882, whilst describing the 8ft 0ins singles, gives some interesting additional information: '*The guide bars* [i.e. slide bars] *are two in number for each cylinder arranged one above and the other below the piston rod, which has a block crosshead between them; the guide bars are far enough apart to permit the play of the connecting rod*'.

Valves

These were of a new design and are described as 'partially balanced'. They were not altogether successful, as Ahrons comments in Chapter VII of *The British Steam Locomotive 1825-1925*: '*The slide valves were partially balanced by means of pistons in the common steam chest. The pistons worked inside a small cylinder open at the ends and were coupled by links to the backs of the valves. The principle objections to this method were the rattling noise, the danger of the link pins coming out and getting into the cylinders and the wear of the balanced piston rings which caused leakage and consequent loss of the balancing effect. Subsequently ordinary unbalanced slide valves were substituted*'.

Sadly, Ahrons does not mention a date when this modification took place but, judging from his comments, I would suggest that the original design had a fairly short life, which leads one to

The 8ft 'Singles' included the 'Iron Duke' Class and the 'Courier' (referred to as 'Amazon' in the text below) sub-class, and also *Great Western*. It is interesting that the two groups are treated individually here, though the contrast between them became blurred over the years. Note the equalising beam attached to the driving and trailing springs. This was only fitted to the Rothwell-built engines and soon discarded.

EIGHT FEET PASSENGER ENGINES.

AMAZON. ALMA. BALAKLAVA. COURIER. CRIMEA. DRAGON. ESTAFETTE. EUPATORIA. HIRONDELLE. INKERMANN. KERTCH. LORD of the ISLES. PERSEUS. PROMETHEUS. ROVER. ROUGEMONT. SWALLOW. SEBASTOPOL. TARTAR. TIMOUR. TORNADO. WARLOCK. WIZARD. [IRON-DUKE. SULTAN. EMPEROR. LIGHTNING. PASHA. GREAT-BRITAIN.] GREAT-WESTERN.

DESCRIPTION

CYLINDERS 18 ins in diamr and 24 in stroke. Steam ports 2 ins by 13 ins. Exhaust 3½ ins by 13 ins.
BOILER (Amazon Class) 10 feet 9 ins long and 4 feet 9 ins in diamr inside. Fire-box 5 feet 6 ins by 6 feet wide.
— do — (Iron-Duke.) 11 feet long and 4 feet 9 ins in diamr inside. Fire-box 5 feet long by 6 feet wide.
— do — (Great Western.) 10 feet 6 ins long and 4. 6 in diamr with 276 Tubes 11 feet long and 2 ins in diamr.
AMAZON CLASS. Tubes. 303. 11 feet 1 inch long and 2 inches in diamr outside.
IRON-DUKE. Tubes 303. 11 feet 5 inches long and 2 inches in diamr outside.
WHEELS. Driving 8 feet in diamr. Leading and Trailing 4 feet 6 inches in diameter.
AMAZON. Heating Surface of I Box 156.56 Sqr feet. Tubes 1611.45 Sqr feet.
IRON-DUKE — do — of I Box 142.80 Sqr feet. Tubes 1647.39 Sqr feet.
AMAZON Class. Area of Fire Grate 25.46 Sqr feet. Iron-Duke. Area of Fire Grate 21.66 Sqr feet.

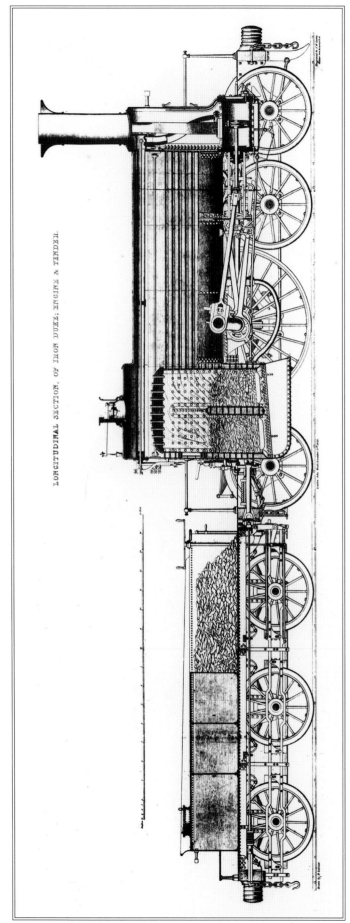

LONGITUDINAL SECTION. OF IRON DUKE. ENGINE & TENDER.

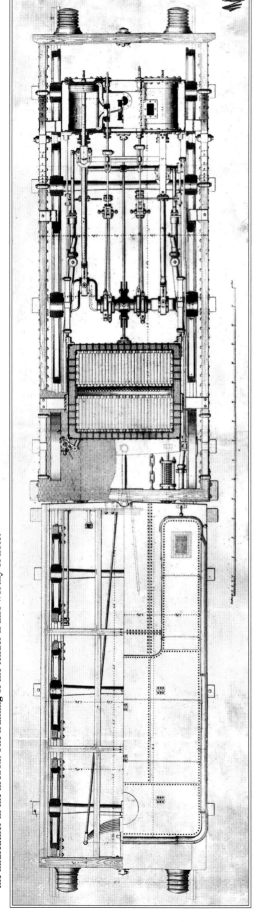

ABOVE: This is the first of a series of sectional drawings made by D. Lavater, engraved by J.W. Lowery and dated 1st February 1849. They were published by John Weale though I am not certain in what publication they first appeared. All the main constructional details outlined in the text are visible here. Of especial note are the arrangements of the regulator, main steam pipe and blast pipe in the smokebox, the direct acting valve gear and the midfeather in the firebox. The design of the iron framed tender and particularly its braking system are also important to note.

BELOW: This vertical section provides an excellent diagrammatic view of the arrangement of the cylinders, the valves and valve gear, along with the crank axle and its attendant support, and again the midfeather in the firebox. The framing of the tender is also worthy of note.

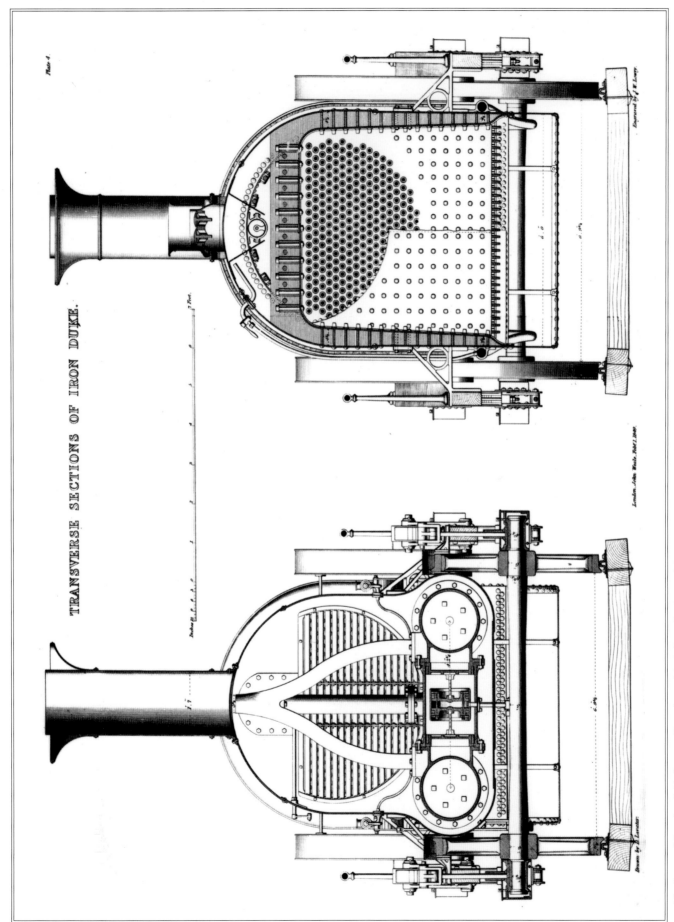

TRANSVERSE SECTIONS OF IRON DUKE.

The front end drawing (left) gives excellent views of the balanced valves and the arrangement of the cylinder, valve and steam pipe design. The inner smokebox shows the arrangement of the system of louvring, which was designed to control the draught through the tubes. The rear view demonstrates the design of the inner firebox and the system of girder and staying support adopted for its suspension.

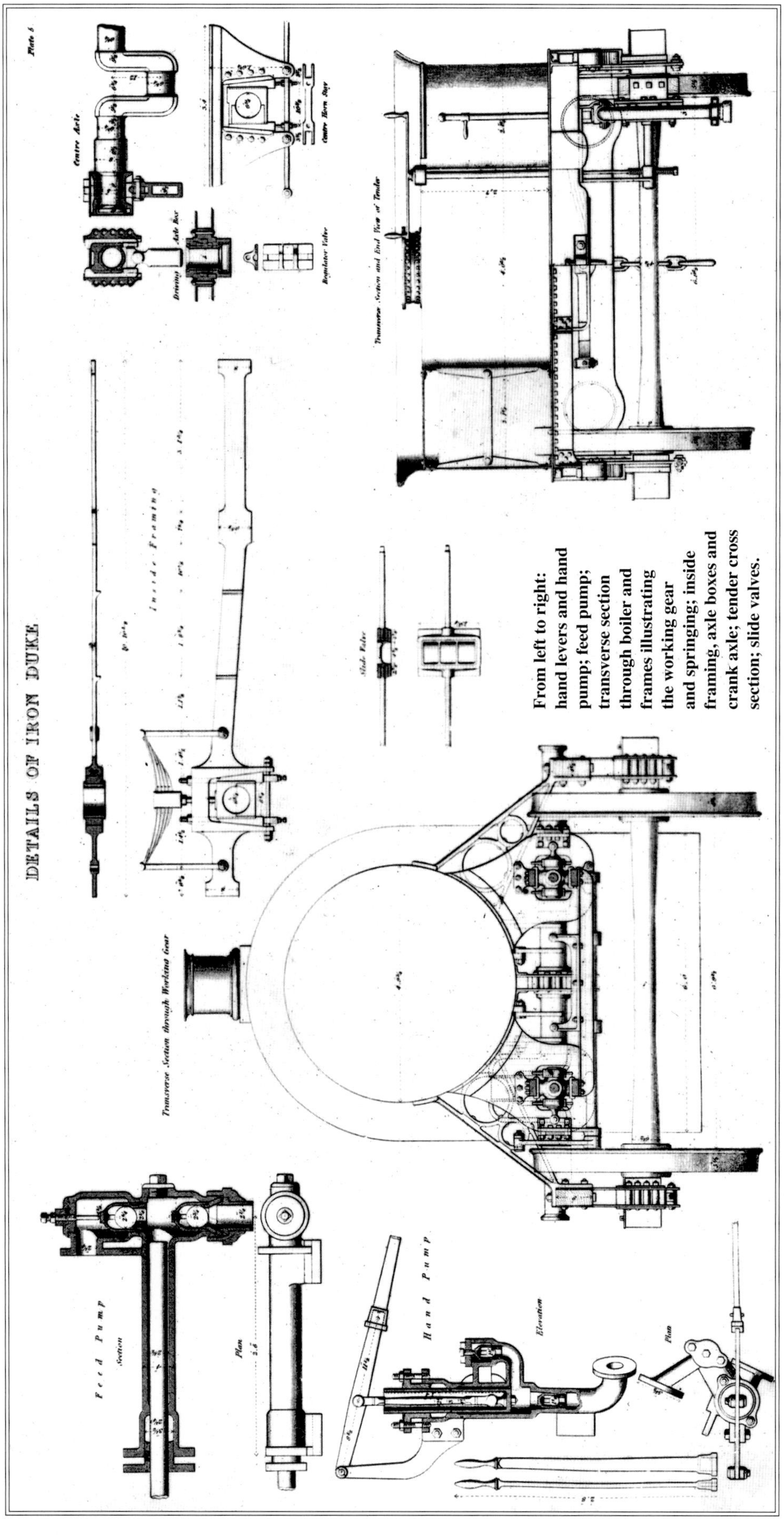

DETAILS OF IRON DUKE

Plate 5

Centre Axle

Centre Horn Stay

Driving Axle Box

Regulator Valve

Transverse Section and End View of Tender

Inside Framing

Slide Valve

Transverse Section through Working Gear

Feed Pump — Section

Plan — 1:8

Hand Pump — Plan — 1:8

Elevation

Plan

From left to right: hand levers and hand pump; feed pump; transverse section through boiler and frames illustrating the working gear and springing; inside framing, axle boxes and crank axle; tender cross section; slide valves.

suspect that some of the later engines ran with the unbalanced slide valves from new. Valve gear was of the normal Gooch fixed link pattern.

Wheels

As mentioned earlier, the leading and carrying wheels were 4ft 6ins in diameter. However, the *RCTS History* states that the rear pair of the leading wheels were of a slightly smaller diameter than the front pair, at least in later days. These wheels were flanged, while the 8ft 0in. diameter driving wheels were flangeless. Fortunately, the pair of wheels which ran under *Lord of the Isles* survived the engine's demise in 1906 and can be inspected today in the entrance hall of Steam Museum at Swindon. These were formed around a cast boss into which each spoke was fixed. The spokes were forged in the form of a 'T', the cross piece of which was slightly curved. Each were hammer welded together and then the steeled tyre shrunk onto the rim. From early records found at Swindon in 1904 and known as the Fawcett List after its compiler John Fawcett, who was a wheelwright, we know who made all these great wheels. Mr Fawcett comments, '*I myself contracted for and made the first 8ft 0in. wheels for the engines* Great Western *and* Lord of the Isles, *Mr J. Waterson and Mr William Hogarth made the remainder and all other driving wheels*'.

Springing

Springing was provided by leaf springs mounted between the frames below the driving axle and above the frames for the leading and carrying axles. The leading wheels were sprung by one large 5ft 0in. long inverted leaf spring mounted alongside the footplate. However, in service these proved to be inadequate and were soon strengthened. The rear spring was lengthened by 6ins and more leaves were provided, whilst the leading and driving springs were also increased in strength with more leaves added. They were all further improved by the addition of underhung dampers, which were of circular section and in

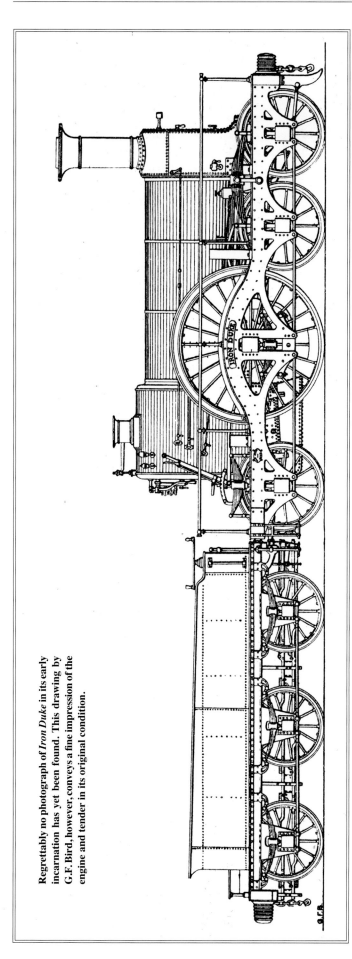

Regrettably no photograph of *Iron Duke* in its early incarnation has yet been found. This drawing by G.F. Bird, however, conveys a fine impression of the engine and tender in its original condition.

which iron washers were interleaved with vulcanised rubber pads and secured by two heavy gunmetal bolts. The vulcanisation of rubber had been perfected by Charles Goodyear in 1843, which rendered it both waterproof and winterproof, and thereby revolutionised its application, as we all have good cause to know. I cannot say if Gooch was the first locomotive engineer to use rubber in this way but he must have been in the vanguard of those who did. Ken Woodham, who perhaps knows more about the construction of the 8ft 0in. 'Singles' than anyone else, suggests that the introduction of these dampers occurred about 1849. He claims to have seen a drawing of *Timour* which shows this innovation. Unfortunately, I have not been able to inspect this item but I have no reason to doubt his assertion, since *Timour* was built in August 1849 and Ken is a meticulous researcher.

Axle Box Covers and Tie-bars

A brief mention should be made about axle box covers because confusion and misinformation has often circulated about them. The simple fact is that they were made of iron and not brass. Initially they were painted black, as they appear in some early photographs. There were always exceptions to these rules, because enginemen would pay cleaners a small bonus to polish axle boxes, buffer heads (after sprung buffers began to replace the leather horsehair buffers in the mid 1850s) draw hooks and even tie-bars, as well as the various brass and copper fittings with which these engines were adorned. *Lord of the Isles*, first an exhibition engine and then often used for Royal train workings, was always given special attention but the rather sparse photographic evidence gives the lie to the oft made assertion that it was alone in receiving such special artistic touches.

Tie-bars were fitted to all members of the class and added an extra element of strength to the frames. They were riveted to the horns of the frames under the axle boxes, between the wrought iron sheets of the sandwich-frames. At the leading end they were also riveted to the 'horn guides' which were, in turn, attached to the leading buffer beam.

Boiler Feed

Two cross head pumps were provided to feed the boilers whilst the train was in motion. These fed water into the boiler via two large brass clacks positioned just behind the smokebox, low down on the front ring of the boiler. On the fireman's side of the footplate, an additional hand pump allowed water to be fed into the boiler when the engine was stationary. This was presumably for use in an emergency, because it was common practice to detach an engine from its train and run forward and backward over a short distance to fill the boiler when a train or engine was standing for any length of time. These pumps were replaced by injectors from the mid-1860s.

The Smokebox

As previously mentioned, the cylinders were jacketed in the lower part of the smokebox. Bird gives the dimensions of *Iron Duke*'s smokebox in the November 1901 edition of *The Locomotive Magazine* in the following way: '… *which, while its length* at the upper part was only 2ft 3ins for a depth of 4ft 8ins, was increased in length at the level of the cylinders to 2ft 9¹/₂ins, this increase extending through 2ft 7ins of the total depth of 7ft 3ins. The lower face of the smokebox casing was 2ft 9ins from the level of the rails, and its diameter at the level of the centre line of the boiler was 5ft 8ins. Its plates were ¹/₄in. thick, except the tube plate, which was ¹/₄in. thick'.

Apart from the blast pipe, steam pipes and regulator, the smokebox also contained a device for controlling the draught through the flu tubes, of which Bird says: 'It should be mentioned that the draught through the flu tubes was controlled at the smokebox end by means of a set of louvres placed one above the other along the tube plate, the opening and closing of which was effected by an outside rod reaching back to the footplate of the engine'.

Blowers were also fitted from no later than the mid 1850s. Smokebox doors were of the then standard 'half-moon' type, which were hinged at the bottom and kept tight by a series of 'dog tags' arranged around the door. However, Courier and all subsequent engines had a redesigned smokebox about which Bird remarks: 'The smokebox had a uniform length at top and bottom of 2ft 9¹/₂ins and a depth below of 4ft 5ins'. The cylinders remained encased in the lower half of the smokebox but the front was now flat, unlike that of the 'Iron Dukes' which curved out over the cylinders. Being wider they obviously also afforded a little more space to fit all the internal piping, etc. Though it is impossible to be explicit, the earlier engines probably received these larger

smokeboxes as heavy repairs became necessary. Photographs of both Sultan and Lightning, taken in the late 1850s or early '60s, suggest that they have received this modification.

Boilers

These were constructed from the best quality wrought iron and were built in three telescopic, sections the largest of which was at the smokebox end of the boiler. G.F. Bird takes up the description again: 'The barrel of the boiler was pitched with its centre line 7ft 2ins above the level of the rails and it was built up of three rings of ³/₈in. plates single riveted as regards the two middle circumferential seams but double riveted to the angle iron rings of the smokebox and firebox casings; the length of the barrel (of Iron Duke) was 11ft 0in. and its diameter outside the largest ring 4ft 9³/₄ins. It contained 303 (brass) tubes each 11ft 6¹/₂ins long and 2ins in diameter, and since there was no steam dome, the upper part of the steam space was occupied by a perforated pipe extending from the front tube plate to the back of the firebox casing, through which ran a rod from the push and pull regulator handle on the footplate to the regulator valve within the upper part of the smokebox. This system (Hawthorn's patent of 1839), which employed a pipe perforated with numerous holes along its upper surface for the purpose of obtaining dry steam for the cylinders, appears to have been markedly successful on these big engines, though it has sometimes seemed conducive to 'priming' when applied to the smaller boilers of the narrow gauge'.

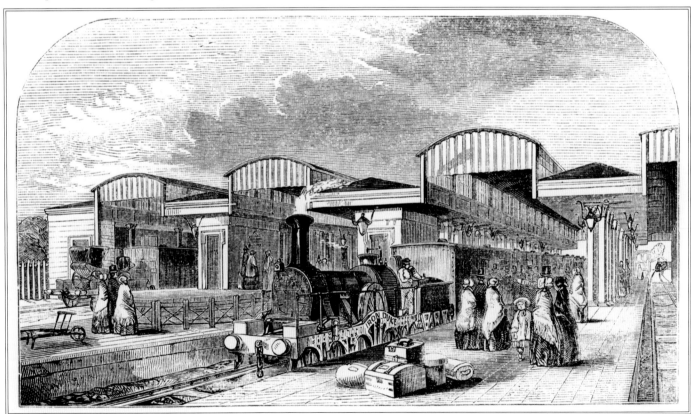

An etching of *Iron Duke* and train calling at the original Didcot station. This opened on 12th June 1844 along with the line from Didcot Junction to Oxford (Old station), increasing the route milage of the GWR by 9 miles and 57 chains. MacDermot makes the following observation: '*On the same day* [12th June] *a large junction station was opened at Didcot consisting of four lines and five very narrow platforms under an 'all over roof' which did duty till burnt down on 11th March 1885*'. This illustration certainly conveys a vivid impression of the contemporary scene which I would date as circa 1850. Note the carriage on a carriage truck, on the far left-hand side, attached to an Up train, which is very typical of the period. This etching was in the GWR's own collection and was also reproduced by MacDermot.

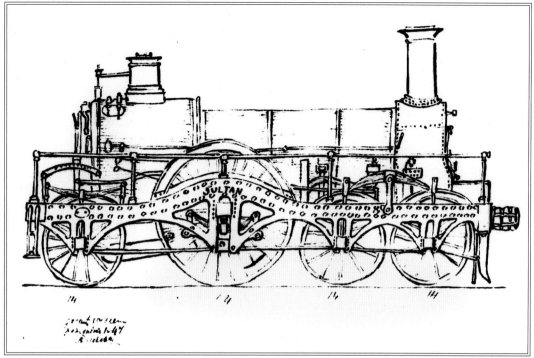

Sultan was the final member of the first batch of 'Iron Dukes', which Swindon termed the '2nd Passenger Lot', to be produced in November 1847. Lane, who must have seen it under construction in the shops, sketched it when it was newly completed, his drawing being dated November 1847. Consequently, we can be confident that it portrays the engine as originally built. When compared to the drawing of *Iron Duke*, you will note that sanding gear has appeared at the front end of the engine, with sandboxes positioned on the front of the running plate adjacent to the smokebox; there were two, one on either side. The leaf springs above the trailing wheels also give the impression of having been lengthened, though the imprecise nature of the sketch may be deceiving. The pair of whistles are shown mounted on the side of the firebox; these were subsequently moved to the now familiar position on top of the firebox probably in the early 1850s. Lest we forget, *Sultan* was the engine involved in the Shrivenham accident on 10th May 1848, in which it was not badly damaged but may have been out of action for some considerable time. In Sturrock's report to Gooch in October 1849, the engine is mentioned under the heading '*undergoing painting and cleating of boiler*'. This implies the last stages of a significant repair, which may have involved more than just the rectification of accident damage.

The later engines of the 'Courier' Class had slightly shorter boilers and therefore tubes, and longer fireboxes which increased the heating surface of these engines, as indicated earlier on. The Rothwell-built engines may have had a slightly rearranged tube layout, which might account for the different heating surface quoted for them. Boiler pressure was initially set at 100psi and later increased to 115psi on the 'Iron Dukes', while the valves on the 'Couriers' were officially set to blow off at 120psi. In the light of the evidence which emerged at the inquiry into the explosion of the boiler of *Perseus* in Westbourne Park shed on 8th November 1862, the actual working pressure of these boilers, at any given time, might be said to be anyone's guess!

Fireboxes

For their time, and for many years to come, these were massive affairs with enormous steam raising capacity. The influence of this design on later engineers' work would prove to be far reaching, a theme which we will explore in a later volume. Once again, referring to *Iron Duke*, G.F. Bird takes up the story: '*The firebox casing measured 5ft 0in. in length and with a width of 6ft 0in., the cross section of that part above the centre of the boiler barrel being semi-circular whilst below the sides were perfectly vertical. At the front end the casing extended 4ft 7ins below the centre of the boiler an 3/8ind the rear end extended 4ft 11 1/2ins below the same datum line. It was built of 3/8in. plates. The firebox itself (i.e. the inner box) was of copper with sides and backplates 1/2in. thick, the tube plate, which at its lower portion was of similar strength, being thickened to 3/4in. to take the tubes, which by the way, were secured in each tube plate by internal ferrules. There was no foundation ring, but the firebox was expanded all round its lower edge to meet the casing and the two sets of plates were securely held together by a double row of rivets. At back and front the water spaces were practically parallel from top to bottom but the sides of the firebox sloped inwards to the extent of giving a water space at bottom of 2 1/2ins and at top of 4 1/2ins. The roof of the firebox was flat and was supported by eleven longitudinal girders. A feature of the firebox consisted of a transverse water midfeather which at the centre line of the engine rose to the level of the fifth row of tubes and thence swept up in a curve either way until it reached the crown plate*'.

It must be remembered that, though the constructional details remained much the same, the 'Courier' Class had larger fireboxes than the 'Iron Dukes' as mentioned earlier. Ahrons contends that the inclusion of such an intrusive midfeather made these engines very difficult to fire; always remembering that the intention was to maintain the rear half of the grate as near to 'white heat' as possible whilst firing the front portion. The back compartment's fire had to be kept relatively thin and very bright, whilst the heavy firing took place in the forward half under the firebox door. Until the early 1860s, coke was the normal fuel which in the circumstances must have made the fireman's job especially difficult. That these hard-working individuals overcame the problems which the challenges of firing these exceptional locomotives presented is evident from the record-breaking performances which they put in!

Finally, it is important to remind readers that with the introduction of the 'Iron Dukes', the old Haycock/Gothic style of firebox was done away with and the roundtop firebox introduced. This type remained standard for the rest of Gooch's superintendency and for many years thereafter.

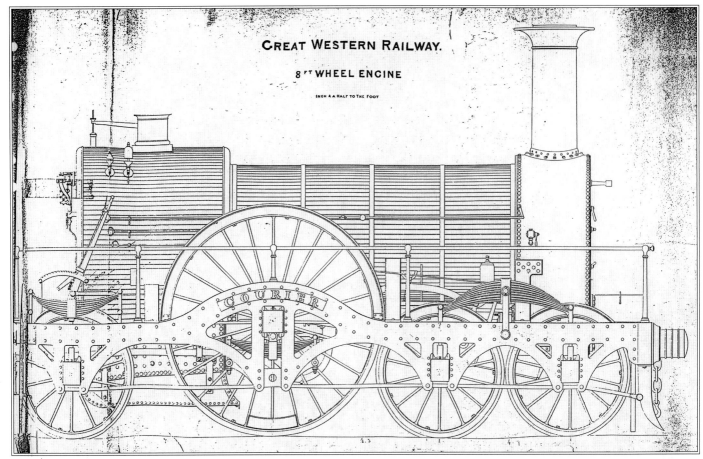

This official drawing of *Courier*, though a poor copy, shows the engine as originally designed. It is not known whether the drawing originates from 1848 or was produced retrospectively but the latter seems, on balance, to be more likely. The boiler is shown clad in wood, as had been the case with the 'Iron Dukes' but a decision was taken to clad, or cleat as the process was then referred to, the boiler and firebox with iron sheets during construction. Consequently, none of the 'Courier' sub-class, known as the '3rd Lot Passenger', actually ran in the condition illustrated here. *Courier* worked until November 1877 and was then replaced by a new engine bearing the same name.

Boiler Backhead Details

Initially, these might be described as 'simplicity itself'. Apart from the 'pull out' regulator handle and the firebox door, the only other major fitting was the boiler gauge glass. On many of the earlier designs this important fitting was placed on the driver's side of the firebox, where only he could easily see it. Clearly it was intended that among his other duties it was his responsibility to ensure that there was sufficient water in the boiler. With the introduction of *Iron Duke*, the gauge was repositioned on the fireman's side of the backhead where it would be visible to both men but implying that responsibility for maintaining the water level of the boiler had passed to the fireman under the driver's supervision. Initially no pressure gauge was fitted. One presumes that the fireman was supposed to use the salter spring balance to determine the pressure but photographic evidence indicates that this shortcoming had been remedied by the mid-1850s. Whistles too were originally placed on the driver's side of the firebox – see the drawing of *Courier* – though they were soon removed to the crown of the firebox, with the brake whistle positioned on the left-hand side. On the driver's side of the firebox, aside from the reversing lever, there were various other hand operated levers that controlled the sanding gear, the louvred draughting arrangement in the smokebox and the feed water. The fireman seems only to

have had access to the sanding gear and boiler feed hand pump. By the mid-1850s, a blower valve handle would also have appeared, as injectors did from the mid-1860s onward.

Footplate Protection

Initially, other than the backhead itself, no protection was provided at all. This soon changed, however, so that by the mid-1850s and perhaps earlier, side sheets began to be fitted, shortly followed by spectacle plates attached to the firebox top. Cabs were fitted to those few members of the class that survived long enough after 1878.

Sanding

Sanding gear was at first fitted to the very front of the running plate, two small sandboxes being positioned on either side of the engine, immediately above the front buffer beam. Sand was delivered to the railhead in advance of the leading wheels, which since they did not provide any traction, proved to be of little value. The problem soon came to light. The *London Evening Standard* for Friday 3rd September 1847, while recording the work of *Great Britain* on a Down train on the previous Wednesday, comments that, '*We observed the driving wheels of the* Great Britain *slip frequently in the trip to Swindon*'. The train encountered a

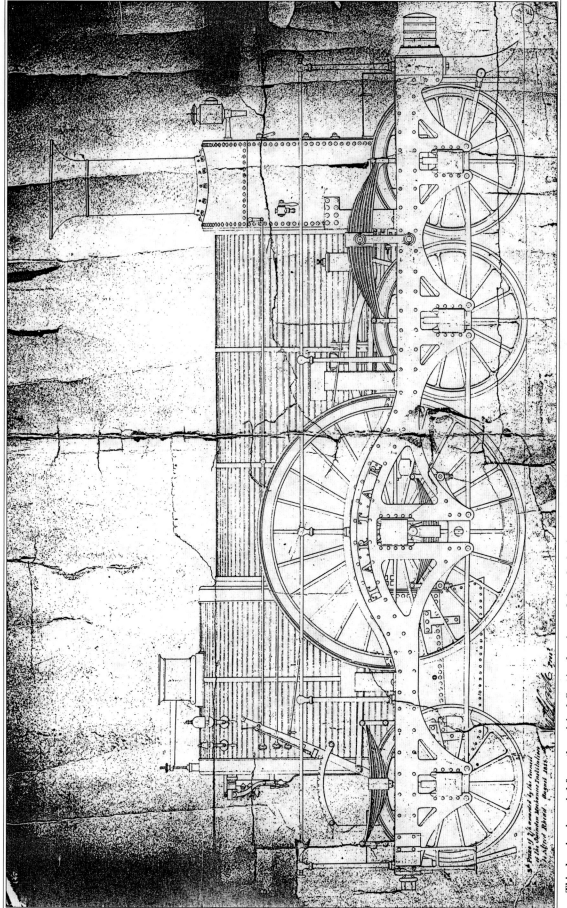

This drawing is copied from the original *Courier* drawing and though also in poor condition is included as a supplement to the official item. It was executed in August 1851 and won for its draughtsman (whose name is not quite legible but looks something like H. Alfred Rhind) 3rd prize in the annual Swindon Mechanics Institution competition, worth 7 shillings and sixpence. The drawing is also signed by Daniel Gooch, who was President of 'the Mechanics' (as Swindonians always referred to the institution). *Tartar* was the second member of the class built, emerging in July 1848 and was replaced in 1876 when the original engine was withdrawn. The major differences between the 'Iron Dukes' and the 'Couriers' (or the '2nd' and '3rd Lot Passengers') related to the design of the smokebox, boiler and firebox. The smokeboxes of the '3rd Lot' were completely redesigned, doing away with the 'piano front' of the '2nd Lot', whilst the boilers were a little shorter and the fireboxes a little larger. Boiler pressure at 120psi was also higher. Though the overall heating surface figures for the '3rd Lot' were a little lower than their predecessors, that of the firebox was larger as was the grate area. Therefore, in theory at least, the later engines should have been more rapid steam raisers than the 'Iron Dukes'.

strong side wind which would have blown the sand away before it could do any good and the small sandboxes would soon have been denuded of supplies. The remedy, soon applied, was to place large sandboxes on top of the footplate in front of the driving wheels, where sand could be delivered directly to the place where it was most needed. The small sandboxes were thereafter slowly removed, a process which seems to have taken some time to implement fully.

Boiler Fittings – Safety Valve Covers

With the 'Iron Dukes', Gooch introduced a style of safety valve cover which remained standard until he resigned in 1864 and remained fitted to the 8ft 0in. singles until 1892. These were attractive items made of brass, with a wide funnel-like body that curved outwards at the top into a shapely rim. The base, which had a less pronounced rim, sat upon a pedestal astride the top of the firebox.

Chimneys

During the lifetime of these locomotives, which began in 1847 and ended with the withdrawal of the much rebuilt *Prometheus* in October 1887, six styles of chimney were fitted:
1 (A-D): The Gooch and early Armstrong type. These were the design usually associated with the class and were

the norm between 1847 and 1875, though the style of chimney cap differed down the years. Initially the caps were made of iron and were of the bellmouth pattern. Copper was sometimes substituted for iron and this later became standard as the styles were refined.
2 (E): The later Armstrong type. This style of slightly tapered chimney with a copper rolled top has a long history but was used at Swindon during the five years 1876-1880.
3 (F): The Dean type. This elegant design was the forerunner of the standard GWR chimney of latter years. It had a parallel barrel and a shallow copper cap of elegant design and proportions.

In the December 1950 edition of *The Locomotive Magazine*, E. W. Twining explored some of the details of the external appearance of the 8ft 0in. 'Singles,' which included drawings of the six variations in chimney styles and types. I have reproduced Twining's drawing here, which beautifully illustrates the sequence of changes and developments outlined above.

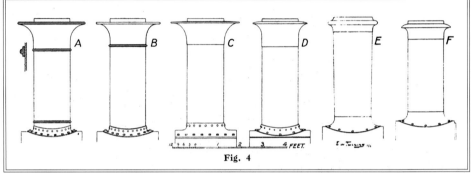

Fig. 4

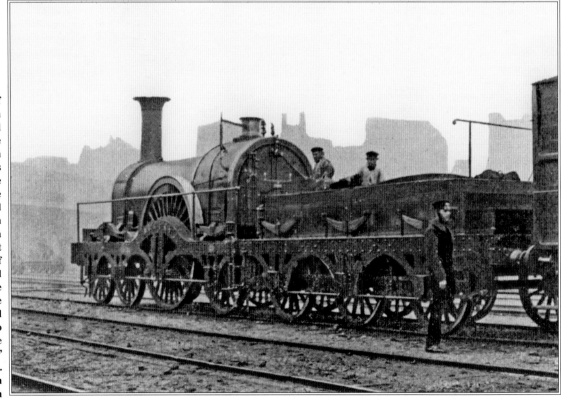

This historic photograph of *Sultan* taken somewhere in the Paddington area is said to have been used by the painter William Powell Firth R.A when he composed his famous painting entitled the Railway Station which he began in 1861 and completed a year later. The photograph predates this by about a decade and is without doubt one of the very earliest views of an 8ft 0in. 'Single'. Compared with Lane's sketch there are one or two differences. The whistles have been moved for example and the 'piano fronted' smokebox may have been replaced by the 'Courier' type straight fronted design. There is also a steam valve on the side of the firebox which when opened fed excess steam back into the tender and so heated the feed-water. The rear sandbox is just visible as a black blob on the footplate while the delivery pipe can just be made out behind the trailing wheel. Though one cannot be certain this photograph may predate the opening of the present Paddington Station, which occurred in two stages in 1854; the Departure side on January 16th and the Arrivals on May 29th. The light rail section and the 'well used' condition of the permanent way suggests the old formation rather than trackwork that has been recently laid.

Other Fittings

As time and technology progressed other fittings appeared, such as boiler feed clacks on top of the firebox – associated with the introduction of injectors – and 'Roscoe' lubricators, used to supply oil to regulator in the smokebox, etc. This is where the paucity of both written and photographic evidence lets us down. It is not known, for example, whether all members of the class received injectors. Some of the very early withdrawals, such as *Swallow* and *Rover*, may not have received this addition for example. Yet since heavy repairs continued throughout the 1860s, one suspects that this important modification was universally applied but we simply cannot be absolutely sure.

Boiler Supports

Early locomotive construction tended toward the view that the boiler constituted a major component of the structure of the engine, thus adding to the strength and rigidity of the frames. To support the boiler, large wrought iron cradles were provided in advance of the driving wheels and on the firebox sides. The former, which were of substantial dimensions, were later hidden behind the large sandboxes, mentioned above. In passing it should be noted that this form of construction, as train weights increased, placed great strain on the integrity of the structure of the engine. With regard to the 8ft 0in. 'Singles', matters came to a head in the 1870s, with a complete redesign of the framing being undertaken from 1878 onwards. We shall return to this matter in more detail in a later volume.

Tenders

The subject of tenders has already received some attention but it is very important to record that the rather scanty Swindon broad gauge tender records indicate that the iron framed, 6-wheeled tenders previously described, were supplied initially to all the 8ft 0in. 'Singles' including those built by Rothwell's in the mid-1850s. G.F. Bird gives the following description of *Iron Duke*'s tender: '*It was furnished with an iron framed tender … this type being known as the 'Ironsides.' The tender was carried on six wheels 4ft in diameter equally spaced over a wheelbase of 12ft and with 1,800 gallons of water and a ton and a half of coke, it weighed 15 tons 10 cwt, the distribution of which is as follows:*

> Leading wheels .. …. …. ….5 tons 7 cwt 2 qrs
> Middle wheels … …. …. ….3 tons 19 cwt 2 qrs
> Trailing wheels … …. …. ….6 tons 5 cwt

Empty its weight was 13 tons 12 cwt 1 qr. This class of tender, as also later patterns, was generally supplied with a hooded seat facing backwards for the use of a guard whose duty it was to keep a watch upon the train throughout its journey'.

With the one major exception of *Lord of the Isles*, the other members of the class eventually received the familiar sandwich-framed tenders. The 1857 specification painting, reproduced below, gives all their dimensional details and describes them as 'Express Tenders' as does the Swindon Works offical drawing dated December 1857, on pages 106 and 107. Braking was provided on the fireman's side only. Many of these tenders were later rebuilt with larger capacity tanks measuring from 2,700 to 3,000 gallons.

Interestingly the records suggest that the iron-framed tenders

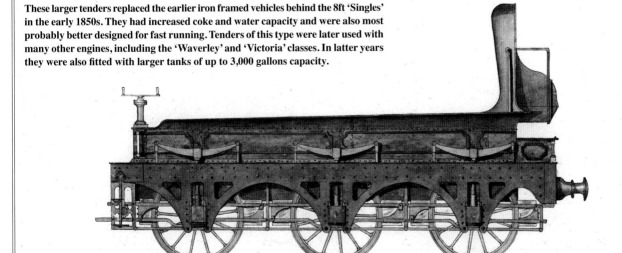

EXPRESS TENDERS.

These larger tenders replaced the earlier iron framed vehicles behind the 8ft 'Singles' in the early 1850s. They had increased coke and water capacity and were also most probably better designed for fast running. Tenders of this type were later used with many other engines, including the 'Waverley' and 'Victoria' classes. In latter years they were also fitted with larger tanks of up to 3,000 gallons capacity.

DESCRIPTION

WHEELS. 6 Wheels 4 feet in diam^r. with 13 arms 7/8" and 1½" thick by 3" and 3⅜" broad.
TANK 16 feet 6 in^s long, 8 feet 3 in^s wide, and 3 feet 3 in^s deep. less coke space 2'-9" by 8 feet 6" by 2'-2".
COKE-SPACE 102·8 cub. feet. **WATER-SPACE** 301·67 cub. feet. Contains 1880 Gallons.
WEIGHT when empty on Leading 2 Tons 18 cwt. Middle 4 Tons 12 cwt. Trailing 3 Tons 6 cwt. Total 10-16-0
WEIGHT when loaded on Leading 7 Tons 3 cwt. Middle 7 Tons 0 cwt. Trailing 6 Tons 17 cwt. Total 21-0-0

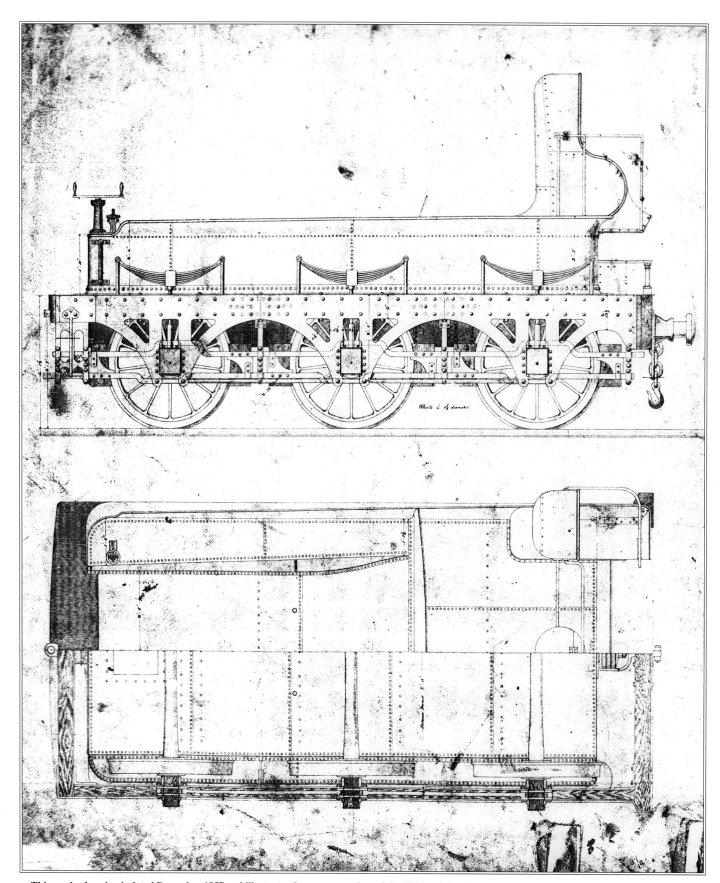

This works drawing is dated December 1857 and illustrates the express tenders of the '7th' and '8th Lot'. In essence, however, these tenders, irrespective of Lots, were very similar and dated back to about 1850. There were, of course, developments particularly to the water capacity, which over the years increased from 1,800 gallons to 2,500 and eventually, circa 1880, to 3,000 gallons. In later builds, the travelling porters 'coffin' was omitted and the vacuum brake fitted. It is important to point out the details of the draw hook fixing, which runs the whole length of the vehicle and appears to form the locomotive

7th & 8th LOTS OF
EXPRESS TENDERS.
SWINDON WORKS, DEC. 1857.

coupling bar. This had the effect of reducing the snatch weight born by the sandwich-frames to the minimum amount possible and helped preserve the vehicles' mechanical integrity. The details of the handbrake and associated pullrods, etc. are also of important significance. It is remarkable that this brake, on the fireman's side, was the only braking apparatus that any tender engine of the period possessed. Little wonder that Brunel described early railway vehicle brakes as 'tolerably useless'!

Lightning on the turntable at the old Oxford, Worcester & Wolverhampton Railway shed at Oxford. The OW&WR became a constituent part of the West Midland Railway on 1st August 1860, which in turn was absorbed by the GWR on 1st August 1863. The engine's condition is consistent with a date in the mid-1860s, in fact being very similar to that of *Sultan*, though there are subtle differences. Most notable is the retention here of the leading sandboxes (in fact, the removal of these fittings on *Sultan* may be an exception to the general rule). Strengthening plates have also been fitted to the frames around the leading and trailing hornblocks, and the works plate has been moved to the far end of the tender frames, rendering it more audible one would hope. Finally, the lined panels on the tender are not painted from spring buckle to spring buckle as was usual but instead as two long rectangles but there are still panels wrapping around the corners. The engine's 'finish' is particularly remarkable. Not only is all the brightwork highly polished but there is what appears to be a copper band around the base of the chimney cap. The boiler bands are also polished as is the driving wheel axle box. The other axle boxes, on both engine and tender, have been painted Windsor brown and lined out in the same manner as the frames, in black edged with a fine vermillion line. One can only conclude that the engine had been prepared for some special purpose, perhaps a Royal working or something similar; does that explain the top-hatted driver and bowler-hatted fireman on the footplate? There are in fact two versions of this photograph – the second is reproduced opposite. Note as well that the line on the far right is standard gauge, whilst everything else is mixed gauge. The two lines to the right of the point lever served the shed.

The second photograph of *Lightning* was taken with a different crew on the footplate, whilst the position of the camera had also subtly changed. The engine was built in August 1847 and withdrawn in December 1877, having run 816,601 miles during its thirty years in traffic. The pictures, which as the map extract below shows were taken looking north with the water tank and coal shed behind, are full of other interesting details, including the mixed gauge trackwork, the double point lever and the gas lamps. Finally, the initials T.W.H. bottom right are presumably those of the photographer.

were in the main cut up as broad gauge vehicles but, conversely, the sandwich-framed variety were converted to standard gauge. This is surprising because one would think that their intricate form of construction would preclude an easy conversion. It is also worth mentioning that a number of the sandwich-framed type were built for the standard gauge in the 1850s and '60s. and many of these attractive tenders could still be found running in the early part of the 20th century.

Modifying and Rebuilding the 8ft 0in. 'Singles'

Before we progress any further it is very important to clarify what we are dealing with under this heading. Various minor modifications were made to the 8ft 0in. 'Singles' over the years and in 1870 three members of the class were given new boilers, two of which also received new frames. This was also a watershed year as far as the class was concerned. Following the reboilering of *Great Britain* in July 1870, no further members of the class

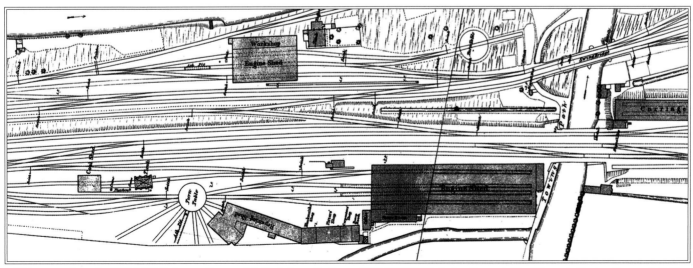

This extract from the 1876 1:500 Ordnance Survey of Oxford shows the the ex-OW&WR/WMR shed on the west side of the main line heading north (left) to Birmingham. The photographer was standing just to the right of the turntable. Opened in July 1850, the shed was closed in 1876.

were rebuilt but were withdrawn, in their turn to be replaced by new engines albeit frequently bearing the name of the locomotive that they had superseded.

The first member of the class to be replaced in this manner was *Rover*, which was built in 1850 and withdrawn in August 1871, with a new engine bearing the same name entering traffic in the same month. Little if anything of the old *Rover* was retained other than the nameplates, which were transferred from the old to the new. Because *Rover* was the first true replacement the whole class are generally referred to as 'Rovers'. This is an unofficial title, however, the GWR continuing to classify any 8ft 0in. 4-2-2, whether old or new, as a member of the 'Alma' Class. The 'Rover' story will be told in a later volume in, I hope, considerable detail. For the moment we remain focussed on the history of the original engines.

As mentioned, three engines were rebuilt in 1870. Two, *Estaffete* and *Prometheus*, were of the 'Courier' group, whilst the other, *Great Britain*, was the second engine built, in July 1847. The rebuilding took slightly different forms, *Great Britain* retaining its original wheelbase.

Estaffete and *Prometheus*

These two engines were both rebuilt between April and July 1870, receiving new boilers of the same dimensions as that also fitted to *Great Britain*. Internally, however, they were not quite the same; that fitted to *Estaffete* is said to have had 271 tubes while the other two had only 270 – hardly a major consideration one would have thought. Though the diameter was more or less the same as the original engines, the reduction in the number of tubes was presumably intended to aid water circulation in the boiler. Construction methods had also changed since the 1840/50s; boiler barrels were still of three rings but each was of the same diameter and were joined together by heavily riveted plates, which overlapped the joints thus greatly increasing the strength and integrity of it. The dimensions are shown in **Table 6.7**, below.

Table 6.7: New Boiler Dimensions 1870	
Diameter	4ft 9ins
No. of tubes	270 or 271
Grate area	24. sq ft
Pressure	140 psi
Total heating surface	1,750 sq. ft approx.

New fireboxes were also provided from which the midfeather was omitted – which may account for the reduction in the grate area compared with the 'Courier' Class's 25.47 sq. ft. These new boxes were, however, larger than those fitted to the first six 'Iron Dukes'. *Estaffete* and *Prometheus* also both received lengthened frames, which increased their wheelbase to 5ft 0in. + 6ft 6ins + 7ft 6ins. However, it is not entirely clear to me why this alteration was considered necessary and it can really only be accounted for if the old frames were in need of replacement. If this is the case, then *Estaffete* and *Prometheus* were virtually new in 1870, which would account for the extended life that these two stalwarts enjoyed.

Great Britain

This engine was rebuilt in July 1870 with a new boiler but retained its original frames and ran for a further ten years until replaced by a new engine, bearing the same name, in 1880.

Apart from the changes already mentioned, these three, and quite probably other members of the class, were brought up to date in other ways. New chimneys were provided with deeper copper caps and shallow rims. Smokebox doors of the old half moon pattern were replaced with the modern circular pattern with central dart and crossbar fixing. This went hand in hand with the provision of new smokeboxes, which were parallel in section and of greater width than those fitted to the original 'Iron Dukes' but resembled the redesigned smokeboxes introduced with *Courier* in 1848 and that were retrofitted to the first six engines in the 1850s.

As noted earlier, Swindon adopted the Wolverhampton pattern tapered chimney with a roll top copper cap in 1876 and most engines received this chimney type as they passed through shops in the late 1870s. This would certainly be true of the three rebuilt engines – we have a photograph of *Great Britain* to prove it – but it would almost certainly have appeared as well on those few unrebuilt engines, such as *Perseus* and *Sebastopol*, which survived until 1880. *Lord of the Isles* was the other obvious candidate but she was such an exception to the general rule in so many ways that we will devote a whole section to her in due course. In this context, however, I can categorically say that the photographic evidence proves that *Lord of the Isles* was not fitted with the roll top chimney. From 1880 or early 1881, the roll top chimney was slowly replaced with the Dean parallel, copper-capped design. *Lord of the Isles* was preserved and equipped with this style of chimney though does not appear to have run in service so fitted. *Prometheus* is the only member of the class likely to have received this chimney but photographic evidence is lacking.

Other than a few experimental designs which appeared in the late 1860s, cabs were fitted at Swindon from 1878. A photograph taken by the Reverend Malan at Newton Abbot circa 1884 of *Prometheus* shows the engine fitted with a cab, roll top chimney and the vacuum brake – probably the only member of the class to receive all these modifications. Incidentally, as might be expected, the engine is still painted in the Armstrong livery of holly green with pea green scafed lining, which shows up rather well in the photograph.

Boiler Explosion

It is well known that the boiler of *Perseus* blew up in Westbourne Park shed on 8th November 1862. Built in 1850 and reboilered in 1855, up to the day of the explosion the engine had been in regular use. The heating surface of the boiler was given in the accident report as 1,768 sq. ft and the working pressure as 115lbs per sq. inch, whilst the engine's weight is recorded as 32 tons. Sadly, three people, two cleaners and the firelighter, lost their lives and the engine was thrown ten yards from its standing position. The boiler barrel more or less totally disintegrated and pieces of boiler plate were being recovered from the surrounding area for some time afterwards. Captain Tyler conducted the Board

In July 1870, *Great Britain* was rebuilt at Swindon with a new boiler of similar dimensions to the original but with a revised layout of the tubes, which at 270 were 33 fewer than originally fitted. Though this slightly reduced the heating surface, the revised internal layout aided water circulation or so it was hoped. Unlike *Estaffete* and *Prometheus*, rebuilt at about the same time, *Great Britain* retained its original frames. The engine also received a new smokebox and design of smokebox door, as clearly displayed here. A Roscoe lubricator has also been fitted behind the chimney to aid the lubrication of the regulator valve in the smokebox. The main water delivery clack valve, seen toward the rear of the first ring of the boiler, had also been moved both upwards and backwards from the position originally adopted. This is one of several small markers which indicate a rebuilt engine, the adjacent oil box on the side of the boiler being another. One archaic feature was the retention of leather buffers at the front end, though spring buffers had been fitted to tenders from about 1850. The driving wheel has remained flangeless though it has been fitted with thicker tyres and there is now a strengthening plate, providing a bulwark to the firebox support bracket, attached to the frames between the driving and trailing wheels. The engine has also been fitted with injectors. The finish of the engine, though generally similar to earlier practise, shows the boiler bands painted black edged in white. The large sandbox has also been lined in a similar way with black edges picked out with white lining. The tender has the pea green lining that had been in use for many years but the 'scafed' Pea green band seems to have become more prominent in the late '60s and early '70s. The location cannot be matched to Westbourne Park as previously thought, so remains to be identified; the building behind appears to have rail access from the far end but lacks any form of smoke ventilation in the roof so is almost certainly not an engine shed.

Great Britain alongside the Swindon Works office block extension built in 1860 which, though much enlarged, still stands today. The engine had just undergone a heavy repair (possibly its last) in perhaps 1876 or '77, in the course of which, it had been fitted with the Armstrong roll top taper chimney, used at Swindon only between 1876 and 1880. Otherwise, little had changed in the *Great Britain's* condition since it was rebuilt in 1870. The livery shows up quite well in this photograph particularly the lining of the frames and the now polished axle boxes. Frames, at this time, were painted Windsor brown with the edges lined in black picked out with a white line, very evident here. The change from red to white lining on the frames occurred, according to a GWR chart, in 1875 and comparison between this and the previous photograph certainly bears this out. Interestingly, the works plate is dated July 1870, suggesting that the engine was considered new when it was rebuilt despite the fact that it retained its original frames.

The famous photograph of *Perseus* at Westbourne Park shed following the disastrous explosion of the engine's boiler on 8th November 1862, in which three people lost their lives, all the result of a poor inspection regime. Sad though they are photographs like this are always useful to historians. Not only can they be accurately dated but they often show features of the engine's construction not visible otherwise. In this instance we can clearly see the details of the smokebox door, cylinder covers and leading sandboxes, items not easily made out in any other contemporary illustration. *Perseus* was the last built member of the 3rd Lot entering service in June 1850 and running until withdrawal in December 1880. It was not replaced and the name not reused.

of Trade inquiry and found that 'grooving' adjacent to a lap joint along the bottom of the boiler's middle ring had weakened the $^{7}/_{16}$in. iron plate to a point (less than $^{1}/_{8}$in. thick) where the internal steam pressure could no longer be contained. Tyler rightly criticised the GWR and, by implication Daniel Gooch, for allowing a boiler to go seven years and five months – during which time the engine had run 175,000 miles – without a full pressure interior examination. Gooch had been warned; he should have been alerted to the problem by the two previous explosions of the 'Fire Fly' Class engines, namely *Actaeon* at Gloucester in February 1855 and *Leopard* at Bristol in 1857. Because these two previous explosions were not accompanied by loss of life, however, a *laissez faire* attitude had been allowed to pervade the system, with tragic and culpable consequences.

As a result of the explosion, *Perseus* was thoroughly repaired, including a new boiler and firebox, in 1863. The frames seem to have emerged from the incident relatively unscathed. As a result of this, the engine remained in traffic for rather longer than many of its sisters, finally succumbing in December 1880. At this point the name *Perseus*, with its tragic overtones, was allowed to lapse, though at least one of the nameplates survived and is now in the collection of Taunton Museum.

Traffic Accidents

There were only two accidents of note which involved engines of the 'Iron Duke' and 'Courier' classes during their lifetime. There were, of course, numerous minor incidents, such as when *Timour* ran down and killed a policeman at the west end of Swindon station on 15th August 1850. This sad event, all too common in the early days, reminds us that railway working up to the late 1860s was still very much in local control, with signals and pointwork under the supervision of railway policemen and their superiors. These worthies regulated all the traffic, which at complicated junctions, like the one at Swindon, would have been truly challenging without the aid of modern safety devices, such as the interlocking of points and signals and in the earlier years telegraphic communication. In the circumstances it is little wonder that minor accidents resulting in loss of life were common occurrences. The wonder is that serious accidents did not occur more often than they did.

In terms of loss of life, the worse accident to involve an 'Iron Duke' 8ft 0in. 'Single' was the collision that occurred at Shrivenham, just to the east of Swindon, on 10th May 1848. The train involved was the 12 noon express from Exeter, which would shortly be widely known as 'The Flying Dutchman'. The

This enlarged portion of the photograph of *Sultan* that features as the title pages double spread is not actually courtesy of modern computer software and scanning techniques but rather was produced as an albumen print seemingly at the same time. Although the name *Sultan* seems an obvious link to the Crimean Warm and the Turkish involvement in that conflict, the building and naming of the engine preceded its start by six years. *Sultan* had clearly recently been through works and received various modifications and additions when compared with the photograph on page 104. The engine had definitely received a 'straight fronted' smokebox and the large sandbox adjacent to the driving wheel had now replaced the smaller boxes by the leading splashers, whilst the cab has acquired a spectacle plate and side sheets. The young lad on the footplate is standing on the rear sandbox. The engine's crew are both on the ground alongside their machine, wearing white fustian clothing. The driver, with his hand on the framing at the front end, appears to be the same man as the driver in the earlier photograph as used by the artist Frith. A close inspection of the engine reveals that the boiler bands are black edged with white, as is the large sandbox, which strongly suggests that it was painted green rather than Windsor brown, the colour of the frames. Finally, note the Roscoe lubricator mounted on the side of the smokebox – this was another innovation which facilitated the lubrication of the cylinders and became a standard fitting for many years to come.

train was running late but the enginemen seemed determined to make up time for they were running fast on a slightly falling gradient. This, after all, was really the start of Brunel's beautifully engineered high speed railway. For the period the train was a heavy one, consisting of a van, three Second and three First Class carriages, weighing in all about 120 tons which included the 200 or so passengers on board. The engine was *Sultan*, then only about six months old and in prime condition.

The direct cause of the accident was a failure of 'local control.' The policeman who was in charge of signalling at Shrivenham was aware that the train was overdue, so he set the signal at the west end of the station to clear and then proceeded to the east end of the formation where a level crossing needed protection from the oncoming express. This was normal practise which all of the station staff should have been aware of. Despite this, and without first checking the position of the adjacent signal, easily seen from the west end of the platform, two porters pushed a horse box and cattle waggon clear of a waggon turntable, which they needed to use, leaving the loose vehicles foul of the main line. Here they were almost instantly struck by the express, which was travelling at between 55 and 60 miles per hour. *Sultan* swept by and was hardly damaged but the debris from the collision tore the side out of the leading Second Class coach, killing six passengers and injuring thirteen more. In those far off days there were no emergency services which could be quickly summoned and help had to come from near and far. In New Swindon, the newly formed Medical Fund retained a doctor, Stewart K. Rea MD. He was called to the scene and rendered significant assistance but it caused him much distress and, on 28th May, he died suddenly though he had been in poor health for some while previously. Gooch records in his diary: '*Rea had not been well for some time and a serious accident we had to our express train on 10th May at Shrivenham by which four people were killed and several seriously hurt* [Gooch is in error here] *caused him a great amount of anxiety and work instead of taking care of himself, and he died on the 29th leaving his widow and child not very well provided for*'.

Not only did the GWR face a bill for significant compensation to those who died and were injured, as well as costly repairs to engine and rolling stock, especially the latter, it also lost the services of a much respected and highly regarded medical practitioner in New Swindon. All this because 'local control' broke down at a critical moment at a wayside station because basic safety procedures were not adhered to. Two otherwise responsible members of staff failed to inform the policeman of their intention to do some 'hand shunting.' He, meanwhile, at his proper post at the level crossing, could not see what was happening in the station yard. With this combination of circumstances an accident was almost inevitable which, without the stability afforded by the broad gauge, could have been considerably worse.

This theme of stability contributed to a remarkably lucky escape from serious death and destruction in our other significant accident, a rear end collision which occurred at Aynho on 20th October 1852. The occasion was the opening of the GWR's broad gauge route to Birmingham and I am going to let L.T.C. Rolt take up the narrative:

'*Just after 9am a special train of ten coaches filled with Great Western directors and officials, their families and friends, pulled out of Paddington. Resplendent at its head was that legendary and magnificent 8-foot single* Lord of the Isles *with Daniel Gooch himself on the footplate. The locomotive had but lately returned from the Great Exhibition where, in the words of the accident inspector, 'its huge proportions and fine workmanship had been so much admired'. The party planned to run to Birmingham and then to return to Leamington for one of those protracted orgies of eating and toasting which invariably accompanied the opening of new lines of railway. Unfortunately the Oxford and Rugby Railway, as it had hitherto been called, had not woken up to the fact that greatness had been thrust upon it; that it was no longer a bucolic cross-country line where time was of little account but had become a section of an important main route. Its signalling and traffic arrangements had not been altered, while it is obvious that whoever was responsible for arranging the timings of the special at Paddington was quite unaware of its dilatory habits. While the glittering* Lord of the Isles *was speeding westwards from Paddington the 9.27 mixed train for Banbury left Didcot thirteen minutes late. In the two years that it had been running this shocking train had never once been known to run to time and this morning was no exception. Regardless of the express which was so rapidly bearing down upon it, the 'mixed' pottered along as usual, stopping every now and again to carry out desultory shunting operations. It stopped to shunt off three wagons at Abingdon Road, dropped three more at Oxford and then picked up some others including a van loaded with cheese and parcels for distribution at various stations north. It dropped off two more wagons at Heyford and then trundled on to Aynho where it arrived thirty-eight minutes late. The special passed Heyford crossing only six minutes behind the 'mixed'. The usual GWR warning signals had not yet been erected at the crossing but the 'policeman' who was stationed there made no attempt to warn the special by hand signal. On the gentle curve approaching Aynho, a thousand yards from the station, there stood a disused signal. It had been installed to protect a temporary siding and had been left there showing 'All Right'. The crew on the special, unfamiliar with the road, thought it gave them a clear run through and put on steam. The guard of the 'mixed' was unloading cheeses from the van and the station staff at Aynho were preparing to unhitch a couple of wagons from the rear when upon this pleasant and rural scene there burst in swift and awful majesty the* Lord of the Isles *running at over fifty miles an hour. For the only time in its disreputable career the mixed train moved very smartly, so smartly indeed that a coupling parted and she left her tail of wagons behind as a kind of defensive rearguard.*

But she was too late. Lord of the Isles *fell upon the wagons, demolished one of them and catapulted the rest forward into the rear of the retreating train.*

Discreditable though this accident was, it demonstrated the extraordinary safety and stability of Brunel's 7-foot gauge. The special was travelling at high speed and on any narrow gauge line such a violent collision would almost certainly have figured in the list of major disasters. Yet at Aynho both trains remained intact upon the metals and only six passengers in the 'mixed' complained of slight injury. The only casualties were the smashed wagons and Lord of the Isles *which broke her front buffer beam and was derailed by a broken wagon axle. The sequel was ignominious. The engine of the 'mixed' drew her train on to Banbury and then returned to rescue the stranded special which had*

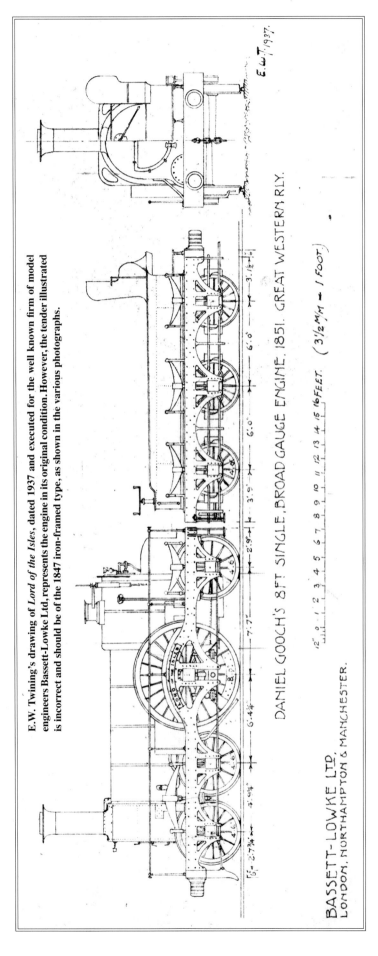

E.W. Twining's drawing of *Lord of the Isles*, dated 1937 and executed for the well known firm of model engineers Bassett-Lowke Ltd, represents the engine in its original condition. However, the tender illustrated is incorrect and should be of the 1847 iron-framed type, as shown in the various photographs.

DANIEL GOOCH'S 8FT SINGLE, BROAD GAUGE ENGINE. 1851. GREAT WESTERN RLY.

BASSETT-LOWKE LTD.
LONDON, NORTHAMPTON & MANCHESTER.

meanwhile been man-handled over a crossover clear of the wreckage. Another locomotive which was telegraphed for from Birmingham was derailed en route with the consequence that the special never reached Birmingham at all. It was the somewhat breathless engine of the 'mixed' which eventually drew the distinguished but rather shaken and disillusioned company into Leamington for their belated banquet.'

As we have seen, *Lord of the Isles* was not much damaged and was soon repaired. Her story is a remarkable one and might now be conveniently told.

Lord of the Isles

In the course of a working life which began in July 1852 (following her display at the Great Exhibition) and came to an end in June 1884, *Lord of the Isles* ran a total of 789,309 miles still, it is claimed, with her original boiler in place. It was the most photographed of all the GWR's early engines and I know of at least six different pictures of the engine taken between 1852 and 1884, all of which are reproduced within these pages. They are invaluable in that they form a record that is indicative of the evolution of the 8ft 0in. 'Singles' (other than the three rebuilds of 1870) but misleading in as much that they give a false impression of the number of livery styles in use during these years. I also mentioned earlier that *Lord of the Isles* was quite possibly unique in that she retained her iron-framed tender for her whole working life and into preservation.

In fact, the story begins with a change of name. The original intention was to call the engine *Charles Russell* after the GWR's much respected chairman. He, however, declined the honour and so *Lord of the Isles* was chosen instead. This was a hereditary title, of Scottish origin, of the Prince of Wales and was also the name given to a racehorse that was well known in the 1850s. The name thus combined royal lineage with the implication of speed, so could not have been a more appropriate choice.

It was Brunel who proposed that the engine should represent the company at the Great Exhibition and what better choice could there be than the latest member of a class of engines that were rightly regarded as the fastest man-made machines in the world. Yet for all its beautiful finish and impressive dimensions, it failed to be awarded a Council Medal, the top award. This went instead to Thomas Crampton's *Liverpool*, which had been built by Bury, Curtis & Kennedy in 1848 for the Southern Division of the L&NWR. Gooch had to be satisfied with a bronze, which he was far from impressed by. His 1851 diary entry expressed his feelings in forthright terms:

'The Great Western Co. sent a locomotive, the *Lord of the Isles*, one of our large class of passenger engines and I am safe in saying she was a beautiful job and has ever since done her work on the line satisfactorily. This cannot be said for most of the engines exhibited. I got a medal for her but the highest class medal was given to Crampton for an engine certainly the most faulty in construction exhibited and which has never since been repeated in this country. So much for the opinion of judges at such exhibitions; favour has generally too large a share in the award of prizes.'

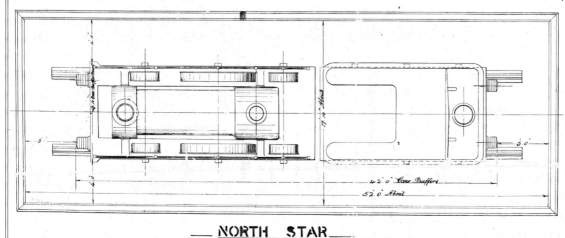

__LORD OF THE ISLES__

__NORTH STAR__

This diagram, produced on 22nd September 1892, shows the profiles from above of both *Lord of the Isles*, top, and *North Star*, below. They were clearly prepared for exhibition purposes, probably to aid those involved in the construction of the display stand, with both engines being transported across the Atlantic for the World's Columbian Exposition, a fair held from 1st May to 30th October 1893 in Chicago, to celebrate the 400th anniversary of Christopher Columbus's voyage to America.

LORD *of the* ISLES' TENDER.

Tenders of this type were built for all of the 8ft 'Singles' but were replaced by the 'Express Tenders' (page 105) from the early 1850s onward. Known also as 'Iron Framed' tenders, one remained attached to *Lord of the Isles* throughout its working life and into preservation,

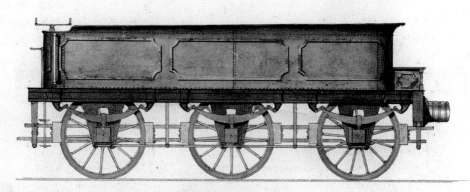

DESCRIPTION

WHEELS. *Six Wheels 4 feet in diam*? TANK *16 feet 6 in? long 8 feet 4 in? wide and 2 feet 7½ in? deep ; less coke space, 7 feet 3 in? long, and 4 feet 2 in? wide by 2 feet 7½ in? deep.*
COKE-SPACE *79·3 cub. feet* WATER SPACE *360·9 cub. feet. Contains 1760 gallons of Water .*
WEIGHT *when empty on Leading Wheels 3 tons 6 cwt 2 qrs Driving 2 tons 5 cwt. Trailing 3 tons 10 cwt 1 qrs Total. 9. 1. 3*
WEIGHT *when loaded on Leading Wheels 6 tons 2 cwt 1 qr. Driving 5 tons 12 cwt 2 qt. „ 5 tons 9 cwt 3 qrs Total. 17. 4. 2.*

One can understand Gooch's feelings, for *Liverpool* did prove to be something of a 'white elephant', yet resplendent in its bronze green livery with all its brightwork highly polished it must have been an impressive sight even if it did flatter to deceive.

As we have seen, the entry of *Lord of the Isles* into traffic in July 1852 was shortly thereafter attended with painful circumstances. Fortunately, there was no loss of life in the Aynho accident and the engine only suffered superficial damage, which was soon repaired. Thereafter it went into regular traffic but was always first choice for any Royal or other prestigious working. One such was the special train – which included some minor royalty – which brought the 1st Guards Division back to London from Plymouth following the conclusion of the Crimea War. This war was brought to an end in March 1856 and the soldiery were returned home via a series of special trains over the following months. There is a famous photograph of the engine, adorned in flags and a crowned headlight of exceptional proportions, on Westbourne Park shed. The occasion has often been mistaken for a visit by the Shah of Persia in 1873, a misunderstanding which was perpetuated by the GWR itself, who published the photograph in the April 1912 edition of the *GWR Magazine* with this inaccurate caption. Clearly no one thought to question the display of flags, which included the French, Turkish and Sardinian colours but not the Persian! This would have been a strange choice to welcome the Shah, who was well known for his bellicosity. Also, apart from the Prince of Wales and other British royalty, the Czar of all the Russians was a passenger too and he would not have been amused by the omission of his standard. Yet the inclusion of

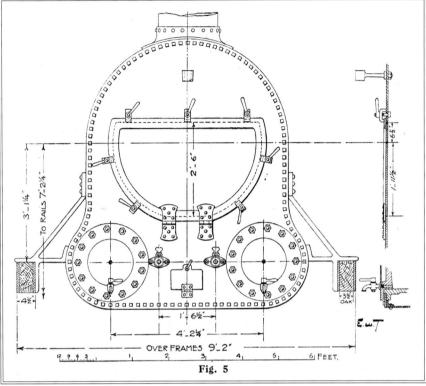

Fig. 5

ABOVE: E.W. Twining's drawing showing the original form of *Lord of the Isles'* smokebox door, which was hinged at the bottom.

BELOW: This 'retouched' photograph is, as far as I can be certain, the oldest that we possess of *Lord of the Isles* and shows it in what must be 'as built' condition or at least very nearly so. I would suggest that it was taken following the repairs necessitated by the accident at Aynho on 20th October 1852. Certainly, the general condition of the engine is consistent with this dating and the lining of the tender, which is in three panels with scalloped corners, supports this contention. The chimney cap is also unpolished and there is no sign of a cab spectacle plate or the large sandbox next to the driving wheel – all fittings that would very soon be making an appearance.

Another well known view, showing *Lord of the Isles* posed in front of St. Mark's Church at Swindon in perhaps 1854 or thereabouts. The engine had probably just emerged from its first heavy repair and has acquired a large sandbox in front of the driving splasher. Most significantly perhaps, the tender frame has the bell for the Harrison chord warning system attached to it. These were first fitted in 1854 and in theory at least rendered the travelling porter's role redundant. In fact, *Lord of the Isles*' tender, which was unique to the engine, retained the porters 'coffin' until it was broken up in 1906.

this photograph led to some interesting letters in subsequent issues of the magazine, none of which questioned the accuracy or otherwise of the caption but that did throw some light on the working of the Shah's train in 1873 hauled by *Lord of the Isles* from Paddington to Windsor. The fireman that day was James Henderson, later an inspector at Swindon, and he wrote in the June 1912 edition of the *GWR Magazine*:

'*I have good reason for remembering the day the photograph was taken* [he was of course misled about this] *June 24th 1873. We left Paddington with the Shah of Persia, the late King Edward with Queen Alexandra, and the late Czar of Russia and his Consort on the train, attended by many distinguished persons. In honour of the Shah's visit a great review was being held at Windsor, and many excursion trains were being run. All went well with the train until we were passing through Slough Station. At that time there was no 'locking gear' there and trains had to pass from the down main line and go through the down platform road to reach Windsor. At the western end of the platform there was a pair of points turned by hand, which led either to Windsor or across the Windsor Branch to the main line. On passing through Slough Station I noticed that these points were wrong, being set for the main line instead of for Windsor. I shouted to my driver "Whoa mate, the points are wrong", and we stopped the train just in time to avert a collision with an empty train coming from Windsor. We put the train back over the* points, *and I jumped down and turned the points myself, the man whose duty it was to attend to them being so overcome that he was unable to do any more work. Mr Tyrrell (then Superintendent of the Line) was on the platform and witnessed the whole affair. He got on the engine and rode with us to Windsor. After we started from Slough, he enquired from my driver who had first noticed that the points were wrongly set, and the engineman, who was Jos Groves, replied "My fireman sir". Mr Tyrrell turned to me and expressed his pleasure at my having observed the position of the points. Subsequently I was sent to Swindon to see Mr Joseph Armstrong (late Locomotive Superintendent) who promised that I should receive recognition for the occurrence. Shortly afterwards I was promoted to be a driver, and before long made a driver on the broad gauge expresses, being the youngest man ever promoted to that position. Many people wondered at the time at my early promotion, but it was the prevention of this collision that led to it. It may be imagined that the occasion on which this photograph was taken stands out as a red letter day in my life. I may say that during my service with the Company I had the good fortune to be the means of preventing five other collisions with passenger trains.*'

Henderson's claim that he was the youngest ever broad gauge driver was challenged by other correspondents, who made the accurate observation that many of the early drivers, recruited from the north, were in their 20s and even late teens. Yet in 1873

Perhaps the best known of all the extant photographs of *Lord of the Isles* and the most misrepresented, this astonishing image is full of interest. We know that it was taken in the late spring or early summer of 1856 and commemorates the return of the Guards Division from the Crimean War. The train originated at Plymouth and was worked from Bristol by *Lord of the Isles*, whilst the photograph was taken in Westbourne Park yard in exactly the same position as that of *Sultan*. There are six flags of which five are identifiable: By the smokebox is the flag of Sardinia, by the footplate the Union Flag and the Royal Standard, and on the rear of the tender the French Tricolour and the Turkish Star & Crescent. These are the flags of the Allies who were involved in the Crimean conflict. The sixth flag is almost certainly that of Piedmont, who combined their army with that of Sardinia and fought alongside the Allies, suffering 10,000 casualties in the process. Evidently members of the Royal Family were on the train, hence the Royal Insignia and the extraordinary headlamp, which seems to represent the orb and crown. From the locomotive history point of view, the engine, which had obviously been

specially prepared mechanically for the occasion, had received a copper top to the chimney, a spectacle plate and the whistles had been repositioned on top of the firebox. The engine had also been repainted and the polished boiler bands are elaborately lined on either side. The lining is painted on the boiler cladding rather than on the bands themselves and seems to consist of a black line on either side edged in white. The tender lining is also newly applied in a non-standard style which comprised a thick straw or light Pea green line, edged probably in black, though it is very hard to be sure. Note the leather bucket with painted GWR lettering hanging from the handrail by the side of the firebox. According to the April 1912 edition of the *GWR Magazine*, the people standing alongside the engine are, from left to right: Mr Kirtley, Locomotive Superintendent (in top hat); foreman J. Heppel; foreman Turner; fireman Hetherington; driver unnamed but believed to be Michael Almond; and foreman Hammond. The District Locomotive Superintendent's house is the large detached villa on the left and Kirtley's son can seen watching the occasion from the window on the right.

This photograph, taken in the yard to the west end of the Swindon Works and shed complex, shows *Lord of the Isles* following a further repaint and as running the later years of the 1850s – mechanically, little if anything has changed since the 1856 photograph was taken. One minor but important difference is the position of the Harrison chord bell on the tender framework, which had been moved closer to the footplate, and the small sandboxes on the front end of the footplate have also been removed. The style of lining on the tender had also changed. There were now three main panels with a fourth carried around the curved front of the tender tank. However, the light colour of this lining is hard to accurately ascertain – was it straw or light Pea green? In fact, one may describe the other, as dried peas are almost straw coloured! It is possible to see that the panels are edged in black and are 'scafed' (to refresh, 'scafed' was where the black line changed from outside to inside the panels at the corners). Interestingly, the engine seems to be 'coaled' with both coal and coke, a combination that was in general use from the late 1850s until coke was rendered superfluous in the mid-1860s. At this time *Lord of the Isles* was regularly allocated to Swindon shed, the only member of the class normally in residence there. Apart from regular workings on the main line and its frequent special duties, it is also known to have worked over the Wilts, Somerset & Weymouth line and is said by W.E. Edwards to have even occasionally reached Weymouth itself.

Lord of the Isles is seen here, at an unknown location (beside a turntable pit?), fitted with a new chimney sporting the shallow lipped cap typical of the late 1860s and early '70s but otherwise the engine's mechanical condition is little different from that visible in the previous illustrations. However, the lining on the tender has changed again and is now of the standard pattern of the period, with a Pea green inner panel picked out in the scafed style with black and white lining. Note that the photograph has been retouched at some stage to pick out the top of the boiler, firebox and dome.

it was most unusual for such a young man to achieve such status, an accolade of which Mr Henderson could be rightly proud.

Although *Lord of the Isles* was a general traffic locomotive, it was used whenever possible for royal duties, many of which, as the standard gauge encroached ever more, were between Paddington and Windsor or vice versa. These came to an abrupt end in 1874, when the GWR built at Swindon a new, standard gauge Royal Saloon for the Queen's use. It was so much preferred by Queen Victoria she ordained that it should henceforth be her chosen mode of travel, thus rendering the broad gauge vehicle redundant other than for possible workings west of Exeter. The engine's relationship with Windsor continued, however. In 1859, Daniel Gooch bought a house at Clewer and though he left the service of the GWR in 1864, he returned in 1865 as Chairman of the Board of Directors, a position he held until his death in 1889. Naturally he travelled up to 'town' on a daily basis. Out of respect for his sensibilities, a broad gauge express was retained in the working time table at a time suitable to his needs which, in its later years of service, is said to have been regularly worked by *Lord of the Isles*.

As previously suggested, *Lord of the Isles*, whilst exhibiting many variations of the standard livery of the time, remained surprisingly little altered mechanically and physically. It was built with the original sanding arrangement but this was soon altered. By 1856 it had acquired a polished cap to its chimney, though whether this was iron or brass is unclear. By the mid 1850s, the engine had acquired a spectacle plate and by the 1860s or early '70s, a shallow copper topped chimney. Presumably injectors were fitted at much the same time. Improved lubrication in the form of oil boxes and Roscoe lubricators appeared progressively from the late 1860s, and a final alteration was made to the tender footsteps in the last few years that the engine was in service, though the tender always retained the porter's 'coffin'. After withdrawal, *Lord of the Isles* spent twenty-two years in preservation, during which time it acquired a Dean chimney, a dished smokebox door with a steel polished ring and had its large sandbox, adjacent to the driving wheel, removed. During this time, it also became an exhibition engine once again, appearing at Edinburgh in 1890, Chicago in 1893, Cardiff in 1896 and Earls Court in 1897, often in company with *North Star*. Regrettably, both engines were broken up in 1906, a decision that was almost instantly regretted. Few parts survived, most significantly being the driving wheels and crank axle. Thankfully these remain today, in the entrance hall of the Steam Museum at Swindon. Next time you pay that emporium a visit, stop and wonder; those wheels were made in the workshops, close to where they now stand, in 1851.

Westbourne Park yard again, with *Lord of the Isles* based at the shed here during its latter years. The photograph must date from about 1882 – note the later pattern of headlamps and whilst the engine still carries the Armstrong chimney of the earlier pattern, it has additional lubricators on top and on the side of the smokebox. Clearly visible in the picture is the driving wheel axlebox cover, which doubled as a works plate and was engraved for the Great Exhibition of 1851.

This 'Works Grey' photograph probably dates from just after *Lord of the Isles* was taken out of service in June 1884. A careful inspection of the engine's condition suggest that it is less than exhibition standard, with ingrained dirt in various places and unpolished fittings and pipework. If I am correct in making this assumption, the comparison with the previous picture will show that during the engine's last overhaul, a new chimney and probably a new smokebox door were fitted. *Lord of the Isles* would also have acquired the post-1880 livery with Venetian red frames, and chrome and black lining on the boiler and tender. It is said that the engine was still carrying its 1851 boiler when withdrawn.

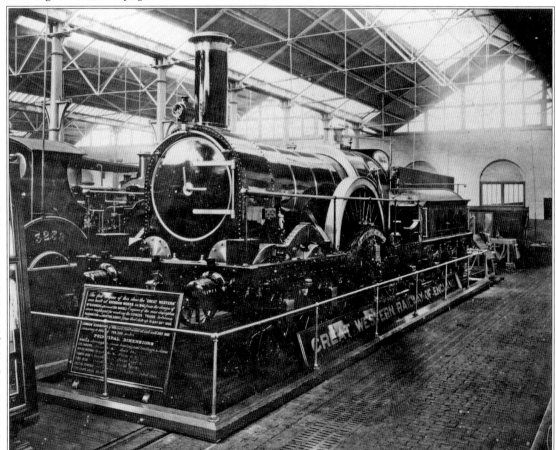

This lovely photograph was taken in the Paint Shop at Swindon when *Lord of the Isles* was being prepared to be shipped to the USA for the 1893 Chicago Exhibition. The engine to the left is '3232' Class 2-4-0 No. 3239, which was built in November 1892 and so helps to date the picture. The general condition of *Lord of the Isles* is that at the time of its withdrawal from traffic, though the Roscoe lubricators have been removed from the smokebox. When you see a beautiful image like this you realise what a terrible sin it was to break the engine up.

This engraving of *Lord of the Isles* shows the engine as prepared for the Edinburgh International Exhibition of 1890. Held between 1st May and 1st November and otherwise known as the International Exhibition of Science, Art & Industry it was organised to mark the opening of the Forth Bridge one year earlier. Unique amongst the class, the engine did not carry a works plate but instead the details of its construction were engraved on the driving wheel axle box cover: 'MANUFACTURED BY THE GREAT WESTERN RAILWAY COMPANY – 1851 – SWINDON WORKS'. One of these covers was saved along with the nameplate and are now in Swindon's Steam Museum (see picture on page 147).

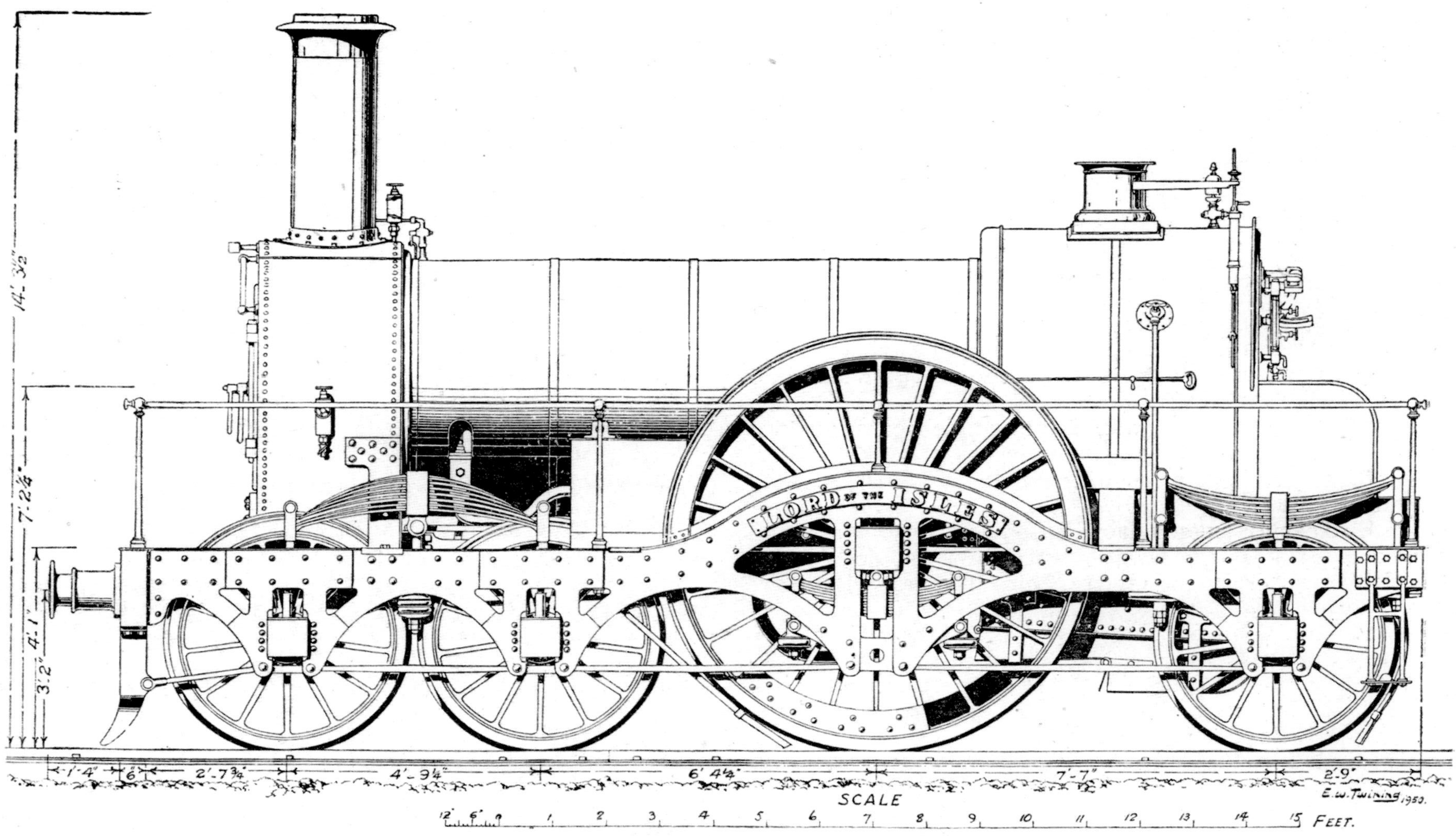

Fig. 1

E.W. Twining's drawing of *Lord of the Isles* depicts the engine at the time of its withdrawal in 1884. Note that it bears a marked similarity to the engraving on the previous page. This drawing, along with those on pages 104, 118, 128 and 140, accompanied an article by Twining entitled the 'Great Western Railway Broad Gauge 8ft Singles' published in the 15th December 1950 issue of *The Locomotive Magazine.*

Front and end elevations of *Lord of the Isles* at the time of its withdrawal.

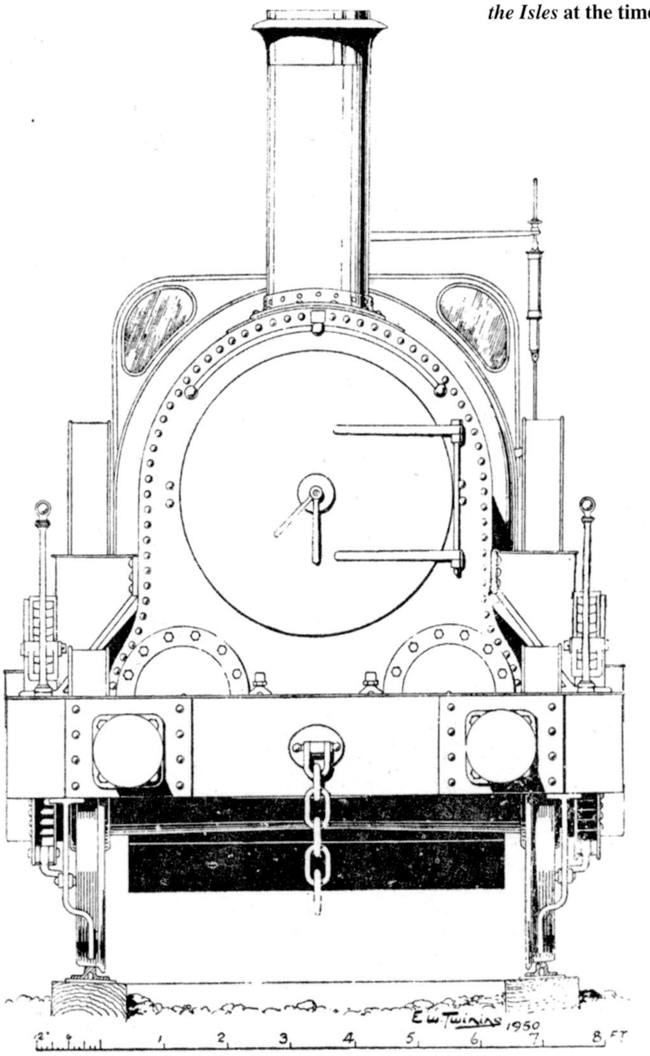

Fig. 2

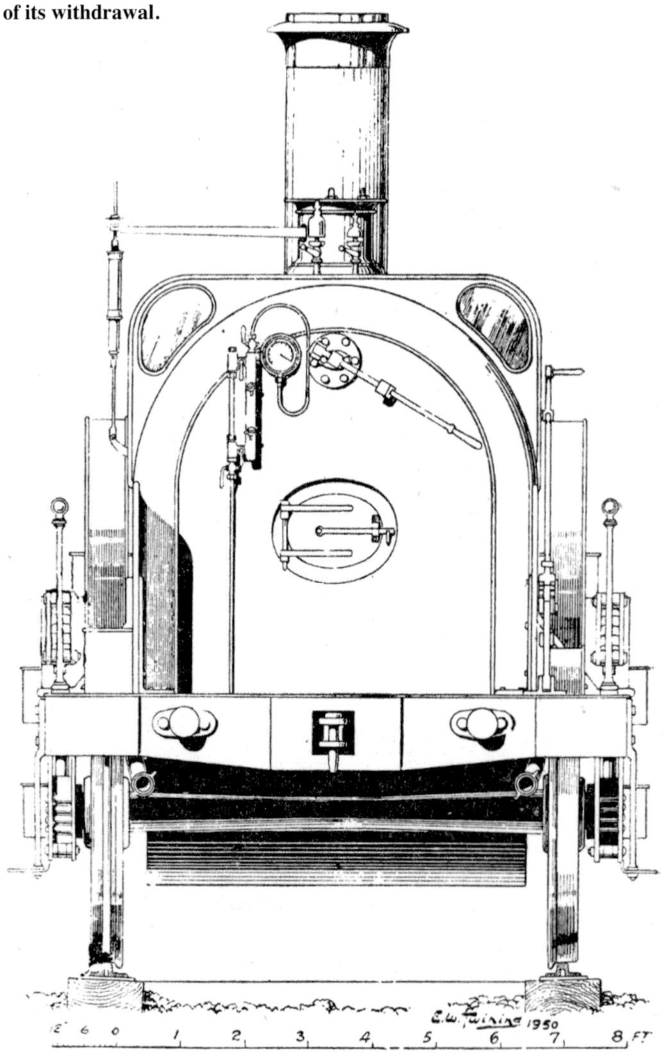

Fig. 3

Early Testing and Running

On Sunday 25th April 1847, *Iron Duke* was tested on Sapperton Bank, albeit before the engine was formally named and before it entered traffic, the tests therefore being in the nature of 'Works Trials'. Several runs were made up and down, first as a light engine then with increasing loads up to 60 tons on the drawbar. Presumably weather and track conditions were good, because the engine is reported to have ascended the bank with this load at a speed of 36 miles per hour.

The engine entered service the following week, on the Duke of Wellington's birthday which was 1st May (Ahrons and others are incorrect saying that he was born on 29th April). The *London Evening Standard* for Monday 3rd May 1847 gives an account of the run, which was from Swindon to Paddington on the 10.00am Up Exeter express. Having given full particulars of the dimensions of the new engine, the paper continued:

'*The* Iron Duke *took the first trip from Swindon with the train that leaves Exeter at 10 in the morning. The train consisted of six carriages, weighing about 60 tons. In a run of about 13 miles to the Faringdon*

Road station a maximum speed of about 57 miles per hour was attained. At Reading eight additional carriages were attached making the total weight of the train about 120 tons. With this load the maximum speed (upon a falling gradient of four feet per mile) over the mile between the 26th and 27th mile post from Paddington was 51.42mph and for the last quarter of the mile 56mph. At this moment one of the eccentrics worked loose and the speed immediately fell below 40mph. This derangement of the eccentric, which occasioned a stoppage of 18 minutes at Maidenhead, prevented the full power of the engine being brought into operation and the rest of the journey was performed at a running average velocity of about 45 miles per hour. The engine was remarkably steady, at the maximum speed of 56mph; and making allowance for the stiffness with which a new engine always works, we have no doubt, judging from the evidence given on Saturday of its capabilities.*'

The final section of the Cheltenham & Great Western Union Railway opened for traffic on 23rd October 1847. A Directors' special train was run from Paddington at 10.10am with *Great Britain*, driven by Daniel Gooch, at its head. The engine worked the train throughout its journey from London to Cheltenham and returned later the same day with its trainload of well fed but no doubt weary guests. Whilst in Cheltenham, the arrangements that had been put in place for mixed gauge working into Gloucester were inspected, a second special train taking them to the junction where Brunel was on hand to explain how the system worked. *Great Britain* performed her part in the day's events in exemplary fashion, though the weather, which was wet, caused difficulties with adhesion. Consequently, the initial aim of running the train nonstop from Paddington to Swindon had to be abandoned and a stop for water was made at Didcot. A strong side wind also played its part in holding the progress of the train back. Despite this, Cheltenham, 121 miles from Paddington, was reached in 2 hours 45 minutes. On the return journey good speed was made as far as Maidenhead despite stops being made at Stroud, Swindon, Shrivenham, Didcot and Reading. Thereafter, the special found itself delayed by an ordinary train which meant a late arrival at Paddington. Despite no less than five stops mainly to set down directors – Lord Barrington left the train at Shrivenham – and to take water, Maidenhead was reached in 2 hours 7 minutes running time, an excellent performance. On the Down journey, the *London Evening Standard* reported that Gooch was accompanied by Francis Trevithick of the Grand Junction Railway, who shared the footplate with him.

As further members of the class entered service, there was much interest in their achievements, which the papers duly reported upon. It must be remembered that each engine had its own crew and there seems to have been an outbreak of competition between the various enginemen to see who could run the fastest, particularly between Paddington and Didcot. The fast morning express to Exeter left Paddington at 9.45am, though from December 1847 this was retimed to 9.50am when ten minutes was knocked off the running time to the Didcot stop, which was brought forward from 10.50 to 10.45. The distance from the old Paddington station to Didcot was $52^7/\text{s}$ miles and the journey was made non stop against a slightly rising gradient. It must be admitted that, by later standards, trains weights were very light, usually about 60 tons and rarely exceeding 100 tons, yet even allowing for this, the new engines achieved some exceptional timings. The fifty-five minutes allowed (from December 1847) was frequently bettered, culminating in a run made on 11th May 1848. In the edition of the *Great Western Railway Magazine* for October 1912, an interesting letter from a Richard Robinson of 96 Goldsmith Avenue, Acton appears, giving much information about Michael Almond, the driver of *Great Britain*, and the events of that day. He writes:

'*It was about the year 1847 that Mr Daniel Gooch (afterwards Sir Daniel) designed broad gauge passenger engines having driving wheels 8ft diameter which became so popular throughout the railway world.*

When these fine engines first made their appearance, the enginemen were naturally proud of them and vied with each other in their attempts to obtain the best speed results. In those days the first express left Paddington at 9.45am and was timed to run to Didcot, $53^1/\text{4}$ miles distant, without an intervening stop. The drivers who worked this train with the new engines used to discuss among themselves the times in which they had, individually, completed the distance between Paddington and Didcot. Michael Almond was one of these men and he determined to show that

his engine, the Great Britain, *could outstrip all others. On the morning therefore of May 14th 1848 he, with the* Great Britain, *left Paddington with five carriages and a guards van at 9.45am and stopped at Didcot at 10.32am thus having covered the $53^1/\text{4}$ miles in 47 minutes giving an average speed including starting and stopping of 68 miles per hour – surely a remarkable performance.*

Unknown to the engineman his chief superintendent, Mr Daniel Gooch, was in the train. While the engine was taking water Mr Gooch, watch in hand, stepped up and said: 'Do you know Michael how long it is since you left Paddington?' Somewhat abashed at the unexpected appearance of his chief the engineman 'supposed that he had not lost any time!' 'Lost time!' exclaimed Mr Gooch 'Why man do you know that it was only forty-seven minutes since you left Paddington?' He then added by way of kindly admonition 'This is all very well Michael just for once to see what your engine can do, but it must not be repeated.'

This incident was related to me nearly forty years ago by old Michael himself.'

In later years the GWR published a certificate (below) detailing the events recorded above. This added a layer of confusion to an already, clearly demonstrated, faulty memory. The card stated that the train concerned on 11th May 1848 was the 9.15am departure for Bristol, not the 9.50 (inaccurately described above as 9.45) and that the train comprised of four coaches and a brake van, not five and a van as stated in the letter. Furthermore, a letter from the Reverend W. J. Scott, a famous timer of trains, appeared in the November 1912 *GWR Magazine*, accurately correcting the distances involved from the old Paddington station to Didcot as $52^7/\text{s}$ miles and amends the average speed if the time was exactly 47 minutes, to 67.5mph. It is not known exactly when the certificate was produced but it must have been after the 9.50 was taken off and replaced by the 9.15 to Bristol – which did not run in 1848. There is only one constant amongst all these contradictions and that is Gooch's assertion that the journey was completed in 47 minutes. In *The British Steam Locomotive 1825-1925*, E.L. Ahrons, tells us that the fireman of *Great Britain*, Richard Denham (who in later years he knew), was adamant that the 47 minutes record was truly achieved. However, the writer was evidently sceptical of this claim and muddied the waters by stating that *Great Britain* covered the 53 miles in $47^1/\text{2}$ minutes at a start to stop average of 66.9mph, which proves that Ahron's

memory was not infallible either. As if damning the achievement with faint praise, he wrote: '*It is just within the bounds of possibility that this may have been done with one of the very light trains of those days, but there is no authentic confirmation of the performance, which was never repeated*'.

I wonder if he would have been brave enough to face Sir Daniel Gooch with his scepticism? What is more, if contemporary newspaper reports are to be believed, there was substantial evidence of very fast runs on the 9.50 from Paddington, even if they did not quite equal Great Britain's record. For example, the *London Evening Standard* reported that on Thursday 27th April 1848:

'SPEED AND POWER OF THE LOCOMOTIVE

FIFTY-THREE MILES WITHIN FIFTY MINUTES

This extraordinary performance was achieved yesterday morning [Wednesday 26th April] *with the usual 9.50 down express train from Paddington. The train consisted of five carriages weighing about 50 tons, and was attached to the* Emperor, *one of the new class of eight feet driving wheel engines with 18 inch cylinders and 24 inch stroke. The train started from Paddington at 9.51.55 and the engine entered Didcot Station precisely at 10.41.45, having therefore run the 53 miles in 49 minutes 55 seconds or at a rate of 64 miles an hour for the whole distance. The greater portion of the journey between the fourth mile post and Reading was performed at nearly 70 miles an hour and several miles were gone over each in 49 seconds, the engine never going over a mile in 48 seconds or at the rate of 75 miles per hour. We believe this speed is the greatest ever maintained, even on the broad gauge.*'

Furthermore, the *Morning Herald* reported that on 29th August 1848, *Courier*, driven by John Heppell and with the L&NWR's '*crack driver*' Jonas Brown on the footplate – an invitation which had been sanctioned by Gooch – completed the journey start to stop in 49 minutes 13 seconds at an average speed of 64.3mph, with 43 miles of the journey said to have been covered at an average of 70.2mph.

The running in the Up direction between Swindon and Paddington was equally good. Working in this direction the falling gradient is in the train's favour, as is evidenced by a report in the *London Evening Standard* of 14th June 1847. Under the heading '*BROAD GAUGE PERFORMANCES*', it reported:

'*It is known that the* Iron Duke, *one of the new eight wheeled locomotives on the Great Western took the express from London to Swindon, a distance of 77 miles, in 71 minutes and from Swindon to London in 70 minutes stopping at Didcot both times. The maximum velocity is said to be nearly 80 miles an hour, maintaining for 8 miles together a rate of 75 miles, and averaging over the whole distance, including twice starting and twice coming to rest a rate of 66 miles per hour – an unrivalled performance for a new engine and having the whole length of boiler, firebox and smokebox within the front and back axles. The steadiness of the engine at these high velocities surprised even those accustomed to other broad gauge engines. The* Great Western *locomotive which has been at work for some time, now also works well and fully rivals the performance of* Iron Duke.'

Notable in this account is the description of *Iron Duke* having the '*whole length of the boiler, firebox and smokebox within the front and back axles*'. This contrasts with other contemporary designs such as the Stephenson 'Long Boiler' engines, where the firebox

was placed behind the rear axle. The steadiness of *Iron Duke's* running, so pointedly mentioned here, was evidently intended to endorse Gooch's design philosophy. It is also interesting to read that *Great Western* 'now also works well'.

A little earlier I mentioned the run of *Courier*, with L&NWR driver Jonas Brown on the footplate, between Paddington and Didcot in late August 1848. On that occasion the engine worked the train as far as Swindon and then returned with the balanced working which, from the Didcot stop to Paddington, was completed in the astonishing time of 49 minutes 13 seconds at an average speed of 67 miles an hour. The report appears in the *Evening Standard* of Tuesday 29th August 1848, which goes on to note that, from the 47th mile post to the 4th, a distance of 43 miles, was performed in 36 minutes 44 seconds at an average speed of upwards of 70 miles per hour. The report continues: '*The whole journey from Swindon* [77 miles] *to London was scarcely less extraordinary than that from Didcot to London. The train left Swindon at 3.9.1pm stopped at Didcot 5 minutes 35 seconds and reached Paddington at 4.28.13. The 77 miles were therefore gone over in 78 minutes 29 seconds including the 5 minutes 35 seconds stoppage at Didcot. The thirteen miles from the twenty-ninth to the sixteenth mile post was performed at the rate of upwards of seventy-two miles per hour*'.

Something exceptional was obviously anticipated, because the paper had sent its own reporter to time the train and a very detailed log of the fastest part of the journey, between Didcot and Paddington, appeared in the article. I am not a train performance specialist but I would hazard a guess that this is one of the first such logs, measured from milepost to milepost, which we possess. It is not known how the log was taken but the recorder must have had the use of at least two stopwatches to make such accurate measurements one would suppose. Since it is of such historical importance the timings, as published by the paper, are given in **Table 6.8**, page right.

To put these times into context, the inaugural timings of the 'Cheltenham Flyer' in 1923, from Swindon to Paddington, non-stop, was 75 minutes!

Gooch was perhaps the first mechanical engineer to attempt what later would be known as 'controlled road testing'. He was also a copious keeper of records, relating to operating costs, which led him to conduct a series of tests between Paddington and Bristol with various members of the 'Iron Duke' and 'Courier' classes, as well as *Great Western*. From these tests a table was prepared, which first appeared in D.K. Clark's *Railway Machinery* in 1855 and are repeated in MacDermot's *History of the Great Western Railway Vol. 1*, as revised by C.R. Clinker.

Ahrons comments that, '*the tables are interesting as showing the high average rates of speed attained by the express trains of 1847 to 1849. But the loads were extremely light, since none of the trains, after deducting the weight of engine and tender, attained 60 tons. For these loads the coke consumption was high*'. Elsewhere he observes that, for coke burning, the firebox of *Iron Duke* was really too big, while there was a tendency to overfire the rear portion of the grate behind the midfeather. For coal burning, however, they proved ideal, particularly after the midfeather was removed. Ahrons continues, '*The highest known maximum speed ever recorded with these engines in*

TABLE 6.8: COURIER RUN FROM DIDCOT TO PADDINGTON AUGUST 1848		
STARTED FROM DIDCOT 3.39.17PM *(i.e. 3.39 & 17 seconds)*		
MILE POST	SECONDS PER MILE	MPH
53		
52		
51		
50	64	56.3
49	59¼	61.8
48	56¼	64
47	55½	64.8
46	55	65.5
45	54½	66
44	54¼	66.3
43	54	66.6
42	53¾	66.9
41	52½	68.5
40	52½	68.5
39	51¾	69.5
38	51¼	70.2
37	52¼	68.9
36	52¾	68.2
35	52¾	68.2
34	52¼	63.9
33	52	69.2
32	51¼	70.2
31	51¼	70.2
30	51¼	70.2
29	50¾	70.9
28	49¾	72.3
27	49¾	72.3
26	49½	72.7
25	48¾	73.8
24	48¾	73.8
23	49	73.5
22	49½	72.7
21	49½	72.7
20	49½	72.7
19	50	72
18	50	72
17	49¾	72.7
16	50	72
15	50½	71.2
14	51	70.6
13	51	70.6
12	51¼	70.2
11	51¼	70.2
10	51	70.6
9	51	70.6
8	51¼	70.2
7	51¼	70.2
6	51¼	70.2
5	51	70.6
4	53½	67.2
3	55	65.5
2	63	57.1
1	71	50.7
ARRIVED AT PADDINGTON 4.28.13		

TABLE 6.9: EXPRESS TRAIN PERFORMANCE 1847 AND 1849				
1. RESULTS OF PERFORMANCES WITH EXPRESS TRAINS BETWEEN PADDINGTON AND SWINDON DURING AUGUST AND SEPTEMBER 1847				
	SPEED & WEIGHT		CONSUMPTION OF WATER & COAL	
NAME OF ENGINE	AVERAGE SPEED WEIGHT ENGINE TENDER & TRAIN MILES PER HOUR	AVERAGE GROSS MILE TONS	AVERAGE COKE PER OF COKE POUNDS	WATER PER LB POUNDS	TEMPERATURE OF WATER IN TENDER DEG. FAHR.
Great Britain	51	103.5	34.4	8.23	109°
Iron Duke	53.4	105	36.6	8.4	91°
Great Western	53	106	36.2	7.4	144°
2. RESULTS OF PERFORMANCES WITH EXPRESS TRAINS BETWEEN PADDINGTON AND BRISTOL DURING MARCH & APRIL 1849				
Wizard	50.19	108.7	38.51	7.04	Temperature
Dragon	51.5	104.2	31.1	7.37	not
Hirondelle	51.5	101	35.4	6.8	given
Tartar	50.19	100.7	37.3	6.28	
Lightning	50.23	101	34.58	7.65	
Rougemont	44.54	101	31.07	7.55	
Emperor	51.3	104.2	38.16	7.36	
Pasha	49.6	101	37.7	8.1	Temperature
Courier	50.19	106	34.26	7.55	not
Wizard	53.1	101	34.4	7.2	given
Warlock	51	101	32.1	8.04	
Dragon	50.3	101	29.4	7.8	
Emperor	49.37	109.2	39	7.28	Temperature
Sultan	50.1	104.2	34.4	7.8	not
Lightning	52.3	104.7	36.1	7.68	given
Pasha	50.9	106	38.7	6.9	
Rougemont	51.9	101	34.3	7.2	
Courier	51.4	104.2	38.16	6.64	
The average weight of engine and tender was 50 tons. The three sections of Table 2 refer to tests with three different qualities of coke.				

the old days was about 78.2 miles per hour down the Wootton Bassett bank of 1 in 100 and this was registered when Brunel and Gooch were testing the engines at the time they were new'. The tables referred to are of considerable interest and are reproduced in **Table 6.9**, above.

There are many other contemporary newspaper reports which give information about the early achievements of the 8ft 0in. 'Singles' but the stories recounted above suffice to give a vivid picture, I hope, of the breadth and depth of the significant impact which the introduction of *Iron Duke* and her sisters had, not only on the GWR but nationally and internationally. Without any doubt these magnificent engines were responsible for working the fastest trains in the world between 1847 and 1852. Thereafter, the economic situation of the country at large and the GWR in particular demanded a severe retrenchment. The train service was cut back and timings increased; for a time in the late 1850s, the old 9.50 Exeter express, known as 'The Flying Dutchman' from 1850, was taken off. The engines continued to work all the best trains for decades to come but their glory days were those of the late 1840s and early '50s when the modern express train, as we understand it today, was created on the Great Western Railway.

Plan of that portion of the Line on w...

Section of...

Experiments with *Great Britain*

Between 1848 and 1850, Gooch used *Great Britain* for a series of tests to determine the potential power output of the engine and to ascertain the optimum size of the blast pipe and choke of the chimney. There was also the question of the valve settings which, of course, affect fuel economy. In addition to these important factors there was, in 1846, the pressing matter of the calculation of wind resistance, which affected the running of trains at differing speeds and thus also has an important economic impact. This latter area of interest and debate acquired particular importance during the gauge controversy. Gooch had made some calculations with *Ixion* of the 'Fire Fly' Class, which suggested that the broad gauge offered an advantage in this quarter but his claim was challenged in a paper given to the Institution of Civil Engineers on 26th May 1846 by the classically trained engineer Wyndham Harding. The arguments were complicated, not least by the obvious desire of Harding to disprove Gooch's claims and, to this end, he was supported by Gooch's old foes Robert Stephenson, George Parker Bidder and John Scott Russell.

The power required to draw a train along a level line depends on the resistance offered by the atmosphere, and the friction of the bearings and wheels. Gooch, in his submission to the Gauge Commissioners, had claimed a figure of 18lbs a ton as the resistance at 60mph. Brunel had gone even further, stating that the Atmospheric System, on which he was then working, offered an even lower figure of 17lbs at a velocity of 60mph. Harding on the other hand, having garnered all the then available information, especially from the likes of Bidder and Russell, refuted these claims,

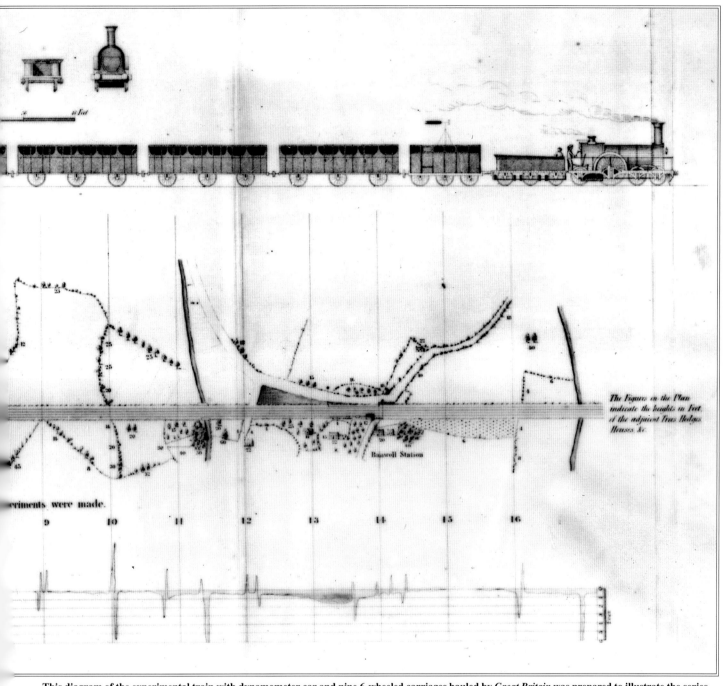

This diagram of the experimental train with dynamometer car and nine 6-wheeled carriages hauled by *Great Britain* was prepared to illustrate the series of tests that Gooch undertook between 1848 and 1850 over a 16-mile stretch of the Bristol & Exeter Railway of almost straight and level main line between Weston-super-Mare and Yatton. As the diagram indicates, Gooch was interested in refining the working of the engine and took special note of the steam distribution, efficiency of the valves, blast pipes, etc. He was also looking into other matters and was particularly anxious to devise a reliable formula for wind resistance relating to broad gauge trains, which was a matter of contentious debate at the time. He took considerable trouble over these tests, which won him much respect among his peers though not the universal approbation that he deserved. I find myself wondering what the rolling resistance of a train of nine 6-wheeled coaches all fitted with grease axleboxes and the dynamometer car would be? It must have been considerable but what a fine spectacle a train of these proportions would have made in the setting of the lush water meadows around this part of North Somerset. It would have been a thrilling sight to behold, for at the time it represented one of mankind's greatest technical and mechanical achievements. Banwell station, shown here on the right of the section of line depicted, had opened on 14th June 1841 but was subsequently renamed several times, becoming Worle in 1869, Puxton in 1884 and finally Puxton & Worle in 1922; it closed on 6th April 1964. The inset map right shows the general area, important because, as can be seen, Banwell station as shown on Gooch's plan was actually at Worle, some distance away from Banwell village, hence its later renaming. Banwell village later shared a station on the Cheddar Valley line with nearby Sandford.

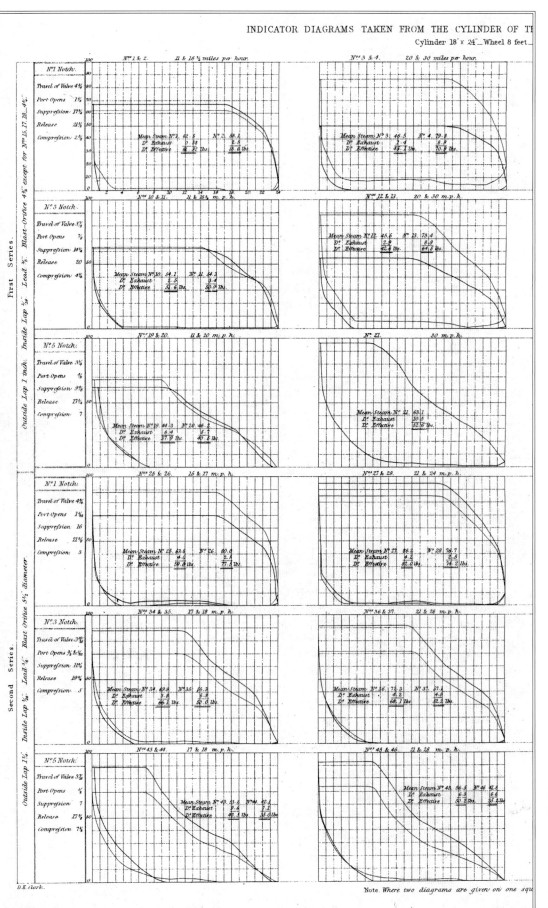

Cross section of *Great Britain*'s blast pipe.

Indicator diagram interpretation. There are many variables – engine speeds (10 speeds noted), cut off (3 variables), etc., and notes are made on lap and lead values throughout the diagrams.

HE GREAT BRITAIN LOCOMOTIVE, ON THE GREAT WESTERN RAILWAY IN 1847_49_50.

Steam ports 13" x 2", Exhaust port 13" x 3½". Lap & Blast-orifice varied.

DIAGRAM — PLATE IV.

Nos 5 & 6.   35 & 42 miles per hour.
Mean Steam Nº 5. 47.4   Nº 6. 48.7
Dº Exhaust   4.3   11.1
Dº Effective   43.1 lbs. 37.6 lbs.

Nos 7 & 8.   52.3 & 53.6 miles per hour.
Mean Steam Nº 7. 59.4   Nº 8. 60.0
Dº Exhaust   17.2   21.2
Dº Effective 42.2 lbs.   38.8 lbs.

Nº 9.   55 miles per hour.
Mean Steam Nº 9. 58.0
Dº Exhaust   19.5
Dº Effective 38.5 lbs.

Nos 14 & 15.   35 & 46 m.p.h.
Mean Steam Nº 14. 48.8   Nº 15. 59.3
Dº Exhaust   5.5   11.4
Dº Effective   43.3 lbs.   47.5 lbs.

Nos 16 & 17.   52.3 & 57 m.p.h.
Mean Steam Nº 16. 58.3   Nº 17. 61.6
Dº Exhaust   15.6   21.3
Dº Effective 42.7 lbs.   60.3 lbs.

Nº 18.   63 m.p.h.
Mean Steam Nº 18. 40.8
Dº Exhaust   12.0
Dº Effective 28.8 lbs.

Nº 22.   35 m.p.h.
Mean Steam Nº 22. 46.4
Dº Exhaust   8.1
Dº Effective   38.3 lbs.

Nº 23.   39 m.p.h.
Mean Steam Nº 23. 34.0
Dº Exhaust   8.0
Dº Effective   26.0 lbs.

Nº 24.   56.2 m.p.h.
Mean Steam Nº 24. 47.4
Dº Exhaust   17.7
Dº Effective 29.7 lbs.

Nos 29 & 30.   27 & 31 m.p.h.
Mean Steam Nº 29. 70.6   Nº 30. 79.6
Dº Exhaust   3.7   5.4
Dº Effective   66.9 lbs.   74.2 lbs.

Nos 31 & 32.   31 & 40 m.p.h.
Mean Steam Nº 31. 73.2   Nº 32. 51.4
Dº Exhaust   5.1   8.0
Dº Effective   68.1 lbs.   43.4 lbs.

Nº 33.   54 m.p.h.
Mean Steam Nº 33. 80.4
Dº Exhaust   12.8
Dº Effective 67.6 lbs.

Nos 38 & 39.   31 & 32 m.p.h.
Mean Steam Nº 38. 60.3   Nº 39. 74.4
Dº Exhaust   7.2   5.7
Dº Effective   53.1 lbs.   58.7 lbs.

Nos 40 & 41.   40 & 61 m.p.h.
Mean Steam Nº 40. 55.7   Nº 41. 49.1
Dº Exhaust   5.1   8.2
Dº Effective   50.6 lbs.   40.9 lbs.

Nº 42.   55 m.p.h.
Mean Steam Nº 42. 62.0
Dº Exhaust   11.2
Dº Effective 50.8 lbs.

Nos 47 & 48.   31 & 36 m.p.h.
Mean Steam Nº 47. 46.5   Nº 48. 39.0
Dº Exhaust   7.4   8.5
Dº Effective   39.1 lbs.   30.5 lbs.

Nº 49.   60 m.p.h.
Mean Steam Nº 49. 34.7
Dº Exhaust   8.5
Dº Effective 26.2 lbs.

Nº 50.   56 m.p.h.
Mean Steam Nº 50. 40.9
Dº Exhaust   11.5
Dº Effective 29.4 lbs.

are the figure in strong lines precedes in numerical order the one in light lines.

Engraved by J. W. Lowry.

ACKIE & SON, GLASGOW, EDINBURGH & LONDON.

Valve and Steam Ports of 'Great Britain.'

Quarter Size

Cross sections of *Great Britain*'s valve and steam ports.

suggesting that a more accurate figure would be in the region of 40lbs a ton at 60mph. Neither Gooch nor Brunel were present at the meeting when Harding gave his address but Gooch responded by letter, giving some more up to date figures obtained from experiments recently undertaken with *Great Western*. He admitted that the figures submitted to the Gauge Commissioners, derived from calculations made from limited data relating to *Ixion*, may have been on the low side. Yet he noted that more scientifically satisfactory calculations made from later testing showed a range of resistance at between 50 and 60mph of 23-30lb tons. These figures were later confirmed by the tests carried out on a flat stretch of the Bristol & Exeter main line between Yatton and Weston Junction with *Great Britain*. Gooch made forty-one runs over a measured mile, at speeds up to 62.4mph with trains weighing between 50 and 100 tons. The resistance figures which he obtained were similar to those of *Great Western* and therefore considerably lower than Harding's. Though vindicated, Gooch felt much aggrieved and when he later fell out with the Institution of Civil Engineers over another but related matter, in which he was certainly the innocent party, Gooch and the ICE parted company once and for all.

Despite these turbulent goings on, Gooch had risen to the top of his profession by demonstrating his intent to scientifically prove his findings and claims. To facilitate this, he had built at Swindon his famous dynamometer vehicle, which he used to great effect in this extended series of tests, along with *Great Britain*, during which he set standards of scientific excellence and impartiality which would stand the test of time. The engine was carefully prepared. Gooch not only wished to calculate the wind resistance but to look into the effectiveness of the valve gear and the efficiency of the cylinders by varying the lap of the valves. Small changes were also made to the diameter of the blast pipe and its height within the smokebox. To enable the cylinders to be 'indicated', i.e. measuring the variation in steam pressure at each stroke of the piston, Gooch designed and had built a cylinder pressure indicator. This beautifully made instrument still exists and is the property of the Science Museum. The cylinder pressure was measured by a spring-loaded piston whose movement was recorded on a chart, driven by the engine wheels and recorded by a pencil. Gooch obtained his results by mounting his indicator on the front of the locomotive and the mechanism was attached

to the cylinder by a tube. By these means Gooch was able to produce a series of test results which pushed the science of locomotive testing well into the future. He records in his diary:

'To enable me to do this satisfactorily I felt a complete series of experiments was necessary, and having the authority of the Board to spend what was necessary I designed and constructed an indicator to measure and accurately record the speed the train was running, and also on the same paper to record the tractive power used by the engine, measured by a spring; also on the same paper the force and direction of the wind ... To check the traction I also, at the same time, took indicator cards from the cylinder of the engine so as to accurately measure the power exerted there. It also gave me the power expended in moving and working the engine. I made a great number of experiments over a level piece of line on the Bristol and Exeter line at various rates of speed and loads. They gave me results very different from those obtained by the narrow gauge [i.e. Harding's calculations] *which however were done more by calculation than by actual experiment.'*

Gooch then goes on to describe his lecture at the Institution of Civil Engineers and some of the fall out of the discussions which fell short of the professional impartiality which should have been observed. He concluded: *'I still keep the original records of these experiments. They cost me a vast amount of labour both in calculations and in making the experiments. It was rather a difficult task to sit on the buffer beam of the engine and take indicator cards at speeds of 60 miles per hour.'*!

Gooch later gave the information that he had gathered to D.K. Clark, who published much of what he received in his well known *Locomotive Machinery* in 1855. There he reproduced the Indicator Diagrams taken from *Great Britain*'s cylinders, allowance being made for the variations in cut off and blast pipe modifications already referred to. The biggest problem that Gooch identified was the relative inefficiency of the slide valves at speeds above 55mph, though at the same speed, the drawbar horse power was measured at 767 tons, indicating a boiler performance equal to many designs of the early 20th century.

There is obviously much more that could be deduced from these experiments by those who are more competent interpreters than I. Therefore, all I can do is to refer you to Clark and Ahrons works, among many others and to D.K. Clark I will give the last word: *'Mr Daniel Gooch is the only experimentalist whose results are worthy of implicit confidence, for he operated with the trains precisely under the conditions of ordinary practise ... It is our conviction that they were conducted with the strictest impartiality and ... the apparatus was elaborated with the utmost care and consideration worthy of the high character of Mr Gooch as an experimentalist and observer'.*

Runaway Engines

The following tale is again from GWR District Locomotive Superintendent T. Houghton Wright's article published in the *Railway Magazine* of October 1898. He writes:

'In 1854 I did some amateur firing with John Hall of the Harpy *and met with several curious incidents. On Saturday June 17th 1854 the engine* Hirondelle *(driven by Robert Harle) was standing in the usual siding, the men being away in the cabin having their food. From some unforeseen cause the regulator flew open, and away she went up toward the station (the engine had been standing at the east end of Swindon Running Shed). The carriage department men were engaged in rolling a pair of wheels for a carriage and seeing the engine coming signalled to stop, but no notice was taken, the engine pushed the wheels aside and continued her course. A ballast engine* Ajax *(driver David Gibb) seeing what had happened followed and overtook the runaway at Farringdon Road (now Challow). Mr Appleby and Mr Andrews (the shed foreman and District Superintendent respectively) followed on the* Great Western *but before their arrival the engine was put in the siding, and my mate took the train up to Farringdon Road, and Harle and his mate came up and went on with their engine to London.*

Following on the above, a few days after, Tuesday 27th June the engine Witch *(engineman Cuthbert Davison) ran away from Didcot, up the Down line, without its tender. This may seem strange but it is true. The turntable at Didcot was too small to take both engine and tender so they had to uncouple and while the tender was being turned the regulator flew open, and the sudden start jerked Davison to the ground, and away she went. Engineman M. Almond, engine* Great Britain, *was standing in the yard and seeing what had happened started in chase up the proper line and overtook her before passing Goring, where he got the switchman to pull over the crossover and so let the* Witch *follow up on the fast line for which feat Almond (a great favourite with Daniel Gooch) was awarded £10 by the Directors.'*

Thankfully, neither of these events resulted in death and destruction, as they so easily might have done. In fact, they display great presence of mind by the various enginemen and others involved and also shine a bright light into the operating practises of the early railway. Neither are they unique; numerous other similar incidents occurred across the railway network in the early days, not unusually with more distressing consequences than those recorded here.

As I mentioned earlier all the engines involved in these stories appear in this volume. *Great Western* and *Witch* you will have just encountered; *Ajax*, a member of the 'Premier' Class which are the subject of a later chapter, was the second GWR engine to bear this name, her predecessor, minus its 10ft 0in. diameter driving wheels,

having been put to stationary use in about 1849. *Harpy* was a member of the 'Fire Fly' Class, described in Part 2.

Later Working Lives and Allocations

As we have already mentioned, initially the 8ft 0in. 'Singles' worked the Exeter expresses throughout. From 1st May 1849, the Bristol & Exeter Railway took over the workings west of Bristol from the GWR, using engines of a similar design but with 7ft 6ins driving wheels. Until the B&ER was absorbed by the GWR, from 1st January 1876, the 'Iron Dukes' and 'Couriers' worked no further than Bristol. As we have seen it was normal practise also for them to work to Gloucester and Cheltenham, though the older 7ft 0in. 'Singles' took a share of this traffic, particularly beyond Swindon. I have seen no records of the 8ft 0in. 'Singles' working into Wales but that is not to say that it never happened. The engines certainly did work over the Wilts, Somerset & Weymouth Railway. W.E. Edwards, writing in the *Railway & Travel Monthly* in a series of articles published in 1918 entitled 'Some Broad Gauge Locomotives on the Wilts Somerset and Weymouth Railway', tells us that *Lord of the Isles*, no less, was an occasional visitor to Weymouth while in the early days of the railway – it opened progressively from 5th September 1848 – a member of the class was regularly shedded at Chippenham, a sub-shed of Swindon.

On 12th June 1844, the line from Didcot to Oxford opened to traffic. In later years Oxford would become a regular haunt for members of the class, which was fortunate from our modern perspective for an unknown individual who possessed an early camera, and the skill and know-how to use it properly, took several beautiful photographs of broad gauge engines on Oxford shed in the late 1850s and early '60s. On 1st October 1852, the broad gauge route to Birmingham opened, with unfortunate

This very poor photograph is copied from a series of articles on the WS&WR in the *Rail & Travel Monthly Magazine* in 1918, the original print having never, as far as is known, turned up. Though the image adds little to our knowledge of these engines, it is included because, other than *Lord of the Isles*, photographs of the '3rd and 4th Lot' engines are so very rare. *Dragon* was built at Swindon in August 1848 and is seen here as it was probably running in the mid 1860s. The chimney appears to have the slightly shallower copper top and the large sandbox on the footplate adjacent to the driving wheel has been fitted. The Harrison chord bell has been moved up to the end of the tender frame and the tender tank has been lined in the conventional way, with four panels which have rounded corners. All these features are consistent with the date suggested above. What seems to be missing is the cab spectacle plate but the photograph has clearly suffered some 'retouching' and it may have been accidentally removed. In any case it would be difficult to see from the angle that it was taken from. *Dragon* ran 670,757 miles in traffic, up to its withdrawal in December 1872. A new engine bearing the same name was built in August 1880.

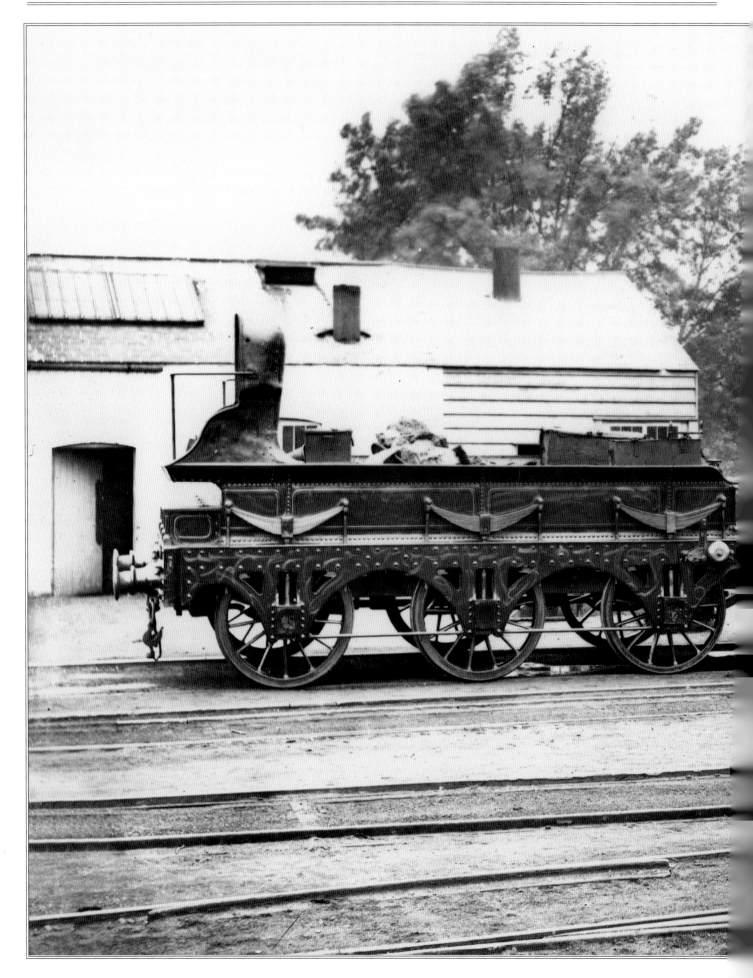

Without doubt this is the finest photograph that we possess of one of the '3rd Lot' engines. *Hirondelle* was the seventh member of the group, entering service in December 1848 and was withdrawn in May 1873, replaced by a new engine of the same name. The location is again at the old OW&WR/WMR shed at Oxford, looking west with the single storey offices forming the backdrop (this was prior to the Repair Shop being built circa 1870) and the photograph probably dates from the mid 1860s, so may in fact have been taken at the same time as those of *Lightning*. The foreground lines are standard gauge whilst *Hirondelle* is standing on mixed gauge track. Judging from the fine external condition of the engine I would think that it had not long emerged from a heavy works repair, though it has not yet received some of the additional lubricators visible on *Lightning*. The Harrison chord bell apparatus has, however, been moved to the later position on the tender frames. The picture also clearly shows off the contemporary livery of the period and may be taken as a good example of the then usual, *i.e.* circa 1865, practise. The boiler bands are black edged in white as is the large sandbox, the cab, spectacles and side sheets. The tender is lined in the normal way, unlike *Lightning*, with four panels which line up with the centre buckle of the springs. The rear tool box is also lined, again normal practise but particularly obvious here. The lining out of the frames is less easy to make out but would be Windsor brown edged in black and picked out with a fine vermillion line. The squiggles on the framing were executed in tallow by the cleaners and were often worked up into very elaborate designs, at the behest of the drivers. There are several different local names given to this practise but at Swindon it was always referred to as 'swizzling'.

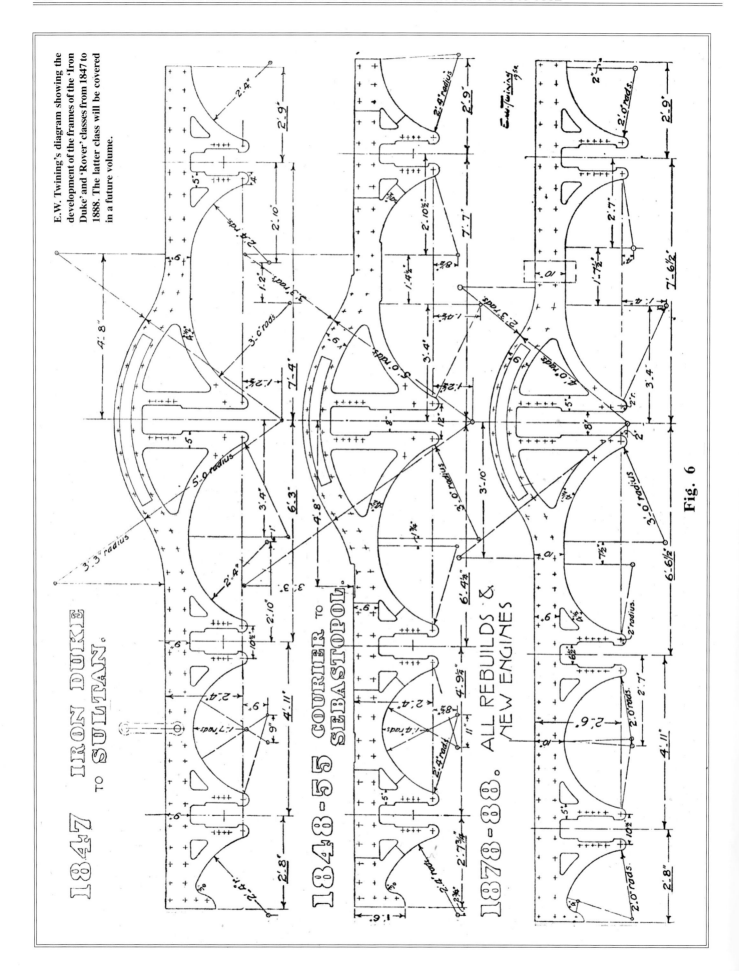

E.W. Twining's diagram showing the development of the frames of the 'Iron Duke' and 'Rover' classes from 1847 to 1888. The latter class will be covered in a future volume.

1847 IRON DUKE TO SULTAN.

1848-55 COURIER TO SEBASTOPOL.

1878-88. ALL REBUILDS & NEW ENGINES

Fig. 6

Prometheus and *Estaffete* were rebuilt at Swindon with a longer wheelbase in May/June 1870. Increasing the wheelbase would have involved making new frames or at the very least radically modifying the old ones, a process which cannot have been very easy or cost effective one would suggest. Both engines were also given new boilers, which differed internally to a very small degree. Cabs were fitted at Swindon to the 8ft 0in. 'Singles' from 1878 onwards and this photograph of *Prometheus*, taken by the Reverend Malan at Newton Abbot on 23rd July 1883, shows the engine as outshopped circa 1878-80 with roll top chimney and the final flourishing of the Armstrong 'scafed' Pea green livery. Despite having been in service for perhaps three or more years, *Prometheus* is still in beautiful external condition, a tribute to the cleaning gang at Bristol Bath Road shed where the engine was based at the time. It was subsequently overhauled again and spent the last three or four years of its working life based at Paddington. Taken out of service in October 1887, *Prometheus* was replaced with a new engine bearing the same name. Interestingly, close inspection of the works plate shows a building date of May 1870, though the engine did not re-enter service until June, when it would have appeared in much the same condition as *Great Britain* in the picture on page 111.

consequences for *Lord of the Isles*, as described earlier. Though members of the 'Prince' Class took a significant part in the running of the Birmingham expresses north of Didcot and Oxford, the 8ft 0in. 'Singles' were nonetheless active on the line and a small number were generally allocated to Bordesley Junction shed.

Broad gauge workings ceased in the West Midlands in 1869, between Swindon and Milford (Neyland) via Gloucester in June 1872 and on the Wilts, Somerset & Weymouth in June 1874, leaving only the main line, with its through connection to the South West, as the focus of broad gauge operations. This was extended to the far west from 1876, when the independent broad gauge companies serving Somerset, Devon and Cornwall were absorbed by the GWR. However, although the broad gauge extended to Falmouth and Penzance, only once did an 8ft 0in. 'Single' work beyond Newton Abbot and that is a story to be told in a future volume.

Of the routes that were regularly worked by broad gauge expresses, the service between Paddington and the West Midlands is, perhaps, the least known. Fortunately, MacDermot gives details of the most important trains, which were the equal of the fast Exeter expresses initially. Paddington to Birmingham via Oxford is 129 miles. In October 1852, two trains were timed to make the journey in $2^3/4$ hours, with stops at Oxford (New station) and Leamington; 70 minutes was allowed for the $63^1/4$ miles to Oxford and 55 minutes for the $42^1/2$ miles thence to Leamington. These trains, unfortunately, ran at such speeds for only a matter of months. Severe flooding in the Oxford area and the general deceleration of services from January 1853 – a consequence of the ever-worsening financial crisis – was their nemesis. Such were the cut backs that the previously world beating timings between London and the South West were also considerably eased. Thus, the best train now took $3^1/4$ hours to reach Bristol and $5^1/4$ hours to Exeter.

Meanwhile, the independent service to the West Midlands was withdrawn altogether. Combined trains ran to Didcot, where the Birmingham portion was detached, and 68 minutes was now the fastest Paddington to Didcot timing. The new overall Paddington-Birmingham time was 3 hours 25 minutes. The rival L&NWR route's best train from Euston to Birmingham Curzon Street made the journey in 3 hours, leaving the GWR an 'also ran' in the competitive market of mid-Victorian rail travel. Matters did not really begin to improve until the early 1860s, by which time standard gauge trains, which worked beyond Wolverhampton to Shrewsbury, Chester and Birkenhead, had commenced running. By 1866, the broad gauge passenger service from Paddington to the West Midlands had been so reduced as to be practically non-existent, the service to Oxford only remaining a broad gauge preserve. One or two stopping trains between Oxford and Birmingham remained for the time being but their days were, alas, clearly numbered.

On the main line to Bristol and the South West, matters had improved by 1866. The best train, 'The Flying Dutchman', left Paddington at 11.45am and arrived at Bristol Temple Meads through platform at 2.33pm. The train ran non-stop to Swindon and called additionally at Bath on its way westward. However,

there was no Up service that exactly mirrored the 11.45am Down. Perhaps the best train was the 12.20pm from Bristol which, in addition to the Bath and Swindon stops, called at Chippenham and slipped a coach at Reading. It was timed to arrive at Paddington at 3.10pm. The next best was the 3.00pm from Temple Meads, which called at Bath, Chippenham, Swindon and Didcot, and was due to arrive at Paddington at 6.15pm.

I have the advantage of possessing an October 1866 *Working Time Table* for the Paddington-Bristol main line. Though it is impossible to know exactly, I suspect that the following trains would have been in the hands of 8ft 0in. 'Singles', as far as Swindon at least:

Departures from Paddington:

6.00am – cheap for Plymouth
7.45am – cheap for Bristol
9.15am – Swindon (detach vehicles for South Wales) & Bristol
10.15am – Bristol
11.45am – 'The Flying Dutchman' for Bristol, Exeter & Plymouth
2.00pm – Bristol
2.30pm – Bristol, slow
4.50pm – Bristol, fast, TM arrival 7.55pm
8.10pm – Bristol, arrive at 12.30am

In addition to these there were several trains that terminated at Didcot or Swindon, no less than seven trains to Windsor – which stopped at intermediate stations – and the 9.00pm 'Special Mail', which was a very light train and was usually hauled by a 'Fire Fly'. By 1866, however, these engines were beginning to be laid aside and were increasingly employed in South Wales, so by 1870 the 8ft 0in. 'Singles' would, no doubt, have taken over this and similar workings. In addition, there were several 'short trains' to either Slough or Reading. Services to South Wales were limited to through coaches detached at Swindon or vice versa. The 8ft 0in. 'Singles' may have taken a turn working trains from Swindon to Gloucester, though these were generally the preserve of the 7ft 0in. engines or the 'Waverley', 'Victoria' or 'Hawthorn' 4-coupled classes. If one includes *Great Western*, as the GWR did when in 1866 all the 8ft 0in. 'Singles' were grouped together as the 'Alma' Class, there were potentially thirty engines available to work the company's most important trains. However, as readers will appreciate, that notional figure was never realised in day to day service. At any one time perhaps as many as ten members of the class would be unavailable for traffic, either undergoing routine examinations, maintenance at their home depot or in workshop hands, generally at Swindon, though before 1869 it is probable that a few light repairs were undertaken at Wolverhampton Stafford Road Works. One can guess that an availability figure of something between 66 per cent and 75 per cent would be the norm, adequate for everyday needs no doubt but at times of heavy traffic, resources must have become rather stretched.

Throughout their working lives the 8ft 0in. 'Singles' were to be found at just a few major sheds. Before 1876, for instance, very few appear to have been allocated to Bristol but there is good reason for this – from February 1855, the 7ft 0in. coupled 'Waverley' Class 4-4-0s were introduced. Ahrons, quoted in MacDermot's *History of the GWR* (Vol. 2, as revised by Clinker,

This drawing, from the *Illustrated London News*, is entitled 'Mail Train 1849'. The GWR's association with mail traffic began no later than February 1840 and was well established by the end of the decade, though the service provided by the railways was not always as reliable as the Post Office desired. Special mail trains, dedicated to post office traffic alone, did not begin to run until February 1855. Prior to this, mail traffic was carried on ordinary trains and was often subject to delay or disruption. From the very beginning, the GWR were keen to accept and facilitate the Royal Mail traffic and designated a number of trains, which carried mail, as 'priority traffic.' Of these the 'Night Mail' left Paddington at 8.55pm and by 1849 served all major towns and cities between London and Plymouth. Mails for Cornwall were also carried, though it would be ten years before they could reach their destination by train. This drawing gives a vivid impression of the 'Night Mail' hauled by an 8ft 0in. 'Single'.

page 272), in a footnote makes the following comment: '*Until 1873 they* [the 8ft 0in. 'Singles'] *seldom ran west of Swindon, the fast trains between there and Bristol being usually worked by the 7ft 0in. coupled Waverleys*'.

As we will learn in Part 4 of this work, about one third of the 'Waverley' Class were stationed at Swindon and Bristol at any one time, which obviously lends credence to Ahron's statement. The 'Waverleys', however, had fairly short working lives, all having been withdrawn by Christmas 1876. By this time most of the original 8ft 0in. 'Singles' had also ceased work, to be progressively replaced by new engines of similar design but increased adhesive weight. What few through workings remained during this latter period were generally the preserve of London-based engines working out and back. Thereafter, there was a rearrangement of working practises and of those few that survived into the 1880s, *Prometheus* is known to have worked regularly between

Bristol and Newton Abbot. Ahrons tells us that it ended its days at Westbourne Park, as did *Estaffete*, which predeceased it in December 1884.

We do not, of course, have complete allocation records covering the period 1847-1887 but those that we do possess are set out below:

1850

Paddington

Engines in steam (two weeks ending 27th July):
Courier, *Great Britain*, *Lightning*, *Pasha*, *Perseus*, *Prometheus*, *Sultan*, *Swallow*, *Tartar*, *Timour*, *Tornado* and *Wizard*

It is almost certain that the majority of the class were allocated to Paddington shed at this time. Seven engines, including *Great Western*, were unaccounted for during this period. By October 1852, two members of the class, *Amazon* and *Lord of the Isles*, were at Birmingham (Bordesley Junction).

1854
Paddington
Engines in steam (two weeks ending 22nd July):
Courier, Dragon, Emperor, Estaffete, Hirondelle, Iron Duke, Pasha, Perseus, Rougemont, Sultan, Swallow, Timour, Tartar, Tornado, Warlock
Swindon
Lord of the Isles, Wizard (on works trial)

1855
Paddington
Engines in steam (three weeks ending 21st July):
Alma, Balaklava, Courier, Dragon, Estaffete, Emperor, Great Britain, Iron Duke, Inkermann, Lightning, Perseus, Pasha, Rougemont, Rover, Swallow, Timour, Warlock

1856
Paddington
Engines in steam (two weeks ending 19th July):
Alma, Courier, Great Britain, Hirondelle, Iron Duke, Inkermann, Kertch, Pasha, Prometheus, Rougemont, Sebastopol, Sultan, Timour, Tornado, Wizard
Oxford
Balaklava, Crimea, Warlock
Swindon
Lord of the Isles

1857
Paddington
Engines in steam (two weeks ending 18th July):
Alma, Balaklava, Dragon, Emperor, Great Britain, Iron Duke, Kertch,
Lightning, Rougemont, Swallow, Sultan, Sebastopol, Tartar
Oxford
Amazon, Crimea, Courier, Eupatoria, Estafette, Inkermann, Perseus, Rover, Timour, Warlock
Swindon
Lord of the Isles

1858
Paddington
Engines in steam: (seventeen days to 17th July):
Balaklava, Courier, Crimea, Emperor, Great Britain, Hirondelle, Kertch, Lightning, Sultan
Oxford
Estaffete, Inkermann, Prometheus, Perseus, Rougemont, Swallow, Tartar, Timour
Birmingham
Alma
Swindon
Lord of the Isles, Rover, Dragon
Bristol
Eupatoria

1859
Paddington
Engines in steam (three weeks to 23rd July):
Crimea, Courier, Emperor, Hirondelle, Iron Duke, Kertch, Lightning, Prometheus, Pasha, Swallow, Sultan, Warlock, Wizard
Oxford
Alma, Balaklava, Eupatoria, Perseus, Rover, Rougemont, Tartar, Timour

Although at first glance this engraving of the old Paddington shed looks of similar date to that from 1846 on page 86, it must in fact have been executed several years later. On the right is *Rover*, one of the '4th Lot' batch of 'Iron Dukes', which was new in September 1850 and lasted in service until August 1871, having run 461,344 miles. On the left is *Elephant*, a 'Leo' Class 2-4-0 tender engine built by R.&W. Hawthorn & Co. (see Part 2) and the first of the class delivered in January 1841. By July 1849, however, it been converted to a 2-4-0 tank engine (although is mistakenly shown here as a 2-2-2).

1860

Paddington

Engines in steam (three weeks to 21st July):

Balaklava, Dragon, Emperor, Great Britain, Hirondelle, Iron Duke, Kertch, Pasha, Rover, Sebastopol, Swallow, Tartar

Oxford

Amazon, Crimea, Estaffete, Eupatoria, Perseus, Prometheus, Rougemont, Warlock

Birmingham

Alma, Inkermann

1862

Paddington

Engines in steam (nineteen days to 19th July):

Balaklava, Emperor, Estaffete, Eupatoria, Great Britain, Hirondelle, Lightning, Perseus, Rover, Tartar, Timour, Warlock, Wizard

Oxford

Amazon, Crimea, Kertch, Rougemont, Sebastopol

Birmingham

Inkermann, Swallow

Swindon

Lord of the Isles

Thereafter, our records come to an end but, nonetheless, we can piece together quite confidently the events that followed. As the broad gauge mileage contracted and therefore the area of activity afforded to members of the class became ever concentrated on the main line to the West, the 'Iron Dukes' congregated at Paddington. Yet this process had hardly begun in earnest when, first, the three rebuildings of 1870 and then the gradual replacement programme, which began in 1871, got underway. By the beginning of 1880, only seven of the original class were still at work and of these, three were the engines *Great Britain*, *Estaffete* and *Prometheus*, rebuilt in 1870. Of these seven, only *Prometheus* would survive beyond 1885, along with the by then preserved *Lord of the Isles*. As previously mentioned, from 1876, following the absorption of the B&ER, South Devon, Cornwall and West Cornwall railways, engine working arrangements were reorganised. For the first time, Bristol gained a substantial allocation of the 8ft 0in. 'Singles', which worked turn and turn about with the former Bristol & Exeter

engines between Temple Meads and Newton Abbot. We know that *Prometheus* spent a period in the late 1870s and early '80s at Bristol and there must surely have been others.

The Engine Sheds

A final word should be said about the sheds themselves. The GWR always referred in official records to its London depot as Paddington. The original shed, a wooden roundhouse adjacent to the temporary station of 1838, was closed and demolished during the reconstruction of Paddington in 1854. The new shed at Westbourne Park opened in March 1855.

The GWR opened its broad gauge shed at Oxford just to the west of the new station on the Up side of the line between the station and the river, it had closed by 1876 and possibly much earlier, when the GWR absorbed the West Midland Railway and gained that company's mixed gauge shed in 1854.

Bordesley Junction shed was on the Down side of the line, just beyond Small Heath & Sparkbrook station and to the east of Bordesley Junction itself. It was replaced by the new depot opened at Tyseley in June 1908.

At Swindon, the original shed was adjacent to the workshops and ran parallel to the main line. Though construction began in 1841, when the temporary shed (a quite substantial building) at Hay Lane was removed to Swindon, it was not completed until 1846. It closed in 1871, though some part of the building may have continued to house the dwindling number of broad gauge engines at Swindon for a few years thereafter. The main reference works, Lyons & Mountford and *The Directory of British Engine Sheds Vol. 1*, are incorrect in their assertion that the shed did not close until May 1892. In fact, a small single road shed was erected alongside the new shed of 1871 and this was used by broad gauge locomotives until the end of operations in 1892.

Finally, as regards Bristol, some uncertainty exists about the initial engine servicing provision. An early map dated 1841 shows a small single road building just to the east of the terminus at Temple Meads, though it is unclear if the shed was intended to be a simple stop gap or a permanent building. It soon proved to be inadequate to the task and was swiftly replaced by a much larger and commodious three-road straight shed in the parish of Barton

The 1855 broad gauge engine shed at Westbourne Park, which replaced the wooden roundhouse at Paddington. Although it looks to have been extended at some stage, the first edition 25 inch OS map of 1869 shows it as this size, so any extension(s) – there may have been one at the far end too – were added prior to that date. The building is seen here empty just prior to its demolition in March 1906. The foundations of many of the original structures at Westbourne Park were recently uncovered by the Crossrail construction engineers.

Hill, about one mile to the east of the terminus. Following the opening of the Bristol & South Wales Union Railway in 1863, it became known as South Wales Junction. Joined by a standard gauge shed in the late 1860s, both closed when all locomotive servicing and maintenance was transferred to the old Bristol & Exeter shed and works site at Bath Road. (See also Appendix 3)

Works Report

This covers the period between April 1866 and November 1870 and only details major repairs:

1866
April. .... *Emperor, Amazon, Lightning*
October .. .... *Balaklava*
December .... *Tornado*

1867
January ... . *Inkermann, Estaffete, Hirondelle*
April. .... *Tartar*
May .. .. *Timour*
December .... *Eupatoria*

1868
March .... *Perseus*
June . ... *Hirondelle, Wizard*
September .... *Swallow*
November .... *Amazon, Emperor*

1869
April. .... *Iron Duke, Dragon*
May .. .. *Lord of the Isles*
August .... *Courier*
November .... *Tartar*

1870
April. .... *Tornado, Prometheus* (renewed)
July .. .. *Estaffete* (renewed), *Great Britain* (renewed)
September .... *Warlock, Eupatoria*
November .... *Crimea*

Notes

1. Interestingly, *Great Britain* is shown as *Great Western* in the records of renewals in 1870. This is a lesson for authors and readers alike, 'official' records are not infallible!

2. The *RCTS History*, following Bird in *The Locomotive Magazine* for 1901, says that *Prometheus* and *Estaffete* were rebuilt in June and *Great Britain* in July 1870.

3. It should be borne in mind that the months mentioned above indicate when the engines concerned were 'in works' and not when they returned to traffic.

Disposal and Final Mileages

Before we proceed with this section of our story, a little clarification is required. I have, correctly, been taken to task by Richard Pender of the Broad Gauge Society for describing engines which are being disposed of as 'cut up'. This phrase, so familiar to many of us from the 1950s and '60s, does not describe the process of disposal as practised in the 19th century. At Swindon engines were taken into the Repair Shop or 'B' Shed as it was properly known, and dismantled so that any usable parts could be salvaged and repaired for future use. Unwanted

TABLE 6.10: 'IRON DUKE' CLASS – FINAL MILEAGAES & WITHDRAWAL DATES		
NAME	**FINAL MILEAGE**	**WITHDRAWN**
Iron Duke	607,412	Oct. 1871
Great Britain	567,760 (to 7/70)	
	426,751 (from 7/70)	Sept. 1880
Lightning	816,601	Dec. 1877
Emperor	690,225	June 1873
Pasha	613,038	June 1876
Sultan	727,300	June 1874
Courier	746,120	Nov. 1877
Tartar	731,817	June 1876
Dragon	670,757	Dec. 1872
Warlock	639,410	June 1874
Wizard	711,908	Nov. 1875
Rougemont	772,401	Aug. 1879
Hirondelle	605,010	Feb. 1872
Tornado	687,997	June 1881
Swallow	569,232	Aug. 1871
Timour	569,893	Nov. 1871
Prometheus	538,025 (to 6/70)	
	(from 6/70) 542,324	Feb. 1887
Perseus	722,458	Feb. 1880
Estaffete	505,544 (to 6/70)	
	442,005 (from 6/70)	Dec. 1884
Rover	461,344	Aug. 1871
Amazon	729,309	June 1877
Lord of the Isles	789,309	Preserved June 1884-1906
Alma	444,608	Feb. 1872
Balaklava	406,425	Oct. 1871
Inkermann	650,220	July 1877
Kertch	326,246	Dec. 1872
Crimea	605,701	Nov. 1876
Eupatoria	618,275	Oct. 1878
Sebastopol	707,148	June 1880

or worn-out items such as boiler barrels, frames, etc., were then dismantled by a team of men who literally broke them up with sledge hammers and cold chisels. The metals could then be recycled in the foundry or the rolling mills. However, there is a strange conundrum at play here; as I write, I have in front of me the GWR's own contemporary records, copies of which were obtained from the National Archives at Kew some years ago. These are hand written yet in the column marked '*how disposed of*', the clerk constantly used the convenient phrase '*cut up*':

The disposal dates given in **Table 6.10**, above, are those of the month in which the locomotive was withdrawn, though that did not mean that the engine always ceased work. *Lightning* is a good example. It was withdrawn in December 1877 but continued to be serviceable until the following April, though how much actual work it did it is impossible to say. Incidentally, *Lightning* achieved the highest mileage of any member of the class other than the three engines that were rebuilt in 1870.

Most of these engines were renewed (i.e. replaced by very similar new builds) between 1871 and 1888. In the majority of cases, the names were perpetuated and the old nameplates refitted. It is easy to spot the original plates, for in every case the first letter (i.e. the 'T' in *Timour*) is larger than the other

When *Lord of the Isles* was broken up in 1906, various items were saved including the nameplate shown here – with those from *Great Britain* and *Great Western* – and the engine's worksplate, which reads '*Lord of the Isles Manufactured by the Great Western Railway Company – 1851 – at their Swindon Works*'. This temporary display had been set up in one of the rooms of the Mechanics Institute at Swindon, probably in advance of these relics being displayed there. All the items shown here are now part of the National Collection and are still in Swindon, at the Steam Museum.

letters. On the later nameplates, such as *Bulkeley*, the letters were all one size. Additionally, not all the names were reused, those discarded being *Pasha*, *Rougemont*, *Perseus*, *Estaffete*, *Kertch* and *Wizard*. *Lord of the Isles* remained in preservation, so that name was not perpetuated either until reappearing on one of the handsome Dean 7ft 8ins 'Singles', No. 3046, in January 1895.

Whilst on the subject of names it is important to point out that *Estaffete* ran for its entire thirty-four years with a misspelt name – the correct spelling is *Estafette*. The name is French in origin and denotes a military courier who was responsible for carrying messages at high speed from one army commander to another. Also of French origin was *Hirondelle* – Swallow in English; thus two of the class effectively had the same name!

Conclusion

Over many years I have been asked to give numerous lectures about the broad gauge. When describing these magnificent engines, I speak of them in terms which describe them as the Concordes of their age – the impact that they had was surely comparable. Just as Concorde shrank the world by reducing the time that it took to fly across the Atlantic, so the 8ft 0in. 'Singles' massively reduced journey times across south western England. In 1838, it might have taken anything between 20 and 70 hours to travel from London to Exeter but ten years later the same journey could be made in less than five hours – surely a phenomenal achievement. E.L. Ahrons summed it up nicely, in the *British Steam Locomotive 1825-1925*: '*The Broad Gauge 8ft 0in. single engines from 1847 until about 1880 undoubtedly performed the fastest running in the country*'.

What better epitaph could there be for this most famous of all classes and for Daniel Gooch their designer. This is how history is made and the world around us changed.

Lord of the Isles driving wheels outside Swindon Works in the 1930s. The picture shows the profile of the spokes, thickness of the tyres and the design of the crank axle. Making such items in the 1840s and '50s was a major challenge involving much hand forging and hammer welding. The Gooch patent steeled tyres also needed grinding, all processes that were very labour intensive and demanding a high degree of skill and physical strength. The wheels are today in the entrance hall of the Steam Museum at Swindon.

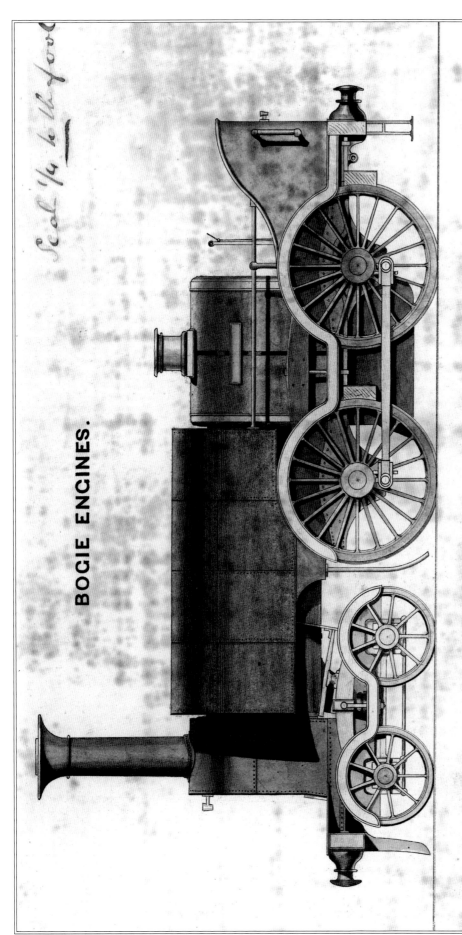

Scal 1/4 to th foot

BOGIE ENGINES.

HORACE . BRIGAND . CORSAIR . EURIPIDES . HOMER . HESIOD . JUVENAL . LUCAN . LUCRETIUS . OVID . SAPPHO . SENECA . STATIUS . THEOCRITUS . VIRGIL.

DESCRIPTION.

CYLINDERS. 17 ins in diam⁹ and 24 inch stroke. Steam ports 1¾ins by 13ins long. Exhaust port 3¼ ins by 13ins.
BOILER. 10 feet 6 ins long and 4 feet 3 ins in diam⁹ inside. Fire-box 4 feet 11 ins long and 3 feet 3½ ins wide.
TUBES. 219 Tubes 10 feet 11 ins long and 2 ins in diam⁹ outside. HEATING SURFACE of Box 121.33. Tubes 1287.7
FIRE-GRATE. area 18.44 superficial feet.
WHEELS. Driving and Trailing 5 feet 9 ins in diameter coupled. Leading 3 feet 6 ins in diameter.
TANK. 10 feet 3 ins long. 1 foot 7 ins water space at bottom, tapering into 1 foot 0 ins over the top, Contains 930.
"BRIGAND" with Tank full. ¾ cwt of Coke on foot plate, and 8½ in⁹ in Class, weighs. 14.14.0 . 11.16.0 . 10.16.0.
Leading   Driving   Trailing

The 'Bogie' Class were broken down into two sub-groups – *Corsair* and *Brigand* had 6ft 0in. diameter driving wheels, whilst all the rest were fitted with 5ft 9ins drivers. However, the wheelbase of *Corsair* differed from *Brigand*, which was the same as the later R.&.W Hawthorn-built engines. Unfortunately, this 1857 watercolour has suffered rather badly from foxing.

CHAPTER 6
THE 'BOGIE' CLASS

Corsair, Brigand and the R.&W. Hawthorn Engines

Following the failure of the Atmospheric System on the South Devon Railway, the GWR, a number of whose directors were also directors of the SDR, were called upon to work the latter's traffic. This arrangement commenced in May 1846 and although James Pearson and his staff managed to get the Atmospheric section between Exeter and Teignmouth to work in 1847, it could not be relied upon and was finally abandoned in 1848. Meanwhile the line was proceeding westward over the batholith of Dartmoor, which involved surmounting some of the fiercest gradients on any main line in England. The extant GWR locomotive stud of the period had hardly been designed with such challenges in mind. Consequently, Gooch set about designing

engines which could cope with the exceptional challenges that the difficult section of the railway between Newton (later Newton Abbot) and Plymouth presented.

Gooch's initial thoughts seem to have turned to a 4-coupled tender engine with 6ft 0in. driving wheels, 17ins x 24ins cylinders and a boiler pressure of only 60psi. The engine and tender together weighed 43 tons and were deemed capable of working a train of 89 tons up a gradient of 1 in 40. However, Gooch soon had second thoughts. He was perhaps influenced by the experience gained from rebuilding the Stothert & Slaughter-built 0-6-0 tender engine *Avalanche* as a saddle tank. As rebuilt, this engine, with its additional adhesion, proved very successful first at Box and perhaps also at Brimscombe, working as a bank

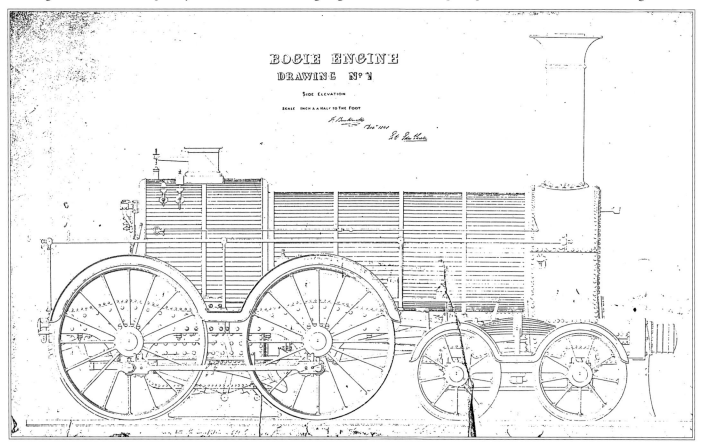

Gooch's first design of the 'Bogie' Class was for a 4-coupled tender engine complete with sledge brake, his initial intention being to build fourteen engines for the South Devon Railway. They were to have 6ft 0in. diameter driving wheels, 17ins x 24ins cylinders and a boiler pressure of 60psi. The engines were to be coupled to a tender weighing 15 tons and were thought to be capable of hauling a train of 89 tons up a gradient of 1 in 40. It was, perhaps, his experience of rebuilding the earlier light locomotives as saddle tanks and the success of the rebuilding of *Avalanche* as the Box Banker that made him realise that the additional adhesive weight offered by a saddle tank was a major advantage. One could hardly dispute this assessment considering the tortuous nature of the South Devon main line. There may also have been other considerations that influenced his decision, not the least of which were the cost implications, as the South Devon Railway had been nearly bankrupted by the failure of the Atmospheric System. Consequently, he redesigned the engines as saddle tanks and built just two initially, *Corsair* and *Brigand*, for trial and development purposes.

engine at both locations. Gooch therefore redesigned his intended 'mountaineer' as a 4-4-0 saddle tank. Despite the inclusion in the design of one or two experimental elements, which were soon discarded, the engine proved an immediate success and was soon joined by a sister. These two, *Corsair* and *Brigand*, would become the prototypes of a type which would serve the broad gauge network through to its sad demise in 1892.

These were among the first passenger tank locomotives built in this country but it must be admitted that they were of a rather primitive design and could hardly be described as handsome. They were, however, an effective product though a number ended up working coal and mineral traffic in the Forest of Dean – a rather different outcome than that which was originally envisaged.

We must now turn to consider the history and details of this ground breaking type, the basics of which are shown in **Table 7.1**, below. *Corsair* and *Brigand* were built at Swindon as the '1st Lot Bogie' and they were then joined in 1854 by thirteen very similar engines but which were built with 5ft 9ins rather than 6ft 0in. driving wheels and constructed by R.&W. Hawthorn Ltd on Tyneside. The main dimensions are shown in **Table 7.2**, right.

Constructional Details
Frames

These were the standard Gooch design of sandwich frames, though set behind the wheels and not outside them. From the rear buffer beam the frames only extended as far as the front

TABLE 7.1: THE 'BOGIE' CLASS

NAME	BUILT	CEASED WORK	REMARKS
Corsair	Aug. 1849	June 1873	Sold
Brigand	Sept. 1849	June 1873	Sold

R.&W. HAWTHORN ENGINES				
NAME	MAKERS NO.	BUILT	CEASED WORK	REMARKS
Sappo	875	June 1854	Dec. 1873	Sold
Homer	876	Aug. 1854	Dec. 1873	
Virgil	877	Sept. 1854	Dec. 1873	Sold
Horace	878	Sept. 1854	Dec. 1880	Sold
Ovid	879	Oct. 1854	March 1873	
Juvenal	880	Nov. 1854	Dec. 1873	Sold
Seneca	881	Nov. 1854	March 1872	
Lucretius	882	Dec. 1854	March 1872	
Theocritus	883	Dec. 1854	Dec. 1873	Sold
Statius	884	Jan. 1855	Oct. 1871	
Euripides	885	Feb. 1855	Dec. 1871	
Hesiod	886	March 1855	Feb. 1872	
Lucan	887	March 1855	Feb. 1872	

NOTES: SALES
Corsair to Cilely Colliery in April 1876
Brigand to Edwards & Suter in August 1873. Returned to the GWR in April 1878 and broken up at Swindon
Sappo to the Staveley Iron & Coal Company, December 1873
Virgil to Dobson, Brown & Adams in July 1874
Horace sold to Cilely Colliery, 23rd June 1881
Juvenal to Dobson, Brown & Adams in February 1874
Theocritus to the Staveley Iron & Coal Company, February 1874
Most were employed as pumping engines or as stationary boilers but further details are lacking

TABLE 7.2: 'BOGE' CLASS – DIMENSIONS

Corsair and *Brigand*	
Driving Wheels	6ft 0in. dia.
Bogie Wheels	3ft 6ins dia.
Hawthorn Engines	
Driving Wheels	5ft 9ins dia.
Bogie Wheels	3ft 6ins dia.
Wheelbase: *Corsair*	5ft 0in. + 5ft 6ins + 7ft 8ins
Wheelbase:	
Brigand and Hawthorns	5ft 0in. + 5ft 6ins + 7ft 6ins
Boiler Dimensions	
These were the same for all engines though the grate area was slightly smaller on the Hawthorns. D.K. Clark's drawing of *Corsair* in his *Railway Machinery* (1855) shows the firebox fitted with a midfeather. Presumably *Brigand* was similar and it is thought that the Hawthorn engines were also fitted with this device.	
Barrel	10ft 6ins x 4ft 3ins, 219 2ins dia. tubes
Firebox	4ft 4¹/₄ins x 4ft 8³/₄ins
Casing	4ft 11ins x 5ft 3¹/₂ins
Tube Heating Surface	1,134.4 sq. ft
Firebox	121.33 sq. ft
Total	1,255.73 sq. ft
Grate Area	
Corsair and *Brigand*	19.00 sq. ft
Hawthorns	18.44 sq. ft
Weight: *Corsair*	35 tons 15 cwt (21 ton 5 cwt resting on the coupled wheels). *Brigand* probably similar
Hawthorns	38 tons 9 cwt (average in working order)

driving wheel. The front of the engine was strengthened by some shallow secondary frames that in turn supported the cylinder/smokebox assembly and the front buffer beam. A third frame, riveted to the underside of the boiler and incorporating an axle box, supported the leading driving wheel. This short frame was in turn attached to the front of the firebox casing and the bogie gusset plate by iron stay rods. The leading driving axle was additionally the crank axle. Thus, Gooch sought to support this vital component with a similar arrangement as that applied to the crank axle of the 8ft 0in. single wheelers.

Boilers

This design utilised the boiler as part of the framework of the engine, a practise or perhaps a concept that had many adherents in the early years of steam locomotive development. It had particular applications in the design of 'road locomotives' or 'traction engines' as they are commonly – but incorrectly – known today. To this end Gooch designed the bogie with a ball and socket joint the weight of which was taken by a double gusset riveted to the underside of the boiler barrel and the steam chest. As Phil Reed put it in the *RCTS History*, '*The boiler barrel formed the connections between the cylinders and the main frames*'. He might have added that it thus became the backbone of the engine.

Smokebox and Cylinders

As was his normal practise, Gooch incorporated the cylinders into the lower part of the smokebox. The cylinders were of 17ins diameter by 24ins stroke and were inclined downwards at an angle of 1 in 14^1/$_2$ins towards the driving axle. The valves were set between the cylinders. The steam ports measured 13ins by 1^3/$_4$ins and the exhaust ports 13ins by 3^1/$_4$ins. The smokebox had a total depth in front of 6ft 4ins, a width at the centre line of the boiler of 5ft 2ins and a length of 2ft 8^5/$_8$ins.

Firebox

The firebox casing was of the normal Gooch 'raised' pattern. It measured 4ft 11ins in length, was 5ft 3^1/$_2$ins wide and had a depth, below the centre line of the boiler, of 4ft 4^1/$_4$ins in front and 4ft 8^1/$_4$ins at the back. The inner firebox measured 4ft 4^1/$_8$ins long, 4ft 8^3/$_4$ins wide and the depth of the firebars were respectively 4ft 4ins at the front and 4ft 7^1/$_2$ins at the back. The firegrate had an area of 19 sq. ft.

The Bogie, Wheels and Springing

As mentioned earlier, the bogie swivelled in a ball and socket joint. The weight of the front end of the engine was supported by two large leaf springs resting on the axle boxes of the bogie. However, the bogie had no provision for side springing so lateral movement was facilitated by making the leading driving wheel flangeless. With *Corsair* and *Brigand*, the driving wheels were 6ft 0in. diameter but the Hawthorn engines, which in other ways were similar to *Brigand*, had driving wheels of 5ft 9ins diameter. Bogie wheels on all of the engines were 3ft 6ins diameter. At the rear end, the support of the frames was achieved by means of compensating levers placed on each side of the firebox, extending from one coupled axle to another and were attached to the strap of an ordinary elliptic spring, the ends of which were secured to the frames. In practical terms therefore, the engine was supported at only three points, on either side of the firebox and at the centre of the bogie.

The Saddle Tank

This was constructed in four courses and was made of iron sheets riveted together. It sat on top of the boiler between the smokebox and firebox and was shaped up over the leading driving wheels. In later years a cut out was made in the front of the tank to accommodate the boiler water delivery clack which was placed on the front ring of the boiler and fed from injectors placed alongside the firebox. The tank originally held 930 gallons of water.

Braking

Initially, *Corsair* was fitted with twin sledge brakes positioned between the two driving wheels and actuated by a lever on the footplate. Realising the severity of the gradients that these locomotives were designed to operate over, Gooch rightly attempted to provide the engines with adequate brake power. Unfortunately, the sledge brake worked all too well nearly lifting the driving wheels off the track when applied enthusiastically. Since the leading driving wheels were also flangeless, there must have been the real likelihood of a derailment occurring. *Brigand* was fitted with wooden brake blocks that bore on the rear driving wheels only. This provision was later increased, with additional brake blocks applied to the leading drivers. No doubt as a direct consequence of this, the Hawthorn engines were built with wooden brake blocks acting on all four driving wheels.

Sanding

As the first of the class, *Corsair* was built with a large sandbox on top of the saddletank positioned exactly in the middle of the tank structure. Here it conveniently fed the railhead just in advance of the leading driving wheel and these large sandboxes would later become a standard fitting on those engines, of a very similar design, built for the South Devon Railway. *Brigand*, however, was fitted with a modified arrangement, with the sandbox positioned ahead of the leading driving wheel and attached to the footplate – where the poor fireman could at least reach it without endangering life and limb.

Boiler Fittings

These were of the standard Gooch design, the boilers of course being domeless. In later years the wide Gooch chimney caps were probably substituted for the shallower Armstrong pattern. Only one member of the class survived in service beyond 1873. This was *Horace*, which fortunately was photographed before its demise in December 1880, by which time the engine carried the standard Armstrong, tapered, roll top chimney.

Weatherboards

Originally no protection was afforded to the unfortunate footplate crew, other than the firebox backhead. Later, probably by the mid 1860s, a weatherboard or spectacle plate was added at the rear of the firebox.

Coupling Rods

Initially these were fitted with brasses enclosed in a circular strap. The photograph of *Horace* illustrates that at some point the design was changed and larger square-ended brasses, with adjustable wedges, were introduced in their place. It is not known if these rods were fitted to all the engines or only to this unique late survivor. This latter option is perhaps the more likely, though absolute evidence is lacking.

Buffers

Leather buffers were fitted to *Corsair* and *Brigand*. The Hawthorn engines came out with sprung buffers with tapered barrels, as illustrated in the 1857 diagram and in the photograph of *Hesiod*. *Horace* is fitted with the parallel barrelled buffers typical of later Armstrong practise but, once again, this engine may have been alone in receiving these fittings.

Working Lives

Initially, both *Corsair* and *Brigand* were, as intended, put to work on the South Devon Railway, operating between Exeter and Plymouth. From 1st July 1851, the SDR, working with the contractors Messrs Evans & Geach, took over the working of their line using engines designed by Gooch that were of a very similar type to *Corsair* and *Brigand*, and of which twelve were

Cross sections of *Corsair*, the first built 'Bogie' Class engine, as shown in D.K. Clark's *Locomotive Machinery* of 1855. Note the midfeather in the firebox, the sledge brake and unique design of sanding arrangement with the sandbox mounted on top of the saddle tank.

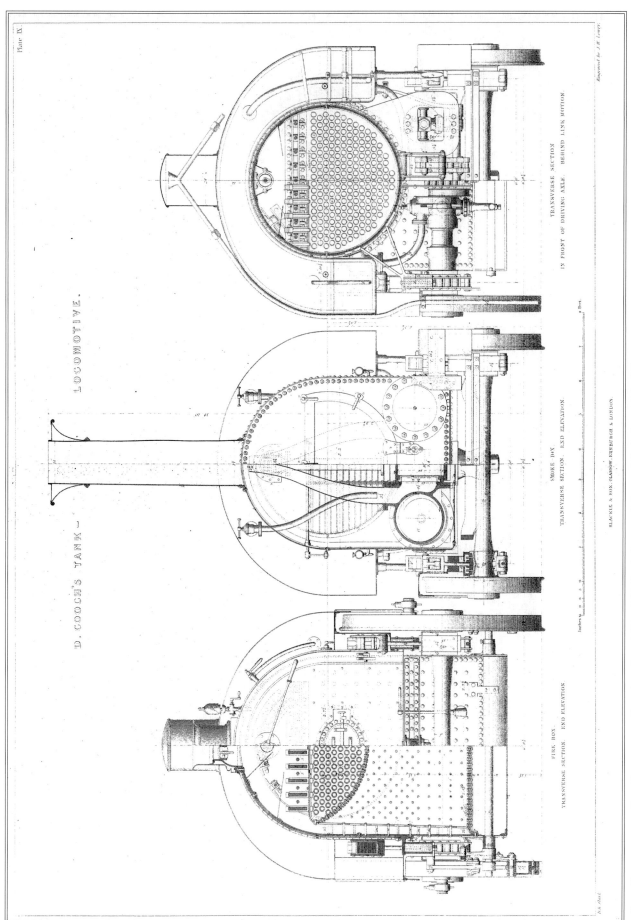

D. GOOCH'S TANK — LOCOMOTIVE.

FIRE BOX. END ELEVATION
TRANSVERSE SECTION

SMOKE BOX. END ELEVATION
TRANSVERSE SECTION

TRANSVERSE SECTION
IN FRONT OF DRIVING AXLE.   BEHIND LINK MOTION

BLACKIE & SON, GLASGOW, EDINBURGH & LONDON.

From the same source, these three cross sections show, from left to right, the firebox, smokebox and the boiler with its 219 tubes.

TANK-LOCOMOTIVE, BY DANIEL GOOCH,

FOR THE

GREAT WESTERN RAILWAY.

CORSAIR.

This drawing is taken from Clark's *Railway Machinery* and shows *Corsair* in its original condition, with tank mounted sandbox and sledge brake. Both of these innovations were not perpetuated by the GWR, though the similar engines built for the SDR from 1851 onward retained the tank mounted sandbox. The drawing illustrates the peculiarities of the design, which might be described as a rail mounted traction engine; the boiler acting as the backbone of the engine with the bogie mounting attached by a double gusset to the underside of the boiler. The driving wheels were balanced by a substantial beam (the leading pair were flangeless) visible in the drawing alongside the firebox. These beams were later removed. *Corsair* and *Brigand* worked successfully between Newton Abbot and Plymouth until about 1852, when they were replaced as the SDR took over the working of its own railway. Later on, *Corsair* spent a number of years based at Hereford working over the route to Gloucester.

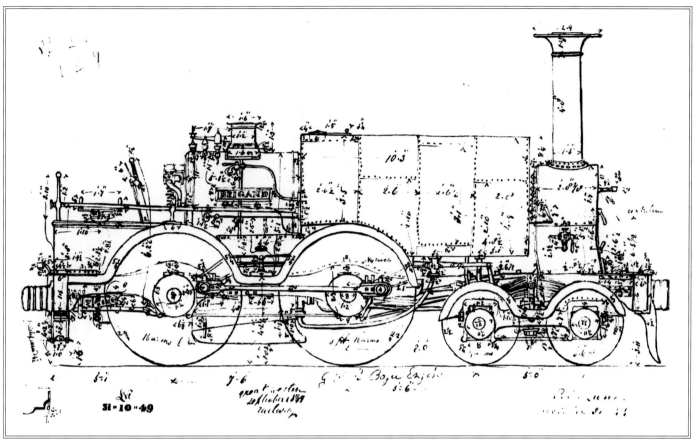

This E.T. Lane drawing of *Brigand* is dated 31st October 1849 and therefore must show the engine as originally built at Swindon, since it had been outshopped only four weeks earlier. Other than the removal of the sledge brake and tank mounted sandbox, the other major difference between *Corsair* and *Brigand* was at the rear end, where the length of the frames was reduced by 2ins. Brakes on *Brigand* were provided on the rear driving wheels.

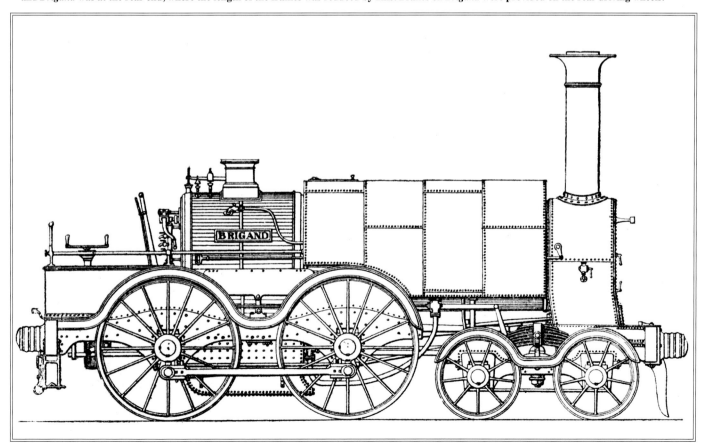

built, by four different manufacturers. They differed from the two GWR engines in various minor ways, the most significant of which was a reduction in the diameter of the driving wheels to 5ft 9ins. In this respect the design was a forerunner of the Hawthorn engines. The first of these new engines were not delivered until November 1851 but it was not until the late summer of 1852 that enough indigenous engines were available for traffic, thereby enabling most of the GWR engines, *Corsair* and *Brigand* among them, to be returned to their parent company. After three years of work over the South Devon main line, both engines would have been in need of a heavy overhaul. There was almost certainly quite a backlog of locomotives awaiting repair or rebuilding at the time and, unfortunately, the return of the engines from South Devon coincided with a period when the Works at Swindon was at one of its lowest ebbs. In 1852, the financial recession was at its peak and the workforce had been severely curtailed. Consequently, engines were standing out of service for many months with priority given those which were most needed in traffic, such as the 8ft 0in. 'Singles' and the increasing number of 0-6-0 goods engines. In all probability, two 4-4-0 saddle tanks would therefore have had to wait their turn, particularly since they no longer had a specific role to fulfil. The reduced capacity at the Works in the early to mid 1850s also accounts for the purchase by the GWR

of the remaining thirteen engines of the 'Bogie' Class from R.&W. Hawthorn and the ten engines of the 'Waverley' Class from R. Stephenson & Co. in 1854-55.

This brings us to the consideration of an important question – what specific traffic requirements, either apparent or perceived, induced Gooch to order the thirteen engines that were supplied by Hawthorns between June 1854 and March 1855? It seems to me that there is not one simple answer but an amalgam of causes, which may be summarised in the following way:

A. *Corsair* and *Brigand* had proved the effectiveness of the design.

B. Gooch's experience with the smaller wheeled South Devon engines, which though primarily passenger engines, also fulfilled a useful 'maid of all work' function.

C. As more route mileage was added to the GWR's network, much of it of a secondary or branch line nature, there was a need for more powerful tank engines to fulfil what later generations would describe as a mixed traffic role, rather in the manner of the '45/55XX' 2-6-2 tanks of a later generation.

D. Following on from the previous point, in 1853-54 the GWR's only tank engines were conversions from small and underpowered 2-2-2 or 2-4-0 tender engines. These might have been be ideal for short out and back branch line work with very light trains but they fell short of the need for the extra power

A panorama of the River Severn from Newnham circa 1910. Bullo Pill engine shed can be seen to the right, surrounded by wagons loaded with coal from collieries at the top end of the Forest of Dean Branch. The branch itself can be seen climbing sharply away from the South Wales main line and curving round behind the water tower. Pill is a term for a river inlet but the tramroad opened in 1810 to bring coal down to be shipped here had originally run to the riverside wharves just visible in the far left distance. The wet dock at Bullo Pill, behind the trees in the middle distance just left of centre, was opened by 1815 in response to the opening of the Severn & Wye Railway's docks at Lydney. Bullo Dock was served by a short branch which dropped down beside the group of buildings just visible in the middle of the picture. 'Bogie' Class tanks would have worked both down to the dock and up the branch to the collieries near Cinderford. The branch was goods only throughout the 19th century, a passenger service only finally being put on in 1908.

demanded by the traffic department as train weights and route mileage continued to grow.

As we have mentioned numerous times already, our knowledge of the workings of the GWR throughout the broad gauge era is far from comprehensive. This is especially true in the case of engines such as the 'Bogie' Class, as the GWR always referred to these 4-4-0 tanks. We can only piece together what little is available, much of which is based on Gooch's 'Coke Returns' for 1854-60 and 1862. Other titbits have been culled from articles in books and magazines, the most significant of which are W.E. Edwards series of writings in the *Railway & Travel Monthly* in 1912. He wrote extensively about broad gauge workings on the Wilts, Somerset & Weymouth Railway and this is of much interest, though some of his assertions, particularly with regard to opening dates of new lines etc., are inaccurate. It is from Edwards that we learn that *Homer* worked the first train on the East Somerset Railway from Witham to Shepton (sometimes erroneously referred to as Shipton) Mallet on 9th November 1858. The *RCTS History* (page B27) infers that a 'Bogie' Class engine was based at Shipton (*sic*) in November 1860. A shed was opened at Shepton Mallet on 9th November 1858 and closed on 1st March 1862, when the extension of the line to Wells (East Somerset) was opened. It is probable therefore that from the 1860s, 'Bogie' Class engines regularly worked this line until the conversion of the gauge in June 1874.

Whilst we are on the subject of new openings, Lyons & Mountford (*A Historical Survey of Great Western Engine Sheds 1837-1947*) tell us that when Bridport shed opened in November 1857, *Hesiod* was the resident engine and that *Homer* was domiciled at Bullo Pill from its opening in August 1854, when the engine had just entered service. A little more information about the Bridport Branch can be found in Gerry Beal's *The Bridport Branch*, wherein he informs us that *Hesiod* hauled an inspection train on 5th November 1857 consisting of two coaches and four waggons on which rode Captain Tyler, of the Board of Trade. He was evidently satisfied with what he saw because he allowed the line to open a week later on Thursday 12th November. Later, *Theocritus* was also recorded to be working on the line, a duty which the 'Bogie' Class shared with 'Leo' Class 2-4-0 tank engines.

The Salisbury Accident, 5th August 1873

It is W.E. Edwards too who recounts the details of a head on collision that occurred about one mile from Salisbury station on Tuesday 5th August 1873.

It occurred because a harassed stationmaster at Wilton, the station next beyond Salisbury, forgot that a telegraphic order, which he frankly admitted he was aware of, had been made arranging to cross an Up Salisbury to Chippenham mixed train with a Down, late running Bristol to Salisbury passenger service at his station. In accordance with instructions, the mixed, hauled by the 'Standard Goods' 0-6-0 *Gladiator*, pulled away from Salisbury at the appointed time of 4.35pm. Meanwhile, the passenger train, behind 4-4-0 'Bogie' Tank *Homer* and running about 28 minutes late, had arrived at Wilton. It was soon sent on its way by the stationmaster who, too late, realised his mistake and frantic efforts were made to stop the train but to no avail. Fortunately, both sets of enginemen reacted quickly when they realised what was happening. The mixed had nearly come to a standstill and the passenger train had slowed to about 15mph at the point of impact. Sadly, however, both the driver and guard of the passenger train were killed, whilst the driver

This view of *Hesiod* was taken at Gloucester, on the viaduct at the west end of the station, where a number of broad gauge engines were photographed in the late 1860s. *Hesiod* is seen here attached to an open carriage truck, suggesting that it was employed on station pilot duties at the time. Built by R.&W. Hawthorn & Co., it was the penultimate member of the class, entering service in March 1855. The Hawthorn engines differed from *Corsair* and *Brigand* principally in that they were fitted with smaller 5ft 9ins driving wheels. As illustrated here, the engine had also undergone some minor modifications. The front of the saddle tank had been cut back to ease access to the inside motion and the boiler feed clack valve, whilst the balance beams had been removed and a cab spectacle plate fitted. Sandboxes are visible attached to the footplate above the leading buffer beam, whilst the spring buffers were fitted when the engine was built. The large, circular projection on the side of the smokebox is rather perplexing and may, in fact, be damage to the emulsion of the photograph rather than anything else.

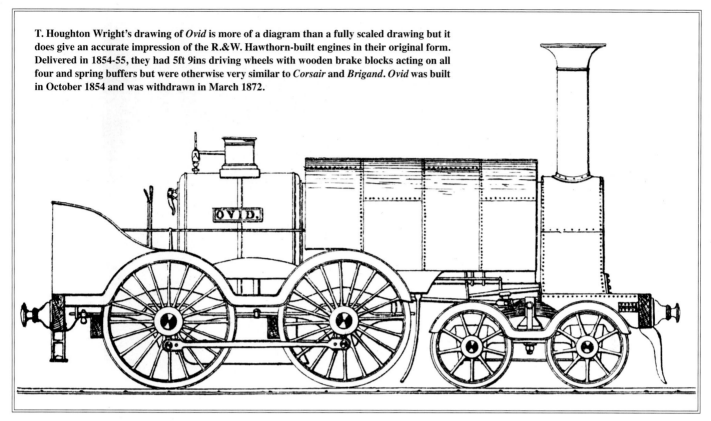

T. Houghton Wright's drawing of *Ovid* is more of a diagram than a fully scaled drawing but it does give an accurate impression of the R.&W. Hawthorn-built engines in their original form. Delivered in 1854-55, they had 5ft 9ins driving wheels with wooden brake blocks acting on all four and spring buffers but were otherwise very similar to *Corsair* and *Brigand*. *Ovid* was built in October 1854 and was withdrawn in March 1872.

of the mixed broke his leg when jumping from the footplate. Twelve passengers complained of slight injury and many more were badly shaken.

Between Salisbury and Wilton, the GWR single track line ran parallel to the London & South Western Railway main line to the South West. Though the GWR and L&SWR were never on the best of terms, it is pleasing to report that the latter gave the GWR considerable assistance in their efforts to deal with the consequences of the accident and afterwards to clear up the mess. There was one other victim of the accident. Both engines were taken to Swindon but whilst *Gladiator* was repaired, *Homer* was deemed 'beyond hope' and was formally condemned in the following December, by which time the remains had probably already been broken up.

The Coke Returns

It is interesting that the records for 1854 available to me, which is the three week period ending on 22nd July, make no mention of either *Corsair* or *Brigand*, or indeed the newly delivered *Sappho*, which may not as yet have entered service. The coke returns only mention engines 'in steam', so not too much should be read into this omission. A significant event, as far as the class was concerned, occurred on 1st August 1854, when the Wycombe Railway opened between Maidenhead and High Wycombe. This line became a regular haunt for the class, with at least two engines usually employed and shown to be allocated to Wycombe shed in all the extant records. However, when the shed opened initially, the first allocation was of two 'Sun' Class 2-2-2s converted to saddle tanks, namely *Aurora* and *Javelin*. They evidently did not prove powerful enough to work the traffic as it

built up though and were replaced by 4-4-0 tanks as they were delivered in the latter part of 1854.

Engines in steam three weeks ending 22nd July 1855:
  Wycombe: *Homer*, *Seneca*
  Reading: *Corsair*, *Horace* (said to be '*ballasting*')
  Birmingham: *Euripides*, *Ovid*, *Statius*
  Cheltenham & Gloucester: *Theocritus* – said to be '*allocated to Goods work*'
  Bullo Pill: *Sappho*, *Virgil*

This is the first survey following delivery of the last Hawthorn engine, when all fifteen of the class might have been available for traffic. The spread of allocations is fairly typical of subsequent reports, though inevitably there were various changes along the way. An obvious omission in 1855 is Hereford. The Gloucester to Hereford line was opened in full on 2nd June 1855 but initially the line was worked by 'Sun' Class 2-2-2 tanks on the passenger service and 0-6-0 tender engines for goods work. This situation soon changed and the 4-4-0 tanks became especially associated with the line's working until its conversion to standard gauge in 1869. Bullo Pill is another place which had a long association with the 'Bogie' Class. From here they worked mineral traffic, mainly coal, to the dock from the collieries on the Forest of Dean Branch and also into Gloucester. Further information about this interesting corner of the GWR, as well as a full list of engines in steam at Bullo Pill between 1854 (the first allocation of *Homer* – soon supplemented by *Virgil* – was made in September) and 1861, can be found in Volume 1 of *The Forest of Dean Branch*.

Elsewhere, *Corsair* based at Reading was perhaps working from Maidenhead on the Wycombe Railway, while the Bordesley Junction allocation were probably working the local traffic

Horace was the one member of the 'Bogie' Class to survive beyond 1873, ending its days working in the South West of England where, fortunately, it was photographed before its demise in December 1880; the actual location is not known. In addition to the modifications already mentioned in the caption accompanying the photograph of *Hesiod*, *Horace* has received an Armstrong roll top chimney, Roscoe lubricators behind the chimney and on the smokebox sides, sandboxes attached to the footplating adjacent to the leading driving wheels – which incidentally are flangeless – and injectors mounted on the side of the firebox with their attendant pipework. The engine's livery is interesting, with each segment of the saddle tank lined, the panels being edged in black picked out with a fine white line. Not all saddle tanks seem to have been lined in this fashion and although it is not conclusive, it may indicate that the engine's previous heavy repair was undertaken at Newton Abbot. The wooden brake blocks bearing on the driving wheels can be clearly seen, a significant improvement in braking power over *Corsair* and *Brigand*. Even so, such a simple arrangement makes their ability to successfully work heavy coal trains down the steeply graded Forest of Dean Branch, for instance, quite remarkable. The prominent works plate is also worthy of note.

between Birmingham and Wolverhampton, as well as the Stratford-on-Avon Branch from Leamington. Surprisingly, the 'Bogie' 4-4-0s seem to have been removed from the Birmingham area by the late 1850s, to be replaced by the older and smaller 'Sun' and 'Leo' classes. The only conclusion that can be drawn from this is that the available traffic did not warrant the additional power of the 'Bogie' Class.

Engines in steam nineteen days to 19th July 1856:
    Wycombe: *Homer, Seneca*
    Reading: *Horace*, 'employed on Goods work'
    Birmingham: *Brigand, Juvenal*
    Hereford: *Hesiod, Statius*
    Bullo Pill: *Sappho*

Engines in steam eighteen days to 18th July 1857:
    Wycombe: *Statius, Theocritus*
    Reading: *Juvenal*
    Birmingham: *Brigand*
    Hereford: *Corsair, Hesiod, Virgil*
    Bullo Pill: *Sappho*
    Neath: *Seneca*, employed 'on banking duties'

Engines in steam seventeen days to 17th July 1858:
    Wycombe: *Homer, Juvenal*
    Reading: *Brigand*
    Hereford: *Corsair, Horace, Ovid, Sappho, Seneca*
    Bullo Pill: *Theocritus*

Engines in steam twenty-three days to 23rd July 1859:
    Wycombe: *Hesiod, Seneca*
    Birmingham: *Lucretius*
    Bristol: *Euripides*
    East Somerset (Shepton Mallet): *Sappho*
    Hereford: *Corsair, Juvenal, Lucan*
    Bullo Pill: *Horace, Virgil*

Engines in steam twenty-one days to 21st July 1860:
    Wycombe: *Euripides, Hesiod*
    South Wales: *Virgil* ('Goods')
    Reading: *Seneca*
    Hereford: *Brigand, Juvenal, Horace, Ovid*
    East Somerset (Shepton Mallet): *Lucan*
    Bullo Pill: *Hesiod, Theocritus*

Engines in steam nineteen days to 19th July 1862:
    Wycombe: *Homer, Lucretius*
    Wells (replacing Shepton Mallet): *Seneca*
    Hereford: *Brigand, Corsair, Theocritus*
    Bullo Pill: *Hesiod, Lucan, Sappho*

Reading through these lists, which at best provide a snapshot of the activities of the class, one is instantly struck by their uniformity. The few exceptions to their regularity, such as the use of *Seneca* as a banker based at Neath in 1857, are noteworthy and in this case unusual. As mentioned earlier, the use of the class in the West Midlands had declined markedly by 1860 but this change to their workload was partially replaced by the opening of the East Somerset line, first to Shepton Mallet and then to Wells. Since only one engine is usually mentioned at Shepton in the returns, it strongly suggests that the branch, initially at least, was worked on the 'one engine in steam' principle.

The one exception to the general rule is found in November 1858, with *Homer* and *Thunderer* shown as allocated to Shepton when the shed first opened. *Thunderer* was a 'Caesar' Class goods 0-6-0, which had most probably been in use as a ballast engine during the line's construction. The part played by Homer in the story is revealed in the following extract from the *Western Daily Press* of Friday 12th November 1858, which records the opening of the line: '*The first train started away from the Shepton Station at seven o'clock and at 9.25 the first down train ran into the station amidst the cheers of hundreds of spectators. Mr R.J. Ward, the engineer of the line, drove the* Homer *engine, a very powerful 'boggy'* [sic] *i.e., an engine whose front wheels are allowed some little play like the free wheels of a waggon and can therefore turn easily at curves'*. The spelling accurately reproduces the original text with its interesting interpretation of the word bogie!

Unfortunately, from 1862 onward we have no formal records but the decline of the class, resulting in the mass withdrawals of 1871-73, can be traced to the conversion of various lines which the engines were associated with, to the standard gauge. This process began with the demise of broad gauge workings in the West Midlands and the conversion of the Hereford to Grange Court Junction (for Gloucester) lines in 1869. The Wycombe Railway followed in 1870 and the South Wales main line, including the Forest of Dean Branch, in 1872.

In the 1860s, the class may have gained some additional work following the opening of the Bristol and South Wales Union Railway in 1863 working from Bristol Temple Meads via Stapleton Road, Horfield, Filton and Patchway to New Passage Pier. This line was, in turn, converted in 1873 by which time the 4-4-0 tanks had largely been displaced by Metropolitan 2-4-0s rebuilt as tender engines. W.E. Edwards records that he recalled seeing a member of the class stabled in the little one road shed at Bath in the 1860's. the engine that he remembered was Homer though there would surely have been others. The Bath engines were used variously on local trains to Bristol and Westbury and for local shunting duties.

The final major conversions, before the GWR assumed control of the railways to the west of Bristol, were the Berks & Hants and the Wilts, Somerset & Weymouth lines in June 1874. By this time only one member of the class, *Horace*, was still at work, perhaps based at Wells before conversion made it redundant. What then happened to this obvious 'survivor' is something of a mystery but it may, in the time-honoured fashion of superannuated tank engines, have become a shunter at Swindon Works. The usual fate of such engines was an encounter with the breakers gang but *Horace* possibly survived so long because of the need to find some suitable support for the very similar South Devon Railway 4-4-0 tanks which the GWR acquired in 1876. The newly amalgamated railways were certainly short of motive power when they were taken over. The GWR cobbled together an assortment of tank and coupled engines, which included *Horace* and three former Vale of Neath Railway 0-6-0s, and sent them to the South West. The 0-6-0s became bankers based either at Newton Abbot or Plymouth Milbay but of *Horace* we hear nothing. It might have been found anywhere from Kingswear to Falmouth or beyond, perhaps working a South Devon or Cornish branch line. Whatever, it survived until December 1880 when the final journey to the breaker's yard was made. (See also Appendix 3)

Works Report

Members of the 'Bogie' Class that received major repairs at Swindon between September 1866 and January 1871:

1866

September .... *Hesiod, Horace*
October .. .. *Homer*
November .... *Lucretius*
December .... *Ovid, Juvenal*

1867

March .... *Statius*
April. .... *Lucan*
May .. .. *Horace*
June . ... *Corsair*
August .... *Virgil*

1868

January ... . *Theocritus*
February . ... *Homer*
November .... *Brigand*

1869

February . ... *Euripides*
August .... *Statius*
November .... *Virgil*

1870

April. .... *Homer*
June . ... *Brigand, Corsair*
July .. .. *Seneca*
August .... *Theocritus*

1871

January ... . *Lucan*

Since the first withdrawals were made at the end of 1871, there could have been few heavy repairs after the early part of that year. The exception to this rule is, of course, *Horace*, which having received no major attention since May 1867 would have been due an overhaul in 1871-72. It seems very likely that it was the last of the class to receive works attention before normal repairs ceased, which explains why it survived beyond 1873. Having, no doubt, been reprieved by the need to send motive power to the South West, it was certainly the recipient of another heavy repair in the mid 1870s. It then acquired an Armstrong

NAME	MILEAGE	CONDEMNED	NOTES
Corsair	387,996	June 1873	**Sold to Ciley Colliery**
Brigand	376,059	June 1873	**Sold to Edwards & Suter Returned to Swindon & Broken up in April 1878**
Sappho	321,256	Dec. 1873	**Sold to Staveley Iron & Coal Co.**
Homer	337,262	Dec. 1873	**Broken up**
Virgil	276,550	Dec. 1873	**Sold to Dobson, Brown & Adams**
Horace	402,968	Dec. 1880	**Sold to Ciley Colliery on 23rd June 1881**
Ovid	301,076	June 1872	**Broken up March 1872**
Juvenal	284,452	Dec. 1873	**Sold to Dobson, Brown & Adams**
Seneca	282,218	June 1872	**Broken up March 1872**
Lucretius	244,895	June 1872	**Broken up March 1872**
Theocritus	359,507	Dec. 1873	**Sold to Staveley Iron & Coal Co.**
Status	302,034	Dec. 1871	**Broken up October 1871**
Euripides	244,342	Dec. 1871	**Broken up**
Hesiod	267,818	June 1872	**Broken up July 1872**
Lucan	293,193	June 1872	**Broken up March 1872**

TABLE 7.3: 'BOGIE' CLASS – FINAL MILEAGAES & CONDEMNED DATES

chimney which only began to be fitted at Swindon from 1876 (Newton Abbot also fitted this pattern of chimney to engines they repaired in the late '70s). No doubt *Horace* was withdrawn when its mechanical condition warranted further heavy works attention. The final mileages and condemened dates for the class are shown in **Table 7.3**, above.

As we have noted with previous classes, there are some discrepancies between condemnation and actual breaking up dates, which seems to be the result of the way that official records were kept. The date 'condemned' relates thus to the time when the locomotive was 'written off' for accountancy purposes, rather than when it was taken out of service.

Conclusion

There is little more to be said. Like so many broad gauge engines designed in the 1840s and '50s, the 'Bogie' Class became victims of the demise of the broad gauge itself. Had the GWR not embarked upon a programme of rapid gauge conversion in the 1860s and early '70s, more members of the class might have survived to enjoy an extended lease of life in the South West of England, as *Horace* did. Sadly, it was not to be, though a number of not dissimilar engines were still at work in May 1892 – a testimony to the soundness of the original design.

SECTION 3: THE GOODS CLASSES DESIGNED BETWEEN 1846 AND 1852
CHAPTER 7
THE 'PREMIER' CLASS

Introduction

Few people, I feel, would argue with the statement that the Great Western Railway was one of the most beautifully engineered railways in the country. Indeed, it is not pushing the bounds of credibility too far to claim that the GWR was the world's first 'high speed line'. Yet, with its easy gradients and sweeping curves, together with its links between the City and Port of London, and the City and Port of Bristol, the railway offered copious opportunities for the rapid movement of goods just as it did for its human patrons.

Initially, goods traffic grew slowly but once the railway opened throughout between London and Bristol and over the Bristol & Exeter line by 1844, the demand for the transit of goods and thus the supply of rolling stock and motive power became ever more pressing. In this context it is worth reminding readers that the very first vehicles produced in Swindon Works were not locomotives but iron goods waggons, the production of which had to be temporarily suspended to enable the first engines to be erected.

Gooch was not the first locomotive engineer to use the 0-6-0 wheel arrangement – that accolade probably belongs to Timothy Hackworth – yet he was certainly in the van of its development. By instructing Nasmyth, Gaskell & Co. to turn out the last four of their order for twenty 7ft 0in. 2-2-2s of the 'Fire Fly' Class as 5ft 0in. 0-6-0s, Gooch, in effect, produced a prototype heavy goods engine. These four engines were an instant success, the first of which, named *Hercules*, markedly outshone its standard gauge opposite number, also named *Hercules*, in the Gauge Trials of 1845-46.

From these small beginnings Gooch went on to develop a standard goods engine which, in its various forms, would continue to serve the broad gauge and, indeed, the railways of Britain for many generations to come. This development began with the twelve engines known as the 'Premier' Class that were built at Swindon between February 1846 and May 1847. They were built in small batches and were contemporary with the 'Prince' Class 2-2-2s but displayed a variety of detail differences which suggests to me that Gooch, along with his design team, were still refining their ideas. Having settled some basic principles Gooch went on to develop the scope of those ideas with two further small classes of 0-6-0s, known as the 'Pyracmon' and 'Caesar' classes of 1847 and 1851. Only six 'Pyracmons' and eight 'Caesars' were built but a slightly enlarged version of the latter became the prototype of the extensive class of engines known as the 'Standard Goods', which eventually numbered 102 members. This design, with further modifications, was perpetuated by Gooch's successor Joseph Armstrong in 1865.

In addition to these increasingly enlarged and standardised engines we will also deal in this section with two miscellaneous builds. The first, *Avalanche*, was built as a tender engine by Stothert & Slaughter in Bristol in 1846 and rebuilt in 1848-49 as an 0-6-0 saddletank. The other, *Bacchus*, has a much more interesting pedigree. It was rebuilt from the 'experimental' R. & W. Hawthorn 10ft 'Single' *Hurricane*. This engine, along with its partner *Thunderer*, carried its boiler on a separate frame from the cylinders and driving wheels. *Bacchus* was built incorporating the boiler and probably the frames of *Hurricane* and Gooch referred to it as '*a powerful and useful goods engine*'. *Bacchus* has already made an appearance in Part 1 of this series but here the engine's story can be told in full.

Let us therefore turn our attention to the engines themselves.

The 'Premier' Class

The 'Premier' Class comprised twelve engines built at Swindon, under the '1st Goods Lot', between February 1846 and May 1847. The first of the class, *Premier*, qualifies as the initial engine turned out from Swindon Works but was not in fact a wholly 'in house' product. The twelve members of the class had boilers supplied by an outside contractor, whose identity has never been incontrovertibly established. *Premier* was fully erected at Swindon and was thus the first new locomotive to be outshopped by the Works but *Great Western* holds the accolade of being the first engine completely built and erected at Swindon. **Table 8.1**, below, gives the build and ceased work dates for the class.

TABLE 8.1: THE 'PREMIER' CLASS		
NAME	**BUILT**	**CEASED WORK**
Premier	**Feb. 1846**	**Nov. 1869**
Ajax	**May 1846**	**Aug. 1871**
Argo	**July 1846**	**March 1866**
Bellerophon	**July 1846**	**April 1870**
Vesuvius	**Sep. 1846**	**April 1870**
Telica	**Oct. 1846**	**July 1870**
Dreadnought	**Oct. 1846**	**April 1871**
Fury	**Dec. 1846**	**Feb. 1871**
Bergion	**Jan. 1847**	**Nov. 1870**
Briareus	**Feb. 1847**	**Dec. 1870**
Brontes	**May 1847**	**June 1872**
Jason	**May 1847**	**Sept. 1870**

An 'Outside Contractor'

The identity of the supplier of the boilers for the 'Premier' Class has never been positively established. I and other researchers have trawled through various national and local

This diagram, taken from Gooch's Notebook, illustrates his initial design planning for what became the 'Premier' Class. A close comparison with E.T. Lane's drawing of *Avalanche* on page 196 is instructive giving, as it will, a clear insight into Gooch's thinking during 1845, when both that engine and the 'Premier' Class were conceived. In effect, this amounted to an enlarged *Hercules* which was itself a 6-coupled 'Fire Fly'. The major changes incorporated into this new design are the provision of inside frames, along with an enlarged boiler and cylinder capacity, and a longer wheelbase. The new engines were also built with expansive gear which, at the time, was also being retrofitted to the earlier engines. In other ways the diagram illustrates Gooch's adherence to tried and tested features such as the Haycock firebox, domeless boiler and regulator set in the smokebox, with the handle visible on the backhead – all proven elements of the 'Fire Fly' design.

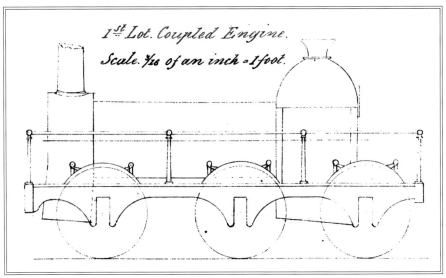

E.T. Lane's sketch of *Premier* was made in February 1846 when it was new and the finished engine deviated from Gooch's original drawing in several ways. Most obviously the shape of the footplating is radically different and there were changes to the layout of the regulator and other fittings. This style of footplating – designated as 'Group 1' in the text – appears to have been applied to the first four engines built: *Premier*, *Ajax*, *Argo* and *Bellerophon*. Though not initially perpetuated, this design became the standard style from 1851 with the introduction of the 'Caesar' Class and remained a norm until 1892.

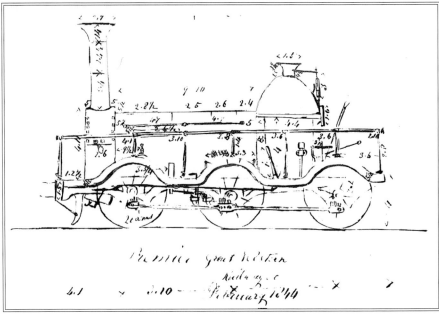

Lane's sketch of *Bellerophon* (note the misspelling) showing the driver's side of the engine is, unfortunately, undated but it illustrates the position of the regulator handle, regulator rod and the addition of a leading sandbox, a fitting which was not included in the original design and is not shown on Lane's drawing of *Premier*. Otherwise, both engines were similar though there may have been some minor differences in the external finish of the Haycock firebox. *Bellerophon* was built in July 1846 and ceased work in April 1870.

archives, so far without success. Many years ago, I asked Alan Peck, who wrote the history of Swindon Works, if he had any idea of the identity of the makers. He told me that he believed, but could not conclusively prove, that the boilers came from R. Stephenson & Co. Stupidly I did not think to ask the next, obvious question, namely *"What basis do you have for making this assumption?"*. Such is the innocence of youth. Being a trusting soul, I took him at his word and in fact, there is no compelling reason to doubt Alan's conclusion. Stephensons could indeed be the contractor, it is just that I can find no firm evidence to corroborate it. By the mid-1840s, the company were the locomotive construction industry's largest manufacturers and the supply of twelve boilers, spread over a period of twelve months or so, would have been well within their scope. They may even have used sub-contractors (a common practice at the time) to supply some of the parts. Yet it should not be forgotten that the GWR were at that time in the midst of the Gauge War with the Stephensons' standard gauge empire. Business, however, is business – a truth that carried as much weight in 1845-46 as it does today.

There is, perhaps, one other possibility. In February 1846, Stothert & Slaughter of Bristol supplied an 0-6-0 goods tender engine to the GWR, named *Avalanche* and rebuilt as a saddle tank a few years later. However, E.T. Lane fortunately sketched the engine in its original form at Swindon in 1848. Though its wheelbase is slightly longer than that of *Premier*, its boiler appears to be very similar in diameter. Stothert & Slaughter's early records have not survived, so there is no possible means of checking whether, at the same time, they had a contract to supply twelve similar boilers but this may explain why evidence of the origin of these boilers cannot be found.

There is also a further conundrum to consider. It might be anticipated that boilers would be delivered attached to the firebox, yet if G.F. Bird is to be believed – and he is the main source of our information – the design of the 'Haycock' fireboxes differed in shape and dimensions between various members of the class. This suggests to me that they were supplied locally from Swindon rather than by a contractor but we simply do not know for sure.

Constructional Details

TABLE 8.2: THE 'PREMIER' CLASS – MAIN DIMENSIONS	
Wheelbase	7ft 7¼ins + 6ft 10¼ins
Wheels – Driving	5ft 0in.
Cylinders	16ins x 24ins
Boiler	10ft 0in. x 4ft 0ins: 178 x 2ins tubes
Firebox Casing	4ft 5ins x 4ft 10ins
Tube Heating Surface	876.27 sq. ft
Firebox	105.91 sq. ft
Total	982.18 sq. ft
Grate Area	13.67 sq. ft
Calculated from the water side the total heating surface would be equal to about 1,081 sq. ft.	

As has just been mentioned, the engines within this class displayed numerous differences from each other, particularly with regard to the design of the footplate and splashers. Following a great deal of research, some of which led up blind and inaccurate alleys, I feel able to cautiously draw the following conclusion: that the twelve 'Premier' Class engines appear to have been turned out from Swindon Works in three distinct groups:

Group 1 – Four engines built at Swindon between February and July 1846: *Premier*, *Ajax*, *Argo* and *Bellerophon*. These all had footplates that curved over the driving wheels, which were supported by a continuous valance that followed the profile of the footplate. This design would later become a broad gauge standard for goods and some classes of passenger engines. The main dimensions are shown in **Table 8.2**, above.

Group 2 – Six engines built at Swindon between September 1846 and February 1847: *Vesuvius*, *Telica*, *Dreadnought*, *Fury*, *Bergion* and *Briareus*. These had straight footplates, with a curved section above the crank pins to allow for the movement of the coupling rods. A solid faced splasher was placed above each driving wheel and the centre splasher displayed the engine builder's plate.

Group 3 – Two engines built at Swindon in May 1847: *Brontes* and *Jason*. These were similar to Group 2 except that the splasher front was left partially open.

Fortunately, E.T. Lane drew four members of the class from life

This drawing of *Jason* is also believed to have been executed by E.T. Lane, though I cannot find it in his archive. Instead, it is copied from G.A. Sekon's *Evolution of the Steam Locomotive* (2nd edition, published by the Locomotive Publishing Co. in 1899). The drawing clearly shows a third variation in the design of the splashers, which I refer to as 'Group 3' in the text. This small section is thought also to include *Brontes* which, along with *Jason*, was turned out from Swindon Works in May 1847. There seems to be no very obvious reason for changing the design of the splashers and framing again, unless it was for experimental purposes. It was not perpetuated in later builds of goods engines, though it bears some resemblance to the ornamental brass splashers fitted to some members of the 'Prince' Class and the later 'Iron Duke' and 'Courier' designs. *Jason* ceased work in September 1870.

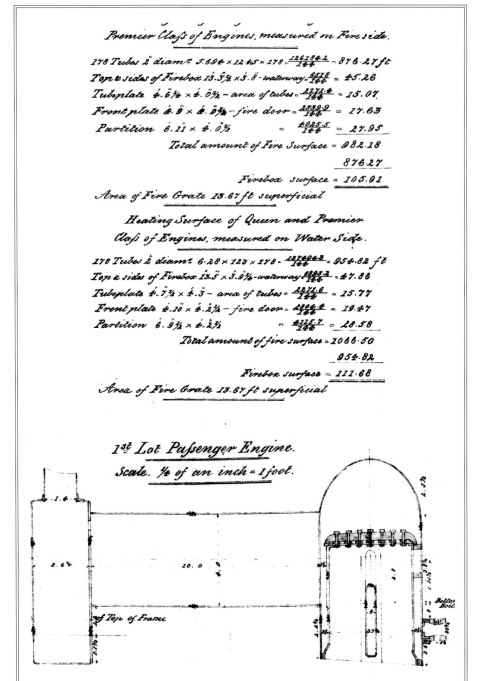

Premier Class of Engines, measured on Fire side.

178 Tubes 2" diam.ᵉ 5.694 × 12.45 × 178 $\frac{126784.2}{144}$ = 876.27 ft

Top & sides of Firebox 13.3¼ × 3.8 - waterway $\frac{6418}{144}$ = 45.26

Tubeplate 4.6¾ × 4.0¾ - area of tubes = $\frac{2171.4}{144}$ = 15.07

Front plate 6.9 × 4.0¾ - fire door = $\frac{2589.0}{144}$ = 17.63

Partition 6.11 × 4.0¾ = $\frac{4025.5}{144}$ = 27.95

Total amount of Fire Surface = 982.18

876.27

Firebox surface = 105.91

Area of Fire Grate 13.67 ft superficial

Heating Surface of Queen and Premier Class of Engines, measured on Water Side.

178 Tubes 2" diam.ᵉ 6.28 × 123 × 178 $\frac{137406.3}{144}$ = 954.82 ft

Top & sides of Firebox 13.5 × 3.9⅝ - waterway $\frac{6895.2}{144}$ = 47.86

Tubeplate 4.7¼ × 4.3 - area of tubes = $\frac{2271.6}{144}$ = 15.77

Front plate 4.10 × 4.2¼ - fire door = $\frac{2406.4}{144}$ = 19.47

Partition 6.9½ × 4.2¼ = $\frac{4115.7}{144}$ = 28.58

Total amount of fire surface = 1066.50

954.82

Firebox surface = 111.68

Area of Fire Grate 13.67 ft superficial

1ˢᵗ Lot Passenger Engine.

Scale. ¼ of an inch = 1 foot.

in 1848-49, *Premier*, *Bellerophon*, *Vesuvius* and *Jason*, which together illustrate the variations that have just been described. There exists but one photograph of a member of the class and that, fortuitously, is of *Premier* itself, a view taken at Westbourne Park in perhaps the early 1860s. Needless to say the photograph confirms the details depicted in Lane's drawing. G.F. Bird, writing in *The Locomotive Magazine* of September 1901, however, either misread Lane's drawings or put the wrong name on the wrong engine, because his illustration of *Premier* is wholly inaccurate, an error which has been perpetuated in the *RCTS History*.

Frames

All members of the class were fitted with inside sandwich frames, constructed in the usual way with iron plates and ash planking.

Cylinders, Valves, Regulators, etc.

These were of the same pattern as those fitted to *Great Western* and the 'Prince' Class, having a bore of 16ins and a 24ins stroke. The valves were placed on top of the cylinders and were worked by means of a rocking shaft. The regulator was in the valve chest and was moved by a horizontal curved lever placed on the driver's side of the footplate, adjacent to the firebox. The regulator rod passed through the smokebox wrapper to actuate the regulator.

Valve Gear

This was of the Gooch fixed link type, arranged to drive the valves by rocking shafts – as previously mentioned. *Premier* was the first new engine to be fitted with this gear.

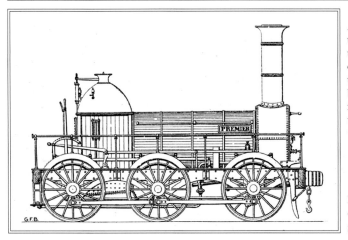

ABOVE: The boilers of the 'Prince' (Gooch refers to them as 'Queens') Class and the 'Premiers' were identical dimensionally. Since the Goods engines predate the Passenger locomotives, I have included Gooch's drawing here, though it is of course equally relevant to Chapter 4. Of particular interest is the design of the inner firebox, with its midfeather and the crown sheets supported by girders bolted to them. I strongly suspect, though cannot prove, that *Avalanche* was also fitted with a boiler of this type and capacity, which underscores my supposition that Stothert & Slaughter were the contractors who provided the boilers for the 'Premier' Class.

LEFT: We have reproduced Bird's wholly inaccurate drawing of *Premier* here in order to emphasise that it should be ignored in future by anyone studying broad gauge locomotive history.

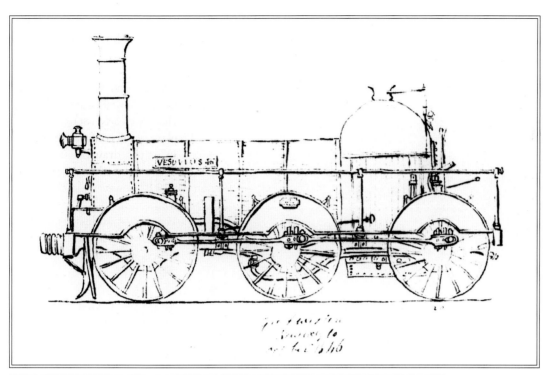

Lane's sketch of *Vesuvius* makes a most interesting comparison with the engine's immediate predecessor *Bellerophon*. Two months elapsed between the entry into traffic of the engines, *Vesuvius* making its debut in September 1846. The change to the splashers and footplating is self-evident and conforms much more closely to Gooch's original concept. In the text, I categorise this design as 'Group 2', within which *Telica*, *Dreadnought*, *Fury*, *Bergion* and *Briareus* are also believed to fall. Note the neater design of the leading sandbox and the shape and positioning of the works plate on the middle splasher. *Vesuvius* ceased work in April 1870.

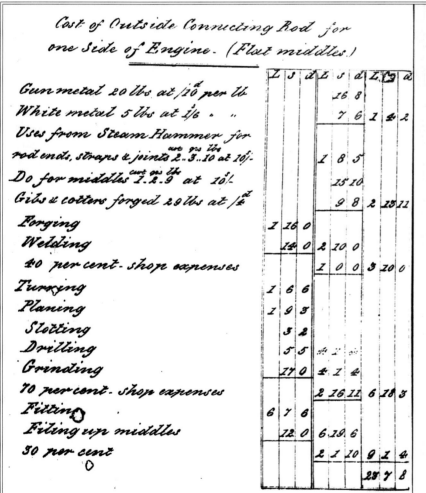

The manufacturing process involved in the construction of the rods is detailed in the cost estimates included with the drawings. They show forging, welding, turning, planing, slotting, drilling, grinding and fitting.

Boiler

As mentioned earlier, details relating to the boiler are sparse. The dimensions quoted are the same as those given for the boilers fitted to the 'Prince' Class with which they presumably were interchangeable. They are officially quoted as being 10ft 0in. long and 4ft 0in. in diameter, and contained 178 brass tubes of 2in. diameter. Externally, the boilers were clad with wood retained by five boiler bands but these timber slats were later sheeted over, as the photograph of *Premier* illustrates.

Smokeboxes

The smokebox had an outside length of 2ft 6ins and rose to a height of 4ft 11ins above the footplate. Including the area of it which enclosed the cylinders, the smokebox measured 6ft 10ins from its highest to its lowest point.

Fireboxes

These seem to have varied externally. The weight and shape of the brass Haycock crowns were of slightly differing profiles but since these complex shapes were made by hand, such minor anomalies should not surprise us. Officially, the dimensions of the firebox are given as 4ft 5ins long and 4ft 10ins wide. In common with the 'Prince' Class and *Great Western*, these were to be the last Haycock-type fireboxes designed into new build engines.

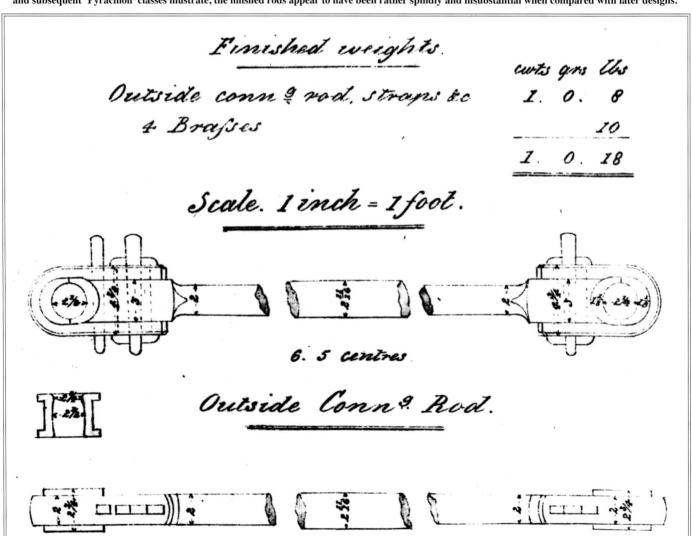

C. E. Outside Conn⁹ Rod. Scale 1 in = 1 foot.

These rods were formerly made without the joint A.

Gooch's drawings of connecting rods and big end bearings, with semi-circular straps and adjustable cotters give us succinct details of the design of the bearings, crank pins, etc. and also demonstrate that they were manufactured from 2⁵/₈ins iron bars. As the various drawings and photographs of the 'Premier' and subsequent 'Pyracmon' classes illustrate, the finished rods appear to have been rather spindly and insubstantial when compared with later designs.

Finished weights.

	cwts	qrs	lbs
Outside conn⁹ rod, straps &c	1.	0.	8
4 Brasses			10
	1.	0.	18

Scale. 1 inch = 1 foot.

6. 5 centres

Outside Conn⁹ Rod.

Lane's detailed sketches showing some of the features of *Premier*: Top Left: The regulator handle and fixing; Top Right: The regulator valve, bracket and lubricator; Bottom Right: The rocking shaft and pivot of the valve gear; Bottom Left: The boiler feed clack, delivery pipe, springing etc.

Sandboxes

E.T. Lane's drawing of *Premier* infers that the engine was originally built without any sanding gear. Quite probably, early experience with the engine suggested that this was an oversight, for his sketches of both *Bellerophon* and *Vesuvius* illustrate sandboxes placed on the footplate ahead of the front splasher, which fed sand to the leading driving wheels. As the photograph of *Premier* illustrates, this engine later received leading sandboxes of larger dimensions than those shown in the drawings. In addition, it was also fitted with a rear sandbox, positioned on top of the footplate alongside the firebox which, via a curved pipe, fed the rails behind the centre driving wheels, evidently to aid backward running. It would be logical to suppose that most, if not all, members of the class received these modifications and additions in due course.

Boiler Fittings

These were of the standard Gooch type, with a tall bellmouth lipped chimney and a squat brass safety valve cover sat atop of the Haycock firebox. The photograph of *Premier* indicates that the height of the chimney and the profile of the cap may have undergone some slight modifications in later years.

Wheels and Coupling Rods

The wheels were 5ft 0in. in diameter, which was to become the standard for broad gauge goods classes. The coupling rods were of a rather spindly design made, it would seem, from iron bar, the manufacture of which involved considerable smithing, slotting, planing and other processes, with each costing £23 7s 8d to make – a considerable sum then. The bearing brasses were enclosed in a circular strap and were fitted with adjustable wedges.

Tenders

For these and later goods classes, Gooch designed a new tender of wood and iron construction, based in part on earlier designs but with plate rather than sandwich frames. Like the earlier vehicles, the tank initially rested on a wooden frame set on top of the underframe. This was soon modified, however, and the wooden framework was discarded, allowing water capacity to be increased by rebuilding the tender tank. Tenders of this sort can be seen in the photographs of *Premier*, *Steropes* and *Bacchus* which follow.

Since these iron framed tenders, referred to as 'Short Tenders' in Gooch's Notebook, were a smaller version of the larger iron framed tenders that were built for *Iron Duke* and her sisters, it seems probable that the earlier members of the 'Premier' Class at least ran initially with the older sandwich framed vehicles, which had been rendered spare by the rebuilding of the 'Sun' and 'Leo' classes as saddle tanks.

Though it is not known exactly when the first of these tenders was built, it must surely be no later than the early months of 1847 and perhaps a little before. Their dimensions, as given on the 1857 specification, are also shown in **Table 8.3**, below.

TABLE 8.3: GOODS TENDERS – MAIN DIMENSIONS	
Wheels	3ft 6ins dia. with 14 spokes
Wheelbase	5ft 0in. x 5ft 0in.
Tank	13ft 9ins L x 3ft 0in. D x 8ft 3ins W
Capacity	1,470 gallons
Coke Space	8ft 5ins x 4ft 0in. x 3ft 0in.
Weight	Empty 7 tons 12 cwt. Full 15 tons 12 cwt

34

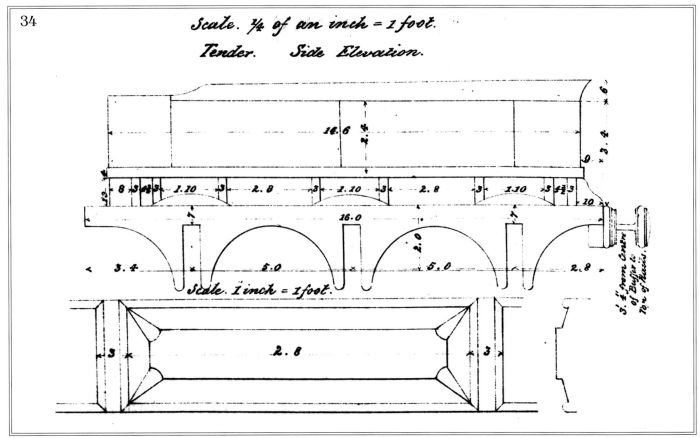

Scale. ¾ of an inch = 1 foot.

Tender. Side Elevation.

Scale. 1 inch = 1 foot.

35

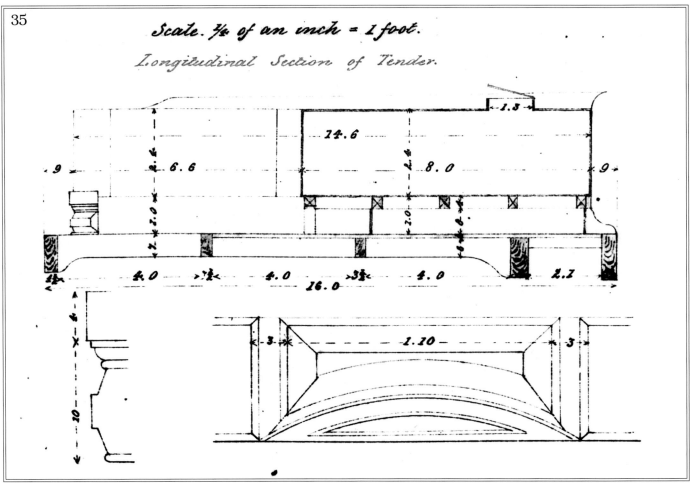

Scale. ¾ of an inch = 1 foot.

Longitudinal Section of Tender.

44

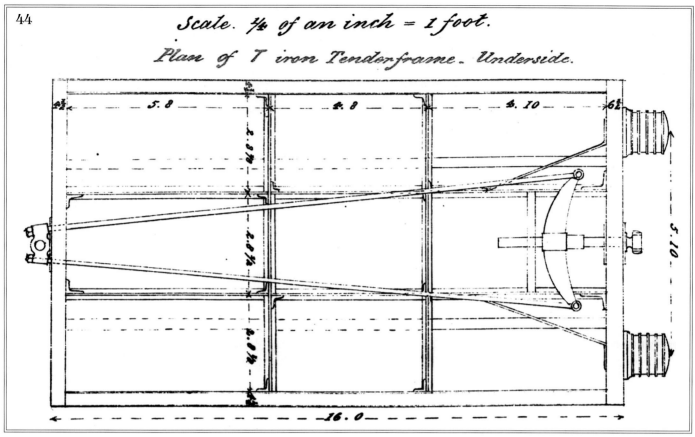

Scale. ¾ of an inch = 1 foot.

Plan of T iron Tenderframe — Underside.

These drawings are all taken from Gooch's Notebook and show the genesis of his design for the short, iron framed tenders with a 5ft 0in. x 5ft 0in. wheelbase, which were intended specifically for attachment to the 'Premier' Class but were then utilised on later classes. The first drawing (No. 34 in the Notebook) illustrates the initial intention which involved mounting the tender tank on a wooden subframe above the iron underframe. Though schemed out it is believed that the proposal was not proceeded, with being superseded after further reflection and experience. Drawing No. 35 shows the longitudinal section of the tender as originally planned and usefully includes all dimensions, the position of the water filler, etc. Drawing No. 44 illustrates the 'T Section' iron underframe design, once again giving useful dimensions along with the design of drawbar springing. Drawing No. 45 shows the revised design for the tender tank omitting the timber subframe, the scheme that was finally adopted. Unfortunately, it is not known how many tenders of this type were built before being superseded by later designs of greater capacity. In fact, the production run may have been quite short, perhaps numbering less than 50 examples.

45

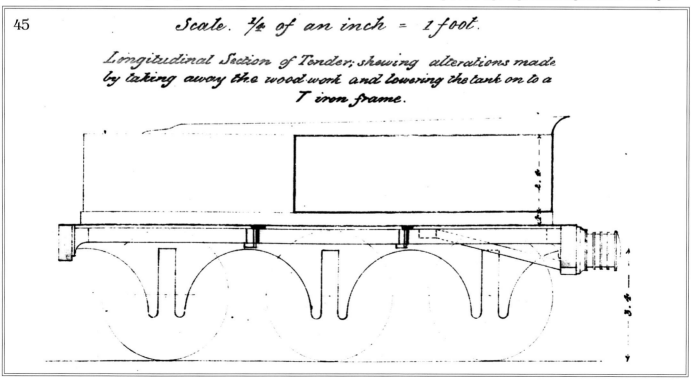

Scale. ¾ of an inch = 1 foot.

Longitudinal Section of Tender; shewing alterations made by taking away the wood-work and lowering the tank on to a T iron frame.

OLD SIX WHEEL⁹ TENDER.

These tenders date from about 1847 and when initially conceived had the iron tank mounted upon a wooden frame, as was the case with the earlier sandwich framed vehicles designed circa 1839-40. The wooden framing was soon discarded and the tender tanks were enlarged giving about another 250 gallons of capacity to the tanks, lifting them to around 1,470 gallons as described here. It is possible that in later years the water capacity was further enhanced by additional rebuilding, though this is by no means certain. This watercoloured drawing from the 1857 specifications book was also reproduced in Part 1 but is included again here for ease of reference.

DESCRIPTION

WHEELS. 6 Wheels 3 feet 6in⁹ in diam⁷. with 14 arms ⅞" and 1½" by 3 inches broad.
TANK 13 feet 9 in⁹ long by 3 feet deep by 8 feet 3 in⁹ wide. Coke space 8".5" X 4".0" X 3".0".
COKE-SPACE 102.0 cub. feet. WATER-SPACE 236.0 cub. feet. Contains 1470 gallons.
WEIGHT when empty on Leading 5..1..1. Middle and Trailing 2..11.1.14. Total 7..12.2.14.
WEIGHT when loaded on Leading 5..7..2 Middle 4..11.2..14 Trailing 6..5. Total 15..12.0.14.

Early Testing

After an initial period of running in and adjustment, *Premier* was put to work and proved an almost instant success. Such was the interest at the time in railway activity, the popular press even published details of the running of goods – or luggage as they are often referred to – trains. For example, the *Berkshire Chronicle* of 21st March 1846 announced that a '*Leviathan train of 46 trucks, on 16th March, arrived at Paddington hauled by* Premier *5ft 0in. driving wheels 0-6-0 built at Sunderland*'. The engine had of course been built at Swindon, a town of which perhaps the paper's editor was unaware! The *Windsor & Eton Express* of 29th August 1846 recorded: '*Monster train on 27th August.* Tityos *hauled 49 trucks on down train* Premier *brought up goods with 40 trucks*'.

Gooch would obviously have been delighted with such successful workings. Yet he was aware that the real challenge that his new designs would be presented with involved working trains in challenging weather conditions, over more difficult sections of railway than that between Swindon and London. He therefore arranged a series of adhesion and haulage tests, on what the *London Evening Standard* of 26th April 1847 referred to as '*the Stroud incline of the Gloucester line*'. This section of railway, which had opened on 12th May 1845, was perhaps the most challenging of the then extant GWR mileage and had the added advantage of being near to Swindon. The *Standard* gave a vivid description of its challenges:

'*The portion of the Gloucester line on which the experiments were made is that lying between the 98¹/₂ and the 95³/₄ mile posts viz. over 2³/₄ miles* [in essence, the starting point was from the site of what

later became Chalford station up to the western portal of the Sapperton Tunnel]. *The line for the whole of this distance is a series of S curves varying from 2,000 to 3,600 ft radius: and the starting point, from which the experiments commenced, viz. the 98¹/₂ mile post, is on a rising gradient of 1 in 105. This gradient extends for a little more than a furlong and is succeeded by a rising gradient of 1 in 75 for about ¹/₂ a mile. There is then a rising gradient of 1 in 70 for nearly ¹/₄ of a mile followed by a rising gradient of 1 in 75 for rather more than ³/₄ of a mile. We then come to a level of about a ¹/₄ of a mile. There is then a rising gradient of 1 in 70 for nearly ¹/₄ of a mile and next a rising gradient of 1 in 60 for nearly ³/₄ of a mile. It was over these severe gradients (all of them on curves) that the power of the locomotives was tested, and in order that the power might be really and commercially tested the train was brought to a dead stand upon this incline of 1 in 105.*'

For these tests Gooch used both *Great Western*, by now running as a 4-2-2, and *Dreadnought*, which had entered service in October 1846 so was well run in. Gooch also had use of his newly commissioned dynamometer coach, though the *Evening Standard*'s recorder used a '*split second hands watch*' made by Charles Frodsham of the Strand. Watches of this sort had two second hand dials one placed under the other, allowing an experienced recorder to make measurements that were said to be accurate to a quarter of a second. There was obviously a little more to this report than mere journalistic and newsworthy interest. The paper's reporters had clearly been invited to attend and they and Gooch, or one of his assistants, checked each other's timings at the conclusion of the tests. At the time Gooch was engaged in an argument, through the Institution of Civil Engineers, about

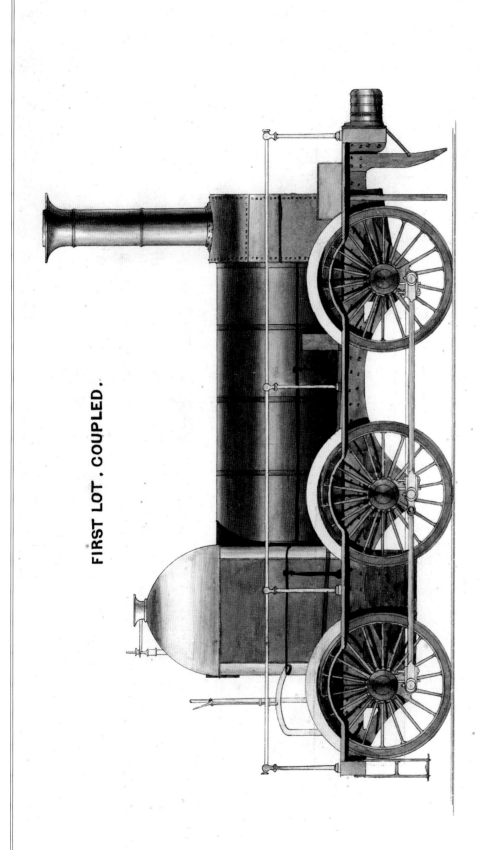

FIRST LOT . COUPLED.

AJAX . ARGO . BELLEROPHON . BERGION . BRIAREUS . BRONTES . DREADNOUGHT . FURY . JASON . PREMIER . TELICA . VESUVIUS .

DESCRIPTION

CYLINDERS 16 ins in diam? Stroke 24 ins. Steam Ports 1½ ins by 13 ins Exhaust 2⅜ ins by 13 ins
BOILER. 10 feet 0 ins long and 4 feet in diam? inside. Fire Box 4½ feet 5 ins long and 4 feet 10 ins wide.
TUBES. 178 Tubes 10 feet 5½ ins long and 2 ins in diam? outside. Heating Surface of Fire Box 105·91. Tubes 876·27.
AREA of FIRE-GRATE 13·67 superficial feet.
WHEELS Driving, Leading and Trailing, all coupled and 5 feet in diam?
BERGION with 6 cwt of Coke and 7 cwt 8 of Water on the Glass. Weighs 10 tons 2 cwt. Driving 9 . 10. Trailing 7 . 0 .

Like the 'Prince' Class, these engines differed in their design of footplating and splashers. The style illustrated here, which I called 'Group 3', was probably only common to the last two engines of the class, *Brontes* and *Jason*.

TABLE 8.4: TESTS ON SAPPERTON BANK WITH *GREAT WESTERN* AND *DREADNOUGHT*, SATURDAY 24TH APRIL 1847				
AVERAGE SPEED MAINTAINED OVER THE LAST QUARTER OF THE FIRST MILE				
GREAT WESTERN	**RUNNING TIME**		**SPEED PER MILE**	
With 50 tons	$30^1/_2$ seconds		$29^1/_2$	
With 60 tons	$33^3/_4$ seconds		$26^1/_2$	
With 70 tons	$42^1/_2$ seconds		21	
Figures not given for *Dreadnought* or the double-headed run				
DETAILS FOR THE ENTIRE CLIMB				
AVERAGE SPEED	*GW*	*GW*	*D-H*	*D*	*GW*
Tons	50	60	111	111	70
1 in 105 for about a furlong	11	10	$11^1/_2$	11	9
1 in 75 for about $^1/_2$ mile	$24^1/_2$	22	22	$19^1/_2$	19
1 in 70 for nearly $^3/_4$ of a mile	$29^1/_2$	$26^1/_2$	$25^1/_2$	$20^3/_4$	21
1 in 75 for about $^3/_4$ of a mile	$33^1/_4$	31	$29^1/_4$	23	26
Level for about $^1/_4$ of a mile	$38^1/_4$	$34^1/_2$	33	$27^1/_4$	31
1 in 70 for nearly $^1/_4$ of a mile	$39^1/_2$	$35^1/_2$	$36^1/_4$	$29^1/_4$	$32^1/_2$
1 in 60 for $^1/_2$ mile	38	33	35	26	31
GW – *Great Western*; D – *Dreadnought*; D-H – Double-Header				
The weather, though reasonably favourable, was changeable and the tests encountered at least one shower of rain				

the wind resistance and friction of the bearings and wheels of a locomotive, which he wanted to prove was, on the broad gauge at least, less than contemporary observers and engineers claimed. Though Gooch was undoubtedly a meticulous recorder and experimental engineer, he also had a keen eye for good publicity – and who could blame him.

The tests themselves, further details of which are given in Chapter 3 which were carried out on Saturday 24th April 1847, were conducted in a series of five separate runs with differing loads. Three were with *Great Western* hauling first 50 then 60 and finally trains of 70 tons. One was double-headed, with *Dreadnought* and *Great Western* hauling a train of 111 tons and then *Dreadnought* working the same tonnage alone. The results obtained are shown in **Table 8.4**, above (Note: This table is a redrawing of that given on page 71, presented here for ease of reference, whilst the *Evening Standard*'s report is given in full over pages 71-72).

Gooch was very happy with the outcome of these test runs, the like of which had never been attempted before. They proved many things, not the least of which was the prowess of his new designs and the merits of building his dynamometer coach; the latter would soon also be put to more extended use in trials with *Great Britain* on the Bristol & Exeter Railway main line.

Both engines, in fact, proved themselves completely. The weight of the trains involved may seem now to be very light but it is worth remembering that all were loose-coupled, running on stiff bulked road track, with iron wheels the axles of which were mounted in grease (i.e. tallow) lubricated axle boxes. The rolling resistance of such trains was considerable, especially that of a 111-ton goods or luggage train. The debate over the gauge question was still a very live one in 1847 and Gooch took every opportunity to play the broad gauge card. In fact these trials were conducted at a time when Parliament was debating the 'Gauge Question' and were therefore a powerful indication of the superiority which broad gauge traction afforded. In other words, they were jolly good publicity of unimpeachable veracity!

Accidents

Minor accidents, derailments, mechanical breakdowns and other *contretemps* were frequent occurrences in the early days of railway operation. Sadly, they often resulted in loss of life. One such event occurred on 29th August 1846, when *Premier* was involved in a shunting accident at Reading. This occasioned the death of one Benjamin Haddrill, whose duties the *Reading Mercury* did not divulge to its readership but presumably he was a shunter or perhaps a policeman. No doubt a thorough search through the archives of local newspapers would throw up many similar incidents.

As far as I can discover, a member of the 'Premier' Class was only involved in one major accident, the unfortunate engine being *Ajax* and the location Wootton Bassett, on Friday 20th September 1850. In many respects the circumstances surrounding the events were similar to those which had previously occurred at Shrivenham, on 10th May 1848, when *Sultan*, on the Up 'Flying Dutchman', ran into a straying cattle truck and horsebox which had been left foul of the main line by a couple of thoughtless porters. On this occasion a horsebox, which had not been properly braked was blown out onto the main line by the wind from a fast-running excursion train. The station at Wootton Bassett, five miles to the west of Swindon, was sited on a gentle falling gradient at an inclination of 8ft to the mile. The siding on which the horsebox was standing was not protected in any way which might have prevented the accident. The station staff claimed that the vehicle had been 'scotched' that is, a piece of timber inserted between the spokes of the wheels to retard its progress but that the timber in question had been stolen; there was a public right of way close to the siding. The accident inspector, Capt. R.M. Laffam RE, was obviously unimpressed by this alleged theft but could not disprove it. In any event, the horsebox was foul of the main line and it was struck by *Ajax* which was working a second excursion train from London to Bristol about 15 minutes after the previous train had passed. The time was about 11.00pm and the accident report described the impact :

'*The body of the horse-box, appears to have been knocked off the wheels by the collision, and to have been thrown forward some 20 or 30 yards, where it fell upon the rails. The wheels jammed in the closed switches appear to have been broken to pieces, – and the engine and train passed on, scarcely feeling the shock. The engine, however, came up with the body of the horse-box a second time, and breaking it to pieces, passed over the fragments; and some of those fragments appear to have thrown the wheels of the engine off the rails. The engine, now in back-gear, but still propelled forward by its own momentum, and that of the heavy train behind, ran on some 60 yards, edging away to the south side of the embankment on which it was running, the right-hand wheels ploughing up the ballast between the rails and smashing all the transverse connecting timbers, and thereby breaking up the roadway and causing all the carriages which followed to leave the line. Finally, the engine reaching the side of the bank, ran down the descending slope, crossed a shallow ditch, and dashed through an earthen bank on the other side, and finally came to a stand in a field about 150 yards from where it left the line. The tender still remained attached to it, and one second-class carriage followed the tender, turning over on its side as it crossed the earthen bank; another*

A most remarkable survivor, this is the only known photograph of one of the class, fortuitously of *Premier* itself. It was taken at Westbourne Park and the locomotive, which is evidently posed for the photographer, with no less than three men on the footplate, had perhaps been engaged in shunting the empty Loco coal waggons seen behind. The picture can be roughly dated – the mixed gauge arrived here in 1861, whilst the engine ceased work in November 1869, and as the trackwork had clearly been in place for some time, I would date it as circa 1865. There are various points to observe. The chimney is of the later Gooch design with the shallower cap, which may be polished though that is unclear. The smokebox illustrates how it was shaped out at the sides to enclose the valves and cylinders. This feature is also visible in the two photographs of *Prince* and *Sylph*, which were contemporary 7ft 0ins passenger engines – see Chapter 5. The leading sandboxes are prominent in the picture and the engine has also acquired rear sandboxes, which fed the middle driving wheels and were positioned alongside the firebox. Most significantly, it appears that *Premier* had been fitted with the later pattern, squared section coupling rods, a design that was introduced with the 'Caesar' Class of 1851. I would imagine that this was an innovation that was applied to all members of the class, as well as the succeeding 'Pyracmon' Class, though there is insufficient evidence to confirm this. It would be interesting to know something of the origins of the photograph itself, from what vantage point it was taken and by whom? A.R. KINGDOM COLLECTION

second-class carriage also reached the earthen bank, and turned over on its side; and two more, running a little further along the slope, came to a stand at the ditch, but remained standing in their proper positions.'

The report goes on to detail the damage to the engine, Capt. Laffan writing: *'The injury done to the engine was slighter than might have been expected; the axles were slightly strained, and the coupling-rods of the driving wheels were bent, the buffers were carried away and the buffer beam sprung; the chimney and ash-pan were also carried away; the eccentric gear and all the rest of the machinery was uninjured. The axles of the tender were bent about a quarter of an inch and the springs were injured; the buffers here were also carried away'.*

Remarkably there was no loss of life though the passengers in the leading coach were badly shaken. Fortunately, the vehicle had an iron frame and sheet iron flooring upon which timber planks were laid. The innate strength of this and the following coach no doubt saved several lives.

From an operational point of view the use of an 0-6-0 on such a train is interesting though not perhaps surprising, always remembering that excursion trains were often heavy yet were easily timed. According to the *Bath Chronicle*'s report of the accident, published on 26th September 1850, *Ajax* had been attached at Swindon. In fact, this was a common working practise at the time, it being quite usual for engines to be changed en route even on fast express trains. Incidentally, it is from the *Bath Chronicle* that we learn of the identity of the engine; the accident report makes no mention of it.

Dreadnought was involved in what must have been a hair-raising

incident on Friday 25th August 1854, when working a ballast train over Winston Green Bridge at Handsworth near Birmingham. The bridge collapsed under the weight of the train after the engine and the two leading trucks had, fortunately, passed over it. The span was of wrought iron tubular construction and it was evidently one of the girders or tubes which failed, bringing down the bridge. Brunel was sent to report on this and on the other bridges between Birmingham and Handsworth. He found five others that either needed rebuilding or strengthening. This work delayed the final opening of the broad gauge link between Birmingham and Wolverhampton, which was due to commence operations on 1st September 1854, until 14th November. More information about this incident, which fortunately did not result in loss of life, and the challenges of extending the broad gauge into the Black Country, can be found in Michael Hale's exceptional monograph (see Bibliography).

Working Lives

The easiest way to describe the distribution of the 'Premier' Class engines around the GWR system is to say that they could be found anywhere from Wolverhampton to Weymouth and West Wales. This general rule applies to all of the 0-6-0 classes, for although they differ in detail and to a degree in power, their utility was, it appears, universal. That said, as the allocation distribution will show, there was a tendency to allot the older engines to more menial jobs such as ballasting and banking.

In the early days the class was distributed along the main line,

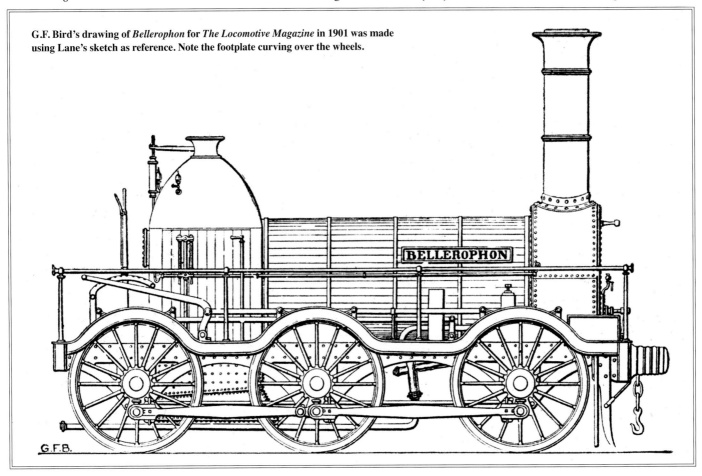

G.F. Bird's drawing of *Bellerophon* for *The Locomotive Magazine* in 1901 was made using Lane's sketch as reference. Note the footplate curving over the wheels.

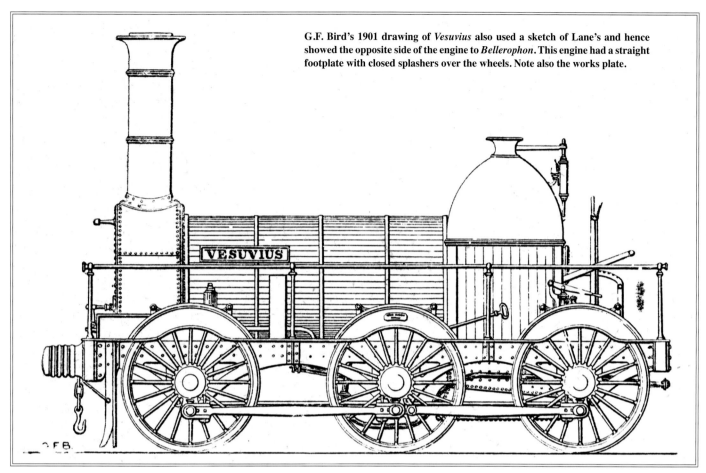

G.F. Bird's 1901 drawing of *Vesuvius* also used a sketch of Lane's and hence showed the opposite side of the engine to *Bellerophon*. This engine had a straight footplate with closed splashers over the wheels. Note also the works plate.

with a concentration at Swindon from where they also worked to Gloucester. Between 1846 and 1st May 1849, workings over the Bristol & Exeter main line would have been a regular occupation for the class, though they do not seem to have ventured into South Devon, except perhaps on an 'out and back' basis. As the network grew so did their field of activity, though as a small class they were usually fairly thinly spread.

Our list of allocations for the class gives an interesting snapshot of their activities between 1854 and 1862. Since the class were all withdrawn by 1871, before the major conversion in South Wales and of the Wilts, Somerset and Weymouth, it would not be unreasonable to assume that, from 1863 until the first withdrawals occurred in 1869, the distribution of class members remained much as it had been over the previous years.

Engines in steam twenty-two days to 22nd July 1854:
Paddington: *Vesuvius* (goods)
Reading: *Premier* (ballasting)
Oxford: *Ajax* (ballasting)
Birmingham: *Briareus* (goods)
Swindon: *Dreadnought* (banking)
Frome: *Bellerophon* (goods)
Engines in steam three weeks to 21st July 1855:
Paddington: *Ajax*, *Vesuvius* (goods)
Oxford: *Telica* (ballasting)
Birmingham: *Bergion* (ballasting)
Hereford: *Premier* (goods)
Gloucester: *Argo* (goods)

South Wales: *Dreadnought*, *Jason* (goods)
Fury (banking)
Engines in steam nineteen days to 19th July 1856:
Paddington: *Vesuvius* (goods)
Reading: *Dreadnought*, *Premier* (goods)
Gloucester: *Bellerophon* (ballasting)
Bristol: *Bergion* (goods)
South Wales: *Fury* (goods)
Engines in steam eighteen days to 18th July 1857:
Paddington: *Bergion*, *Vesuvius* (goods)
Devizes: *Dreadnought*
Gloucester: *Jason* (goods), *Brontes* (ballasting)
South Wales: *Ajax*, *Fury*, *Premier*, *Telica* (goods)
Engines in steam seventeen days to 17th July 1858:
Paddington: *Bergion* (goods)
Reading: *Briareus* (goods)
Oxford: *Argo*, *Vesuvius* (goods)
Gloucester: *Jason* (goods), *Brontes* (ballasting)
Bristol: *Telica* (goods)
Neath and Swansea: *Ajax*, *Premier* (banking)
Engines in steam twenty-three days to 23rd July 1859:
Paddington: *Briareus*, *Vesuvius* (goods)
Reading: *Jason* (goods)
Devizes: *Premier*
Gloucester: *Fury* (goods)
South Wales: *Brontes* (goods)
Neath and Swansea: *Ajax*, *Bellerophon* (banking)

Engines in steam three weeks to 21st July 1860:
  Paddington: *Vesuvius* (goods)
  Reading: *Premier* (goods)
  Gloucester: *Telica* (goods)
  Chippenham: *Briareus* (ballasting)
  Bristol: *Jason* (goods)
  South Wales: *Bergion*, *Fury* (goods)
  Neath and Swansea: *Ajax*, *Brontes* (banking)
Engines in steam nineteen days to 19th July 1862:
  Reading: *Ajax*, *Bergion* (passenger)
  Reading: *Briareus*, *Vesuvius* (goods)
  Wycombe: *Bellerophon* (passenger)
  Gloucester: *Telica* (goods)
  Neath and Swansea: *Brontes*, *Fury*, *Premier* (banking)

There is little further to add other than to observe the unusual allocation of *Ajax*, *Bergion* and *Bellerophon* to passenger work at Reading and Wycombe in 1862. The Reading engines may have been working the Wycombe Branch from its southern end or perhaps employed on the Berks & Hants line to Hungerford, an extension to which, as far as Devizes, was due to open in November that year. The Wycombe Railway was also in the process of enlargement, the extension of the line to Thame opening on 1st August 1862. Work at the High Wycombe end may have impacted the water supply for a short time, necessitating the use of tender engines. Interestingly, it appears that the 'Premier' Class may have been specifically chosen for these workings. There must be a technical reason for this choice, most probably their axle loading, which was less than later 0-6-0s, or perhaps their length. (See also Appendix 3)

Works Report

The reports that still exist only cover the period from September 1866 until the early months of 1870. The first member of the 'Premier' Class to cease work was *Argo*, which had been taken out of service in March 1866, so there were only eleven engines in service when our records commence. The class was obviously still valued, for there are twelve entries between October 1866 and September 1868 after which, it appears, heavy repairs ceased. The register contains the following entries:

1866
October .. .. *Bergion*, *Ajax*
December .... *Brontes*
1867
January ... . *Fury*
August .... *Vesuvius*, *Premier*
November .... *Jason*
1868
February . ... *Dreadnought*, *Ajax*
March .... *Telica*
July .. .. *Bergion*
August .... *Briareus*
September .... *Fury*

Withdrawal, Final Mileages and Disposal

There is an illegible entry in the register relating to the disposal of *Bergion*, which may suggest that the engine saw some use after November 1870, when it certainly ceased work, possibly as a stationary boiler. The entry in the register about the disposal of *Argo* is another oddity as, in effect, it spent more than five years on the scrap line. There is no indication that it was put to use in a stationary capacity during this time, so perhaps it was used as a source of spares or as a works shunter but we will probably never know for sure. In the mid-1860s, the 'Premiers' became part of the 'Fury' Class.

After ceasing work, several of the class were broken up before they were officially withdrawn. The relevant dates, along with their recorded mileages, are all given in **Table 8.5**, below.

TABLE 8.5: 'PREMIER' CLASS – WITHDRAWAL, FINAL MILEAGES & DISPOSAL			
NAME	**MILEAGE**	**BROKEN UP**	**DATE WITHDRAWN**
Premier	379,931	Nov. 1869	**July 1870**
Ajax	390,858	Aug. 1871	**Dec. 1871**
Argo	250,457	Sept. 1871	**March 1866**
Bellerophon	347,468	April 1870	**July 1870**
Vesuvius	315,648	April 1870	**July 1870**
Telica	329,220	July 1870	**July 1870**
Dreadnought	378,901	April 1871	**June 1871**
Fury	352,146	Feb. 1871	**June 1871**
*Bergion**	316,931	——	**Dec. 1871**
Briareus	375,866	——	**Dec. 1870**
Brontes	373,593	Oct. 1872	**June 1872**
Jason	343,277	Sept. 1870	**Dec. 1870**

Conclusion

When built, these engines were heralded as an advance in size and power over their smaller predecessors. The *Bristol Mercury* of 23rd May 1846 made the following announcement: '*Mammoth GWR engines* Great Western, Queen *built Swindon 7ft 0in. driving wheel 16ins x 18ins cylinder engine empty 25 tons tender empty 9 tons, luggage engine* Premier 0-6-0 *with 5ft 0in. driving wheel surpassing the strength of* Hercules *involved with gauge commissioners*'.

These were indeed exciting times. The railways were already transforming Britain by greatly reducing transit times for people and goods, thereby aiding the nation's progression from a largely rural society to a largely urban one. To feed our growing towns and cities, rapid bulk transit became an increasing necessity as the second stage of the industrial revolution gained impetus. The 'Premier' Class might almost be called the progenitor of the modern goods engine, as they and their successors provided the power, the speed and utility that has helped create the modern world.

CHAPTER 8

THE 'PYRACMON' CLASS

In the same way that the 'Premier' Class goods engines had been contemporaries of the 'Prince' Class passenger locomotives and had therefore incorporated similar technical elements, so the 'Pyracmon' Class were scions of the 'Iron Duke' and 'Courier' classes, incorporating the various technical developments which had been introduced with the former and refined in the latter. Out, therefore, went the Haycock fireboxes, with the cylinders being redesigned and the valves placed between them, so that they could now be driven directly without the complexity of rocking arms, etc. The regulator was placed in the smokebox and was operated by a 'pull out' handle located in the rear of the firebox backhead. The 'Pyracmons' were both heavier and more powerful than their immediate predecessors and therefore mark a third stage in the development of the broad gauge goods engine.

The class, of which there were only six examples, were all built

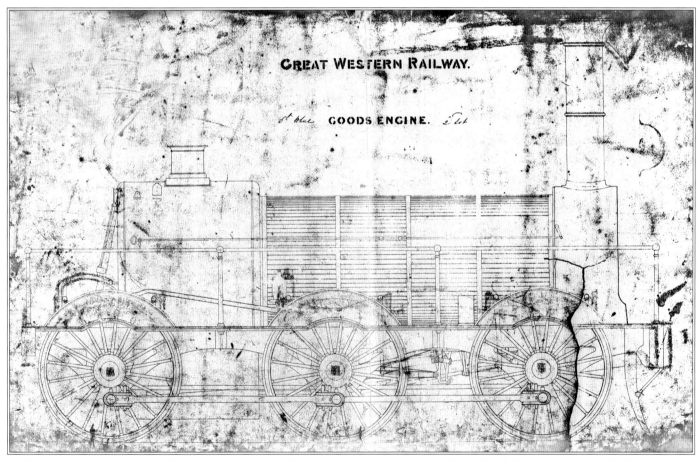

This drawing, from the Swindon Works archives, though stained and damaged, illustrates the 5ft 0in. 'Goods Engine 2nd Lot' as initially conceived. The building of these engines followed on directly after the erection of *Sultan*, the last of the '2nd Lot Passenger' or 'Iron Duke' Class. Consequently, the design incorporated features which had been developed in the passenger engines, including redesigned cylinders with the valves positioned between them. The valve gear was also reconfigured, enabling a direct-action layout to be evolved thus eradicating the need for rocking shafts, etc. The regulator valve was repositioned in the smokebox actuated by a 'pull out' regulator positioned on the backhead and the smokebox also had the pronounced 'piano front', another feature of the 'Iron Dukes' in their original form. The design of the footplate and splashers – common to all six members of the class – followed the pattern referred to as 'Group 2' in the previous chapter dealing with the 'Premier' Class. Another feature common to both goods classes was the design of the coupling rods, which are well illustrated in this drawing. They were forged from 'bar' section and are particularly well illustrated in the photograph of *Steropes* off the road at Llanwern. A major departure from previous practise, following the lead given by the 'Iron Dukes' was the introduction to a Goods class of the round topped firebox. This type, produced in various styles, would remain normative for the following fifty years, until the introduction of the Belpair design in the late 1890s. One omission, soon rectified, was the total absence of any form of sanding gear from the original design. The 'Pyracmons', with their larger boilers improved cylinders and valve gear layout, and much increased heating surface, were a substantial step forward from previous designs and as such are the real prototypes for all the goods classes both broad and standard gauge which were to follow them.

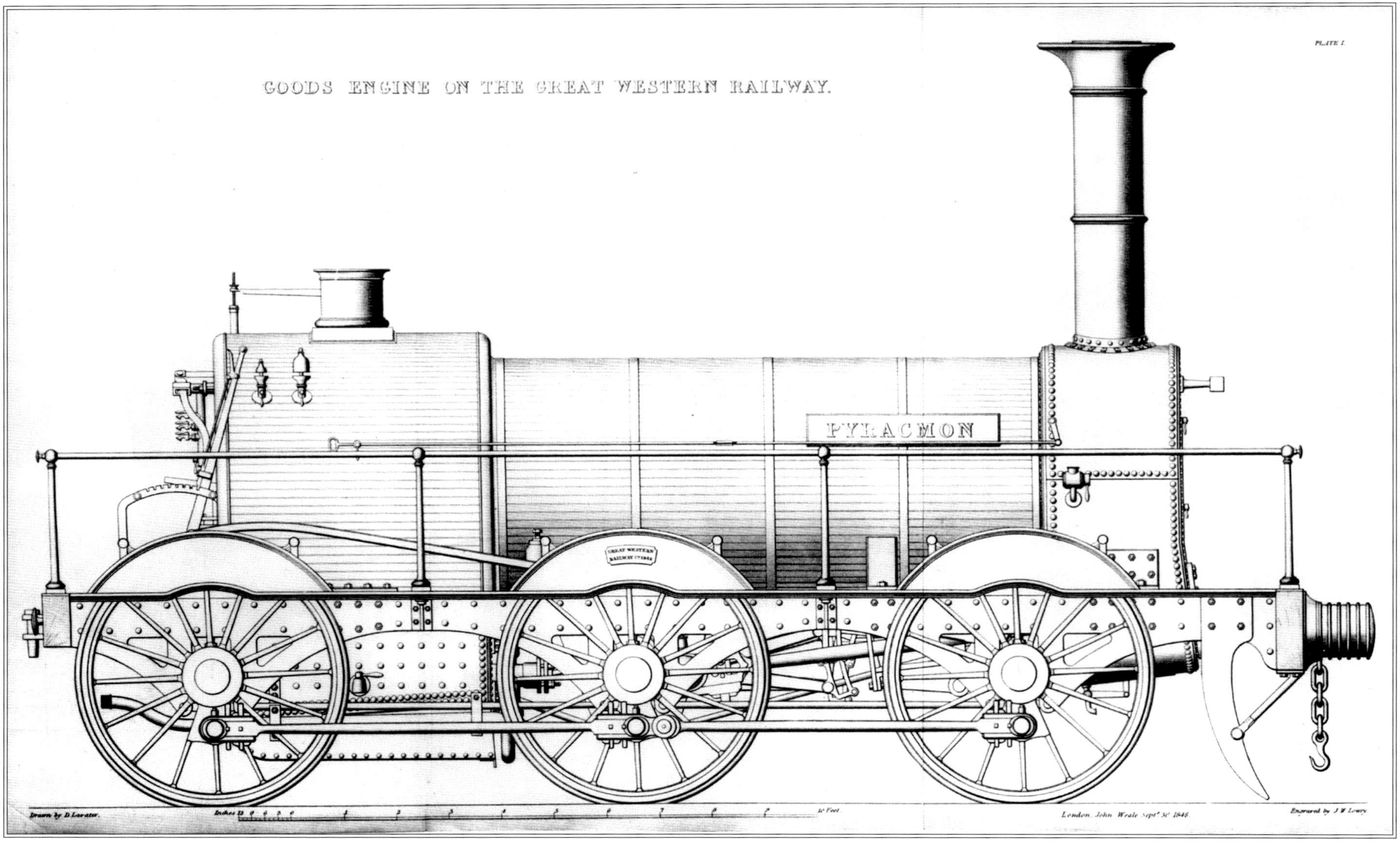

GOODS ENGINE ON THE GREAT WESTERN RAILWAY.

PYRACMON

Drawn by J Lavery.   London, John Wrale, 1 Sept. 30. 1848.   Engraved by J. H. Lavery.

This and the two following drawings first appeared in D.K. Clark's *Railway Machinery* in 1855. Drawn and engraved by J. Lavery, they are dated 30th September 1848 and were published initially by John Wrale of London. The drawings benefit by not only being beautifully clear but also from being scaled, a great assistance to model makers. Executed only months after *Alligator*, the last member of the class entered service, this drawing illustrates a major difference from the official one on page 179 in that the design of the smokebox front has lost its 'piano shape'. It is therefore reminiscent of the style introduced in June 1848 with the '3rd Lot Passenger' engines normally referred to as the 'Courier' Class. As we have noted, this style of smokebox front displaced the earlier design as smokebox renewal fell due. As far as the Goods engines were concerned, this modification may not have been made for some considerable time. *Steropes* for instance still appears to have have the 'piano front' in one the 1857 photographs of the engine derailed at Llanwern. As noted in the text, the 'Pyracmon' Class were the last class to be built fitted with the timber cladding exposed to the elements. Iron cladding was subsequently added. Lane's watercolour of classmate *Behemoth* can be found on page 13, in the colour section at the front of this book.

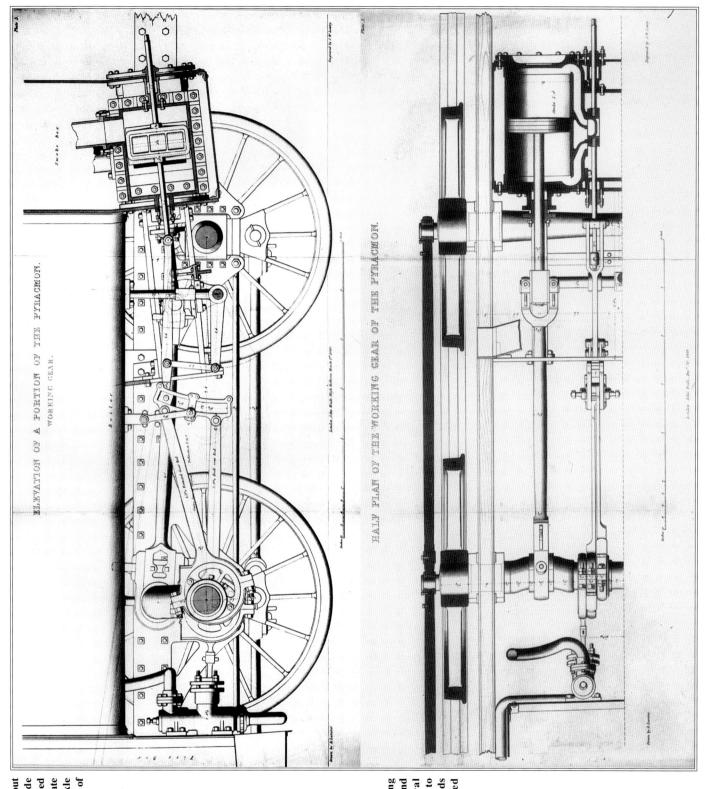

ELEVATION OF A PORTION OF THE PYRACMON.
WORKING GEAR.

HALF PLAN OF THE WORKING GEAR OF THE PYRACMON.

This drawing shows the layout of the valve gear and slide valves. Note how the boiler feed pump is worked from a separate eccentric on the middle axle and is attached to the front of the firebox.

The crank axle, connecting rod, cross head, cylinder and valve layout. This general arrangement would apply to all the later designs of goods engines that incorporated Gooch valve gear.

at Swindon and are detailed in **Table 9.1**, below. Officially they were termed the '2nd lot Goods'.

TABLE 9.1: THE 'PYRACMON' CLASS			
NAME	**BUILT**	**CEASED WORK**	**NOTES**
Pyracmon	Nov. 1847	March 1872	
Steropes	Jan. 1848	Aug, 1871	
Caliban	Feb. 1848	April 1873	Sold
Behemoth	March 1848	Dec. 1873	See Table 9.?
Mammoth	April 1848	July 1872	
Alligator	July 1848	Dec. 1873	See Table 9.?
Note: *Caliban* was sold to the Severn Tunnel Railway Company, presumably for use as a pumping engine.			

Constructional Details
Framing, Footplate and Splashers

The main frames were of the now standard, for goods engines, inside sandwich pattern. In this sense they were similar to the 'Premiers', though the wheelbase was longer at 7ft 4ins x 8ft 1in. The wheels were 5ft 0in. diameter.

The footplate and splashers were arranged in the form described as 'Group 2' in the previous chapter. That is to say that they had straight footplates with a curved section above the crankpins to allow for the movement of the coupling rods. Splashers had solid faces and the works plate was mounted on the middle splasher on each side of the locomotive. All six engines were the same in this and just about every other aspect of their construction.

The Cylinders and Valves

These incorporated the valves, set between the cylinders. The dimensions of the cylinders were the same as the 'Premiers' at 16ins x 24ins. It is possible that the engines were initially fitted with the balanced pattern of valves used on the 'Iron Dukes' but, if so, they were rapidly changed, for a drawing dated 1849 shows the plain pattern as fitted to the 'Courier' group of 8ft 0in. 'Singles' and retrofitted to the 'Iron Dukes'.

Valve Gear

This was the standard Gooch fixed link gear, which now drove the valves directly and thus more efficiently than the previous arrangement adapted for the 'Premiers' and other contemporary classes.

Boilers

The boilers were slightly larger than their predecessors and measured 10ft 6ins long with a diameter of 4ft 3ins. They contained 219 2ins tubes and contemporary drawings show the boilers lagged with wood, the 'Pyracmons' probably being the last new class to be treated in this way. The wood lagging was later sheeted over with iron cleats, as was the general practise of the late 1840s and early '50s. Boiler pressure was set at 115psi. Steam collection was effected by means of a perforated pipe set in the upper section of the boiler.

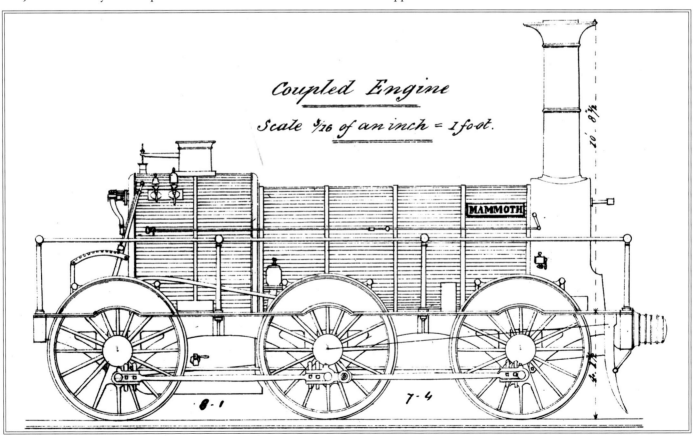

This drawing of *Mammoth* is taken from Gooch's Notebook – in reality a dossier of drawings, specifications, costings and other details, including ideas which did not necessarily come to fruition or were subsequently modified. From our perspective, this drawing's main value is in the arrangement of the smokebox, with its 'piano front', which again confirms the original design of this feature. It is also our only illustration of this particular engine, though it is fair to say that the whole class exhibited an admirable degree of standardisation. Of the six 'Pyracmon' Class engines, only *Caliban* is missing from the catalogue of drawings or photographs of them. *Mammoth* entered service in April 1848 and ceased work in July 1872.

Smokebox

This was of the usual pattern which incorporated the cylinders in its lower portion. The blast pipe orifice had a diameter of $4^7/_8$ins and the regulator valve was set in the upper part of the smokebox.

Firebox

The 'Pyracmons' were the first Goods class to be fitted with the new standard raised, round top firebox. The casing was 4ft 11ins long and the grate area was 18.44sq. ft. A midfeather divided the grate across its centre line and the heating surface was calculated on the fireside as 121.33 sq. ft.

Sandboxes

A sandbox was initially fitted to the footplate in front of the leading splasher. It would be reasonable to suppose that a second sandbox would later have been fitted to facilitate backward or tender first running. On the 'Caesar' and later classes, this was fitted to the rear of the frames, adjacent to the footplate and attached to the back splasher. Unfortunately, the available photographic evidence is, to say the least of it, sparse and does not confirm the supposition made above.

The photograph that keeps on giving! An enlargement of the 'Pyracmon' Class engine *Alligator* from one of the two famous views taken at Cheltenham shed circa 1848-49 (the full picture is given in Part 1). These are rare and valuable illustrations not only of the locomotives featured but also of early railway workings. This rear three quarters view of *Alligator*, uncoupled from its tender, affords us a glimpse of its rear drawbar and tender coupling with attendant leather buffers. Unfortunately, the driver standing on the footplate partly obscures the backhead of the firebox but it is just possible to discern the gauge glass, regulator fitting, Salter safety valve spring and the whistles mounted on the driver's side of the firebox. As per common practise at the time, the turntable at Cheltenham was not long enough to turn engine and tender together – most early turntables were only about 25ft long but, in later years, a 40ft one was installed here. The two photographs are often dated as 1849; however, *Javelin*, the 'Sun' Class 'Single' glimpsed on the right was at Swindon in the latter half of that year undergoing conversion to a saddle tank. So with the trees in full leaf and with *Alligator* having entered service in July 1848, I would suggest that the picture may well in fact date from August/September of that year. *Alligator* ceased work in December 1873.

Boiler Fittings

These were of the standard Gooch design, with flared iron topped chimney and polished brass safety valve cover. The boiler feed was via two clacks fitted just behind the middle splasher, on the lower part of the rear boiler ring. Maintenance may have proved difficult or there may have also been a problem with scaling or internal water circulation in the boiler, because the delivery clacks were later moved to a position on the side of the firebox. This alteration is visible in the photograph of *Steropes* taken at Llanwern on 6th May 1857 following a derailment. Injectors were probably fitted from the mid-1860s onward, if it was thought worthwhile. Both whistles were originally positioned side by side on the driver's side of the firebox, as was normal practise in the 1840s. Again, these may have been moved to what we now consider to be the appropriate position, on top of the firebox, in the early 1860s. Perhaps this modification coincided with the fitting of spectacle plates, which likewise date from about this time.

Rather pleasingly, in common with the 8ft 0in. 'Singles', the brass cleating bands at the front and the rear of the firebox were generally highly polished, as was the brass beading around the splashers. E.T. Lane's coloured drawing of *Behemoth* shows the splasher fronts painted in 'red brown' colour. Officially the colour of the frames, etc. is described as Windsor brown, which has more of a chocolate hue. Whatever, one thing seems certain, they were not painted green – as might have been expected. The accuracy of Lane's drawing is confirmed by the 1857 specification, which shows the frames and splashers coloured Windsor brown.

Wheels and Coupling Rods

Wheels were 5ft 0in. diameter with sixteen spokes. No balance weights are visible in any of the illustrations. Coupling rods were of a pleasing but rather insubstantial profile,

with crankpin bearing brasses enclosed in a circular strap with adjustable wedges.

All the main dimensions are shown in **Table 9.2**, below.

TABLE 9.2: THE 'PYRACMON' CLASS – MAIN DIMENSIONS	
Wheelbase	7ft 4ins + 8ft 1ins
Wheels – Driving	5ft 0in.
Cylinders	16ins x 24ins
Steam Ports	1½ins x 13ins
Exhaust Ports	2¾ins x 13ins
Boiler	10ft 6ins x 4ft 3ins (inside): 219 x 2ins tubes
Boiler Pressure	115lbs per sq. inch
Firebox	4ft 11ins x 5ft 3½ins
Tube Heating Surface	1,134.40 sq. ft
Firebox	121.33 sq. ft
Total	1,255.73 sq. ft
Grate Area	18.44 sq. ft
Calculated from the water side the total heating surface would be equal to about 1,081 sq. ft.	

Commonly with these early designs, some figures vary. G.F. Bird gives the boiler length as 10ft 9ins and the firebox casing as 4ft 10⁷⁄₈ins. The water side heating surface has variously been estimated as 1,363.14 and 1,373 sq. ft.

Tenders

The observations and descriptions given in the previous chapter relating to the 'Premier' Class tenders are equally relevant here. The 'Pyracmon' Class engines were probably from

This first view of the Llanwern accident of 6th May 1857 is especially useful for not only does it illustrate a derailed coal truck on the opposite side of the embankment – suggesting that as the tender broke away it jack-knifed and threw the following train away from the engine – but also the damage to the engine and importantly the 'piano front' of the smokebox, which is otherwise hidden by the sandbox in the other illustrations. Incidentally, the valve visible on the side of the firebox (fixed only on the fireman's side) allowed the crew to divert excess steam into the tender, so heating the feed water.

Unfortunately, little is known about the circumstances of the accident, though there can be little doubt that it was caused by the fracture of the tyre of the leading driving wheel (visible here). No-one was killed or seriously injured, so it did not attract any major press attention nor has an accident report been found. Other than minor damage to the front end, the engine escaped fairly lightly. The tender on the other hand broke away and turned upside down which suggests that the train was travelling at a fair speed when the derailment occurred. The footplate crew were fortunate to avoid being fatally injured, probably being saved by the engine remaining upright, becoming embedded instead in the soft bank of a drainage ditch at the side of the railway. Had the fracture occurred a few yards further on, when the train was passing through Llanwern station, the consequences would have been far worse. Note the spindly nature of the coupling rods, the thin footplating and the splasher design, with the polished worksplate on the middle splasher, the shaping of the nameplate support to the contours of the boiler, the spring hangers positioned behind the splashers and the riveting of the smokebox ring and wrapper.

new coupled to the iron framed tenders mentioned in the 1857 specification. Tenders were, however, frequently exchanged so that members of this and other Goods classes could and did run at various times with the earlier sandwich framed vehicles which had been taken from rebuilt 'Sun' and 'Leo' class engines, as illustrated by the photographs of *Premier*, *Steropes*, *Dido* and *Bacchus*.

Accidents

As far as it is possible to be sure, no member of this small class was involved in any accident where loss of life was incurred. There were, of course, the minor mishaps which were an almost daily occurrence in early railway operations. The *Bristol Mercury* of 25th November 1848, for example, recorded a shunting accident when *Steropes*, which was running tender first, collided with the rear vehicles of another train. The newspaper report is a little muddled and we do not learn much about the consequences of the accident, other than that *Steropes* was due to work a train to Bridgwater and then return piloting another train. Because the engine was too long for the Bridgwater turntable, it was due to make its outward journey tender first. The driver's name is given as Robert Hale, who had been a footplateman for eight years, the last four of which he had served as a driver.

Steropes is also the engine which appears in the series of classic

photographs taken of the derailment at Llanwern on 6th May 1857. A close inspection of one of the pictures reveals that the tyre of the leading driving wheel is missing, so one presumes that the tyre had disintegrated whilst the train was in motion, causing the accident. Little is known about the results of the derailment but self evidently the engine broke away from its train and from its tender which, unlike the engine, turned over and came to rest upside down. There are three known photographs of this incident, all presented here. In one there appears to be an upturned coal waggon on the opposite side of the line from the engine. Undoubtedly there is more to this story than I have, so far, been able to unearth. Incidentally, *Steropes* was known as 'Old Stirrups' by enginemen in the Wiltshire area, who evidently found pronouncing names garnered from classical mythology something of a challenge!

Working Lives

Like all of the other 0-6-0 goods engines, members of this small class might have been found anywhere on the broad gauge network. As the newest and most powerful engines of their type they would have found employment on main line goods workings as far west as Exeter. As time progressed and new broad gauge mileage was added to the system, their range obviously widened considerably. Their numbers were soon supplemented

This final photograph graphically demonstrates how close to a real disaster the accident came to be – Llanwern station, visible on the left, was but a few yards away! The rudimentary nature of the station is visibly apparent and was typical of the facilities provided by the cash strapped South Wales Railway. Though the engine and rolling stock were still awaiting recovery, the line had evidently been reopened to traffic as the disc & crossbar signals are 'off', suggesting that trains were expected in both directions. *Steropes* was heading towards Newport so derailed on the south side of the line. Note the coal truck is visible again through the engine's footplate handrail, lettered 'S W R' on its end.

by the eight members of the 'Caesar' Class – to be described in the next chapter – and then the slightly larger 'Standard Goods' classes, which we will study in the next volume.

Allocations

Although probably largely based at Swindon initially, from the limited information so far unearthed, the following list of engines in steam between 1850 and 1862 can be made:

Engines in steam two weeks to 27th July 1850:

 Reading: *Mammoth*

 October 1852: Carmarthen Junction, when the shed opened:

   Caliban (probably ballasting)

Engines in steam twenty-two days to 22nd July 1854:

 Paddington: *Alligator*, *Steropes* (goods)

 Swindon: *Mammoth* (on test from Works)

Engines in steam twenty-one days to 21st July 1855:

 Paddington: *Caliban*, *Mammoth*, *Pyracmon*, *Steropes* (goods)

 Bristol: *Alligator* (goods)

 South Wales: *Behemoth* (goods)

Engines in steam nineteen days to 19th July 1856:

 Paddington: *Alligator*, *Mammoth*, *Pyracmon* (goods)

Engines in steam eighteen days to 18th July 1857:

 Paddington: *Mammoth* (goods)

 Bristol: *Behemoth*, *Steropes* (goods)

Engines in steam seventeen days to 17th July 1858:

 Paddington: *Alligator* (goods)

 Gloucester: *Steropes* (goods)

Engines in steam twenty-three days to 23rd July 1859:

 Paddington: *Alligator* (goods)

 Birmingham: *Mammoth* (goods)

 Gloucester: *Pyracmon* (goods)

 South Wales: *Caliban* (goods)

Engines in steam twenty-one days to 21st July 1860:

 Paddington: *Behemoth* (goods)

 Brentford, *Steropes* (goods)

 Birmingham: *Mammoth* (goods)

 Gloucester: *Pyracmon* (goods)

 Weymouth: *Caliban* (goods)

Engines in steam nineteen days to 19th July 1862:

 Llantrisant: *Alligator*

Though these records are interesting in their own right, they only provide a snapshot of the availability and activities of the class, which vary considerably, reaching an especially low point in the summer of 1862, when these engines still had a further ten years of useful life ahead of them. Few hard and fast conclusion can be drawn from the geographic spread of the allocations, though Llantrisant is an interesting inclusion. The shed was opened in 1860 by the Ely Valley Railway, which the GWR first worked then leased in 1861. A short broad gauge branch led from Llantrisant to Tonyrefail and was opened for goods traffic on 2nd August 1860. The Mwyndy & Brofiscin Branch opened in July 1862. No doubt *Alligator* was employed working mineral traffic on these lines. (See also Appendix 3)

Works Report

This partial record only covers the period between September 1866 and February 1871, and gives details of engines which have received heavy repairs,

1866

September .... *Steropes*

October .. .. *Alligator*, *Mammoth*

November .... *Pyracmon*

1867

January ... . *Caliban*

April. .... *Alligator*

December .... *Steropes*

1868

May .. .. *Caliban*

December .... *Pyracmon*

1869

March .... *Behemoth*

October .. .. *Mammoth*

All six members of the class appear at least once in this list. *Behemoth* is the last to make an appearance, in March 1869, implying that its previous heavy repair had been just before the date that our records commenced, perhaps in the summer of 1866. It would also seem reasonable to suppose that a decision was made at the end of 1869 to discontinue repairs to these and other older 0-6-0s and to withdraw them as heavy repairs fell due or became necessary. Their final mileages and disposal are shown in **Table 9.3**, below.

TABLE 9.3: 'PYRACMON' CLASS – FINAL MILEAGES & DISPOSAL			
NAME	**MILEAGE**	**BROKEN UP**	**DATE WITHDRAWN**
Pyracmon	385,109	March 1872	June 1872
Steropes	423,271	Oct. 1871	Dec. 1871
Caliban	408,679	Sold	June 1873
Behemoth	420,960	Dec. 1873	
Mammoth	365,506	July 1872	Feb. 1872
Alligator	436,826	Dec. 1873	
NOTES:			
Caliban was sold to the Severn Tunnel Railway in April 1873 but was returned to Swindon in August 1873 and presumably then broken up.			
Behemoth and *Alligator* were sent to 'Hockley Hydraulics'. I take this to mean the complex of sidings at Hockley, the next station on from Birmingham GWR heading towards Wolverhampton, where there were waggon lifts giving access to the Soho Branch of the Birmingham Canal. Presumably they were used for pumping or stationary boiler purposes.			

Conclusion

The 'Pyracmon' Class were built to satisfy a growing need for powerful goods or luggage engines, as they were then known. They mark a small but significant step forward in goods locomotive design, which would be further developed in the coming years in the 'Caesar', 'Caliph' and 'Ariadne' classes. In the 1860s, the 'Pyracmons', along with their slightly larger sisters, were all integrated into one large class under the 'Caesar' heading.

As with many other classes, it was the demise of the broad gauge which brought about their downfall, especially the conversion of the South Wales Railway in 1872, which rendered this useful but small class, surplus to requirements.

THIRD LOT. COUPLED.

CAESAR . DIDO . DRUID . FLORENCE . HERO . NORA-CREINA . THUNDERER . VOLCANO.

─── *DESCRIPTION* ───

CYLINDERS. 16 ins in diam. and 24 inch stroke. Steam ports 1½ ins by 13 ins. Exhaust port 2¾ ins by 13 ins.
BOILER 10 feet 6 ins long and 4 feet 3 ins in diam. inside. Fire-box 4 feet 11 ins long and 5 feet 3½ in wide.
TUBES. 219 Tubes 10 feet 11 ins long and 2 ins in diam. outside. **HEATING SURFACE** of **BOX** 121.33 Tubes 1287.7
FIRE-GRATE. area 18.44 Superficial feet.
WHEELS. Driving and Trailing 5 feet 9 ins in diam. coupled. Leading 3 feet 6 ins in diameter.
CAESAR with ⅓ cwt of Coke and 8 ins of Water in the Glass, weighs Leading 10.2.2. Driving 10.10.0. Trailing 7.14.0

We have now arrived at what might be termed the quintessential broad gauge Goods engine and these eight 'Caesar' Class locomotives really did provide a platform for further development by both Gooch and Armstrong. Though designated Goods engines, they fulfilled a mixed traffic function, handling perishables and excursion traffic as well.

CHAPTER 9

THE 'CAESAR' CLASS

This class of eight engines, which in Swindon records are referred to as the '3rd Lot Goods', were an enlarged development of the 'Pyracmon' Class. In their turn' they became the prototypes of the larger 'Ariadne' and 'Caliph' classes (usually collectively referred to as Gooch's 'Standard Goods'), which numbered in total 102 locomotives.

The building of the 'Caesars' – and subsequent classes – reflected the growing tonnage of freight traffic that was now being handled by the railway, as well as its anticipated growth in mileage as the main lines in South Wales and the West Midlands opened from 1852 onwards. The eight engines were built at Swindon between June 1851 and February 1852, and are detailed in **Table 10.1**, below.

TABLE 10.1: THE 'CAESAR' CLASS		
NAME	**BUILT**	**CEASED WORK**
Dido	June 1851	Dec. 1872
Volcano	June 1851	June 1874
Thunderer	July 1851	June 1874
Caesar	Aug. 1851	June 1880
Florence	Nov. 1851	June 1874
Nora Creina	Nov. 1851	May 1872
Hero	Dec. 1851	June 1871
Druid	Feb. 1852	March 1879

Constructional details
Framing, Footplate and Splashers

In this respect, these eight engines differed from their immediate predecessors of the 'Pyracmon' Class but mirrored the first batch of the 'Premier' Class and this design was referred to in Chapter 7 as 'Group 1'. The footplate curved over the driving wheels and was supported by a continuous valance that followed the contour of the footplate, exposing the wheels.

Cylinders and Valves

The cylinders were encased in the lower part of the smokebox, as usual practise dictated. The dimensions were initially the same as the 'Pyracmon' Class at 16ins x 24ins but the diameter was later increased to 17ins. The valves were set between the cylinders, whilst the steam ports measured $1^1/_2$ins x 13ins and the exhaust ports $2^3/_4$ins x 13ins.

Valve Gear

This was of the now standard pattern of Gooch fixed link valve gear. It was arranged in the same way as that utilised on the 'Pyracmon' Class, as illustrated in the drawings on page 181.

Boilers

These were of the usual wrought iron telescopic design, measuring 10ft 6ins in length by 4ft 3ins in diameter and 219 tubes were contained within. Boiler pressure was set at 120psi.

Fireboxes

These were of the now standard round top pattern and measured 4ft 11ins long and 5ft $3^1/_2$ins wide. A midfeather divided the lower part of the firebox. The firegrate was calculated to be 18.44 sq. ft and the heating surface as 121.33 sq. ft

Smokebox

This was of the usual 'built up' construction, incorporating the cylinders in their lower half. Detailed measurements do not appear in any of the extant diagrams. Though no doubt similar to the 'Pyracmon' Class dimensionally, they were of a revised design which eliminated the previous piano front styling.

Sandboxes

Initially these were placed on the front of the frames, with a straight delivery pipe in front of the leading driving wheels but later, rear sanding was provided. A sandbox was positioned on the back of the frames and delivered sand behind the rear driving wheels.

Boiler Fittings

These follow all the established, norms though it is not known if the whistles were initially placed on the side of the firebox; they were certainly later moved to the crown of the firebox. Also in later years, chimneys perhaps became a little shorter and were fitted with copper caps, whilst blowers were fitted from the early to mid 1850s – always assuming that they were not fitted from new. Spectacle plates appeared from the mid 1850s onward, the fitting of which may have coincided with the removal of the whistles to the firebox crown.

Frames, Wheels and Balance Beams

The frames were of the usual sandwich type fitted behind the driving wheels. The wheels were 5ft 0in. diameter with sixteen spokes, the photograph of *Dido* illustrating that balance weights were fitted, though whether this was from new is unknown. G.F. Bird states that this class was fitted with compensating beams between the '*leading and driving axles*' but the 1857 specification does not show this fitting, which it does for later Goods lots. In the absence of corroborative evidence therefore, I am inclined to doubt this statement, despite the

Dido, the first member of the 'Caesar' Class, was built at Swindon and entered traffic in June 1851. Basically enlarged 'Pyracmon' Class engines, there were important differences in the design of the footplating, splashers and the much improved coupling rods, with their 'fish belly' profile, thus creating a much stronger and more workmanlike component. This is the only known photograph of a member of the Caesar Class. It is a mistake to assume that the following 'Standard Goods' engines, introduced in 1852, are one and the same class because the GWR unfortunately grouped all the 'Pyracmon', 'Caesar' and 'Standard Goods' together in 1864 under the 'Caesar' heading. In fact, the later engines, though outwardly very similar, had a longer wheelbase and slightly larger boiler and firebox. The photograph, I would suggest, was taken toward the end of the engine's working life, perhaps as late as 1870, as it had received the whole range of additions and modifications. Beginning at the front end, *Dido* has been fitted with double buffers and a sliding coupling to enable it to shunt mixed gauge stock. The sandboxes were probably fitted from new but it has received a new front end with larger cylinders and longer smokebox. The chimney is of the later pattern with shallower lipped copper top but the engines of this class were probably equipped with blowers when built. The cab has acquired a spectacle plate and rear sandboxes – the driver is resting his right leg on one. The tender is one of the rebuilt and much enlarged sandwich framed vehicles that dates back to the early 1840s, with the frames strengthened by the addition of patches around the horn blocks, whilst the tender sides show signs of considerable replating and patch repairs. The livery is the standard Holly green upper works with Windsor brown frames. The tender body is lined with two equal panels with scafed Pea green, black and white lining. The rear tender panel would have been similarly lined. Unfortunately, we have no knowledge of where the photograph was taken. Though the background gives the impression of a rural setting the engine, which is standing on mixed gauge track, seems to be posed near the throat of a marshalling yard or perhaps some industrial complex. Since the photograph dates from the mid-1860s or later it could almost be anywhere from the West Midlands to the London area. *Dido* ceased work in December 1872.

fact that Bird included this feature in his drawing of *Hero* (see page 193).

Coupling Rods

These were of a more substantial nature than previous designs, being of 'fish belly' section for enhanced strength. The crankpin bearings were retained in a semi-circular strap with adjustable wedges.

Boiler Feed

Our only photograph of a member of the 'Caesar' Class is of *Dido*, probably taken towards the end of its working life in 1872. In this picture, a large clack valve is visible on the lower half of the boiler between the leading and middle wheels. There

TABLE 10.2: THE 'CAESAR' CLASS – MAIN DIMENSIONS	
Wheelbase	7ft 4ins x 8ft 0ins
Wheels	5ft 0in.
Cylinders	16ins (later 17ins) x 24ins
Boiler	10ft 6ibs x 4ft 3ins: 219 x 2ins tubes
Firebox Casing	4ft 11ins x 5ft 3¹/₂ins
Tube Heating Surface	1,134.40 sq. ft
Firebox	121.33 sq. ft
Total	1,255.73 sq. ft
Pressure	120psi
Grate Area	18.44 sq. ft
Caesar, with 7cwt of coke and 8ins of water in the glass, is said to have weighed:	
Leading Wheel	11 tons
Driving Wheel	11 tons 15 cwt
Trailing Wheel	9 tons 14¹/₂ cwt
Total	32 tons 9¹/₂ cwt

is no sign of any injectors, so I can only assume that this is an original fitting and positioning thereof.

Springing

Large leaf springs were positioned behind the driving wheels and framing, above the axle boxes.

Main Dimensions

The weight figures quoted in **Table 10.2**, left, are those of the RCTS which contradict those given on the 1857 specification drawing of leading wheel – 10 tons, 2 cwt 2 stone; driving wheel – 10 tons 10 cwt 0 stone; trailing wheel – 7 tons 14 cwt 0 stone. However, they are almost certainly the correct version, since the 1857 specification also suggests that the wheels are respectively 3ft 6ins, 5ft 9ins and 5ft 9ins, i.e. a 2-4-0 – which is nonsense!

Tenders

These engines ran both with the much rebuilt sandwich framed type, illustrated in the photograph of *Dido*, as well as the later iron plate framed variety described in Chapter 7 – known as 'short tenders' because of their 5ft 0in. by 5ft 0in. wheelbase. Both tender types enabled these and sister classes to access the short turntables of around 40ft diameter or less which were then commonplace around the system.

Names

The names of seven of the eight members of the class are fairly straightforward, with their origins easy to trace, albeit from a variety of seemingly unrelated sources – *Dido* after the first queen of Carthage, *Florence* presumably after the Italian city which had

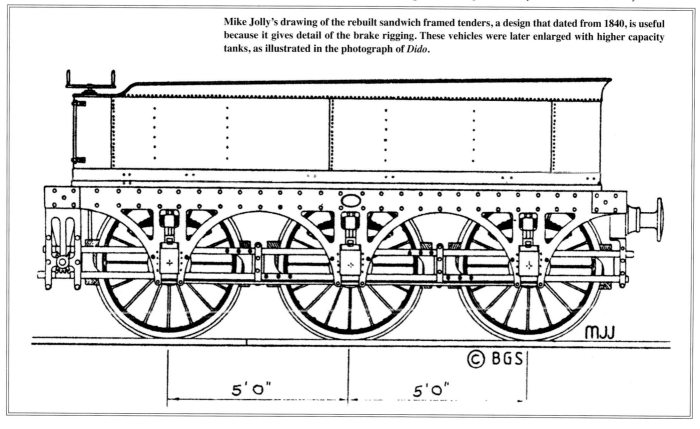

Mike Jolly's drawing of the rebuilt sandwich framed tenders, a design that dated from 1840, is useful because it gives detail of the brake rigging. These vehicles were later enlarged with higher capacity tanks, as illustrated in the photograph of *Dido*.

© BGS

5'0"   5'0"

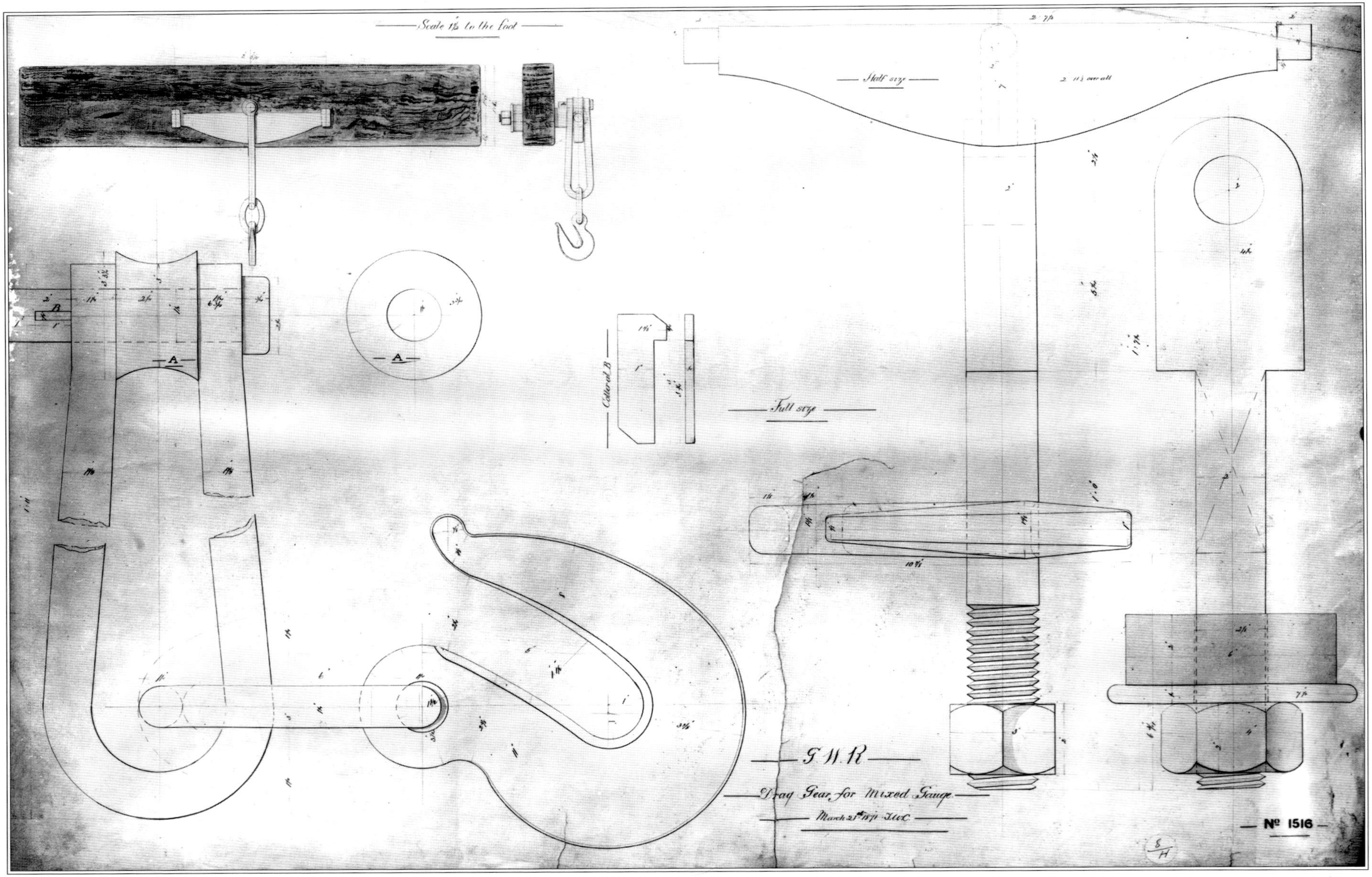

The photograph of *Dido* illustrates the engine running in the last year or so of its life fitted with double buffers and the device illustrated here, for hauling and shunting both broad and standard gauge stock. This was trialled in the late 1860s and perfected by March 1871 when this drawing was made. Fitting to engines involved in shunting, piloting and banking duties, where mixed gauge working was increasingly encountered, commenced immediately. The system incorporated a half-moon shaped arm that could pivot through ninety degrees and was attached to the drag beam. An elongated link, with a bearing set in the top, ran along the arm allowing the coupling to 'centre', so that either broad or standard gauge vehicles could be hauled. This fitting could be found on both broad and standard gauge locomotives, as well as on some specially adapted 'converter vehicles', and remained in use until broad gauge workings ceased in 1892.

Roman origins (Florence Nightingale did not attain her Crimean War fame until three years after the engine was built) and so on. Not so, however, with *Nora Creina*. An online search threw up a few possibilities, all of them seemingly obscure: a popular 18th century Irish air; a sailing ship; and Nora Creina Bacon, whose portrait was painted by the noted artist William Frith Powell in 1845 when she was aged twenty-one. However, the 18th century Irish air had become a well known ballad in the 19th century, after words were added to the tune by the poet Thomas Moore in 1810, under the title *Lesbia Hath a Beaming Eye* and in which form it was commonly sung in Victorian drawing rooms. Interestingly, the tune was also picked up by Beethoven around the same time, who used it to honour a commission. So who was Nora Creina? The answer to this seems to be that no one knows, if there even was an actual Nora Creina in the first place – she may have been a fantasy of the unknown composer of the original air.

Working Lives

I have been unable to trace any major accidents which involved these engines though, no doubt, there was the usual clutch of minor incidents and derailments which were the norm on the 19th century railway.

However, a most remarkable account of a near miraculous escape from imminent disaster, involving *Volcano*, *Etna* of the 'Leo' Class and a third unnamed engine, which occurred on Sapperton Bank on 8th July 1851, has come to light. I must thank Mike Fenton for making me aware of this incident and then very kindly sending me a copy of the report of the 'near miss', which was printed in the *Stroud Free Press* on 18th July 1851. Before

turning to this sensational story I would comment that, at the time of the events recorded, *Volcano* was only a matter of perhaps two or three weeks old. *Etna* had been built by Fenton, Murray & Jackson in June 1841 as a 2-4-0 tender engine and had been rebuilt as a saddle tank at Swindon in either late 1849 or 1850. Though not named, the engine of the Mail Train would most probably have been a member of the 'Fire Fly' Class. It might be added that *Volcano*, at the head of the excursion, was fulfilling its role as a powerful mixed traffic engine, an important aspect of this type of locomotive's workload. Let us turn therefore to this most remarkable description of near disaster:

'SINGULAR ACCIDENT TO, AND NARROW ESCAPE OF, AN EXCURSION TRAIN

On Tuesday 8th July, an excursion train for London left Cheltenham, Gloucester and Stroud with about 1,500 passengers. The train, consisting of 23 carriages, was drawn by the Volcano, one of the most powerful engines upon the line, assisted up the incline, which commences at Brimscombe, by Etna as pilot engine, and left Brimscombe Station at 8.55pm.

The engine laboured heavily up the steep gradients, which vary from 1 in 100 to 1 in 60. When about two-thirds of the way through the tunnel, and within a few yards of the summit level, the middle coupling of a composite carriage gave way, and the chains on either side also snapped. The last twelve carriages immediately ran backwards, to the consternation of the passengers, who regarded a frightful sacrifice as inevitable, and whose fears were augmented by the knowledge of the mail being nearly due. Many had been in the highest spirits on the journey up, but now shrieks succeeded laughter, and those who had been foremost in obscenity, were loudest in their prayers.

Twenty minutes after the departure of the excursion train from

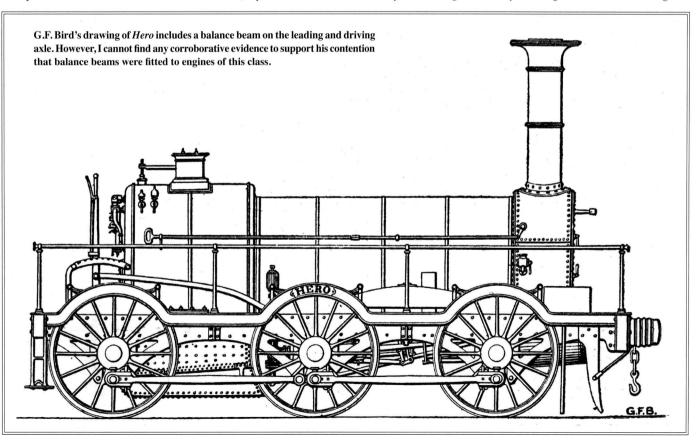

G.F. Bird's drawing of *Hero* includes a balance beam on the leading and driving axle. However, I cannot find any corroborative evidence to support his contention that balance beams were fitted to engines of this class.

A view across the Chalford Valley at Frampton circa 1890, with the railway climbing Sapperton Bank on the far side, past Frampton Crossing. The west portal of Sapperton Tunnel can just be discerned in the left distance and it was down this section of line that the excursion ran away in 1851, to what those on board thought would be their inevitable doom. However, the Up Mail train ascending the hill behind them was able to stop, reverse and then gently bring the runaway carriages under control as they caught up – a remarkable escape. In the foreground, the Thames & Severn Canal climbs towards its own tunnel.

Brimscombe, the mail train followed. When about a mile and a quarter from the tunnel the driver received the caution signal from Mr Folly, the inspector of the line, and immediately got upon the splasher which covers the engine wheel, to keep a sharp lookout. He proceeded steadily up to within a quarter of a mile of the tunnel, when he got a signal from the policeman, who had caught sight of the returning carriages, and was running back to warn the driver to reverse his train.

This was done about 200 yards from the tunnel, and the mail had proceeded backwards as far as Frampton viaduct, half a mile distant, before it was caught up by the descending carriages, and the consequent collision was exceedingly slight.

Several ladies, and others, got out of the train when it stopped, and were hospitably sheltered by W. Baker, Esq., of Hattons, where they received every attention. Two passengers, Mr Dye, a plasterer and slater, of Lynn, Norfolk, and a Mr Jowlings, of the firm of Messrs J. & E. Barnard, of Lightpill, jumped out, and were seriously injured. W. Barnard, Esq., of Holcombe, also stepped out on the platform outside the carriage to signal the driver of the mail, and seeing he should be unable to return to his place before the collision should ensue, jumped off, receiving in the fall several bruises about the hands and face.

The pilot engine upon the return down the line, instead of meeting with mangled bodies and broken carriages as was expected, found both trains at a standstill completely under the command of Wilkinson, the driver, who returned with the whole to Brimscombe Station.

The Volcano, on emerging from the tunnel, and arriving at Tetbury

Road, left the excursionists in a state of great anxiety as to the fate of their companions, which was not relieved until the passing of the mail with the gratifying signal 'all right', and returned for the runaway carriages, which reached the station in the course of a couple of hours, and were greeted with loud cheers.

The Volcano then resumed its journey, and the whole train safely reached Paddington about three o'clock. Too much praise cannot be awarded to Wilkinson, the driver of the mail, and to the policeman at the tunnel, to whose coolness and intrepidity under providence, the avoidance of a calamity scarcely equalled in the annuls of railway accidents be attributed.

Subscriptions for a testimonial to Wilkinson have been set on foot in Ross, Gloucester, Stroud, Cirencester and Swindon, and are progressing very favourably. The injured passengers are rapidly recovering.'

Like their forebears, these engines worked the length and breadth of the GWR's broad gauge system, from Wolverhampton to Weymouth and West Wales. Most of their work would have been on general goods or mineral trains but, as we have already noted, they took their turn on excursion and special workings as the needs of the time dictated. With this in mind we will move on to view a snapshot of their distribution around the system, as the extant information from the Gooch Coke Returns record: Engines in steam for twenty-two days to 22nd July 1854:

Paddington: *Caesar, Hero, Nora Creina* (goods)
Birmingham: *Volcano* (goods)
Swindon: *Thunderer* (on trial)

Engines in steam for twenty-one days to 21st July 1855
    Paddington: *Caesar, Dido, Druid, Hero, Thunderer* (goods)
Engines in steam for nineteen days to 19th July 1856
    Paddington: *Caesar, Florence* (goods)
    Wiltshire & Somerset: *Druid* (ballasting)
Engines in steam for eighteen days to 18th July 1857
    Paddington: *Hero, Nora Creina* (goods)
    Weymouth: *Druid, Volcano* (ballasting)
    Oxford: *Caesar* (goods)
Engines in steam for seventeen days to 17th July 1858
    Paddington: *Druid, Hero, Volcano* (goods)
    Westbury: *Thunderer*
    Bristol: *Nora Creina* (goods)
Engines in steam for twenty-three days to 23rd July 1859
    Paddington: *Thunderer, Dido* (goods)
    Devizes: *Hero*
    Hereford: *Volcano*
    South Wales: *Florence* (goods)
Engines in steam for twenty-one days to July 21st 1860
    Oxford: *Dido, Hero* (goods)
    Gloucester: *Druid, Nora Creina, Volcano* (goods)
    Westbury: *Florence*
    South Wales: *Caesar, Thunderer* (goods)
Engines in steam for nineteen days to 19th July 1862
    Paddington: *Hero* (goods)
    Oxford: *Nora Creina* (goods)
    Salisbury: *Druid* (goods)
    Westbury: *Thunderer*
    Neath and Swansea: *Caesar, Dido* (both ballasting)

There is, unfortunately, little more that we can add other than to observe that, as the 1850s rolled into the 1860s, the availability of the class seemed to markedly improve. This was almost certainly the result not so much of mechanical reliability but the increased demand for locomotive power as the railway's mileage expanded and the country continued to emerge from recession.

It would be interesting to know where the two late survivors ended their working lives. Both *Caesar* and *Druid* could have found their way to the wild South West, in far flung Falmouth or piratical Penzance! We may never know but it is provoking to speculate.

Works Report

The available records cover the period from September 1866 until February 1871. The engines recorded below will have received a heavy repair.

1866
September ....*Thunderer*
November ....*Caesar*
1867
October .. ..*Nora Creina*
December ....*Florence*

1868
October .. ..*Dido*
1869
March ....*Volcano*
August ....*Thunderer*
October .. ..*Caesar, Nora Creina*
1870
May .. ..*Thunderer*

It is interesting that, of the eight engines in this class, neither *Hero* nor *Druid* received main works attention during the four and a half years covered in these records. This fact may account for *Hero*'s relatively early withdrawal, though obviously *Druid* was considered worth repairing again. I suspect that it was the condition of the frames which had a major bearing on an individual engine's future by 1871. *Hero* may even have become involved in some minor accident – we simply do not know. Whatever, the engine was withdrawn in June 1871, a year and a half before any other member of the class succumbed, as broad gauge mileage began to wither on the vine.

Withdrawal, Final Mileages and Disposal

TABLE 10.3: 'CAESAR' CLASS – FINAL MILEAGES & DISPOSAL			
NAME	**MILEAGE**	**BROKEN UP**	**DATE WITHDRAWN**
Dido	424,758	s/b*	Dec.1872
Volcano	420,856	June 1874	June 1874
Thunderer	427,453	Sept. 1874	June 1874
Caesar	369,705	—	June 1880
Florence	415,581	Sept. 1874	June 1874
Nora Creina	341,517	May 1872	June 1872
Hero	385,846	July 1871	June 1871
Druid	428,177	—	March 1879
* *Dido* was put to work as a stationary boiler in Swindon Waggon Works in February 1873.			

The mileage recorded against *Caesar*'s name seems inordinately low considering its length of service. Unfortunately, the entry in the register is a little indistinct, it may just read 869,705 which appears to be inordinately high! However, there may be some error here. The mileage record of *Druid*, the other survivor, has been altered in the register from 399,859 to 428,177, so perhaps a similar correction was missed with Caesar.

Conclusion

The small 'Caesar' Class became the harbinger of the large Gooch-designed 'Ariadne' and 'Caliph' Classes, all of which, along with the 'Pyracmons', were merged into one substantial group numbering 116 engines in the mid 1860s under the 'Caesar' classification. The original group of eight locomotives did good, solid, albeit unspectacular work, over a period of nearly thirty years. No 19th century locomotive designer could have expected any more and they certainly served the GWR well, which is all that could be asked of them.

E.T. Lane's 1848 drawing of *Avalanche* is of immense value, for it is the only known illustration of the engine. The style is very strongly 'Gooch' and in so many ways could be described as the prototype for much of what was to follow. Built for the GWR by Stothert & Slaughter, so similar is this engine to the 'Premier' Class that I am increasingly drawn to the conclusion that this company were also the suppliers of the boilers for those locomotives too. No evidence has ever been found in the records of other companies, such as Stephensons, that boilers were built and supplied for the 'Premiers', whilst the records of Stothert & Slaughter were lost at a very early stage.

CHAPTER 10

MISCELLANEOUS ENGINES: AVALANCHE AND BACCHUS

Alongside the Gooch inspired engines that were designed between 1846 and 1851, the GWR acquired two other locomotives – both 0-6-0s – in the same period. The two engines, named respectively *Avalanche* and *Bacchus*, are to a degree shrouded in mystery. In the case of *Avalanche*, we do not know when it was ordered from Stothert & Slaughter of Bristol, or indeed why it was acquired. *Bacchus* was rebuilt from the experimental T.E. Harrison-designed *Hurricane* in May 1849 although apart from the boiler, how much of the original engine was reused is uncertain.

TABLE 11.1: MISCELLANEOUS ENGINES			
NAME	DATE BUILT	BUILT BY	CEASED WORK
Avalanche	Feb. 1846	Stothert & Slaughter	Aug. 1865
Bacchus	May 1849	Rebuilt Swindon	Nov. 1869

Avalanche

This engine was originally built as an 0-6-0 tender locomotive and fortunately, E.T. Lane drew it, minus the tender, on 18th November 1848, no doubt when it was standing in Swindon Works yard. This date is significant, for in October 1849, *Avalanche* is known to have been at work as a banker at Box, by which time the general assumption is that it had been rebuilt as a tank engine. If this assumption is correct, which seems reasonable, then we can cautiously conclude that *Avalanche* was rebuilt between November 1848 and October 1849.

I mentioned at the start that nothing is known about the ordering and acquisition of *Avalanche*. That said, the engine, as represented in Lane's drawing, bears more than a passing resemblance to some members of the 'Premier' Class. It has inside sandwich frames, a Haycock firebox, a wood lagged boiler of what appears to be ample proportions and other typical 'Gooch style' fittings. It differs from the 'Premiers' in the positioning of the regulator, which is on the backhead. There is nothing in the drawing which gives any indication of what type of valve gear was fitted. though it is reasonably safe to assume that the engine acquired Gooch fixed link gear during its rebuilding, if it had not been built with it. In other respects, *Avalanche* was unusual. It had a straight footplate and fully closed in splashers, with sandboxes positioned at the front of the footplate, just behind the buffer beam, feeding the leading driving wheels. The works plates were attached to the middle splashers. Sadly, few dimensions were recorded – the wheelbase, which has been calculated from Lane's drawing, equates to 7ft 8ins x 7ft 9ins, whilst the wheels are said to have been 5ft 0in. in diameter and the cylinders 17ins x 24ins.

One possible explanation for the purchase of the engine was the increasing difficulties that were being experienced with the available motive power at Box. Banking had been introduced from the opening of the line in June 1841 but problems were encountered more or less immediately. More powerful engines with increased adhesion were obviously required and this became even more urgent following the opening on May 12th 1845 of the Cheltenham & Great Western Union Railway between Kemble Junction and Gloucester, which included the long, stiff climb up Sapperton Bank.

Banking requires a locomotive with a high power to weight ratio and a boiler capable of producing a high steaming rate in short bursts. There is also a considerable amount of light engine and tender first running combined with periods of relative inactivity. All of these factors, when added together, suggest that a tank engine rather than a tender engine is more suited to the required task. Swindon Works was already in the middle of a conversion programme that saw the small 'Sun' and 'Leo' Class engines converted to saddle tanks, so *Avalanche* was an obvious candidate for similar attention.

No details of the conversion have come to light but it must have been a fairly rudimentary affair, which involved lengthening the frames at the rear end and providing a bunker. The saddle tank would have been fitted between the smoke and fireboxes and would have been of about 700-800 gallon capacity. Other than the previously mentioned dimensions for wheelbase, wheels and cylinders, nothing more is known about the engine. The 1857 specification includes it with the later built saddle tanks of the 'Banking' Class under the generic title 'Bank Engines'. Though perhaps sharing some dimensional similarities, *Avalanche*, with its closed in splashers and Haycock firebox, would have presented a somewhat contrasting appearance to the four 1852-54 members of the group.

Working Life, Mileage and Disposal

Until it was laid aside in 1865, *Avalanche*, which was always based at Swindon, seems to have divided its time between banking at Box and local goods or pilot duties at its home station. I have no record of it working as a banker from Brimscombe, though that is not to say that such was never the case. Considering its relatively restricted sphere of operation, however, the engine achieved a very respectable 375,556 miles during its operating life of just under twenty years, up until withdrawal in August 1865; it was broken up in the following month but was not officially removed from stock until July 1870.

This photograph of *Bacchus* was most probably taken whilst the engine was working either from Gloucester or possibly Birmingham, which would date the picture to the early 1860s. Note the shallow design of framing visible between the leading and centre wheels, and the non-standard design of boiler, which certainly came from T.E. Harrison's *Hurricane*. The engine had also been fitted with a spectacle plate and other additional modifications, such as a blower just about visible behind the chimney. The tender is of the 1846-47 design, which Gooch described as 'short tenders', but appears to have been modified by the fitting of a larger tank (see pages 170-72). Note the engine crew in their white fustian jackets, the wearing of which was common practice in the 1850s and '60s. After this, their use became less common, not surprising when one considers that the working week had to be started with a pristine jacket which gradually became grimier as the week wore on!

Bacchus

To my mind, *Bacchus* is a most interesting engine though, like *Avalanche*, there is much that we are uncertain about regarding its constructional details. Fortunately, there is a rather faded photograph of the engine which gives a vivid impression of its appearance but which also throws up some further questions.

As an 0-6-0 tender engine, *Bacchus* entered service in May 1849 and, according to the *RCTS History*, a report made to the GWR Board by Gooch, dated 19th November 1849, contains the following entry: '*1 engine recently entirely rebuilt the boiler only being retained. This engine was originally made with the boiler and engine on different carriages and is now a powerful and useful goods engine*'.

The original engine referred to here is *Hurricane*, which had been built to an intriguing design by R.&W. Hawthorn of Newcastle under a patent held by T.E. Harrison. With its 10ft 0in. diameter driving wheel, the locomotive had been laid aside as long ago as December 1839, though there is some evidence to suggest that it may have, initially at least, been used after its retirement for experimental purposes.

TABLE 11.2: *BACCHUS* – KNOWN MAIN DIMENSIONS	
Wheelbase*	7ft 6ins x 7ft 6ins
Wheels	5ft 0in.
Cylinders	16ins x 24ins
Boiler	8ft 8½ins x 3ft 8ins: 135 x 1⅝ins tubes
*Calculated from the photograph – appears to be the same as the boiler carriage of *Hurricane*	

Constructional Details – Frames

Though it is impossible to be certain, the photographic evidence strongly suggests that the engine was fitted with a shallow type of plate frames. They are so unlike the standard Gooch practise of the time that writers have been prone to speculate about their origin, suggesting that they may also have been retrieved from *Hurricane*. However, no matter how likely this suggestion appears, we simply cannot be certain about this.

Cylinders and Valve Gear

These were the then standard product, with the valves set between the cylinders and driven by Gooch fixed link valve gear.

Footplate

This mirrors the design of *Avalanche* in that it is straight with closed in splashers. From the photograph, the splashers seem to be decked with a brass rim or bead around their circumference.

Boiler and Firebox

This, as Gooch's report made clear, was originally built for *Hurricane* and had a 'manhole' casing positioned above its middle ring. It is said to have been 8ft 8½ins long, with a diameter of 3ft 8ins and contained 135 1⅝ins diameter tubes.

Judging from the photograph, the firebox might not have been transplanted for it bears a striking resemblance to the design fitted to the 'Pyracmon' Class 0-6-0s. In its later years it was fitted with a spectacle plate, though the whistles and other fittings, appear to have remained on the firebox side under the driver's control.

Smokebox and Boiler Fittings

The smokebox is of the standard Gooch built up type incorporating the cylinders in its lower part. Boiler fittings are also of the usual Gooch design, though the chimney, as illustrated in the photograph, is of a later pattern with what appears to be a copper cap.

Sanding

A sandbox was positioned on the front of the frames, a little forward of the leading splasher and fed the rails in advance of the driving wheels.

Tender

The tender appears to be one of the surplus 6-wheeled type, rebuilt with an enlarged iron tank, which were common to all early goods engines – see Chapter 7, pages 169-172.

Working Life

As *Bacchus*, the engine entered traffic in May 1849 and must have quickly moved away from Swindon for it is not mentioned in Sturrock's report of October 1849 to Gooch – see Appendix 3. However, it was in steam at Swindon (goods) during the twenty-two days to 22nd July 1852. I have no records of the engine for 1853 and 1854 but in the eighteen days to 18th July 1857 it is shown as '*ballasting*' at the same place. It is probably safe to assume therefore that it had spent the previous two years working from Swindon. By 1858, the engine had moved to Gloucester (possibly following a much needed heavy repair) and was in steam there during the seventeen days to 17th July 1858, employed on goods work. Subsequently, the engine seems to have remained there, for it next appears for the twenty-one days to 21st July 1860, when it was recorded at Gloucester ('*ballasting*'). It must have then undergone another major repair, because it next appears during the nineteen days to 19th July 1862, engaged on '*passenger work*' at Birmingham.

Thereafter, we have no more records of the engine though it may be significant that broad gauge workings ended in the West Midlands in November 1869 and *Bacchus* was withdrawn from service that very same month. The engine may have been due a heavy repair by the time of its withdrawal, as it had not received any major attention, at Swindon at least, during the preceding three years. It is very possible too that *Bacchus* had retained its original boiler, built more than thirty years earlier, which was therefore probably nearly life expired in 1869. At the time of its withdrawal, the engine had accumulated 204,762 miles in traffic and was finally officially removed from stock in July 1870.

Conclusion

Both *Avalanche* and *Bacchus* are interesting and fascinating engines in their own right, the latter especially so. They have an air of mystery about them, particularly *Avalanche* about which so little is really known. To see *Avalanche* working hard at the rear of a goods train up through Box Tunnel; or *Bacchus* perhaps pulling through Birmingham on a cattle train bound for Hockley – oh to be able to step back in time!

SELECT BIBLIOGRAPHY

Magazines

Railway Archive No. 27, 'The Broad Gauge at Gloucester 1844-1872', Neil Parkhouse, 2010

Railway Archive No. 43, 'The Broad Gauge in Cheltenham 1844-1872', Roger Langley, 2010

The Broadsheet: The Journal of the Broad Gauge Society, various issues

The Engineer, 1895

The Great Western Railway Magazine, various issues

The Locomotive Magazine, 1901

The Railway Observer, RCTS, various issues

The Stephenson Locomotive Society Magazine, various issues

Books

Ahrons, E.L., *The British Steam Railway Locomotive 1825-1925*, Locomotive Publishing Co, 1927

Ahrons, E.L., *Development of British Locomotive Design*, Locomotive Publishing Co, 1914

Betjeman, J., Grinsell, L.V., Tallamy, H.S. & Wells, H.B., *Studies in the History of Swindon*, Swindon Borough Council, 1950

Bennett, A.R., *The Chronicles of Boulton's Siding*, Locomotive Publishing Co, 1927

Brunel, I., *The Life of Isambard Kingdom Brunel*, Longmans, Green & Co., 1870

Cattell, J. & Falconer, K., *Swindon, The Legacy of a Railway Town*, HMSO, 1995

Clark, D.K., *Railway Machinery*, Blackie, 1855

Clifford, D., *Isambard Kingdom Brunel: The Construction of the Great Western Railway*, Finial, 2006

Crittall, Elizabeth, Rogers, K.H. & Shrimpton, Colin, *A History of Swindon to 1965*. Wiltshire Library and Museum Service 1983

Darwin, B., *A Century of Medical Service, The Story of the GWR Medical Fund 1847-1947*, Great Western Railway, 1947

Fuller, Rev'd Dr F., *The Railway Works and Church in New Swindon*, The Swindon Press, 1987

Hale, M., *Brunel's Broad Gauge in the Black Country*, Woodsetton Monograph Series, 1997

Institute of Mechanical Engineers, *Engineering Heritage Vol. 1*, Heinemann, 1963

Karau, P., *The Henley on Thames Branch*, Wild Swan, 1982

Lowe, J., *British Steam Locomotive Builders*, Goose, 1975

Lyons, E. & Mountford, E., *An Historical Survey of Great Western Engine Sheds 1837-1947*, Oxford Publishing Co., 1979

Marion, J. & Pearse, S., *Twyford and the Great Western Railway*, Twyford & Ruscombe Local History Society 1994

MacDermot, E.T., revised by Clinker, C.R., *History of the Great Western Railway*, Vols 1 & 2, Ian Allan, 1966

Matheson, Rosa, *Death, Dynamite & Disaster*, The History Press, 2014

Matheson, Rosa, *Women and the Great Western Railway*, Tempus Publishing, 2007

Matheson, Rosa, *Trip, The Annual Holiday of the GWR's Swindon Works*, Tempus Publishing, 2006

Measom, G., *The Official Illustrated Guide to the Great Western Railway*, London, 1860

Peacock, Thomas A., *Great Western London Suburban Services*, Oakwood Press, 1970

Peck, A., *The Great Western at Swindon Works*, Oxford Publishing Co., 1983

Platt, A., *The Life and Times of Daniel Gooch*, Alan Sutton, 1987

Potts, C.R., *Windsor to Slough. A Royal Branch Line*, Oakwood Press, 1993

Reed, P.J.T. (compiled), *The Locomotives of the Great Western Railway, Part Two, Broad Gauge*, RCTS, 1952

Sekon, G.A., *The Evolution of the Steam Locomotive 1803-1898*, Railway Publishing Co., 1898

Sekon, G.A., *A History of the Great Western Railway*, Digby, Long & Co., 1895

Sharman, M., *The Broad Gauge of the GWR etc., A Selection of 7mm Drawings*, Oakwood Press, 1985

Sharman, M., *The Crampton Locomotives*, Sharman, 1983

Sheppard, G., *Broad Gauge Locomotives*, Broad Gauge Society, 2008

Simmons, J. (edited), *The Birth of the Great Western Railway. Extracts from the Diary of G.H. Gibbs*, Adams & Dart, 1971

Swift, A., *The Ringing Grooves of Change*, Akeman Press, 2006*

Tippett, N. & de Courtais, N., *The Abingdon Branch*, Wild Swan, 1985

Tredgold, T., *Locomotive and Stationary Engines*, James S. Virtue, 1850

Vernon, T., *Archibald Sturrock; Pioneer Locomotive Engineer*, Tempus Publishing, 2007

Warren, J.G.H., *A Century of Locomotive Building by R. Stephenson & Co.*, R. Stephenson & Co., 1923

Waters, L., *The Great Western Broad Gauge*, Ian Allan, 1999

Wilson, R.B. (edited), *Sir Daniel Gooch: Memoirs and Diary*, David & Charles, 1972

Wishaw, F., *The Railways of Great Britain and Ireland*, Wheale, 1840 & 1842

*Anyone wishing to read a much fuller account of the building and operating of the line between Bristol and Bath is directed to Andrew Swift's *The Ringing Grooves of Change* (which is a quote from Tennyson's poem about the opening of the Liverpool & Manchester Railway), which is full of excellent source material.

Also consulted

The Library of the Institute of Mechanical Engineers

The National Archives at Kew. RAIL 254 files

The Great Western Trust Archive, Didcot, *Gooch's Coke Returns 1854-61*

In addition, I have consulted *North Star*, the journal of the Friends of Swindon Railway Museum and in particular Vols 8 and 9 which include articles by Jack Hayward about the origins of 'B Shed' and its later history.

APPENDIX 1

THE EXPERIMENT WITH GREAT WESTERN

From *The Railway Times*, 20th June 1846

On Saturday a public experiment for the purpose of exhibiting the economy and tractive capacity of the broad gauge locomotive was made on the Great Western line to and fro between London and Bristol. The experiment was an extremely valuable one, inasmuch as it is the first by which the Great Western Company have had it in their power to test the capacity of the broad gauge engine against that of the narrow gauge engine. In the experiments made on the Great North of England Railway under the superintendence of the Gauge Commissioners, the narrow gauge party worked their passenger trains of 50 and 80 tons with a locomotive that had had applied to it every improvement of which the narrow gauge engine was considered to be capable to enable it to run at high velocities. But with 50 tons not more than a maximum velocity of 56 or 57 miles per hour, nor more than an average of about 48 miles per hour, could be attained, while with 80 tons the maximum speed was about 50, and the average speed about 44 miles per hour. At these speeds the motion of the engine was considered so dangerous that Professor Airy, one of the Commissioners, declined to ride on her a second time. These speeds, it will be recollected, were some miles per hour below those attained by the old broad gauge engine upon similar gradients, and with similar loads. The world has now to compare them with the working of the new broad gauge engine – the first of a class – called the *Great Western*, some details of the speed and power of which were given a few days since in the *Morning Herald*. It will be found, from the comparative working given below, that the *Great Western* takes a passenger train of something more than one hundred tons, at seven miles faster per hour than the new narrow gauge locomotive propelled fifty tons; that she took the one hundred tons eleven miles faster per hour than the new narrow gauge engine carried the eighty tons, and that the work was done at less than half the cost at which the narrow gauge engine works.

The great national importance of these two facts must be evident to those who consider that the amount of railway traffic on the trunk lines of this country is increasing with extraordinary rapidity, that the London and Birmingham cannot manage its present traffic with speed and regularity which the public have a right to expect, and that in truth the propriety of constructing a second double line between Euston Square and Birmingham has for some time been seriously contemplated. Such a passenger train as the *Great Western* can propel at a maximum speed of 70, and an average speed of about 50 miles per hour, would require two or three narrow gauge locomotives to propel it at 38 or 40 miles per hour. But the use of more than one engine has been pronounced by Sir Frederick Smith himself to be dangerous, and the expense of their use shuts them, in a commercial point of view, entirely out of comparison with the economical working of the new broad gauge engine. The other important advantage of the *Great Western* arises from the amount of surplus power she would always have at command in running passenger trains of – say 80 tons, at an average rate of 45 miles per hour; that is, from platform to platform – a performance utterly beyond anything that the new narrow gauge engine could approach in the ordinary working of a train. This surplus power is of the most serious commercial advantage. It enables the engine driver to keep his time at the stations, and therefore ensures regularity, as a matter of as much moment as speed itself. Punctuality at stations in railway travelling is the means of avoiding accidents, many of the most serious of which have, if I recollect rightly, arisen from trains being late between station and station. A locomotive like the *Great Western*, able, as she has proved herself, to run under a serious disadvantage, with 100 tons, 116 miles (as she did down on Saturday), *viz.*, from the 1st to the 117th mile post, including 9 minutes lost in stoppages, in 142 minutes, or at about 49 miles per hour, and to run (as she did likewise on Saturday) from the 118th to the 1st mile post, including upwards of 16 minutes stoppages, in 155 minutes, or at 45 miles per hour, will, when she gets into proper order, be able to maintain in ordinary seasons and under ordinary circumstances an average speed of 50 miles per hour over a line of any length, whether it be one from London to Exeter, or from London to Edinburgh.

The train attached to the *Great Western* on Saturday, consisted of ten carriages, seven of them were weighted with pig iron, and the three other carriages took down a full complement of passengers.

Among the gentlemen who went down were Mr Charles Russell, MP, the Chairman of the Company; the Marquis of Chandos, Lord John Scott, Major General Pasley, Mr R.F. Gower, Mr W. Tothill, Mr H. Simonds, Mr John Roskell, Mr Brunel, Mr C.A. Saunders, Mr D. Gooch, Captain Claxton, Mr T. Holroyd, &c.

The train started from Paddington at 11 hours 47 minutes 52 seconds. It passed the first mile post at 11 hours 51 minutes 1 second, and came abreast of the 52nd mile (immediately after which the breaks were put on for stoppage at Didcot), at 12 hours 45 minutes 24 seconds, running, therefore, the 51 miles, with a rise of 118 feet, in a few seconds over 54 minutes, or at an average speed of upwards of 56 miles per hour. Perhaps the best mode in which the tractive power of the broad and narrow gauge engines can be conveyed to the mind of the reader is that of placing in juxtaposition the working of the new narrow gauge engine with loads of 50 and of 80 tons, and that of the new broad gauge engine with one hundred tons. I take the working of the narrow gauge engines from the returns delivered unto the Gauge Commissioners by the narrow gauge party. I will first take the working of the narrow gauge 50 tons train.

The following figures give the respective workings of the narrow gauge engine with 80, and of the broad gauge engine with 100 tons:

Mile Posts	MPH Narrow Gauge with 50 tons	MPH Broad Gauge with 100 tons
2	30	40
3	40	48
4	44	53
5	55	56
6	55	58
7	53	57
8	51	57
9	54	59
10	52	59
11	51	60
12	48	61
13	48	60
14	47	63
15	56	62
16	57	62
17	51	62
18	51	50
19	52	63
20	50	60
21	49	59
22	52	58
23	50	60
24	47	60
25	48	60
26	51	57
27	51	60
28	49	60
29	50	60
30	49	62
31	52	62
32	52	53
33	51	52
35	49	55
36	43	55
37	45	56
38	46	51
39	48	61
40	48	57
41	45	53
42	46	48
43	41	60

Mile Posts	MPH Narrow Gauge with 80 tons	MPH Broad Gauge with 100 tons
1	—	—
2	26	40
3	42	48
4	42	53
5	45	56
6	48	58
7	47	57
8	49	57
9	49	59
10	49	59
11	51	60
12	49	59
13	48	60
14	45	63
15	47	62
16	49	62
17	48	62
18	45	50
19	45	63
20	43	60
21	43	59
22	44	58
23	45	60
24	47	60
25	45	57
26	43	60
27	47	60
28	47	60
29	46	62
30	45	62
31	44	52
32	46	53
33	48	54
34	48	55
35	45	55
36	44	56
37	41	55
38	40	55
39	39	61
40	41	57
41	47	53
42	40	48
43	41	60

At Didcot a stoppage of 5 min 15 sec took place. The mile-post beyond Didcot, viz., the 54th, was passed at 12 hour 54 min 27 sec., and the 75th mile-post, just after passing which the brakes were put on for stopping at Swindon, was reached at 1 hour 18 min 6 sec., the distance of 21 miles having been passed over in 23 min 39 sec., or at the average rate of upwards of 54 miles an hour. At Swindon there was a stoppage of 4 min 27 sec. The 78th mile-post was passed at 1 hour 29 min 30 sec and the 98th mile-post, which is a short distance on the Paddington side of the Box tunnel, was reached at 1 hour 49 min 26 sec., the 20 miles having therefore been accomplished in 19 min 56 sec., or upwards of a mile per minute. The train came abreast of the 117th mile-post at 2 hour 12 min 3 sec. This gives the time occupied in running distance between the 78th and 117th as 42 min 33sec for the 39 miles, or something like 53 miles per hour.

The maximum speed on the down journey was obtained between the 83rd and 92nd mile posts. From the 80th to the

Whilst Maidenhead Bridge is the most famous of Brunel's Thames' crossings, he designed two other viaducts to carry the Great Western main line across the meandering river, at Moulsford and here at Gatehampton, between Pangbourne and Goring. J.C. Bourne's print was entitled 'Bassildon Bridge', which was actually a miss-spelling of its alternative name, Basilden. A wide-beamed barge and two narrow boats head for the centre arch.

85th mile there is a falling gradient of 8 feet per mile, and from the $85\frac{1}{2}$th to about the $86\frac{1}{2}$th mile there is a falling gradient of about 1 in 100, and a fall of 8 feet per mile then reaches to about the $90\frac{1}{2}$th mile post; a rising gradient of 8 feet per mile then succeeds, and extends beyond the 92nd mile post. The train came abreast of the 83rd mile post at 1 hour 34 min 56 sec., and passed the 92nd mile post at 1 hour 43 min 8 sec., performing the 10 miles in 9 min and 8 sec., or at an average speed of nearly 66 miles per hour. The 87th and 88th miles on a falling gradient of 8 feet per mile were run over at the rate of sixty-nine miles per hour. I made the speed of the train over the 88th mile seventy miles and a half per hour. Mr Samuda (the patentee of the Atmospheric), who kept time the whole of both journeys, made the speed 70 miles per hour, while a gentleman who attended from one of the narrow gauge Companies made it $69\frac{1}{2}$ per hour; but these slight differences will always occur when running at such velocities, seeing that the variation of only half a second by two persons keeping time will give a decrease or increase of more than half a mile per hour.

A few minutes after the arrival of the experimental train at Bristol, the Company partook of a very elegant dejeuner that had been prepared in the long-room of the station. It was supplied by Mr Niblett, the well-known proprietor of the White Lion Hotel. The turtle, hock and champagne were – particularly to those who had been occupied by the dusty duty of timing the velocity of the engine – as acceptable as they were excellent. About 100 gentlemen sat down at table. Mr C. Russell presided.

The speed of the engine over the up journey was, from Bristol to Paddington, exclusive of 16 minutes lost while at a state of rest at Swindon and Didcot, about 50 miles an hour. The consumption of coke for the day's work of 237 miles was equal to about 42lb per mile. The cost of coke per mile, taking the coke at 20s per ton, would be about 4d per mile. Taking the other expenses, as stated in the returns exchanged between various Railway Companies, and given in evidence before the Gauge Commissioners, the items would stand thus:

Coke.	4.0 pence per mile
Engine and fireman's wages.	1.3 pence per mile
Cleaning engine, & other general charges	1.9 pence per mile
Repairs	<u>2.5 pence per mile</u>
TOTAL	9.7 pence per mile

or about $9\frac{3}{4}$d per mile, for 100 tons, at the above high velocities. The cost of working the new narrow gauge engine that ran on the Great North of England line is stated to have been 1s 7d per ton per mile, or more than twice the expense of the *Great Western*.

The motion of the carriages, at the maximum velocity – *viz.*, 70 miles per hour, was perfectly easy. There was not anything approaching the unpleasant oscillation too frequently experienced while travelling in the express trains on the narrow gauge, particularly when the outside cylinder engine is employed.

8

Six coupled Goods Engine, wheels 5 ft. 1 in. in diameter, inside cylinders 17½ in. by 24 in., inside bearings. Designed by Mr. P. Stirling, and built by the Great Northern Railway Company, at Doncaster, in 1872.—No. 187 (50).

Six coupled Engine, wheels 5 ft. 1 in. in diameter, cylinders 17½ in. by 26 in., inside bearings. Designed by Mr. P. Stirling.—No. 647 (110) (built by the Great Northern Railway Company, at Doncaster, in 1880), No. 738 (100) (built by Messrs. Dubs & Co., Glasgow, in 1882).

Six coupled Saddle Tank Engine, wheels 4 ft. 6 in. in diameter, inside cylinders 17½ in. by 26 in., inside bearings. Designed by Mr. P. Stirling, and built by the Great Northern Railway Company, at Doncaster, in 1881.—No. 672 (122).

GREAT SOUTHERN AND WESTERN RAILWAY (IRELAND).
(Gauge 5 ft. 3 in.)

Four coupled Passenger Engine, coupled wheels 5 ft. 6 in. in diameter, inside cylinders 16 in. by 20 in., inside bearings. Designed by Mr. A. McDonnell, and built by the G. S. & W. Ry. Co., at Inchicore Works, in 1873.—No. 21 (539).

Four coupled Passenger Engines, with leading bogie, coupled wheels 16 in. by 20 in., inside bearings, wheel base about 21 ft. 4 in. Designed by Mr. A. McDonnell, and built by the G. S. & W. Ry. Co., at Inchicore Works.—No. 15 (533) (1875), No. 2 (532) (1877). N.B.—No. 2 is taken without tender.

Four coupled Express Passenger Engine, coupled wheels 6 ft. 6 in. in diameter, inside cylinders 17 in. by 22 in., inside bearings, total wheel base 14 ft. 9 in. Weight, empty, 29 tons 6 cwt. Weight, in working order, 32 tons 7 cwt. Designed by Mr. A. McDonnell, and built by the G. S. & W. Ry. Co., at Inchicore Works, in 1875.—No. 64 (534).

Four coupled (in front) double bogie single boiler "Fairlie" Tank Engine, coupled wheels 5 ft. 7½ in. in diameter, inside cylinders 15 in. by 20 in., inside bearings, total wheel base 25 ft. 7 in. Weight, in working order, 35 tons 17 cwt. Designed by Mr. A. McDonnell, and built by the G. S. & W. Ry. Co., at Inchicore Works, in 1869.—No. 33 (536).

Four coupled (in front) Tank Engine, with bogie at trailing end, coupled wheels 5 ft. 6 in. in diameter, inside cylinders 17 in. by 22 in., inside bearings, total wheel base about 23 ft. 6 in. Designed by Mr. A. McDonnell, and built by the G. S. & W. Ry. Co., at Inchicore Works, in 1879. The 100th locomotive built at Inchicore Works.—No. 40 (538).

Six coupled (in front), ten-wheeled, Side Tank Engine, with bogie at trailing end, used for piloting goods up the Inchicore incline, coupled wheels 4 ft. 6 in. in diameter, inside cylinders 18 in. by 24 in., inside bearings. Weight about 45 tons Designed by Mr. A. McDonnell, and built at Inchicore Works, in 1881.—No. 205 (535).

GREAT WESTERN RAILWAY.
(7 ft. gauge.)

Passenger Engine, with single driving wheels 7 ft. in diameter, inside cylinders 16 in. by 18 in., outside bearings. Weight, empty, 16½ tons. Weight, in working order, 18½ tons.—"NORTH STAR" (285) (Stephenson, 1837).

Passenger Engine, with single driving wheels 8 ft. in diameter, inside cylinders, outside bearings. Built by Tayleur & Co., Warrington, in 1837.—"VULCAN" (283A).

Passenger Engine, with single driving wheels 7 ft. in diameter, inside cylinders, outside bearings. Built by Jones, Turner & Evans, 1840.—"FIREFLY" (284A).

Eight-wheeled Express Engines, with single driving wheels 8 ft. in diameter, inside cylinders 18 in. by 24 in., outside bearings, total wheel base 18 ft. 7½ in. This class was designed by the late Sir (then Mr.) Daniel Gooch, and the first of the class came out 1846.—"GREAT BRITAIN" (267 and 268) (built by G. W. Ry. Co., Swindon, 1847, re-built 1880), "COURIER" (266) (built by G. W. Ry. Co., Swindon, 1850, "LORD OF THE ISLES" (265) (built by the G. W. Ry. Co., Swindon, 1852, exhibited at the Exhibition of 1851, and commenced work July, 1852), "TARTAR" (276) (built by G. W. Ry., Swindon, re-built 1876), "EUPATORIA" (274) (built by Rothwell, 1855, re-built 1878), "DRAGON" (370) (1880), "SEBASTOPOL" (269), "IRON DUKE" (271), "INKERMAN" (272), "SWALLOW" (275), "LIGHTNING" (378), "BALACLAVA" (379), "WARLOCK" (380), "TORNADO" (1611), "PROMETHEUS" (1612) (both 1888), "EMPEROR" (1613) (1880).

9

Four coupled Passenger Engines, coupled wheels 6 ft. in diameter, inside cylinders 16 in. by 24 in., inside bearings.—"GOOCH" (291) (1865), "HAWK" (301A) (Swindon, 1865), "PHLEGETHON" (152) (both Swindon, 1866), "WOOD" (340), "AVONSIDE" (1615) (Avonside Engine Co., 1865), "HACKWORTH" (332) (Avonside Engine Co., 1866).

Four coupled Saddle Tank Passenger Engines, coupled wheels 5 ft. in diameter, inside cylinders 17 in. by 24 in., inside bearings. All built by the Avonside Engine Company, 1865. Originally same class as preceding.—"CERBERUS" (302), "PENN" (296), "HEDLEY" (293), "MELLING" (298A).

Four coupled Saddle Tank Engine, with leading bogie, "Corsair" type, coupled wheels 6 ft. in diameter, inside cylinders 17 in. by 24 in., inside bearings, wheel base 18 ft. 2 in. Built at Swindon, 1855.—"HESIOD" (292).

Six coupled Goods Engines, wheels 5 ft. in diameter, inside cylinders 16 in. by 24 in., inside bearings.—"ETTON" (361) (built 1853, renewed 1869), "TAY" (361A) (built 1858), "XERXES" (362A) (built 1858).

Six coupled Goods Engines, wheels 5 ft. in diameter, inside cylinders 17 in. by 24 in., inside bearings. Built at Swindon.—"EUROPA" (385) (built 1853, renewed 1869, Nos. 1196 (375), 1198 (374), 1199 (394), 1201 (373), 1204 (353), 1205 (392), 1207 (364), 1212 (399), 1213 (351) (all 1876).

Four coupled Passenger Engine, coupled wheels 7 ft., inside cylinders 20 in. by 24 in. Built at Swindon, June, 1888. No. 16 (1616).

Four coupled (behind) Side Tank Engines, coupled wheels 5 ft. in diameter, inside cylinders 17 in. by 26 in., inside bearings for coupled wheels, outside bearings for leading wheels. All built at Swindon, in 1885. Designed by Mr. Dean.—Nos. 3501 (344), 3502 (316), 3503 (325), 3504 (318), 3505 (317), 3506 (303), 3507 (328), 3508 (321), 3510 (320).

Four coupled (in front) Saddle Tank Engines, coupled wheels 5 ft. in diameter, inside cylinders 17 in. by 24 in., inside bearings. Designed by Mr. Dean, and built at Swindon, 1889.—Nos. 3541 (323), 3547 (297), 3555 (295), 3557 (333).

Four coupled Tank Engine, with bogie at trailing end, coupled wheels 5 ft. in diameter, inside cylinder 17 in. by 24 in., inside bearings. Built at Swindon. 1889. No. 3560 (1617).

Six coupled Saddle Tank Goods Engines, wheels 4 ft. 6 in. in diameter, inside cylinders 17 in. by 14 in., inside bearings. All built at Swindon.—Nos. 1229 (355), 1231 (380), 1236 (371), 1238 (1618), 1240 (350), 1241 (363), 1244 (372), 1245 (1619), 1246 (377), 1247 (384), 1250 (368) (all built 1876-1887), 1562 (358), 1563 (1620), 1566 (381), 1567 (1621), 1271 (1622), 1573 (312), 1576 (383), 1578 (369), 1580 (367) (all built 1879).

GREAT WESTERN RAILWAY. (4 ft. 8½ in. gauge.)

Four coupled Passenger Engines, coupled wheels 6 ft. 6 in. in diameter, inside cylinders 17 in. by 24 in., outside bearings, no dome. Built by Messrs. G. England and Co., 1862.—Nos. 152 (135), 155 (221).

Six coupled Goods Engines, wheels 4 ft. 6 in. in diameter, inside cylinders 17 in. by 24 in., outside bearings. Built by the Great Western Railway Company, Swindon Works, 1862.—Nos. 123 (524), also 87 (527) (renewed 1878), also 126 (428), 130 (523).

Six coupled Goods Engines, wheels 5 ft. in diameter, inside cylinders 17 in. by 24 in., outside bearings. Built at Swindon.—Nos. 136 (487) (1862), 313 (436) (1864), 59 (403) (built 1862, renewed 1874), 60 (432) (built 1862, re-built as a tank engine, 1877).

Six coupled Goods Engines, wheels 5 ft. in diameter, inside cylinders 17 in. by 24 in., outside bearings. Built by Beyer, Peacock & Co.—Nos. 338 (528) (built 1865, renewed 1883), 327 (464) (built 1864, re-built and altered to a goods tank engine by the G. W. Ry. Co., Wolverhampton, 1879).

Four coupled Passenger Engines, coupled wheels 6 ft. in diameter, inside cylinders 17 in. by 24 in., inside bearings. Built by the Great Western Railway Company, at Wolverhampton.—Nos. 1009 (235) (1866), 30 (209) (1886).

Passenger Engines with single driving wheels 7 ft. in diameter, inside cylinders 17 in. by 24 in., outside bearings. Designed by Mr. J. Armstrong, built by the Great Western Railway Company, Swindon Works.—Nos. 378, "SIR DANIEL" (160) (1866), 471 "SIR WATKIN" (172), 479 (218), 480 (255), 586 (257) (all built in 1869).

APPENDIX 2

THE BLEASDALE PHOTOGRAPHIC COLLECTION
(NEIL PARKHOUSE)

Richard Henry Bleasdale was born in 1837 and resided in Warwick before later moving to Birmingham. He was almost certainly the very first railway enthusiast/photographer and was described by the late Ken Hoole as having been active taking pictures from 1857 up to 1892. He died in 1897 but his son, R.E. Bleasdale, continued taking railway pictures and also sold postcard copies and possibly larger copy prints too of his father's photographs. The cover of one of his catalogues is reproduced right. He also lived in Warwick where he is thought to have been in business as a chemist.

In 1924, probably after retiring, Bleasdale sold the entire negative collection to the Locomotive Publishing Company, in which archive they are held uncredited. However, in more recent years the discovery of original prints of a handful of the pictures within the archive has thrown light on who actually did take some of these photographs and it was not Bleasdale. We should not necessarily be surprised by this, photographers the world over have swapped with and collected pictures taken by other like minded individuals almost since photographs began to be taken. However, as this discovery pertains in particular to the broad gauge pictures (the broad gauge listing from the catalogue is shown page left), it was thought worthwhile to explain all this in an appendix to this volume.

Firstly for those who know little of the Bleasdale Collection, the purchase of it merited a short article in *The Locomotive Magazine* (published by the LPC) of 15th August 1924, which gave the following detailed description of it:

'THE BLEASDALE COLLECTION OF LOCOMOTIVE PHOTOGRAPHS

A by no means negligible adjunct to the dissemination of locomotive information and more especially in regard to design, is the photograph; and when we consider the vast number of fine engines that have passed to the scrap heap, it is of some consolation to know that many faithful reproductions of famous and historic locomotives are preserved to us in this form.

Mr R.H. Bleasdale, who made the collection of photographs of locomotives, of which these notes are the subject, was one of the few pioneers in this direction: many of the earlier negatives made by him under the wet plate process, and under all sorts of conditions, being as beautifully

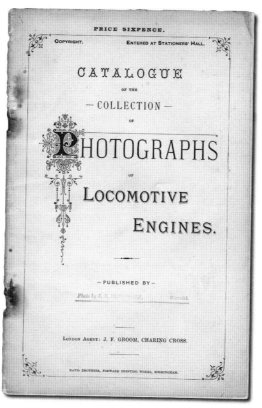

PRICE SIXPENCE.
COPYRIGHT. ENTERED AT STATIONERS' HALL.

CATALOGUE
OF THE
— COLLECTION —
OF
PHOTOGRAPHS
OF
LOCOMOTIVE
ENGINES.

— PUBLISHED BY —
Photo by R. E. BLEASDALE, Warwick.

LONDON AGENT: J. F. GROOM, CHARING CROSS.

DAVIS BROTHERS, FORWARD PRINTING WORKS, BIRMINGHAM.

clear now as they were when first produced in the seventies. To examine the collection in detail is tantamount to a review of the history of the locomotive to about 1892: for we had to find such embryonic machines as Murdocks', Trevithicks', Blenkinsop's and Brunton's original models, such transitional types as those designed by Mr Edward Bury and Mr T.R. Crampton, and such finished products as the London & North Western 3-cylinder compounds of the 'eighties, and those efficient 4-4-0 engines of the London & South Western and the Midland Rys.

Previous to 1872, Mr. Bleasdale had photographed such types as Hedley's Puffing Billy, *Stephenson's Killingworth locomotives, the early Stockton & Darlington engines beginning with* Locomotion, *many of the named locos of the East Lancashire and Lancashire & Yorkshire Rys, Dundee & Newtyle* Earl of Airlie. *Shutt End Ry* Agenoria *and the Bristol & Exeter 9ft 4-2-4 Tanks. In 1872 he was occupied at Crewe and Wolverton with L&NWR engines designed by Messrs Allan, Trevithick, McConnell and Ramsbottom. The locomotives built to the order of Mr Matthew Kirtley on the Midland system next engaged his attention: an interesting photograph of this period being the interior of the shed at Derby shewing characteristic Kirtley engines. Following the MR, Mr Bleasdale transferred his operations to Wolverhampton where many of the old Great Western, and others of the Oxford, Worcester & Wolverhampton Ry were 'taken'. He next visited the GWR. sheds at Swindon, where the famous 4-2-2 engines designed by Mr, afterwards Sir Daniel Gooch, were photographed. This was in 1877: between this date and 1890 all types on the Great Western Ry were exhaustively treated, both broad and narrow gauge. In 1878 the North of England and Scottish border were worked with the object of adding some of the locomotives designed by Mr Fletcher (North Eastern Ry), Mr D. Drummond (North British Ry), Mr J. Stirling (Glasgow & South Western Ry) and Mr B. Connor (Caledonian Ry). Between 1878 and 1881 the Samson, Newton, Precedent, and Precursor classes (L&NWR) and Mr S.W. Johnson's latest designs on the Midland Ry were added. In 1881 Mr Bleasdale was at the Stephenson Centenary at Newcastle-on-Tyne, photographing the principal exhibits: at which time the two surviving sons of Mr William Hedley were photographed with* Wylam Dilly *previous to its removal to Edinburgh Museum. In 1882-3 attention was given to engines designed by Mr J. C. Craven and Mr W. Stroudley on the London, Brighton & South Coast: by Messrs Martley and Kirtley on the London, Chatham & Dover: and by Messrs Cudworth, Watkin and Stirling, on the South Eastern Rys. Then, with intervals devoted to the*

GWR and L&NWR, followed the Great Eastern, with engines designed by Messrs Sinclair, Johnson, Adams, Bromley and Worsdell. In 1887 a new departure was made: the Rhymney, Taff Vale, Monmouthshire and Festiniog Rys were visited; the remarkable double-bogie engines of Fairlie's patent on the famous narrow gauge railway, together with other motive power, rolling stock and views of the important features of this railway were fully recorded; some fine negatives being made. In the following year Mr Bleasdale was at Doncaster (GNR) and reproductions of Mr P Stirling's famous 8ft singles, and other types, including some of the older locomotives designed by Mr A. Sturrock, were obtained. In the same year, at Stoke-on-Trent, many North Stafford engines designed by Messrs Clare and Longbottom were also photographed. Succeeding these, in 1889 the West of England claimed his attention with the result that a number of Bristol & Exeter, South Devon, and Somerset & Dorset locomotives were 'taken'. At Gorton works in 1890, and at Lincoln many photographs were made of Mr Sacré's fine 7ft 6in. singles and other types characteristic of the Manchester, Sheffield & Lincoln, subsequently the Great Central Ry. In 1891 Mr. Bleasdale was photographing in North Wales and Cheshire, on the Cambrian and Mersey Rys: and in 1892 he was concentrating on the express engines of the more important lines. A great number of all types of London & South Western Ry engines, designed by Messrs Gooch, Beattie and Adams, were photographed at this time, and in previous years. Exigencies of space do not permit of more details being given now; but as the foregoing particulars indicate the character and scope of the collection, which numbers upwards of 3,000, its historical importance and value will be realised. The negatives are now producing excellent 8 x 6 silver prints, and selections of these are now available. They will be submitted on approval upon request being made to the office of this Journal.'

Several photographs of broad gauge locomotives are known showing engines posed on what clearly appeared to be a viaduct, The brick parapet in the foreground is distinctive and common to all the pictures but most had the background blanked out. This, incidentally, was quite common with early

photographs, in order to focus attention on the subject. One of the locomotives had even had its crew cut out of the picture, whilst those which did show some background still gave little clue to a location. One appeared in a publication on the early days of the GWR some years ago, where it was stated that the location was probably in South Wales. However, around twenty years ago, two original *carte-de-visite* style photographs turned up which, in the style of the day, had the photographer's details printed on the reverse, which at last provided the answer as to the location – it was Gloucester and, more specifically, the viaduct which carries the South Wales line across London Road at the north-west end of the station.

The photographer was one R.H. Barrett of George Street, Gloucester. The pictures were obviously taken in the 1860s but *Kelly's Directory* for 1885 lists Richard Henry Barrett of George Street as '*photographer and registrar of births and deaths for the St. Nicholl's sub-district of Gloucester*'. A glance at the 1896 street map of the city, below, shows that George Street ran parallel with the viaduct – Richard Barrett was taking photographs out of his rear studio window! To date, six pictures are known, several of which will appear in the next volume in this series. Of the engines depicted – *Hesiod*, *Stephenson*, *Bury*, *Saturn*, *Lagoon* and *Cambyses* – only one, *Hesiod*, actually features in the Bleasdale list but clearly they must all have been taken by Barrett. Further, apart from the picture of *Stephenson*, from which a later printer blanked out the driver and fireman as well, all of the crews are looking at the camera and the engines are stationary. This would have taken a few minutes, given the nature of early photography, and was thus deliberate (as well as obviously being a regular occurrence) – these men knew they were being photographed, although this was all almost certainly without the GWR's official blessing. Some arrangement with the signalman and possibly station staff, however, must have been necessary.

Although only the *Hesiod* picture (page 158) appears on the list, other postcards at this location are certainly from the Locomotive Publishing Co. and later Locomotive & General Real Photograph Co. archive,; this later went to Ian Allan, and the whole L&GRP collection has since gone to the NRM at York. Whether any negatives for these Gloucester views exist amongst them is not known at the present. The likelihood is that one of the Bleasdales also bought in prints or the glass negatives of early railway interest from other sources and it is now clear that R.H. Barrett of Gloucester took the photographs of *Lagoon* and *Cambyses* and can therefore be credited with the other four views too.

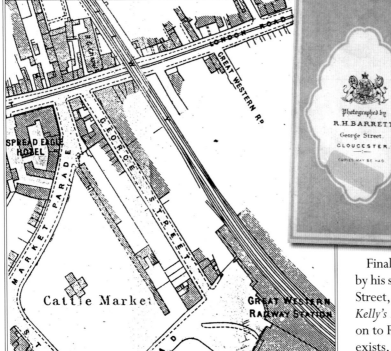

Finally, it appears that Barrett was succeeded in his business by his son, Henry Arthur, who is listed as trading from 8 George Street, again as photographer and as the local registrar, in the 1902 *Kelly's Directory*. Perhaps it was him who sold the photographs on to R.E. Bleasdale in Warwick. George Street itself no longer exists, replaced by the Bruton Way dual carriageway.

APPENDIX 3

GWR ENGINE STOCK, OCTOBER 1849

Chippenham station in 1841, shortly after opening, with a 'Fire Fly' Class calling at the head of a Bristol-bound train. Note the waggons at the entrance to the goods shed on the left, a broad gauge era scene not often depicted/

It is inevitable that while writing a series of books such as *The Broad Gauge Engines of the Great Western Railway*, ongoing researches throw up material that might have found its way into previous volumes. Such is the case here, for whilst searching for something completely different, I came across a list prepared for Daniel Gooch by Archibald Sturrock, detailing the GWR's engine stock in October 1849. At the time, Sturrock was Works Manager at Swindon and the Works was engaged in rebuilding many older engines – in particular the 'Sun' and 'Leo' classes as saddle tanks – as well as general maintenance and a limited amount of new construction. The year 1849 was also that in which there was a considerable reduction in the workforce at Swindon, due to the financial crisis of this and following years. The list, which is handwritten, is a little difficult to interpret but has been transcribed and is presented in **Table A1**, right and overleaf, which will make it more readable.

Based on the list, I therefore estimate that on 26th October 1849, the GWR had 165 engines in stock. However, it only lists seventy-two engines in total, which leaves ninety-three unaccounted for. There would probably have been between ten and fifteen engines at work in South Devon and on loan to the South Devon Railway. The remainder, one assumes, would have been in everyday use

and would have been included in returns provided by the District Locomotive Superintendents and sent separately to Gooch. Clearly Sturrock is simply reflecting the situation at Swindon, though it is interesting that he includes engines under repair at other sheds for which, perhaps, he took some responsibility.

To my mind there seems to be an inordinate number of engines 'in stock', including four 8ft 0in. 'Singles'. This status usually reflected the prevailing traffic needs and included engines which were awaiting reallocation following repair or construction, as well as engines temporarily surplus to requirements but serviceable. The numbers may therefore reflect the on-going fall off in traffic because of the recession in the nation's and consequently the GWR's finances.

This report is a major rediscovery, as far as I am concerned. Unquestionably it is one of the 'lost' reports which Phil Reed refers to in the RCTS history, *The Locomotives of the Great Western Railway, Part Two, Broad Gauge*. It also allows us to peer into the past during an especially difficult period in the life of the GWR, in the development of Swindon Railway Works, and in the lives of those who had travelled the length and breadth of the country to find work there, albeit only temporarily, to which the long list of engines out of service bears testimony.

Engines in good order and at work (*presumably from Swindon*)

NAME	CLASS
Damon	Fire Fly
Priam	Fire Fly
Mentor	Fire Fly
Milo	Fire Fly
Bright Star	Star
Pollux	Fire Fly
Pyracmon	Pyracmon
Ajax	Pyracmon

Engines in stock

NAME	CLASS
Great Britain	Iron Duke
Iron Duke	Iron Duke
Great Western	Iron Duke
Shooting Star	Star
Fire Fly	Fire Fly
Evening Star	Star
Dog Star	Star
Leopard	Fire Fly

Actaeon	Fire Fly
Castor	Fire Fly
Elk	Prince
Load Star	Star
Stromboli	Leo
Eagle	Sharp Roberts
Mercury	Fire Fly
Dart	Fire Fly
Hercules	Hercules
Mammoth	Pyracmon
Brontes	Premier
Caliban	Pyracmon
Stag	Fire Fly
Jason	Premier
Gorgon	Fire Fly
Falcon	Fire Fly

Engines painting and 'cleating of boiler:

NAME	CLASS
Ganymede	Fire Fly
Belona	Fire Fly
North Star	Star
Sultan	Iron Duke
Greyhound	Fire Fly
Hesperus	Sun
Mazeppa	Fire Fly
Virgo	Leo

Engines undergoing repair including an estimate of the number of days required to finish the repair:

NAME	CLASS	DAYS
Achilles	Fire Fly	10
Sun	Sun (Tank)	None given
Eclipse	Sun (Tank)	None given
Vesta	Fire Fly	6
Medusa	Fire Fly	10
Teign (Viper)	Haigh Foundry	8
Arab	Fire Fly	4
Centaur	Fire Fly	6
Javelin	Sun	8
Stiletto	Sun	14
Rocket	Sun	4
Swallow	Iron Duke	6

Engines requiring more than two weeks repairs:

NAME	CLASS
Pegasus	Fire Fly
Hecla	Leo
Stentor	Fire Fly
Minos	Fire Fly
Spit Fire	Fire Fly
Vulture	Fire Fly
Atlas	Sharp Roberts
Exe (Snake)	Haigh Foundry
Panther	Fire Fly
Aurora	Sun
Antelope	Sun
Djerid	Sun
Elephant	Leo
Lynx	Fire Fly
Fire Brand	Fire Fly
Pasha	Iron Duke
Etna	Leo
Royal Star	Star
Prosperine	Fire Fly
Tityos	Hercules
Sampson	Hercules
Goliah	Hercules
Leo	Leo
Comet	Sun
Gazelle	Sun
Premier	Premier
Vesuvius	Premier
Wolf	Sun
Zebra	Sun
Behemoth	Pyracmon

Sturrock comments that he has no reports for *Wolf*, *Zebra* and *Behemoth*, which I understand to mean that he cannot estimate yet how long they will be out of service or the extent of repairs required.

Engines undergoing repairs at Sheds

NAME	CLASS	SHED
Bellerophon	Premier	Paddington
Yataghan	Sun	Didcot
Avalanche	Misc.	Box